Oman – The Islamic Tradition

Oman is the inheritor of a unique political tradition, the *imāma* (imamate), and has a special place in the Arab Islamic world. From the eighth century and for more than a thousand years, the story of Oman was essentially a story of an original, minority, movement, the *Ibāḍi*. This long period was marked by the search for a just *imāma* through the *Ibāḍi* model of the Islamic State.

The *imāma* system was based on two principles: the free election of the *imām* leader and the rigorous application of *shūrā* (consultation). Thus, the *imāma* system, through its rich experience, has provided us with the only example of an Arab-Islamic democracy.

Hussein Ghubash's well-researched book takes the reader on a historical voyage through geography, politics and culture of the region, from the sixteenth century to the present day. Oman has long-standing ties with East Africa as well as Europe; the first contact between Oman and European imperialist powers took place at the dawn of the 1500s with the arrival of the Portuguese, eventually followed by the Dutch, French and British.

Persuasive, thorough and drawing on Western as well as Islamic political theory, this book analyses the different historical and geopolitical roles of this strategic country. Thanks to its millennial tradition, Oman enjoys a solid national culture and stable socio-political situation.

Dr Ghubash is the author of several books and the U.A.E. ambassador to UNESCO. He holds a PhD in political science from Nanterre University, Paris X.

Durham Modern Middle East and Islamic World Series
Edited by Anoushiravan Ehteshami
University of Durham

1 **Economic Development in Saudi Arabia**
Rodney Wilson, Abdullah Al-Salamah, Monica Malik and Ahmed Al-Rajhi

2 **Islam Encountering Globalisation**
Edited by Ali Mohammadi

3 **China's Relations with Arabia and the Gulf, 1949–1999**
Mohamed Bin Huwaidin

4 **Good Governance in the Middle East Oil Monarchies**
Edited by Tom Pierre Najem and Martin Hetherington

5 **The Middle East's Relations with Asia and Russia**
Edited by Hannah Carter and Anoushiravan Ehteshami

6 **Israeli Politics and the Middle East Peace Process, 1988–2002**
Hassan A. Barari

7 **The Communist Movement in the Arab World**
Tareq Y. Ismael

8 **Oman – The Islamic Democratic Tradition**
Hussein Ghubash

Oman – The Islamic Democratic Tradition

Hussein Ghubash

Translated from French by
Mary Turton

Routledge
Taylor & Francis Group
LONDON AND NEW YORK

First published 2006
by Routledge
2 Park Square, Milton Park, Abingdon, Oxon, OX14 4RN

Simultaneously published in the USA and Canada
by Routledge
270 Madison Ave, New York NY 10016

Routledge is an imprint of the Taylor & Francis Group

Transferred to Digital Printing 2008

Typeset in Times New Roman by
Newgen Imaging Systems (P) Ltd, Chennai, India

British Library Cataloguing in Publication Data
A catalogue record for this book is available from the British Library

Library of Congress Cataloging in Publication Data
Ghubash, Hussein.
[Oman. English]
Oman – The Islamic Democratic Tradition / Hussein Ghubash.
p. cm. – (Durham modern Middle East and Islamic world series ; 8)
Includes bibliographical references and index.
1. Democracy–Oman. 2. Oman–Politics and government.
3. Ibadites–Oman–History. 4. Oman–History. I. Title. II. Series.

JQ1843. A91G48 2006
320.95353–dc22 2005013201

ISBN10: 0–415–37568–1 (hbk)
ISBN10: 0–415–48132–5 (pbk)

ISBN13: 9–78–0–415–37568–9 (hbk)
ISBN13: 9–78–0–415–48132–8 (pbk)

To Mona

Contents

Acknowledgements

I would like to express my deep appreciation to Professor Maurice Robin for his remarks and advice, which were of essential help in giving this work its final form.

I would also like to express my appreciation to Mrs Moazimi for her moral support and encouragement, and the late Samah Ghanim Ghubash for her indispensable spiritual backing.

I wish to thank the Eminent Sheikh Hamad bin Ahmed al-Khalīlī, mufti of the Sultanate of Oman, and the Eminent Sheikh Ahmed bin Sa'ud al-Sayyabi, for their pertinent remarks. My gratitude goes also to Ali al-Sharhan for his important and valuable opinions.

I would like to thank my friends Jean-Dominique Mellot, Ali Annun, Ali Umran, Ali al-Khalafi, Amel Benhamla and Zeina Torbey for their support and assistance. Finally, I wish to express my gratitude to all those who helped me to achieve the task of completing this book, which took ten years of research and writing.

Transcription system according to the Arabic alphabetical order

a	أ	ḍ	ض
b	ب	ṭ	ط
t	ت	dh	ظ
th	ث	ʿ[ʿain]	ع
j	ج	gh	غ
ḥ	ح	f	ف
kh	خ	q	ق
d	د	k	ك
d̲	ذ	l	ل
r	ر	m	م
z	ز	n	ن
s	س	h	ه
sh	ش	w	و
ṣ	ص	y	ي
		’[hamzah]	ء

Notes

Arabic long vowels: *ā*, *ū*, *ī*.

The *tā’ marbūṭa* has been transcribed by the letter ‘*t*’, but only in the annex.

Most common words such as Qur’ān, Sunna, Sultanate etc., have been kept in their Europeanised form, and sometimes anglicised. The same applies to the names of some recognised persons, towns or countries, like Muscat, Abu-Dhabi, Bahrein, etc.

The *ʿain*, and the *hamzah*, they took the form of an accent: ʿ(= ʿain) and ’(= *hamzah*).

Ibn (*bin* or *ben*) means ‘son of’.

Introduction

The history and culture of Oman (*'Umān*) have a number of original features and are very often misunderstood. From the second century of the Hegira (AD eighth century) and for a span of more than a thousand years, it was essentially the story of an original movement stemming from a minority Islamic doctrine, the *Ibādi* (Ibadhite) movement. This long period was marked by the search for a just and efficient *imāma* (imamate) through the *Ibādi* model of the Islamic State.

Very early on, the Ibadhite movement identified its doctrine and ideals. Having upheld the principles of the *shūrā* (consultation) and the free election of the *imām* – the principle of *al-ijmā' wal-ta'āqd*, 'consensus and contract' – this movement could see itself as the true heir of the system of the Rashidi caliphs (AH 11–40/AD 632–661) with special reference to the period of Abū Bakr and 'Umar ibn al-khattāb.

For the *Ibādis*, the Rashidi State represented the ideal and exemplary period of the Islamic State after the death of the Prophet Mohammed. For them, as for others, it was the sole point of reference for Islam and the Ibadhite movement derived its vision, legitimacy, principles and the constitutional laws for establishing an ideal Islamic state and society from it, through the creation of the *imāma* system. So, from the first *imāma*, that of al-Jalanda bin Mas'ūd (AH 135/AD 751), Omani history and culture rested on three fundamental and unchanging principles.

The first principle established the system of authority, or the *imāma* system; this was built on *al-ijmā' wal-ta'āqd* (consensus and contract) and on the principle of the free election of the *imām*, and was itself based on the principle of *shūrā* (consultation). This first set of principles was to form the fundamental basis of the 'Omani democracy', an ethically and spiritually inspired system, which can be more accurately called 'Omani Islamic democracy'.

The second principle is identified with the actual concept of the homeland: *al-watan*. The removal of the Ibadhite movement and its *'ulamā'* (religious scholars) from Basra to Oman, and the transfer of part of the Islamic intellectual centre in Mesopotamia towards the end of the first century AH, rendered Oman the '*spiritual home*' (*al-watan al-rūhi*) of the *Ibādis* and a place of refuge for Muslim Arabs fleeing the oppression of the Abbassid authorities. In other words, the concept of a homeland took shape at an early stage among the Omanis.

The third principle, that of independence and sovereignty, became a reality with the separation of Oman, first from the Umayyad state and then from the Abbassid state in the latter half of the second century of the Hegira.

These three principles, applied and practised over twelve centuries, forged Omani history and culture, and were instrumental in moulding the psychological component of the Omani character. Oman was distinguished too by its written history. At a very early stage, Omani historians took the initiative of chronicling the events and achievements of their homeland in the service of the ideals and principles characteristic of the country and of 'Omani democracy': *shūrā*, the *imāma*, sovereignty.

Islamic democracy would thus constitute one of the mainstays of Omani history and distinguish the political culture of the country. So an in-depth treatment of this question implies reflecting on the concept of democracy itself.

Democracy and *shūrā*

Democracy is a human and cultural value. However, when the question of democracy is raised, the model that most often springs to mind is western parliamentary democracy. A democracy that, through its constitutions and modern institutions, guarantees civic and political liberties and, especially, personal freedom.

This concept of democracy usually harks back to a political philosophy peculiar to the modern western state. The question then arises whether, outside the strict framework of modern political theory, there exists a democracy of a different order, a democracy that differs from the western model. Are there other societies or human experiences that have satisfied their demands for justice, equality and law within a democratic framework of their own?

Perhaps no other phenomenon has required so much effort to determine its nature and identity as democracy. In political theory, it has been identified essentially with a set of processes aimed at achieving political, social and economic justice and with an elective parliamentary regime that guarantees the rights of the citizen through direct or indirect participation in the election (demand for representativeness), while preserving the common good of the nation. It has been defined theoretically in this same process as 'government of the people, by the people and for the people'. Still others have seen democracy as the rule of the majority over the minority, although this simplistic definition has been firmly refuted, for it is undeniably the case that the majority of the people never rules the minority, even in modern democratic systems. In this connection, Jean-Jacques Rousseau notes 'Taking the term in its strictest sense, a true democracy has never existed and will never exist. It is contrary to the natural order that the large number should govern and the small number be governed.'[1]

But in our opinion, the most appropriate definition is that of Alexis de Tocqueville: 'According to the true meaning of the words, [democracy consists in]: a government in which the people plays a part, whether larger or smaller'. And he specifies 'Its meaning is intimately linked with the idea of political liberty', while asserting that 'liberty is not what peoples whose social status is democratic chiefly and constantly desire. What they love with an undying love is equality'.[2]

Moreover, if we consider democracy to be a set of laws established in line with a country's particular culture, traditions and values, we may advance the idea that this is the essence of democracy, of whatever kind. Montesquieu observes in this regard:

> In general, law is human reason, insofar as it governs all the peoples of the earth; and the political and civil laws of each nation must be just particular cases to which that human reason has been applied. They must be so peculiar to the people for whom they were formed that it would be a great stroke of luck if those of one nation could suit another.[3]

If each society has its own special character, its traditions, convictions, values and a culture of its own, that means that each society also possesses its own vision of what it needs if it is to achieve fulfilment through the justice, equality and security of its members. Hence we may infer, in the case that concerns us here, that Arab and Muslim societies – each in its own way and according to its historical and cultural characteristics – have been able, even forced by circumstances, to secrete and construct their own democracy.

In the final analysis, and if we distance ourselves from the current strictly legal definition, Western democracy does not necessarily provide an exemplary alternative to the way other societies function. That does not, of course, mean that we should not profit as far as possible from the positive and negative features of Western experience – insofar as they are relevant to each country – since different cultures and experience are the heritage of all mankind.

But does not democracy, by its very nature, require a secular system of government? And is not the secular a *sine qua non* of the sovereignty of the people, of their power and their freedom? The concept of the secular is not univocal. In the field of politics it refers in particular to the separation of the temporal from the spiritual, of Church and State. A secular power structure, then, presupposes chiefly: first, that the state's legislative sources are not based on divine law but on temporal (positive) law, and second, following on from this, that no religious institution is able to influence the management of the state.

In this form, the concept of secularism emerged only late in western Europe, where, every nation royalty (sometimes said to be by divine right) exercised direct control over the Church, until the French Revolution made secularism (religious neutrality) one of the foundations of citizenship and then secularised power by first separating Church and State.

Meanwhile, in this modern Western world, religious and spiritual values have yielded pride of place to reason 'natural law' and man's material development. By thus subjecting human relationships to reason, man has achieved sovereignty and became 'master' of his destiny. For him, humanity and the world are no more than a historical projection.[4]

Secularism is the product of the history and culture of Christian Europe. If secularism was a pre-condition for the advent of European democracy, it was not necessarily so for Arab-Islamic 'democracy' and in any case it was certainly not so for the 'Omani democracy' that we are discussing here. If the course of Islamic history has not been the same as that of Europe, it must also be recognised that the role of Islam has not been defined institutionally in the same way as Christianity, which has been so to speak embodied in the Church and its clergy. Islam has never, strictly speaking, known priestly power. That is why the question of secularism has never arisen in Muslim culture. And yet the question of the separation of powers is still of paramount importance in an Islamic State.

So in Islam, the State is not theocratic. The position of caliph has never been seen as divine and according to the *sunna*, the caliph must be freely elected by the community, the people. The relationship between the caliph and the people is defined and determined by a contract (*'aqd*) characterised by allegiance (*bay'a*). The caliph thus derives his legitimacy from the people, and those who grant legitimacy can also withdraw it. The *umma*, or community, is the source of legitimate power in Islam.

Furthermore, the delegation of power in Islam is plainly set out: 'O believers, obey Allah and obey the Apostle and those in authority among you.'[5] But if believers must obey those in authority, they in turn must above all, consult the community, the *umma*. 'So... consult them in the conduct of affairs.'[6] The Koranic precept gives legitimacy to the collective power of the *umma*, the community, and so to its sovereignty and its freedom.

The precept: 'Obey those in authority among you' is always subject to the proviso: if they govern you in accordance with the law. The 'virtue of justice', *al-'adāla*, is one of the fundamental requirements of the caliph. In this respect, the exercise of legitimate power is founded on 'justice' (*'adl*), regarded as the observance of the Koranic precepts.[7]

Rashid Rida observes that power to legislate exists in Islam; this power has been sanctioned by God, entrusted to the community and is exercised, subject to consultation, by all those who have won recognition for their learning, their judgment and their ascendancy. Power, in fact, belongs to the community, since, on any matter on which it is possible to consult the community and on which it adopts a unanimous stand, its decisions are binding.[8]

According to 'Abduh, Islam has no other authority but the power to enjoin good and forbid evil. Yet that power is delegated by God to every Muslim.[9] For every man is God's caliph on earth. Addressing his Emissary, God in fact said: 'We have sent you forth in truth, as a bearer of good news and a warner'.[10]

The famous *khuṭba* (speech) delivered by Abū Bakr after he was proclaimed caliph is highly significant from this point of view: 'Now I have been placed over you to govern you. I am not the best man among you. If I follow the straight path, assist me; if I wander, show me the right way again.'[11]

Islamic political theory definitively precludes any form of theocracy, whether embodied in a clerical party or in a sovereign by divine right. The temporal, relative and contractual nature of power is, on the other hand, clearly set out. Although temporal, it is not necessarily secular; on the contrary, it is accountable – in principle – to a community of believers. It is this very accountability to a people defined by religious affiliation that can open the way to a democratic system. It is indeed the basis of democracy.

This being the case, the question is whether religion is able to make the citizen-believer sufficiently aware of his responsibilities to produce genuine political life and democracy. To this question Islamic political theory and the experience of the Omani Islamic democracy have given an affirmative answer. Omani democracy really did constitute a living embodiment of Islamic democracy.

Aside from the important part played by the principles of *shūrā* (consultation) and *ijmā'* (consensus) in the social harmony and unity of the people, the practice of consultation in itself affirms the citizen's place and acknowledges his true value, as well as that of his representative, the *imām*. Both thus assume responsibility and human dignity: two key concepts for the unity and stability of the *umma*.

The presence and role of Islam in society are of the utmost importance, not only for keeping a watchful eye on the power of the state, but also as the most important source of social and moral values.[12] Indeed, in Islam and contrary to the habitual outlook of western thought, the notion of a free man will appear as a legal, rather than a metaphysical concept, based primarily on a very strong and unwavering sense of the absolute equality of rights between all the members of the Muslim community. All believers are equal before the law because they are brothers.[13]

Virtue, justice, equality, consultation and consensus thus form the basis of Islam. A people that entertains these values, as an ideal cannot be a people without sovereignty, freedom and democratic aspirations. Are not the principles of justice and equality the characteristics and foundation of democracy? Furthermore, social equality, which underpins the message of Islam, is an essential basis for political equality. 'And if you judge between people, judge justly'.[14]

The firm belief remains that religiously inspired authority is incompatible with democracy. Can democracy, as generally understood, be identified with Islamic principles, in particular the *shūrā*? On this point, the Islamic religion provides several answers, including the verse: 'Their affair being a counsel among themselves'.[15]

It is known that the Prophet Mohammed himself set great store by rigorous application of the *shūrā* principle. Rashid Rida notes that the Prophet made the principle of consultation the legal basis for the general public interest.[16] In the words of the Prophet: 'Neither God nor I have need of it; God gave it as a mercy to my community. He among them who takes counsel shall not lack wisdom, and he who abandons it shall not lack darkness'.[17]

Recourse to consultation is therefore a necessity for the development of the *umma*, a pre-condition if society is to achieve wisdom. It is also a guarantee of the values of justice and equality. And it is above all an essential requirement for the proper functioning of political power in Islam. That is why the *shūrā* is both a mercy and a necessity in order for men to live in peace and dignity.

Furthermore, the Prophet had told the Muslims 'You are the best judges of the affairs of your temporal life [here below].'[18] We may point too to the famous statement he made to Abū Bakr and 'Umar: 'If you unite concerning a certain matter, I shall not go against you.'[19] The essence of these remarks is that the Prophet himself accepts the opinion of the majority. 'I am but a man like you'.[20]

What wisdom inspired the Prophet to leave the management of the *shūrā* to the *umma* without laying down any rules? According to Rashid Rida, the *shūrā* system has to evolve so as to adapt to the development of the *umma* in its various social aspects and general interests. Still according to Rida, if the Prophet had laid down permanent rules, the Muslims would have applied them even against the general interest.[21]

In the Islamic context, from the end of the Rashidun caliphate and the beginning of the Umayyad state, the implementation of the principles of consensus and contract (*ijmā' wal-ta'aqd*) was in fact suspended. And later, in certain periods of Islamic history, the Arab caliphs themselves would be appointed by the Ottoman military (Turks). The *Ibādis* of Oman, on the other hand, continued to apply these principles within the *imāma*, that is to say the state, for all matters from as early as the AH second century (AD eighth century). In other words, the practice lasted for twelve centuries in Ibadhite Oman, with interruptions due to circumstances that we shall be examining in this book.

Now, if we accept that full application of the principles of consultation and free election of the leader of the *umma* – consensus and contract – is proof of democracy, the *Ibāḍi imāma* of Oman may be held to be the longest democratic experience in the history of mankind, and is the more noteworthy in that, for the Omanis, this experience has served as an ideal, even a myth, for the greater part of their history, to the point of being identified with that history.

In short, it can be argued that the essential difference between East and West is, in fact, cultural and comes down primarily to a question of ethics. We know that, in the West, man is now deemed to find fulfilment by asserting his individuality, by his actions and by achieving personal happiness. This is supposed to guarantee modern democracy. In the East, self-fulfilment is conceived only through realisation of the aims and demands of the community or membership group.[22]

As a result of this view, there is now virtual consensus that the question is not whether Western democracy can be applied in Muslim-Arab countries, but rather, which democratic forms are best suited to those societies and what is the fundamental purpose of democracy. Democracy should not be restricted to an electoral system beginning and ending with purely political boundaries without engaging man in his essence and soul. In other words, democracy should also be ethical. If we study its history closely, the autonomous Omani model seems to pre-figure that form of democracy.

However, before describing the development of the Omani experience in broad outline, we must point out that it is not the intention of this work to limit its account of the *Ibādi imāma* system to a comparison with 'Western democracy'. Moreover, the *Ibāḍi imāma* does not conform to the same criteria and requirements as its Greek and Roman predecessors and the Western systems that came after them. Any such attempt at comparison would be as demeaning as it would be anachronistic. For it is precisely due to its originality in its day that the *Ibāḍi* experience is of value. In order to understand this, it is preferable to resituate the 'founding act' of Omani spiritual democracy in the Islamic context which saw the emergence of that democracy and inspired its expansion.

Omani Islamic democracy

From its inception, Omani democracy set out to obey as faithfully as possible the values of a moderate, tolerant Islam and the noble Arab traditions. To that end it was structured in the framework of the *imāma* around seven basic pillars:

- the principle *of al-ijmā' wal-ta'āqd* (consensus and contract) and *al-shūrā wal-bay'a* (consultation and allegiance),
- the principle of the free election of the *imām*,
- *al-dustūr*, the constitution,
- *al-majlis*, the institution of the *imāma*,
- the principle of the independence of the law and of equality before the law,
- the law of *zakāt* (legal alms),
- the suppression of the army in time of peace.

Alongside these fundamentals are other basic elements: for example, the tribal component of Omani society as a political institution and a political society; this institution has played a positive role in supporting the *imāma* system and ensuring its continuity. Mention should also be made of the administrative and legislative self-determination (ahead of its time) of the regions, which submitted to the central government of the *imāma* only as a last resort or in affairs that concerned the whole country. This set of principles and factors has gradually given shape to a 'general will' in the culture and values of Omani society, helping to define the actual framework of the political culture of the nation.

In the management of affairs of state and of society, the *imāma* system is based on implementation of the *shūrā* principle, which constitutes a continuing and mandatory law. This principle of justice and equality reflects the spirit of political power in Islam; it aims at the unification of the nation and of society through effective participation by the citizens. It also aims to realise the principle of consensus.

Finally, the *imāma* system is based on the free election of the *imām*. And if the constitution does not stipulate that the *imām* must belong to the *'ulamā'*, although that is preferable, it does require him to be a man of integrity, religiously and morally upright and virtuous, regardless of the colour of his skin or of the tribe and the family or society to which he belongs. These are the conditions of *al-bay'a* (allegiance). The *bay'a* represents *al-'aqd*, the written contract between the *imām* and the *umma* presented by the *'ulamā', ahl al-hall wal-'aqd*, 'those who can make and break'. The *bay'a* is thus a constitutional and contractual text, mandatory for the *imām* and bearer of the general will of the *umma*.

The Ibadhite constitution is the first of its kind in the Arab and Islamic world, indeed, one of the first in the world. The first foundations of this constitution were laid down in the second half of the AH first century (AD seventh century). It is thought to have been drafted, and then added to in the AH fifth and sixth centuries and it provided a general framework for the *imāma* and its institutions. It enabled them, in the course of time, to settle how they should function. And, despite its simplicity, it met the needs of society, the *imāma* and the nation. It has become the true expression of the spirit of Omani Islamic democracy.

The *majlis* (councils) of the *imāma* were also the first of their kind to be established in the Arab and Islamic world, as early as the second half of the first century AH. They consisted of a *majlis* of the *'ulamā'* (senate), which was also called the supreme council, then *al-majlis al-'ām* (general council) and traditional local *majlis* in the regions and towns. Within these institutions, the chief role belonged to the *'ulamā'*, known in history by the name of *ahl al-ḥall wal 'aqd* (those who can make and break), who formed a permanent assembly with legislative powers in the country. It is worth pointing out that this group played a pioneering role in the first Islamic state, that of the caliphate (AH 11–40 / AD 632–661). Their activity was later paralysed by the advent of the Umayyad, and then the Abbassid states. But in Oman, this group which assumed responsibility for the maintenance and extension of the *imāma*, continued to play a vital role for almost twelve centuries. These *'ulamā'* were the leaders of society and its conscience.

So we shall give pride of place in this account of Omani institutions, not to their juridical or constitutional nature, but to the way they function and the various roles they have assumed. Despite the absence of detailed and precise constitutional frameworks to regulate them, these institutions have proved to be consistent, durable and effective. Over a period of time they have created a model of communal life and have also set out the conditions necessary for political participation in power. They have guaranteed harmony, too, between the leaders and the population. They have not only ensured the legitimacy of the *imām* and the continuity of the *imāma*, they have also, by their very existence and function, stood as one of the foundations of Omani democracy.

The *imāma* system is founded equally, it must be said, on the tribal component of Omani society. It is important to draw attention to the fact that this tribal institution, which intellectuals – and more particularly Arab intellectuals – have often failed to understand, is the prime political institution (the one most inspired by, and attached to liberty). That, of course, is why it has welcomed the principles of consensus, contract, *shūrā* and the free election of the *imām* and has found them satisfactory. It is also the source of the *'urfs* (common law). And this tribal institution has likewise been seen to be the repository of democratic values that are practiced even in the most mundane affairs of everyday life.

It is important to stress this, for the tribal framework is the place where the characteristics of political society first find expression; it is at the tribal stage that all, or almost all individuals start to take part in consultation and collective decision-making in matters that concern them. This is in harmony with the logic of *Ibāḍi* thought, which requires centralisation only in specific circumstances. But it should also be pointed out that when there is a lack of tribal balance in the *imāma*, the tribe then generates a corporate spirit that can lead to the fall of the *imāma* itself.

As for the *imāma* system, which represented a kind of continuous expression of the caliphate State, it offered an ideal of the Islamic State. The *sharī'a* (legal code based on the *shar'*, 'revealed law')[23] was the main source of its legislation; however the rigorous application of the principles of consensus and contract had ensured the separation of legislative and executive powers, thanks to the *'ulamā'* which, throughout history, had formed a permanent legislative assembly in the state.

To conclude this introductory account of Omani democracy, we must emphasize that the political responsibility of the individual and his community in the *imāma* system is a significant factor. For, the almost total submission of the individual to his community does not imply that he enjoys no status as a citizen and a free man. Quite the contrary, this submission to the supreme ideal represents an affirmation of his citizenship and individuality as a quite separate person in a society that is held to be completed only through his person. By thus submitting himself, a man can even attain a higher form of humanity, according to this logic. By the same token, this submission does not imply the negation of individual freedom but rather its affirmation, since individual freedom can only be achieved here by the achievement of collective freedom.

Any attack on such an individual-citizen is an attack on his community, on his society itself. In his voluntary renunciation for the good of the community, the citizen finds a kind of personal honour. The more he gives of himself, the more he is fulfilled. These objectively democratic values evolved by Omani society cannot be understood by anyone unaware of their interaction with the social, moral, cultural and even spiritual values stirring deep in different members of the social corpus.

So democracy came into Oman with the *Ibādi* doctrine, in other words, with religion. This form of democracy, the first of its kind, is embodied in the *imāma* system – moderate, constitutional, capable, through the constitution – of ensuring the continuation of democracy and seeing it gradually take root in Omani culture. And this form of democracy has, in its turn, ensured the continuity of the *imāma* over a span of twelve centuries, although not without interruptions.

Oman and the challenges of her modern history

Geography often determines politics and sets its mark on history. Throughout ancient and modern history, Oman's strategic situation has imposed different historical roles, at times even burdens, on its population. And if, from Antiquity, the Omanis have played a fundamental role as intermediaries between the civilisations of Mesopotamia, Asia and Africa, during the colonial period, Oman became one of the most coveted countries, and the Omanis had to confront the expansions and challenges of the imperialists.

At the dawn of the sixteenth century, the end of a period of decay extending over almost four centuries and marked by the absence of a unified *imāma*, the first contact between Oman and the European imperialist powers took place with the arrival of the Portuguese in the Gulf region. The Portuguese were motivated, by their own admission, by the spirit of the Crusades and the idea of a 'reconquest' of the East, and they saw in Oman, because of its favourable geographic situation, the ideal fulcrum for their domination of the Gulf and their strategy directed towards the East. In relation to Oman, an Arab Islamic country, the politico-religious discourse of the Portuguese justified savage military action and a century and a half of occupation.

For its part, the Ibadhite movement, still inspired by the ongoing myth of constructing an ideal *imāma* for the Islamic State, would struggle for centuries to regain its cohesion. With remarkable perseverance, it managed to maintain the practice of the election of *imāms* in the interior of the country and finally, at the beginning of the seventeenth century, its efforts were crowned with the installation of the Yaʿrūbi *imāma* (1624–1741) to rule over the whole country and to put an end to the Portuguese occupation, liberate the region of East Africa and found the Omani–African State.

From the beginning of the seventeenth century, several waves of colonialists, Dutch, French and English, succeeded each other in the Gulf region. This military and politico-economic expansion was inspired by a long-term strategy. It rested on a colonialist ideology that saw the European presence not just as beneficial and necessary for the colonial powers, but as a civilising mission *vis-à-vis* the occupied peoples. This ideology did not merely fail to recognise the difference, the autonomous civilisation and the independence of those peoples, it categorically denied them.

As for the English, who had only recently achieved their own national identity, they were not in a position to identify the concept and demand of 'other' peoples' independence, still less to recognise and respect their values. For them, as for the other colonial powers, the peoples of the Gulf, like other emerging countries, were seen primarily as backward and so deserving only to be dominated.

From the mid-eighteenth century, Oman was to live through a period of decisive socio-political change: the transition from the *imāma* system to that of the sultanate. While this change in the Omani regime and in the internal political context was going on and a new national and cultural identity was taking shape, Oman had to suffer the backlash from the colonial conflicts between France and England. Thus the signing of the treaty of 1798, the first agreement between an Arab country and Great Britain, was one of the results of Napoleon Bonaparte's expedition to Egypt.

So the beginning of the nineteenth century proved decisive for British strategy. Great Britain gained almost complete control of the shipping lanes of the Indian Ocean and the Gulf. She was thus able to establish her colonial domination over the ports of India and a large part of eastern Asia, and to put an end to the Omani-African State. With all these developments, Oman was to enter into a period of marked decline.

Meanwhile, the first British strategic equation was becoming clear: in order to keep hold of India and eastern Asia, it was essential to lay hands on the Gulf, the strategic access route. It was only with the discovery of oil at the beginning of the twentieth century that the Gulf took priority over the other colonial stakes.

The Ibadhite movement was the only patriotic force able to face up to this increasing ascendancy. It had become almost standard that whenever those in

The birth of the Sultanate / by country split in two

power reached an impasse, the general will of the Omanis found expression in regrouping around the Ibadhite movement, which offered a steadfast historical alternative. Serious attempts to revive the country were made along those lines, notably the revolution of ʿAzzān (1869–1871) and later, al-Kharūsi's long revolution (1913–1920).

Silencing revolutions and preventing occupation

In order to preserve her hegemony, Great Britain put an end to the first attempt and contained the second with the signature of the treaty of al-Sib (1920), by which the country was divided into two parts: the ʿimāmaʾ of Oman' in the interior and the 'sultanate of Muscat' on the coast. Although the unity of a 'state', the *imāma*, had been recognised, this treaty nevertheless tended to isolate it and led in time to its disappearance.

If the question of democracy is one of the essential aspects of this book, it is not the only one to claim our attention. We shall attach particular importance to analysing and assessing the fertile soil of this democracy, namely the Omani civilisation, the *Ibāḍi* civilisation, taking time to study the roots and foundations of *Ibāḍi* thought. This research will focus, too, on the experience and achievements of the Ibadhite movement – the *imāma*s – on its evolution, the challenges and trials it has encountered, the causes of its unusual longevity as well as of its ultimate failure in our own day, under the pressure of British colonialism.

Given that Omani history is, for the most part, the history of the Ibadhite movement, in the context of the *imāma*, we shall have to study and portray Omani political history as a whole, so as to trace the course of the movement through the various historical stages.

It must ultimately be acknowledged that, although much has been written about Oman, most of it has been content to deal with certain periods or special aspects of Omani history, for example, the Ibadhite movement alone, or the history of the sultanate, or, again, the history of Oman and Great Britain and so on. Moreover many of these works have been written by colonial historians like Lorimer, Kelly and others, and start from a colonial perspective. Without disregarding their contributions, we have tried to present another point of view, more objective and more scientific.

We would point out, while on that subject, that Arab historians, and more especially those who have dealt with Islamic history, have failed, whether from ignorance or by design, to mention and still more to emphasise the importance of the *Ibāḍi* experience in Oman. So it will be for us to insist, among other things, on the fact that this pioneering experience offers a rare heritage to Islamic thought and culture.

The specific nature of this book and the demands of objectivity and method have led us to have recourse to various sources, which have mostly not been much used or even known; among them French and English diplomatic archives, most of which are used for the first time here.

The literary contribution of the Ibadhite movement has until recently been unrecognised, by both Arab and foreign specialists; however it appears today that the Ibadhite movement was one of the richest and most fertile in Islam in the literature of ideas, whether in the field of legislation and jurisprudence, in matters concerning the history of the caliphate and the schools and groups issuing from it, or, again, by its written testimony to the historical process of the *imāma* in Oman and the history of Ibadhism in certain Arab regions. This is all attributable in the first place to the contribution of the Omani *'ulamā'* (scholars).

Finally, this study will be chiefly concerned with the modern political history of Oman, from the beginning of the sixteenth century to the end of the 1960s (the advent of Sultan Qābūs in 1970). It will develop the political dimension in the framework of international relations and, more precisely of Franco-British antagonism, while trying to clarify both Anglo-Omani and Franco-Omani relations.

Last of all, we would remind readers that the chief aim of this work on Oman is to propound an in-depth study of the Islamic experience in Oman, both as a system of power and as an Arab-Islamic democratic heritage. It is true that the *Ibāḍi* position, notably on the question – which as we shall see is fundamental – of the arbitration of Ṣiffīn (AH 37/AD 657) and the 'exit' of the Khārijites, differs from that of other schools, the Sunnis and the Shi'ites. These few divergences of opinion and doctrine, however, must not make us forget that the path traced by the Ibadhism of Oman is an integral part of Islamic history. The *Ibāḍi* experience in Oman, original and pioneering as it is, draws its very inspiration from Islam, and as such concerns every Muslim. More than that, it is an original contribution to the history of the democratic ideal and its progress.

Part I

The *imāma* state from its formation to the British colonial order

and if you judge between people, judge justly.
(Sura 4 Women (An-Nisā') verse 58)

We shall start by describing the *imāma* system, about which little is known and which has proved particularly stable ever since its inception. Its *majlis* (councils), a novel Arab-Islamic institution, saw to it that the principle of Islamic *shūrā* with its democratic implications was implemented. And, from the outset, these institutions met the moral requirements of the *Ibāḍi* doctrine for justice and equity, so that Oman became their spiritual homeland. The *imāma* system thus provided the general framework for Omani history as well as a national and cultural reference point.

Why, and under what conditions has this system stood the test of time and adversity? This will be the main subject of discussion in this part. With the help of a rapid survey from the early beginnings of the *Ibāḍi imāma* and the first challenges it met (notably the fall of the *imāma* of al-Ṣalt ibn Mālek in the AH third/AD ninth century and its consequences), we shall seek to illustrate one of the major characteristics of Omani Ibadhism, namely how it functions as a living myth as well as an experiment in power.

A minority movement in Islam, initially persecuted, Ibadhism has shown that it could cope with times of internal or external adversity. It has proved that it could manage periods of consensus and of power, thanks in particular to the strong religious basis of its legitimacy and to strong-minded *'ulamā'*.

Oman's first internal test took the form of a long civil war when tribal loyalties were uppermost. The country was then divided into several semi-autonomous regions. But *Ibāḍi* identity was never really threatened throughout that period. Nor was it swamped by the Portuguese invasion of Oman (1508–1650). Yet the Portuguese were to occupy all the coastal towns and ports of Oman and this intrusion would strike a fatal blow to local trade and disrupt the general situation in the region. It would also introduce international piracy into the region for the first time. By destroying the peace and security that had reigned until then, moreover, it left the Gulf vulnerable, after a century and a half of oppression, to the succeeding stage of Western colonial occupation.

Despite five centuries during which the nation was torn apart, despite the bitterness of foreign occupation, the Ibadhite myth showed itself quite unaffected by these vicissitudes. Throughout the period, the movement had never ceased electing its *imāms* in the interior of Oman; it even proved capable of bringing about national reconciliation and of establishing with the Ya'rūbite state (1624–1741), not just an era of unity and independence for the country, but also an *imāma* that was an exceptional example for the Islamic state.

However, these achievements were not to last long. The election of *imāms* from the same line tended to transform the *imāma* into a dynastic system. The logic of events set it irreversibly adrift until the state itself was fractured. Oman embarked on another civil war. The fall of the Ya'rūbite *imāma* marked a decisive turning point in its political history and that of the Gulf. Oman would have to forge a new political and cultural identity for itself.

Disillusioned by the new nature of power, the Ibadhite movement began to turn in on itself, even in some circumstances returning to a traditional and almost voluntary state of *al-kitmān* (dissimulation). However, true to its principles and commitments, the movement continued to keep watch on developments in the situation of the country, marked by a general decline, and it kept alive its hope in the ideal, while waiting till it could renew its historic role.

Meanwhile, Western colonial antagonisms in the region had increased in scale and would be settled in favour of Great Britain, who would apply a steady, yet flexible strategy in pursuit of her aims. There was no lack of pretexts for intervention and it was in the name of the fight against slavery, or against the arms trade and later against piracy that Great Britain would work towards the systematic destruction of the fleets of al-Qawāsim and then of Oman.

From then until the middle of the nineteenth century, British strategy would have three main goals in view: to consolidate her complete domination of the shipping routes; to weaken Oman so as be sure to subjugate the whole country; lastly to strike at the fleet of al-Qawāsim in order to arrive at political and military domination of the region of '*Sāḥel Oman*' and of the Gulf by imposing colonial treaties.

Preliminary chapter

Oman lies at the entrance to the Arabian Gulf, on the east side of the Arabian Peninsula; the country is surrounded on three sides by coastline extending to 1700 km, from the frontier of Ra's al-Khaymah, near Ra's Musandam on the Arabian Gulf, then from the Gulf of Oman via the straits of Hormuz and the Arabian Sea to the frontier of the Yemen. It currently covers 320 000 square kilometers.[24] Its population exceeds 2 million and, according to the British historian, J.B. Kelly, it houses about 200 principal tribes and innumerable lesser ones.[25]

Oman enjoys an outstanding commercial and maritime position in the region of the Gulf and the Indian Ocean. The country has a relatively strong economy, based on limited exports of oil and gas, in addition to an agricultural economy built on exporting dates and citrus fruit and on fishing and pasturage. If we add the advantages of an important strategic position, Oman today, as in the past, enjoys a national economy combining internal productive resources with the inevitable commercial role of intermediary on the trade route from the Gulf to the Indian Ocean.

The civilisation of ancient Oman

This strategic land has a rich history going back, according to historians and archaeologists, to at least 3 millennium BC, when Oman is mentioned under the Sumerian name of Magan. With a much bigger territory than present-day Oman, the kingdom of Magan existed together with the kingdom of Dilmun, modern Bahrein, and the civilisation of Melukha in India. Earlier, Dilmun had been occupied by the Phoenicians before they moved away to Greater Syria and Palestine. The two civilisations of Magan and Dilmun maintained close links and were in active contact with the great civilisations dominating the region of Mesopotamia: Sumerians, Akkadians, Babylonians and Elamites.

The existence of human settlements in Oman in the third millennium is well established now. In 1973, an archaeological mission from the university of Harvard located some twenty sites, scattered over an area of around 5000 square kilometres, from Bahla in the interior of Oman to al-Mintirib in Sharqiya.[26] We know, too, that Magan, as an exporter to Mesopotamia, had explored sites for smelting copper. In other words, an ancient civilisation grew up on what is now the territory of Oman and was based not just on agriculture and the export of mastic to Egypt or copper to Sumer, but was engaged in ship building and sea-borne trade.

One of the tablets of Sargon, king of the Akkadians (2371–2316 BC) shows ships from Magan, Delmun and Melukha berthing in the port of Akkad,[27] further proof of the existence of a shipping industry in Magan. This opinion is reinforced by the sign of the king of the Sumerians, Dungi, on a tablet in the town of Lagash in 2050 BC, testifying to the existence of boat builders at that period.[28] So, although it has left no particular cultural legacy, this civilisation appears at least to have been productive, active and open to exchange.

Oman's vocation as a maritime state thus seems to be heralded very early and we may visualise the site of Oman playing a considerable part in communication between the various civilisations of the region for 5000 years. The English historian, Miles, relates how, thanks to the inhabitants' experience in maritime matters, the region now called Oman had contributed to exchanges between Mesopotamia and India and vice versa.[29]

We know, too, that in Antiquity the influence of what is now Oman was not restricted to the Gulf and the Indian Ocean; it extended to the Mediterranean Basin as well. Miles notes that the Omani fleet would have been secondary to those of Tyre and Cordoba. Thanks to this important contribution, the commercial activity of ancient Oman was undoubtedly a driving belt between the civilisations of Mina and Babylon and from Susa to India. It was from these civilisations that the Indians derived astronomy, philosophy, alchemy and mathematics.[30]

From the fourth century BC it is possible to follow the trading activities of the ancient Omanis as far as China. We know that they had establishments in Canton and the relations between Oman and China continued from then till the end of the Middle Ages, when new internal and external circumstances, due to the arrival of the Portuguese in the Indian Ocean and the Arabian Gulf put an end to relations between the two countries. However, if we look a little further back, it is fair to think that the Magan civilisation began to decline with the end of the Mesopotamian civilisations. The occupation of the Indus Valley by Indo-European invaders around 1500 BC and the subjection of Mesopotamia, after hard-fought and destructive wars, first to the Assyrians in about 1200 BC then to the Achemenid Persians around 580 BC brought about a genuine decline in commercial exchanges throughout the Arabian Gulf.[31]

Omani origins

A return to prehistory so as to get some idea of the population and civilisation of ancient Oman is merely a necessary preliminary to the main thesis of this book. Our investigation in fact looks at the more immediate origins of the Omani identity. First, according to the Muslim historian Sayeda Kāshef, the inhabitants of Oman would be of ancient Arab origin, going back to vanished peoples like the ʿĀd, who inhabited the al-Aḥqāf region between Oman and Hadramawt and whose Prophet was Hūd.[32]

According to Wilson, Sumerians are thought to have settled in Oman in the course of the four millennia BC. Wilson calls them 'faithful' because they paid tribute regularly to the governors of Sumer.[33] It was they who gave the name Magan to the region. We know moreover that Oman was subject to the Humerite kingdom that had followed the kingdom of Saba'. The Abyssins, too, settled in Oman for a short while after overthrowing the Humerite kingdom and Miles states that the Kūshāns, mentioned in the Gospels had settled in those parts.[34]

Furthermore it is suggested that several waves of migrants flowed from the Yemen into what is now Oman in the course of the centuries. Kelly states that the migration of Arab tribes from the south of the Arabian Peninsula towards Oman may have started at the beginning of the ninth century BC and continued throughout the following centuries.[35]

Historians often observe that there were two great waves of migrants. The first Yemenis to arrive in Oman were the Yaʿrūbites from Qaḥṭāṇ in the reign of Yaʿrūb, who imposed their rule over all the south of the Arabian Peninsula, including Oman and Hadramawt in the eighth and seventh centuries BC.[36] Then, in a second phase, the Yemeni migration to the Arabian Peninsula, Oman and Iraq intensified and in the end changed the demographic map of the whole region after the fall of the famous Ma'rib barricade at the beginning of the second century, which marked a decisive turning point in the way the history of those three regions, and more especially of Oman, evolved.

It is generally accepted that most of the Arab populations of modern Oman go back to the Yemeni tribes of al-'Azd. These tribes migrated as far as the Oman region under the leadership of Mālek bin Fahm. When he arrived, Fahm found the Persians dominating the Omani coasts and trading ports, more particularly the port of 'Ṣaḥār',[37] a name attributed to one of the sons of the Prophet Noah. Fahm drove the Persians out and established his sway in the Omani territories. Moreover, the Azds gave Oman its name; according to Omani historians it comes from the name of a plateau the tribes of al-'Azd lived on near Ma'rib.[38]

Indeed Omani historians claim that these tribes reached Oman in the AD fourth century. Perhaps the al-'Azd tribes of the second migration were the ones that Mālek bin Fahm is said to have led at the beginning of the fourth century, that is after the fall of the Ma'rib barricade.

Be that as it may, power was transferred to Oman definitively after Fahm who, according to al-Azkaui, ruled for seventy years[39] until the advent of the kings of al-Jalanda. During the reign of those kings, the Persians (Sassanids) again set about occupying the Omani coasts and renamed Oman Mazūn, a name which in fact applied only to the coasts of Oman where they were dominant. Perhaps this name was attributed to the Mazūn tribes in Oman. As for the Azds, they kept control of the interior, a situation that lasted till the arrival of Islam.

Oman and the early days of Islam

At the time of the birth of Islam, ʿAbd and Jyfar, the two sons of the king of Jalanda al-Maʿuli, were ruling Oman. The Prophet Mohammed sent ʿUmar bin al-ʿĀṣ to them with a letter in which he asked them to adopt the Islamic religion. The exact date of this letter has been the subject of historical controversy (sixth or eighth year of the Hegira).[40] It seems more likely to have been the sixth year.

The Prophet's envoy had no difficulty in convincing the rulers of Oman of Mohammed's prophecy and of his message. The brothers ʿAbd and Jyfar embraced the Islamic religion unreservedly and in a little while the population of Oman had become Muslim. By this voluntary acceptance, Oman again differed from the rest of the Arab and other lands. Moreover, Oman and the Omanis were to occupy a special place in the early history of Islam. And this was the period when the Omanis succeeded in driving the Persians out for good.

In accordance with the orders of the Messenger, ʿUmar bin al-ʿĀṣ stayed in Oman to spread the Islamic religion and oversee its application. He only left the country following news of the death of the Prophet.

The Prophet had blessed Oman and everything indicates that he had granted it a privileged place in his heart. According to the prophetic *ḥadīth* (traditions)[41] mentioned in the writings of the historians and the Omani *ʿulamā'*, the Messenger predicted the Omanis' attachment to Islam and their respect for its laws. One of the sayings of the Prophet, when he was informed of the voluntary adoption of Islam by the Omanis was (literally): 'Happy is the man who has believed in me and seen me, happy and happier still is the man who has believed in me and not seen me, nor seen a man who has seen me and God will make Islam to grow among the Omanis.'[42] After the Prophet, the caliph Abū Bakr also valued and praised the Omanis. On the return of ʿUmar bin al-ʿĀṣ from Oman, speaking to the Omani chiefs accompanying him, he said: 'What charity is more virtuous than yours and what action is more honourable than yours; the word of the Messenger of God, may God bless him, is honour enough for you until the Last Day.'[43]

Later, contrary to what had been agreed, the caliph Abū Bakr (AH 11–13/ AD 632–634) discharged the Omanis from paying taxes to the Islamic state. Those taxes were distributed among the poor of Oman in homage to its people.

From the dawn of Islam, the Omanis played an active part in strengthening and spreading the faith. They helped repress 'renegade' movements in the time of the Prophet. They took part in the spread of Islam in Asia as well as in Africa and subsequently worked to reinforce Islam in North Africa.

Oman was also distinguished by the number and quality of the *ʿulamā'* it gave Islam in the very early days. Among the most prominent Omani personages, mention must be made of the judge of caliph ʿUmar bin al-Khṭāb in Basra, Kaʿb bin Ṣūr, and al-Muhallab bin Abī Ṣafrā who saved Basra from the extremist group of al-Azāriqa. According to the Sunni historian al-Shahrestani, al-Muhallab fought against al-Azāriqa for nineteen years, until they were liquidated in the time of al-Ḥajāj (the *wāli* of the Umayyads)[44] and so, as the historian al-Sālmi tells us, Basra was called Basra of al-Muhallab.[45] The contribution of the Omani *ʿulamā'* to the influence exerted by that centre was by no means negligible.

The birth of the Ibadhite movement and its context

From the very first century of the Hegira, the name of Ibadhism has been associated with Oman. So it is appropriate to set out briefly the context in which the Ibadhite movement and doctrine unfolded. Non-Ibadhite historians have often played down the scope of the movement, content to link *Ibāḍis* with Khārijites, recalling their refusal to give their backing to the caliph ʿAli, their 'exit' from 'Islamic legitimacy'. To clarify the long drawn out nature of this process, we must turn to the writings left by the *Ibāḍi 'ulamā'* on this – for them – all-important point.

The framework of events is well known: during the year AH 38/AD 658 and following the battle of Ṣiffīn (AH 37) which had seen him opposing Muʿāwiya the *wāli* of al-Chām (Syria), the fourth legitimate caliph, ʿAli, the last of the Rashidites, accepted the arbitration that was to put an end to the bloody wars and give a ruling on the legitimacy of the caliphs. It was then that a group of Muslims, allied until then to ʿAli, refused to follow him. This was not to mark a protest against his legitimacy as caliph, but in protest against his having accepted a proposal of arbitration with Muʿāwiya.

This group, to use its own words, denied that human arbitration should be preferred to that of the book of God. Hence the name by which the group was known: *al-Muḥakimah*, 'the party of the *arbitrators*', but their opponents called them '*khārijites*' ('leavers', 'secessionists') and that name stuck.

The khārijites included first class scholars and *fuqaha'* (legal experts), amongst them a number of companions of the Messenger himself and his circle. They had all previously given allegiance to ʿAli for the caliphate and supported him. They had even followed him into the wars against his adversary Muʿāwiya and had only denied ʿAli's legitimacy as caliph after he had renounced it himself by accepting arbitration. And on that supremely important point we must bring in the writings of the Omani Ibadhite historians, still largely unknown but often contemporaries of the facts. According notably to al-Qalḥāti, there was then an exchange of correspondence (to which we shall return) between ʿAli and the khārijites. ʿAli admitted that on this occasion he had fallen into a trap by accepting the famous arbitration. He begged the khārijites to return to him and form an alliance against Muʿāwiya. But the khārijites refused; while reaffirming his legitimacy, they still held ʿAli responsible for the error of accepting arbitration.[46]

However, Caliph ʿAli was unwisely advised to fight them and have done with them. Al-Qalḥāti ends his account by asserting that after fighting the khārijites and dispersing them, ʿAli regretted what he had done.[47]

If we adopt this version of the facts, it becomes difficult to lay the whole responsibility for secession on the khārijites. For if they had really rejected 'Islamic legitimacy' out of hand, would ʿAli have asked them for an alliance to uphold the law and that same Islamic legitimacy? The testimony of the Ibadhite historians, which moreover has only recently come to light, provides vital clarification of this decisive stage – perhaps the most decisive in Islamic history – and must be taken into account by anyone with the slightest claim to objectivity.

The first leader of the Ibadhite movement, sheikh Abū Bilāl Mirdās bin ʿUdayya Al-Tamiimi, one of the survivors of the battle of Nahrawān, regrouped the faithful shortly after it in the Basra region. He it was who organised the movement and instilled in it its 'vocation', whence the name of *ahl al-daʿwa* (people with a vocation), used by the faithful to designate themselves. Several people of note joined him; amongst them ʿAbd Allāh bin Ibāḍ (hence *Ibāḍis*) and Abū al-Shaʿtha

Jāber bin Zayd al-'Azdi al-'Umāni, who took up the torch. The fact that he belonged to the al-'Azd tribes helped greatly in spreading the movement in Oman, where he received the active support of the family of al-Muhallab. Jāber bin Zayd played a decisive role as spiritual father and first *imām* of the movement. With him and after him, notably in the *imāma* of Abū 'Ubayda, *ahl al-da'wa* continued to extend their influence to the Yemen, Oman, Khorassan and North Africa.

Throughout the Umayyad period (AH 41–132/AD 661–750), if we except the caliphate of 'Abdel Malik bin Marwān (AH 65–86), the situation in Oman remained quasi stable. But with the start of the doctrinal and political troubles and the rebellions of the shi'ites, Azariqa and others, the rulers of Oman, Sa'id and Sulaymān, the sons of 'Abad bin al-Jalanda, launched into a revolution against the Umayyad state. To counter it, 'Abdel Malik then appointed al-Ḥajāj bin Yussef, a *wāli* renowned for his harshness, who removed the sons of al-Muhallab from power in Iraq. He then invaded Oman in order to snuff out the revolution but the attempt ended in failure.

By way of reprisal, al-Ḥajāj set about tormenting the Azds of Iraq at Basra and imprisoning their *'ulamā'*, including Jāber bin Zayd, whom, according to *al-'ālim* al-Samā'īlī, he had already prevented from spreading 'the spirit of liberty'.[48] Jāber bin Zayd was exiled with certain *'ulamā'* of his movement to Oman, where the Ibadhite doctrine was already widespread. In fact, the exile of the doctrinal leaders in Oman did not disarm the movement; rather it helped to reinforce the vocation of Oman, which supplanted Basra as a bastion of the Ibadhite doctrine.

Thanks to the *ḥamalat al-'ilm* (bearers of learning and knowledge), the Ibadhite movement was able, in AH 128–129/AD 747, to launch a first revolution in the south of the Arabian Peninsula and extend from Hadramawt and Ṣan'ā' as far as Mecca and Medina, but the rising came to an end after two years.[49] In the Maghreb, the Omani *Ibāḍis* played a preponderant part in stabilising the Islamic conquest.[50] Ibadhite writings indicate in particular that Sulma biṇ Sa'd was the first to carry the Ibadhite doctrine there.[51]

During the first half of the second century of the Hegira, by dint of several revolutions, the Ibadhite movement succeeded in founding three *imāma*s at Qayrawān (Kairouan) and Tripoli, all of which disappeared following bloody conflicts in which the *Ibāḍis* sacrificed many martyrs. Their clandestine action was crowned for a while by the establishment of the Rustamite state (AH 144–296/AD 761–909). But its fall was to leave the *Ibāḍis* of the Maghreb with only a few scattered pockets in Algeria, Tunisia and Libya; however they still maintained links with Oman.

Oman from the eighth to the sixteenth centuries: unity unaccomplished

In Oman, in AH 132/AD 750, the Ibadhite movement unleashed a revolution against the Umayyad state which resulted in the declaration of a first independent *imāma* with al-Jalanda ibn Mas'ūd as the elected *imām*. This *imāma*, however, with territories stretching from Oman to Hadramawt and the Yemen, had only a brief lifespan. The Abbassid military leaders crushed it in AH 134/AD 752.

There followed an Abbassid occupation of more than forty years, which formed the worst phase in the early history of Oman. For the Abbassid rulers used tyranny and oppression against the populations, persecuting the Ibadhite *'ulamā'* in particular; this obliged many of them to flee and migrate to East Africa. They brought their doctrine and determination with them to those regions and were even able to set up Islamic emirates which remained populated and prosperous until the arrival of the Portuguese at the beginning of the sixteenth century.

Despite these vicissitudes and the diminution of power it experienced following the fall of its first *imāma* and the humiliations imposed on the *'ulamā'*, the Ibadhite movement maintained a solid base in Oman. Kelly observed: 'Ibadhite theory had been so firmly anchored in the consciousness of the Omanis that it was impossible to uproot it, especially as the theory was associated in their mind with independence.'[52] And he adds: 'the long struggle, lasting from the ninth to the tenth century AD, between Ibadhism in Oman and the Abbassid caliphs, endowed the imama system with a "secular aspect" which dominated the religious aspect.'[53]

Thanks to new *ḥamalat al-'ilm* (notably the famous al-Bashīr b. al-Mundhir), sent to the province by Abū 'Ubayda's successor, al-Rabi' b. Ḥabib, and also the action of Mūssa b. Abī Jāber, the *Ibāḍis* took courage and resumed their activities in Oman. The centre of this new movement was the town of Nazwa. It was there that, on the occasion of a council presided over by Mūssa b. Abī Jāber al-Azkani in AH 177/AD 793, Muḥammad b. 'Affān, a member of the Azdite tribe, was proclaimed *imām* of Oman.[54]

Throughout a century of prosperity and stability from this successful election until the days of al-Ṣalṭ ibn Mālek (AH 237–273/AD 851–886), the sixth *imām*, the *Ibāḍis* elected their *imāms* without let or hindrance, in line with the principle of *shūrā*, and this enabled them to hold on to a valuable asset: the unity of the Omani nation. The example of Oman stands in contrast, from that point of view, to the political practice of the Abbassid state, in which recourse to the principle of *shūrā* and to that of free election had been suspended ever since the days of the Umayyads.

This period of prosperity and stability was of short duration, however. The *imāma* of al Ṣalṭ ibn Mālek (AH 237–273/AD 851–886) was overthrown by Mūssa bin Mūssa, who demanded that al-Ṣalṭ retire on the grounds of senility. The *imām* complied so as to avoid armed disputes. But in a letter to his companions, the *'ulamā'*, he confided that his retirement from the *imāma* did not mean that he abandoned or renounced it. In other words he did not consider himself deposed. He even accused Mūssa bin Mūssa of wanting to misappropriate *bayt al-māl* (public assets).[55]

Mūssa bin Mūssa imposed Rashed ibn al-Nadhir as the new *imām* in place of al-Ṣalṭ. But the *'ulamā'* would accept neither Mūssa bin Mūssa's challenge to the *imāma* nor the isolation of *imām* al-Ṣalṭ and, so as to put an end to that state of affairs, they resolved to punish Mūssa. Thus Oman embarked on a long civil war which put an end to the rule of the al-'Azd *imāms* in the *Ibāḍi* Islamic State.

These *imāms* had, in the course of a century, established a unified system for the *imāma*, its frontiers extending from Bahrein to the Yemen; they had been steadily developing the maritime strength of the country. This whole edifice was endangered when, at the request of a group of Mūssa bin Mūssa's followers, the Abbassid state intervened and sought to impose its power over Oman for a time. The expedition the Abbassids sent on this occasion was accompanied by one of the most terrible massacres in the history of Oman.[56]

This conflict spawned two schools of thought, that of Rustāq and that of Nazwa. In the opinion of certain contemporary *Ibāḍis*, the former was essentially 'fundamentalist'; it insisted on condemning Mūssa bin Mūssa's group and regarding them as renegades. On the other hand, the Nazwa school tended towards moderation, appealed to people to leave the past behind and restore the unified *imāma*.[57] So the constitutional debate on the dismissal of the *imām* remained unresolved.

The practice of electing the *imām*s continued. But the internal differences were still not settled. So Oman entered the Middle Ages torn apart both politically and geographically, with the *imāma* maintained in the interior and a usurping dynasty, the Nabhānites (Banī or Banū Nabhān) seizing the coastal regions and imposing their dominion from 1154 on. The political fragmentation reached its peak with the occupation of strategic coastal regions, including Muscat, by the Portuguese (1508–1650). In fact, Oman was not completely united, her *imāma* re-established and her laws restored until the advent of the Ya'rūbite *imām*, Nāṣer ibn Murshed, in 1624.

The fact remains that in Oman the constitutional dialogue between the two schools of Nazwa and Rustāq led to much thought being given to legitimacy and its conditions and to the development of a rich juridico-political culture.[58] And it is to that culture, glimpsed in the presentation of the historical origins of Ibadhism, that we must turn our attention in a first chapter devoted to the Ibadhite doctrine and the functioning of its institutions, before examining in the following chapters the historical process that developed from this doctrinal framework.

1 The *Ibāḍi* doctrine

Origin, thought and tradition

So . . . consult them in the conduct of affairs
Sura 6 The Family of 'Imrān (Āl-'Imrān) verse 159
Those who answer their Lord, perform the prayer – their affair being a counsel among themselves
Sura 42 The Counsel (As-Shūrā) verse 38

The traditions of the *imāma*

Al-dustūr: the ibadhite constitution

Ibadhite thought has been deeply rooted in Islamic history ever since the caliphates state in the second half of the first century of the Hegira (cf. the preliminary chapter). Unlike the other main schools, the Sunnis and the Shi'ites, Ibadhism is the only doctrine, after that of the khārijites, to have insisted on maintaining over the centuries and through the *imāma* system the application of the principles of *al-ijmā' wal-ta'āqd*, consensus and contract. This chapter will look again at the origins and specific nature of Ibadhite thought and deal with the main questions concerning the constitution of the *imāma* and its institutions.

Ibadhite origins or *Al-ibāḍiyyah*

Islam did not hand down any precise form for the caliphate or system for the Islamic State but entrusted that task to Man himself, while asserting that any affair between men is a subject for consultation (*shūrā*). So the state of the Rashidite caliphs (*the well-advised caliphs*) (AH 11–40/AD 632–661) was the standard and model for the Islamic State. But twelve years after the death of the Prophet (AH 11/AD 632), from halfway through the reign of the third caliph, 'Uthmān ibn Affān, the state experienced its first deviations from Islamic traditions and its first real crises. At this point, 'Uthmān was killed. Then, at the start of the reign of the fourth and last of the Rashidite caliphs, 'Ali ibn Abī Tālib (AH 36–40/AD 656–660), the cousin and son-in-law of the Prophet (the husband of Fatima), his power has been challenged by Mu'āwiya ibn Abi Sufyān, who had in turn obtained *al-bay'a* (the allegiance) of the populations of al-Chām. The two camps embarked on bloody wars which were ended provisionally by resorting to arbitration at Ṣiffīn (AH 37/AD 657). The *imām* 'Ali accepted the idea of this arbitration, hoping thereby to avoid shedding the blood and to safeguard the unity of the Muslims.

The position of al-Muḥakimah *(the «arbitrators »), the Khārijites*

The fact that 'Ali accepted this arbitration at the request of his adversary Mu'āwiya – so as to put an end to their disagreement on the subject of the caliphate – brought about a major turning point in Islamic history. Following his decision, a group of his companions broke away from him. This group was known as *al-Muḥakimah* (the *arbitrators*) or Khārijites or *muḥakkimīn*. The Khārijites saw the decision to accept arbitration as impugning the legitimacy of caliph 'Ali himself, as well as deviating from the caliphate state. For them, their 'exit' was a duty demanded by religion. It was a protest against a deviation. But it was not, at least in theory, a question of irrevocable secession. The Ibadhite sources mentioned in the preliminary chapter provide valuable clarification on this point.

According to these sources, before going to that extreme, the Khārijites tried very hard to make 'Ali go back on his decision. In fact at the outset they managed to dissuade him: 'Ali then relinquished the idea of arbitration, as they put it. In return the Khārijites renewed their support for him and their willingness to fight against his adversary Mu'āwiya. But 'Ali 'broke' his agreement with the Khārijites and again concurred with the decision to arbitrate. The Omani scholar, al-Qalḥāti tells us on this point:

> They had reproached him. They had obstructed him and protested against him. 'Ali had repented and manifested his repentance. They had followed him after this repentance, had supported him and accepted him. Then 'Ali resorted to arbitration in spite of their acceptance after his repentance and return. And he did that after they had noised abroad that 'Ali had refrained from arbitration.[59]

This version of the facts challenges and even refutes a host of writings by non-Ibadhite Muslim historians, more particularly some who state that the Khārijites had encouraged 'Ali to accept the principle of arbitration.

Moreover, when the Khārijites were informed of 'Ali's return to the decision to go to arbitration, they parted from him, invoking the arbitration of God with the words: 'There is no arbiter but God'. To which 'Ali replied: 'that is a true word invoked for the wrong reason.'[60] To which Abū Obeida Muslem, one of the early founders of the Ibadhite movement retorted: 'Since 'Ali knew that their slogan expressed the truth, who told him that their intention was wrong?'[61]

The Khārijite group consisted of former *Anṣār* (aids or auxiliaries),[62] *Muhājirūn* (immigrants) and a few Omani personalities. They settled in the al-Nahrawān region, near Kūfa in Iraq. According to al-Qalḥāti, they numbered 10 000[63] at that time and elected the Omani 'Abd Allāh ibn Wahb al-Rāsibi al-'Azdi as their *imām*. According to al-Shahrestani, the 'Khārijites' were all those who had risen against the *imām* ('Ali) appointed by the community.[64]

Linguistically, there is no objection to this definition, but *al-muḥakkimīn, al-khawārij*, or the Khārijites preferred to be called '*barterers*', in the religious meaning of the term, the *barterers* being those who 'went out' for the triumph of Islam and those who sold their souls here below and bought the after-life by resorting to the koranic verses: 'Let those who sell the present life for the life to come fight in the way of Allāh'[65] 'Allāh has bought from the believers their lives and their wealth in return for Paradise'.[66]

For the French orientalist Louis Gardet: 'The *khawārij*, the "leavers" were those who refused to accept the Ṣiffīn arbitration. Former supporters of 'Ali, they would not forgive him for having submitted power that stemmed from God to human arbitration.[67] They were equally unwilling to obey Mu'āwiya and took refuge in the absolute values of the Koran (...) Western historians present them as "the Puritans of Islam".'[68]

Be that as it may, the arbitration, as we have seen in the preliminary chapter, took place after the battle of Ṣiffīn (AH 37/AD 657). But it is accepted that this arbitration was nothing but a 'huge confidence trick'. The *imām*'s representative, Abū Mūssa al-Ash'ari, in fact declared that he agreed with the representative of Mu'āwiya, 'Umar bin al-'Āṣ, that both men should be deposed and a re-election held. But the latter denied this and proclaimed that he had indeed agreed with 'Ali's representative, but that the agreement was that 'Ali be isolated and Mu'āwiya confirmed.[69]

And yet, according to the Ibadhite writer, al-Qalhāti, 'Ali then wrote to the people in al-Nahrawān, the Khārijites: 'Their arbitration runs counter to what God has revealed and God has disavowed them, as has his Messenger and so have I.'[70] By this letter, published by al-Qalhāti in his book *al-Kashf wal-Bayān*, 'Ali asked the Khārijites to return to him and join the common fight against Mu'āwiya, as they had previously declared it was their intention to do.

To this, al-Rasbi, the *imām* elected by the Khārijites, replied:

> From the imam of the Muslims to 'Ali ibn Abi Talib, having deposed himself:
> We have received your letter in which you say that [the arbitrators] have turned their backs on the Book of God and made an arbitration that runs counter to what God reveals (...) Their dealings fell short of the truth from the outset (...) You have stated that you are consulting the truth, that you give your consent and that you are returning to the first matter and we do not reject your repentance.[71]

Al-Rasbi, who could see that 'Ali's letter contained a clear retreat as far as his previous attitudes to them were concerned, and even repentance, nevertheless turned down his rallying call. Instead, he asked 'Ali to rally to the Khārijites under himself as *imām*, arguing from the fact that 'Ali had stood down from his caliphate (which his due repentance did not expunge) and that meanwhile a new *imām* (al-Rasbi) had been elected by *al-Muḥakimah* who had refused to submit, as 'Ali had done, to the rigged verdict of the arbitration. But 'Ali, for his part, could not accept al-Rasbi's appeal if he believed he was still the legitimate caliph of the Islamic *umma*. From this difference of opinion on the principle of arbitration, a doctrinal schism arose that would later harden between the Khārijites and the Shi'ites, supporters of 'Ali.

Following *imām* al-Rasbi's reply, caliph 'Ali sent his son Ḥassan to fight the Khārijites. The Omani Ibadhite scholar and historian al-Shammakhi reports that when Ḥassan ibn 'Ali arrived at the head of an army to fight them, al-Rasbi went to meet him and said: 'You want to fight us because we named your father the prince of believers and he stood down and we refused to depose him.'[72]

This harangue was enough, the sources say, to turn Ḥassan from his intention. He refused to fight the Khārijites and returned to his father. 'Ali was on his way to go and fight Mu'āwiya in al-Chām, but nevertheless he launched an expedition against the Khārijites. We know that he inflicted a definitive defeat on them at the battle of Nahrawān (AH 38/AD 658), in the course of which several thousand Khārijites perished and the survivors could only scatter. Some Sunni sources claim that the victims numbered a thousand since some of them had withdrawn from their positions during the discussions between them and 'Ali.[73]

However, according to al-Qalḥāti, caliph 'Ali bitterly regretted having fought the Khārijites. He repented that action and said several times at the end of the battle 'wretches that we are to have done what we have done, we have killed the best from among us and our fuqaha (legal experts)'.[74] Al-Qalḥāti adds that several of 'Ali's companions left him after this episode. Indeed some of them were afraid and others were aware of the gravity of their action and made their repentance manifest.[75]

It may have been after this event that 'Ali gave expression to his will, saying 'Do not fight the Khawārij after my death for we should not confuse those who fell into error with those who succeeded in their plans by relying from the outset on injustice.'[76] It must be noted, moreover, that 'Ali did not consider the Khārijites to be secessionists, idolaters or hypocrites. They were, in his eyes, 'our brothers but they tyrannised us and that is why we fought them.'[77]

Thus the arbitration ended and with it the era of the four Rashidite caliphs: Abū Bakr al-Ṣaddīq (AH 11–13/AD 632–634), 'Umar ibn al-Khattāb (AH 13–23/AD 634–644), 'Uthmān ibn Affān (AH 23–35/AD 644–656) and 'Ali ibn Abi Tālib (AH 35–40/AD 656–661).

The disagreement over the notion of arbitration and its consequences gave rise to several sects and schools of thought and to three main doctrines, each of which defined the general framework of the process of Arab-Islamic history down to the present day: the Sunni, the Shi'ite and the Khārijite doctrines.

From the Khārijites to the ibadhites

As a result of the rout of the Khārijites at the battle of Nahrawān (38 AH /658 AD), the remainder of the group dispersed into certain Arab and Islamic lands. It is thought that the majority moved to Basra. In AH 65/AD 685 the Khārijites (or what remained of the *muḥakimah*) split up. Several groups were derived from it: *al-Azāriqa, al-Najdāt, jamā'at al-Muslimīm* ('the community of Muslims') and *Ahl al-Da'wa* ('the people with a vocation'). This latter group was subsequently, because of special circumstances, to be known by the name of the 'Ibadhite movement', a reference to one of its symbolic figures, 'Abd Allāh ibn Ibāḍ.

Ibadhism, which is descended from Kharijism (the *muḥakimah* party) nevertheless shows marked differences. In the view of certain *Ibāḍis*, the origins of their movement lie as far back as the period in which opposition was developing to the third caliph, 'Uthmān (AH 23–35/AD 644–656), who, six years into his reign, is thought to have been responsible for 'deviation'. Several *Ibāḍi*-inspired writings indeed echo the criticisms incurred at the time by 'Uthmān (cf. later, the letter from 'Abd Allāh ibn Ibāḍ to 'Abdel Malik ibn Marwān).

Whatever the reason, in the course of this long period of open and clandestine doctrinal and political struggle, the movement gained greatly in maturity and experience. It succeeded in elaborating the doctrinal, ideal and organisational foundations of a movement independent of all other groups and currents, from Shiism to Sunnism. Ibadhism thus appears as a doctrine that evolved entirely apart from, though at the same time as, or even earlier than, the so-called principal doctrines.

Five personalities were at the forefront of the movement and set their mark on its history. Sheikh Abū Bilāl Mirdās ibn 'Adyat al-Tamimi was the first of them all; he was one of the survivors of the battle of Nahrawān, moved to Basra and there began his 'vocation' aimed at organising *ahl al-da'wa*. He was thus at the start of the Ibadhite movement, an outstanding scholar and soldier. His date of birth is not known but he died in the course of the revolution against the *wāli* of Basra in AH 61.

A second personality was the scholar Abū al-Sha'tha Jāber bin Zayd al-'Azdi al-'Umāni[78] (21–93/AH 98) – a native of the town of Feraq near Nazwa; he joined AH 98 the troop of the *al-da'wa* people shortly after their arrival in Basra and it was not long before he became their leader. Every one took orders from him, including Abū Bilāl himself.[79] Although he was very young, he became the spiritual father of the movement and its first *imām*. He is credited with having contributed to the enrichment of Islamic jurisprudence and established the Ibadhite school of law.

Abū 'Ubaydah Muslim bin abi Karimah was the third prominent personality in the movement. The greatest contribution of this *'āli*, the second Ibadhite *imām*, was the setting up of the *majlis* and especially the *hamalat al-'ilm*, 'the bearers of knowledge', whose task was to spread the Ibadhite doctrine in the Arab and Islamic countries. In the words of Ennami, 'the development of the Ibadhite doctrine, the growth of their organisation and the rapid expansion of the movement in the Yemen, Oman, Khorassan and North Africa are unquestionably due to Abū 'Ubaydah and his innate talent as a man of learning and a statesman.[80] Abū 'Ubaydah died in the period of Abi Ja'far al-Mansour.

'Abd Allāh bin Ibāḍ al-Murri al-Tamimi, who gave his name to the doctrine, is the fourth outstanding personality. A pupil of Jāber bin Zayd, he was also a *'ālim* and made a name as an active defender of the movement. Coming, perhaps, from

Najd, it seems likely that he was one of the ṣaḥabites (companions of the Prophet).[81] The title of *Imām* of *al-Muslimīm* or *Imām al-Qawm*, given him in the *Islamic Encyclopaedia*, can only refer to the time when Ibāḍ took part in the defence of Medina (AH 64); the *kitmān* state to which all *Ibāḍis* were restricted after 65AH seems to exclude any possibility of the existence of an *imāma* in the political sense. Perhaps we should see in that title an allusion to the role of president that ibn Ibāḍ occupied in a kind of secret Ibadhite theocratic government called *Jama'at al-Muslimīm*.[82] Moreover, after the death of Abū Bilāl one year later, it was no doubt ʿAbd Allāh ibn Ibāḍ who became the leader of the moderates.[83] He died towards the end of the reign of the Umayyad caliph ʿAbdel Malik ibn Marwān (AH 86/AD 707).

The last personality who should be mentioned here is the *'ālim* al-Rabīʿ ibn Habib al-'Azdi al-ʿUmāni, the doctrinal authority of the Ibadhite movement. He lived mostly in Basra before returning to his country, Oman, where he died in the second half of the second century of the Hegira.

But following the split in the party of the *muḥakkimīn* in AH 65/AD 685, the Ibadhite movement, the most moderate, was obliged to affirm its doctrinal position in the face of other groups, more particularly, the extremist group of al-Azāriqa. ʿAbd Allāh bin Ibāḍ, enjoying the protection of his strong tribe, was given that task, while Jāber bin Zayd, the true *imām* of the movement, continued his clandestine work so as to avoid exposure. This was when the movement was given the name 'Ibadhite'.

The period of construction

Throughout the long period of doctrinal construction and political and organisational preparation that preceded the stage of the building of the *imāma*, three different councils were set up to fulfil different roles and missions: *majlis al 'ulamā'*, the council of the *'ulamā'* – a sort of 'senate'; *al-majlis al-'ām*, the 'general council' and *majlis ḥamalat al-'ilm*, the 'council of the bearers of knowledge'.[84] It is useful to stress that these *majlis* were secret at the time so as to avoid oppression by the state. A clandestine movement from the very beginning of their history, the *Ibāḍis* had to have a keen sense of organisation and an unfailing spirit of discipline.

These councils, the first of their kind, laid the organisational and doctrinal foundations of the movement. We may assume that a great many of the articles of the Ibadhite constitution were formulated during this phase of so-called dissimulation, although the actual constitution only appeared complete and in writing in the third century of the Hegira and following the fall of the *imāma* of al-Ṣalt ibn Mālek in Oman (AH 237/AD 851). Indeed, this fall sparked off a constitutional dialogue which went on for centuries. And it is during this stage that the Ibadhite *'ulamā'* wrote their best doctrinal, legislative and constitutional works.

Among the fundamental doctrinal principles defined by this movement and which distinguished it, three important points must be stressed. First, Ibadhism insisted on demanding moderation as a fundamental principle of its reasoning and its work. Contrary to other groups, Ibadhism rejected the principle of *al-khurūj* (the principle of 'leaving'), in other words it refused to attack any other group or wage war on any party except in self-defence. Quite the opposite, it ratified a principle known as *al-Qa'ūd* (quietism). It preferred to spread the Ibadhite doctrine through peaceful and often clandestine activity. Second, the movement was anxious not to rebel against the rulers in power so long as they were just and saw that Islamic laws were observed. On the other hand, the movement took on the doctrinal obligation to declare the *imāma* of *al-ḍuhūr* (demonstration) in order to overthrow a despotic ruler and replace him with the *imāma*. Third, the movement held the *al-kitmān* stage to be important for preserving the integrity of the doctrine and the security of the movement against persecution.

It was in the course of this phase, which extendes over more than half a century, that the Ibadhite *'ulamā'* are thought to have ratified the four stages or states of the *imāma*: *al-kitmān* (dissimulation), *al-shira'* (sacrifice), *al-ḍhūr* (demonstration) and, lastly, *al-difā'* (defence); they called these *masālek al-dīn* (the paths of faith). And these states were later to become firm rules in the Ibadhite constitution.

This stage of doctrinal, ideal and organisational construction would last for more than half a century. And so it was that the Ibadhite movement was marked from the outset by its organisation, planning and discipline, and also, of course, by flexibility and moderation, features still inherent in Oman today.

It is noteworthy that Jāber bin Zayd enjoyed a place of eminence among the *'ulamā'* of that period. He played a vital part in the organisation and doctrinal construction of the movement, as well as in its expansion. At his death, 'Ins bin Mālek, one of the companions of the Prophet, who had been Jāber's sheikh (one of his teachers) even declared 'Today the most learned man of all the peoples on earth has died'.[85]

Even before his death, the Ibadhite 'vocation' had become a considerable Islamic movement. The tribal and ethnic loyalties of most of the followers had been replaced by doctrinal convictions. The movement was no longer restricted to the Azdite or Tamimite tribes; it had found its way into other lands, thanks to the proselytising work of the *ḥamalat al-'ilm*,[86] who had themselves received instruction from the *'ulamā'* in Basra. From then on, Oman would be the centre of this development from which the doctrine radiated out. And the time had come for the Ibadhite movement, now grown to adulthood, to take its stand on loyalty to the principles defined during the time of the construction of ideals.

Letter of 'Abd Allāh bin Ibāḍ to the Umayyad Caliph 'Abdel Malik ibn Marwān (AH 65–86/AD 685–705)[87]

Through the whole of 'Abdel Malik ibn Marwān's reign, the head of the Ibadhite school, 'Abd Allāh bin Ibāḍ, kept up a correspondence and discussions of ideas with him. He raised questions specifically concerned with the crisis in the Islamic caliphate and with the doctrinal and philosophical position of the Ibadhite movement in the face of that crisis. Characteristic of this period was an effort to construct ideals through the emergence of the Ibadhite movement and its increasingly powerful positions. From it, a clear vision of the Islamic State and its foundations would emerge.

The long letter below discusses, among other things, four main points that lay at the centre of the Muslim dialogue on ideals at that time, and perhaps still do so today: the attitude to be adopted towards the caliph ʿUthmān ibn ʿAffān (AH 23–35/AD 644–656) in the matter of arbitration and the appearance of the Umayyad state, towards the *khawārij* and lastly towards the Azraqite sect or *al-Azāriqa*.[88] To all this, ʿAbd Allāh ibn Ibāḍ's testimony brings a clarity which is the more vivid for being contemporary with the events it is dealing with.

At the start of the letter, ʿAbd Allāh ibn Ibāḍ recalls the reign of ʿUthmān ibn ʿAffān and exposes, as he puts it, the Muslims' criticisms of him. Among other complaints is the fact that ʿUthmān ibn ʿAffān drove certain Islamic personages from the towns of Kūfa and Basra, the seizure of the lands of the poor and the use of the *bayt al-māl* (public property) as well as the money of the poor as gifts to his cronies. ʿAbd Allāh ibn Ibāḍ ended his comments: "ʿUthman's judgment was opposed to that handed down from God and transgressed the teaching (Sunna) of the Prophet of God and the two pious caliphs, Abū Bakr and ʿUmar.'[89]

In another paragraph, he adds sternly, addressing himself to the Umayyad caliph directly:

> I shall show you, ʿAbdul Malik ibn Marwān, what the believers have rejected from the works of ʿUthman and what has caused our separation. I shall show you the acts of insubordination that ʿUthman made lawful. It might be that you are unaware of them, that you are still following in ʿUthman's path and are his enthusiastic admirer! You must not be carried away, Abdul Malik ibn Marwān, by your enthusiasm for ʿUthman, thereby denying and refuting the signs of God.[90]

ʿAbd Allāh ibn Ibāḍ then tackles two major questions. First is the attitude of the *Ibāḍis* to the deviation of ʿUthmān, the third caliph, from the path and principles of the Muslims. Second, he clarifies the Ibadhite position regarding the Umayyad state, whose legitimacy Ibadhism does not recognise.

As to the attitude of the *Ibāḍis* to the Khārijites, the head of the Ibadhite movement himself continues, still addressing ʿAbdel Malik ibn Marwān:

> In your letter you attacked the Khārijites (the leavers). You have claimed that they are over zealous in their religion and so set themselves apart from the Muslims. You have also claimed that they follow a different path from that of the believers. So I should like to show you their path. They are ʿUthman's companions who split off from him because they rejected his modification of the Prophet's teaching (Sunna). They abandoned ʿUthman, in fact, when he dropped the judgement of God and disobeyed his God. The Khārijites are also the companions of ʿAli ibn Abi Taleb. They abandoned him when ʿAli accepted the arbitration of ʿAmro ibn al-'Aas and abandoned the judgement of the Book of God.[91]

And he adds 'Those who knew the Khārijites and saw their works knew that the Khārijites were the best of all by their actions, and that they were the most courageous in the struggle to defend the way of God.'[92]

Following this, ʿAbd Allāh ibn Ibāḍ defines the attitude of the *Ibāḍis* to the Khārijites in these words: 'We call on God and the Angels to witness our oath. We are the enemies of their enemies and the friends of their friends and we prove it with our hands, our tongues and our hearts.'[93]

By adopting this position, ʿAbd Allāh ibn Ibāḍ, settles the long-running dispute amongst historians on the subject of the attitude of Ibadhism to the Khārijites, and he spells out another position of the *Ibāḍis*, this time towards the Azraqites, to which the Khārijites' enemies were attempting to assimilate them. 'We confess before God that we have no link with Ibn al-Azraq and his supporters. They left with the others but they abandoned Islam and then blasphemed, saying that they were believers.'[94]

From a historical and doctrinal point of view, this letter is of the greatest importance. Its author is not a historian writing *a posteriori*, he not only lived through these events, he played a vital part in them. Furthermore he is one of the master thinkers of the Ibadhite movement. In the light of this letter, it appears that the Ibadhite movement structured its doctrinal and philosophical viewpoint during the caliphate of ʿUthmān ibn ʿAffān (AH 23–35/AD 644–656). We know he later approved the accession of ʿAli ibn Abī Tāleb (AH 35–40/AD 656–661). And yet he diverged from ʿAli on the question of the Ṣiffīn arbitration which would open the way to schisms pregnant with consequences. For that reason we must now look at the Ibadhite position in relation to other Islamic doctrines.

Ibadhism in the context of Islamic doctrine

The Shiʿites are a group that attached itself to *imām* ʿAli and became his disciples after the arbitration of Ṣiffīn. This *jamāʿa* (community) is distinguished by its intransigence in clinging to a hereditary caliphate. The caliph, the *imām*, can only come from *Quraysh, 'min ahl al-bayt'* (people of the house) and the caliphate must only go to that one tribe. For the Shiʿites the office of *imām* is divine and cannot be subject to election.

Their position is based on the following consideration: like the Prophet, the *imām* must be infallible so as to be able to pass on faithfully the doctrine and the *sharīʿa* after him. Now Shiism states that at the death of the Prophet,

> ʿAli alone was infallible for no sacrilege emanated from him and before Islam he did not worship idols, so he had to be imam. The imam must be the best ʿalim (scholar) of his day. ʿAli was that and so the imam had to be ʿAli.[95]

The Sunnis, ahl al-sunna (people of tradition), in a majority, had stated, like the Shiʿites that the successor to the Messenger had to come from *Quraysh*, provided that he did not neglect to observe the precepts of the Muslim religion and that the majority of the Muslims accepted him.

The three conditions mentioned earlier came to guide the reasoning of the Shiʿites but were rejected by Sunnites. There is nothing, according to the Sunnis, that can establish these conditions, neither the infallibility of the *imām* nor the fact of him having previously committed no impious act. And as for the condition that the *imām* should be the most learned man of his day, all he needs is to be competent to carry out the missions of the caliphate and for *ahl al-ḥall walʿaqd* (those who make and break) to elect him.[96]

Moreover, for the Sunnis it is established that 'the existence of a despot is preferable to having a *fitna* (sedition, crisis) at the heart of the *umma*'.

In fact, Sunni historians will be very severe towards the policy of Muʿawiya and even more so on the person and role of his son Yazid who was responsible for the defeat and death of Hussein at Karbela. But, faced with the claims of the dissidents, the Sunni attitude will be one of accepting the facts, whatever they may be, so long as they do not contravene the instructions of the Koran.[97]

But it is important to stress that Sunnism only became embodied in a doctrine in the second century of the Hegira, after the fall of the Umayyad state,[98] in other words at a date when the Ibadhite doctrine had already been formed.

As to the *Khārijites*, we know that they rejected the principle of appointment and would not accept that the *imāma* should be the exclusive prerogative of *Quraysh*, that is to say hereditary, or that it was divine. Instead, they insisted on the principle of the free election of the *imām*, whatever his class or tribe ('even if he were an Abyssinian slave'). For them, the main condition required for this office was that the *imām* be the most pious. But should the *imām* fail to respect the religious laws or the state fail to respect its obligations to the Muslim *umma*, the Khārijites adopted an unyielding position: the *imām* must then be deposed, or, if he refused, he would be executed.

> An 'unjust' and hence illegitimate caliph deserves death (hence the assassination of ʿAli by an Azraqite). For a caliph or imam does not wield power in his own name (. . .) And this is perhaps one of the most characteristic features of the Khārijite mentality: they take the notions and values of the Koran literally and carry them to extremes.[99]

As for the Ibadhite position regarding the question of the *imām*, it is similar to that of the *khawārij* in refusing the principles of appointment and heredity. In the first place, the office of *imām* is not divine but temporal. The *Ibāḍis* base this position on antecedents drawn from the period of the Muslim caliphate and stand firm on it as an unchanging point of reference in law. They see that the enthronement of the first caliph after the death of the Prophet, Abū Bakr al-Ṣaddiq, and of the second caliph, ʿUmar ibn al-Khattāb, did not take place by appointment but rather by consulting the companions, *ahl al-ḥall walʿaqd*.

As for the second aspect, namely whether the caliph must come from *Quraysh*, the *Ibāḍis* hold that the enthronement of the first two caliphs took place not because they belonged to *Quraysh* but because they obtained the *al-bayʿa* of the *Muhājirīn* (emigrants) and the *Anṣār* (supporters).

Finally we should note that the *Ibāḍis* have a very moderate position in relation to the other Islamic schools, notably the Sunnis, unlike the Khārijites and the Azraqites. Marriage of members of those sects with *Ibāḍis* is not ruled out or illegal, and they may inherit. This is a fundamental principle that clearly distinguishes the *Ibāḍis* from the Khārijites. It was when their great doctrinal lines were being worked out during the *al-kitmān* period that the *Ibāḍis* in fact differed from the Khārijites.

The *imāma* system: from the choice of the *imām* to the four states of the *imāma*

Ibadhism is not a sect in the strict sense of the word, but rather a school of thought based on five legislative sources: the Koran, the *Sunna* (tradition), *al-ijmā'* (consensus), *al-qiyās* (reasoning by analogy) and *al-istidlāl* (induction).

These sources provide the *Ibāḍis* with spiritual inspiration, the basis for their political constitution and the spirit of social philosophy. The question of the *imāma* is a pillar of the Ibadhite doctrine. It is a duty. But is the *imāma* really an obligation? The answer is yes and no. Theoretically yes. The *imāma* is an obligation in the Book, in the *Sunna* and by consensus. But for Ibadhism, unlike the Khārijites, a just ruler – even if he is not an elected *imām* – must be obeyed:

> If the imam of the Muslims, whether by the process of shura or otherwise, is just, he must be obeyed and any divergence is a depravity. If he becomes iniquitous, it is possible to remain under his sway but he cannot be obeyed if he disobeys God. It is even accepted that he should not be obeyed.[100]

And if there is at least one just ruler, there is no need to set up the *imāma*. In other words, according to this text it is not a duty. But there is another principle by which if the ruler changes into a despot, he must be disobeyed and the *imāma* of *al-shirā'* declared after meeting all the required conditions, like the *ijmā'* of the forty *'ālims* ('ālim is the singular of *'ulamā'*). In that case the *imāma* becomes a duty.

This remains a very delicate question and cannot be settled other than by the *'ulamā'*. One of the *Ibāḍi 'ulamā'* has summed the matter up theoretically: 'The imamate is sunna before the contract has been established. If the contract is established, it is a duty.'[101] In the same way, the *imāma* is assimilated by certain *Ibāḍi fuqaha'* to marriage: 'Marriage is sunna but becomes a duty when it has taken place.'[102]

The 'states' *or* 'paths' *of the* imāma

For *Ibāḍis*, there exist four *states* of the *imāma*, also called four religious *paths*. The first one, the state of *al-kitmān* (dissimulation) occurs when the Ibadhite movement is in a clandestine situation or in recession. This state seems to have been recognised for the first time after the failure of Abū Bilāl Mirdās' revolution (AH 61) and it will often come about following the fall of an *imāma*; it enables the movement to avoid being exposed to oppression or persecution by those in power. The movement then goes into the *al-kitmān* state: there is no overt *imāma* and no *imām*. Notable features peculiar to this state include the ebbing of political activity of the movement, which is then limited to the activity of the *'ulamā'* in their religious and social missions only. However, the *'ulamā'* keep in touch and correspond with each other so as to study their own situation and that of the country, while they wait to move on to another stage. This state can last for years, if not a century.

More than once in the history of Oman the Ibadhite movement has entered the *al-kitmān* state. For example, the first time was after the fall of its first *imāma*, that of al-Jalanda ibn Mas'ūd between 132 and 135 of the Hegira; the *al-kitmān* stage then lasted for about forty years, until AH 177/AD 793. More recently the movement experienced the *al-kitmān* state after the fall of the *imāma* of 'Azzān ibn Qays (1871) until the proclamation of the *imāma* of al-Kharūsi (1913–1919).

The second state is that of *al-shirā'*, or sacrifice. The literal meaning of *al-shirā'* is 'he who sells the world for the after-life or who buys the after-life with the world'. In other words, the *al-shirā' imām* is faced with carrying out the *imāma* or sacrifice. For the path of sacrifice (*al-shirā'*) is that of men who 'deliver their souls to God for his paradise' and who 'cannot rest until God's order has been made manifest [by the path of Manifestation], even though they die for it'.[103]

Two questions then arise in connection with this state of exception. The first is that the Ibadhite movement takes the decision to move to the *al-shirā'* stage – that is in fact to declare war on the ruling power – only when that power has become intolerably despotic. These circumstances weigh on the conscience of the *'ulamā'*, and they are bound by their religious and moral duty to the *umma* (the community or nation) and the *waṭan* (the fatherland). But there is a vital condition that must be fulfilled when that step is taken. Forty *'ālims* must be in agreement on the necessity to move to the state of *al-shirā'* and consequently be willing to contribute to a rebellion against those in power. In no case can the decision be taken without the consent of those forty, because the Messenger did not reveal his message until his companions numbered forty and the one who completed the number was 'Umar ibn al-Khaṭṭāb. This decision of the Messenger has become part of the *sunna*, on which Ibadhism is founded, as on an unchanging constitutional principle.

The second question has to do with the election of the *imām* of *al-shirā'*, that is the *imām* who may not draw back even if his companions desert him. He must persevere in the fulfilment of the *imāma* or else die. This is the state of absolute religious and political *jihad* (effort) among the *Ibāḍis.*

The third state, *al-ḍuhūr*, translated as the state of manifestation and sometimes as the 'state of glory'[104] came quite naturally after the states of *al-kitmān* and *al-shirā'*. It is in this state that the *imāma* determines customs and the movement sets up *Ibāḍi* codes and laws. This is the 'natural' situation of the Ibadhite movement.

In the state of manifestation, the situation of the *imām* himself is transformed: from *al-shirā' imām*, he becomes *al-ḍuhūr imām*. On this point, North African Ibadhism differs from its Omani parent for it demands that, after the state of *al-shirā'*, a new *al-bay'a* ceremony is held, either the *al-shirā'* *imām* is re-elected or an entirely new *imām* is appointed.

Finally, a fourth and last state of *al-difā'* (defence) comes into play when the Ibadhite movement is in power and an external menace threatens the country and the *imāma*. The state of *difā'* may also be proclaimed when the Ibadhite movement is not in power and feels threatened by the government of the country. At the proclamation of *difā'*, an *imām* is then elected.

In short, the institutional purpose of these states, that of *kitmān* among others, is the continuity of the *imāma*. The Ibadhite movement is concerned that *al-umma* should not be left with no current point of reference, without an *imāma*. So the link between the people and their religious and spiritual rulers, the *'ulamā'*, those who break and make, is permanent in all the states and throughout the centuries.

Different kinds of imāms *and the paths of their* bay'a

> And we appointed some of them as leaders, guiding by our command, when they stood fast and believed firmly in our signs.[105]

According to the Ibadhite constitution, the *imām* must be just, wise, courageous, honest, capable of administering justice to the people and of guarding their rights and interests, in short of governing them in all justice according to the religious laws. The *imām* must not be jealous, or vindictive, or miserly, or over zealous, or wasteful or perfidious. Nor must he be cunning, infirm, blind, dumb or deaf.[106]

As we have noted previously, in Ibadhite political thought there exists two kinds of *imām*, – the *imām* of *al-shirā'* and the *imām* of *al-difā'* – and, in function of transitions, these may be transformed into *imām* of *al-ḍuhūr*.

Alongside all these required conditions, already mentioned, two important characteristics are looked for in an *imām*. First, and as a general rule, the *imām* must be the most pious man of his day and the most *'ālim* in the field of the *fiqh*. The *imām* endowed with that quality is recognised as an *imām 'ālim*, that is to say *al-qawī*, 'strong', and the text of his *bay'a* does not, therefore, indicate that he must have recourse to the *ahl al-ḥall wal-'aqd*, the people who make and break, the *'ulamā'*, before making any decision.

Second, if the first and most prized quality is not forthcoming, then pride of place is given to those with the military competence required for the defence of an *imāma* threatened with constant dangers. It may seem paradoxical that this *imām* is acknowledged to be *da'īf*, 'weak'. But in fact, in *Ibāḍi* logic, it is because he does not belong to the *'ulamā'* and is not considered to be of religious or spiritual eminence among the *ahl al-ḥall wal-'aqd* that he is reputed to be weak. Hence, in the terms of his *bay'a*, he is required to have recourse to the legislative institution of the *imāma*, that is *ahl al-ḥall wal-'aqd* before taking any decision concerning the *imāma* or the *umma* (whether the decision be religious, judicial or political).

> The minimum conditions placed on a weak imam, and then not in a restrictive sense, are: that he receives no money and order no expenditure; that he does not appoint a wāli or have one appointed; that he does not train or command an army; that he may not judge or submit to judgement without consulting the Muslims, the 'ulamā', ahl al-ḥall wal-'aqd.[107]

The Ibadhite position on this question is clear cut; it is subordinate to the unchanging principle of the *shūrā*. 'The conditions placed by the Muslims on the power of the imam are obligatory duties. If he abandons them, he is apostate. His imāma ceases to be and the obedience of his subjects lapses.'[108]

Independent of the nature of the *imām*, the principle of *shūrā* is imprescriptible for the Ibāḍis. The pious and *'ālim imām* whose *bay'a* does not set conditions of recourse to the people of *ahl al-ḥall wal-'aqd* is not thereby denied that recourse; on the contrary, the *imāms* drawn from the *'ulamā'* and considered 'strong' are often the most meticulous in applying the principle of *shūrā* and having recourse to their *majlis*. In the last resort, of course, the decision belongs to the strong *imām* but the principle of *shūrā* remains fundamental to the way the religious and political affairs of the *imāma* are managed. On the other hand, the fact that some *imāms* may be considered *da'īf* does not mean that their *imāma* is weak; on the contrary, it proves that it is firmly and prudently settled on a strong principle, that of recourse to the *shūrā*. That is the basis of participation and of the search for consensus.

So the principle of *shūrā* appears to be central in *Ibāḍi* political thought; it is even characteristic doctrinally of the spirit of the *Ibāḍi* school. *Al-dustūr*, *Ibāḍi* the constitution, sums it up clearly and demands that the 'shūrā of the imam is a duty, whether he be 'ālim or da'īf; and to abandon it is apostasy'.[109]

Procedures for the election of imāms

In the *Ibāḍi* system, the procedure for electing an *imām* breaks down into three stages. In the first, if the *imām* dies or is deposed, the *Ibāḍi 'ulamā'* hold a consultation concerning the names of the persons proposed as candidates for the post. No time limit is set for this consultation stage; the time varies, depending on the circumstances. Certain tribal rulers may take part in the consultation with the *'ulamā'*. But in theory they have no influence on the ultimate decision. That belongs to the *'ulamā'* alone.

In the second stage, when the aforesaid required conditions are found in one person, the candidate is presented by one of the *'ulamā'* and it is mandatory that he have the agreement and support of a minimum of six other *'ulamā'*. When agreement on the candidate for election is not reached, then, obviously, the candidate does not present himself at the *bay'a* ceremony if the minimum number of votes (i.e. six) has not been in his favour.

But what is the legislative basis for the principle of an elective quorum of six votes? As has already been pointed out, the *Ibāḍi* school and *Ibāḍi* thinking are based on five legislative sources, including *al-sunna* and *al-ijmā'*. And if the *Ibāḍis* rest their decision on the principle of six votes, this is in deference to what they have called the way of the second caliph, 'Umar ibn al-Khaṭṭāb, which conforms to both *al-sunna* and *al-ijmā'*. On his death bed, 'Umar had to present a candidate for succession to the caliphate. He chose six men[110] from among his friends and entrusted to them the task of meeting three days after his death to elect a caliph of the Muslims. 'Umar laid down in precise detail how he should be chosen.[111] True to this precedent, the quorum of six votes has become a permanent principle for the *Ibāḍis*, and even one of their constitutional articles.

Another interpretation of this principle consists in deeming it to be sufficient for a candidate to garner five votes in order to obtain the *bay'a*, his own making up the sixth. But this point of view comes within the framework of minor constitutional debates.

In the case of several candidates being presented, all of whom have all the required qualities and conditions, the *'ulamā'* must choose between them in the light of the situation. If the *imāma* and the country are enjoying stability, then the favoured candidate will be a scholar, learned in the *fiqh* and the *sharī'a*. If the *imāma* and the country are going through a troubled period, the candidate most readily selected will be the one who has the qualities of a ruler and the abilities of a military man.

The fact that a non-*'ālim* candidate can be elected *imām* is indicative of the flexibility and tolerance of the *Ibāḍi* doctrine. Thus – and the point is worth stressing – the *imāma* system cannot be held to be theocratic; it is clearly temporal as well.

Moreover, *ahl al-ḥall wal-'aqd* insist on the need for elections that are free of any pressure and untrammelled by tribal and clan influences. In this way the accession to power of a candidate by application of the principle of free election is guaranteed; this in turn is founded on the principle of consensus. But, on the other hand, once chosen, the candidate does not have the right to refuse, that is to say to shy away from the *imāma* for, in the *Ibāḍi* view, that would lead to division among the Muslims. The candidate who withdraws loses his place, not just within the *'ulamā'* but amongst the Muslims too, that is to say among the Omani people; henceforth he is considered to be a rebel and is no longer worthy of the trust of the *'ulamā'*; he may even incur death.[112]

After the first and second stages, the *'ulamā'* move on to perform the third and last phase. The chosen candidate presents himself to the *ahl al-bilād*, or people of the country (citizens) to perform the ceremonies of the *bay'a*, which take place in the presence of the *'ulamā'* and the chiefs of the tribes in the region. Although the mode is ceremonial, the *bay'a* itself is equivalent to a referendum, and when it is over, the candidate must take the oath. One of the *'ulamā'* holds the candidate's hand while uttering the text of the *bay'a*. If the *imām* presented is *al-shirā' imām*, this must be mentioned in the *bay'a*, otherwise he is considered to be *da'īf*. Here is an example of the *bay'a* text, modelled on the one for the oath of allegiance of *imām* 'Azzān ibn Qays (1869):

> We have elected you on the basis of obedience to God, respect to good and the prohibition of evil. We have elected you our Imam and the Imam of all people for their defence and on condition that you take no decision, pass no judgment and carry out no decision without the approval of the Muslims and according to their advice. We have elected you on the condition that you obey the will of God and that you impose His teaching, collect the taxes, read prayers and provide relief for the oppressed. Let nothing interfere and deter

> you from the service of God. Let the strong be weak until the rights belonging to God are given by Him and let the powerful be meek until the judgment they deserve has been passed. You shall continue in the path of right and shall give your soul to it. We ask you to give us your pledge to this for all Muslims.[113]

At the end of the ceremonies, the *imām* receives the reins of power and the people are obliged to obey him. Indeed, the rule lays down that if the *imām* has obtained the acceptance and support of the *ahl al-ḥall wal-'aqd*, any opposition can only be rejected. For example, in the case of the consensus of the *'ulamā'* concerning the candidate, the tribes present do not have the right to oppose the outcome of the *bay'a*. These tribes, like the others, must bow to the decision of the *'ulamā'* who represent the supreme legislative and moral power.

The absence of the tribes in the ceremonies of the *bay'a*, moreover, is considered to show approval. In the case of opposition on the part of the tribes, the new *imām* is obliged to subdue them by force. And we have at least two examples of this trial of strength, the first in the period of Nāṣer ibn Murshed (1624–1649) and the second, later, in the time of *imām* 'Azzān ibn Qays (1868–1871).

> As well as being regarded as head of State, the Imam is the ulal amer, or the legitimate repository of all authority, and is mentioned in prayers in this capacity. His authority embraces all fields – religious, political and judicial – and he exercises it in accordance with Islamic law.[114]

Exclusions from the imāma

Not just any one may accede to the *imāma*, and, leaving aside the conditions considered above, a certain number of exclusions from the candidacy exist. Ibadhism does not accept the *imāma* of a slave. It refuses to elect one to the office of *imām* from a simple principle: how can a man who does not enjoy freedom govern others? So the constitution asks: 'How could a man who does not dispose of his person or have control of himself dispose of others?'[115] If, on the other hand, the conditions for the *imāma* come together in a man who is black but free, the *'ulamā'* do not oppose his *bay'a* on grounds of colour. 'If they have reached agreement on a man belonging to the people of al-salah (of virtue) and of knowledge, they entrust him with the imamate, even if he is black'.[116]

In the same spirit, the *imāma* of a son of adultery is unacceptable, as is the *imāma* of a minor.

> The imamate of a minor is in no way accepted, for his imāma (as leader in prayer) will be rejected at the time of prayers. And how could he be an imam and make judgements when he is not his own master?[117]

Another text adds: 'How could a man who is not accountable or is subject to chastisement be accountable to the people and chastise them?'[118]

Unlike the Shiʻites, who accept the *imāma* of a minor, the *Ibāḍis* are inflexible on this point: the Ibadhite constitution is categorical. However, the text of the constitution is not decisive in all cases. Concerning, for example, acceptance of the election and *bay'a* of an *imām*'s son (when the required conditions are fulfilled in him), the *Ibāḍi* constitution provides no explicit instructions.

Because of this gap in the constitution, Bel'arab ibn Sulṭān, the son of the *imām*, and national hero Sulṭān ibn Sayf I (1649–1688), was elected in 1688. This election led in practice to the adoption of a dynastic system and to the flouting of Ibadhite traditions. Following this, Oman entered a long civil war (1718–1737), the vicissitudes and effects of which we shall examine in Chapter 3, devoted to the Yaʻrūbite state.

The possibility of dismissing the imām

According to the constitutional principle, 'the imām cannot dismiss himself without occasions' any more than 'his subjects can dismiss their imam without occasion'.[119] This principle goes back to the *shūrā* and the *ijmāʻ*. In a time of political stability and respect for *Ibāḍi* values, the dismissal of the *imām* can only occur in conformity with the rules of consensus of the *'ulamā'*. In other words the only source of legitimacy of the *imām* and his *imāma* is the *ijmāʻ*, the consensus.

In theory too, the *imām* loses office when he is afflicted with any physical infirmity such as deafness, blindness, mutism or senility. His dismissal is not arbitrary and must have been the subject of consultation among the *'ulamā'*. Moreover, if they are of the opinion that his infirmity is not such a handicap that he cannot perform his mission satisfactorily, he is not removed from office.[120]

What is more, the Ibadhite constitution requires that, if the *imām* loses his sight and the *'ulamā'* agree to his remaining in office, he may be kept on the sole condition that someone helps him in the practical and executive tasks of the *imāma*.[121] So it was decided in the ninth century that ʻAbd Allāh ibn Ḥamayd (AH 208–226/AD 824–840), although he was old, should continue in office.

But if the question of the possible dismissal of the *imām* acquires such importance in *Ibāḍi* theory, it is because the *imām* is not just the head of state; his religious, spiritual and ethical role is considerable and his possible failure is more serious in that it also involves the spiritual authority of the people. Hence the rigorous attitude of the *'ulamā'* to this question; so provision is made that, in the case of an *imām* failing in his practical conduct to respect the religious and doctrinal precepts, the first care of the *'ulamā'* should be to attempt to bring about a change of heart on his part and repentance.

> If he repents, he returns to his imāma (...) If he persists and does not repent, the Muslims have the right to isolate him. If he refuses both to repent and to be isolated, it is then licit to fight him and shed his blood.[122]

Resipiscence is precisely a return to *ijmāʻ* to consensus, that is to say a return to the sources of doctrinal and political legitimacy.

Thus the power of the *imām* is the more incontestable, in theory, as the holder of the title holds to the constitution and Islamic values.

The institutions of the *imāma*

Generally speaking, there are two distinct ideas of a state: the state in the traditional historical concept and the modern state, in the juridical and constitutional meaning, as it has gradually emerged from the sixteenth century on. The *Ibāḍi* state, the *imāma*, is exceptional in that it borrows from both notions. Although its institutions do not operate, for example, in line with written constitutions or published laws, none the less they exist and operate in conformity with constitutional rules and traditional customs that are clear, cannot be set aside or indeed violated and are actually sacred. As such, these institutions have guaranteed stability and social peace as well as harmonious and cooperative relationships between the people and their rulers. More than that, they have ensured the survival of the *imāma* over more than a thousand years.

ʿUlamāʾ *and* majlis

The *imāma* system rests on one fundamental institution, the *ahl al-ḥall wal-ʿaqd*, made up of *Ibāḍi ʿulamāʾ*. These assembled *ʿulamāʾ* represent the supreme legislative authority and the juridical, doctrinal and political standard of reference. It is under their aegis that the election or dismissal of the *imām* is accomplished. They are directly responsible for managing all the affairs of the *imāma*. They control the application of the *shūrā* principle and prevent any deviation from it. They are judges, historians, teachers and it is from among them that most well-known poets and revolutionary leaders have been recruited. Last and by no means least, they are the spiritual and moral mentors of society and its conscience.

It is important to stress in this connection that, unlike other persuasions, (e.g. Shiʿite), no strict hierarchy exists within the *ʿulamāʾ*. Instead, in order to be recognised as *ʿālim*, it is generally necessary to have a good knowledge of the *fiqh*, which implies having been the pupil of other recognised *ʿulamāʾ* or having studied in certain schools.

In the exercise of his powers, the *imām* is assisted by a *majlis* of *shūrā* (upper council), probably consisting of fifteen members. Its chairman is the *imām* and its members are either ministers (*wazara*) or councillors. It meets as occasion requires, sometimes weekly, sometimes monthly. The *imām* can do nothing without asking the advice of this upper council. Sheikh Ṣāleḥ al-Ḥārthi (one of the leaders of the 1955 revolution) has described this system as 'consultative democracy'. All decisions have to be unanimous.[123]

There is also an assembly (*al-majlis al-ʿām*), which includes the members of the upper council, the *ʿulamāʾ* and the tribal chiefs. It meets when the *imām* considers it necessary and examines questions put to it by the *imām*.

Important decisions are taken only after the tribal chiefs have consulted their tribe. Thus the people share with their chiefs the responsibility for important decisions.[124]

Al-wūlāh: *the* wālis *(governors)*

> The administration of the country is carried out by the Imam through 'wālis' and tribal leaders. The wālis are appointed by the Imam, with the assistance of the Higher Council. After a wāli has been chosen, the people of his province (manāṭq) are asked if they approve him. If they do not, another is chosen.[125]

Moreover the *wāli* may be challenged by the population of the constituency to which he has been nominated, on condition that the objection is for motives that the *imām* and the *'ulamā'* find appropriate and convincing.

The appointment of the *wālis* follows the same model as the *bay'a* of the *imām*. These commitments reconcile the responsibilities and duty of the governor to his people and to the *imām* on the one hand and the *imām*'s responsibilities towards them on the other. The commitments stipulate again the equitable application of the law and indicate clearly the existence of the rights of *al-muwātn* (the citizen) and the need to preserve them.[126]

Traditionally, the *wāli* is supported by local notables, the *'ulamā'* and tribal chiefs. They constitute a restricted, quasi consultative council but with no official authority. Even so, they play a preponderant part in the administration of the affairs of the region or the village; they give their backing, usually effectively, to the governor in his duties.

Furthermore, each region has an autonomous 'consultative council' which is an almost exact replica of the *majlis* attached to the person of the *imām*. This council, consisting of notables and tribal chiefs, represents local authority and may be considered to be the legitimate representative of its community. Its mission is to assist the *wāli* and the judge in their duties. In certain instances it may also enjoy legislative power.

Al-quḍāh:[127] *The* qāḍīs *(judges)*

In Oman as in other Islamic countries the judge constitutes an institutional mechanism of prime importance. So judges are appointed directly by the *imām*, without *bay'a* or any particular ceremony. Of course, the other members of the *'ulamā'* help to choose them and present them as candidates. It may well be that a group of *'ulamā'* close to the *imām* recommend this *qāḍī* or that. But, once chosen, the judge (and his jurisdiction) enjoy a marked independence. Why? Because the judges are often recruited from the *'ulamā'* who fulfil the role of an independent legislative and juridical power. Recourse to the *imām* of course is still a duty but in particularly important causes.

Justice is administered in accordance with the law by the *Imām* and the *qāḍī*. Disputes between individuals are heard by the *qāḍīs* but disagreements between tribes are settled by the *imām*. The *qāḍīs* have the power to condemn to death but execution cannot take place without the approval of the *imām*.[128]

But in the end, what deserves emphasis is the independence, integrity and strict application of the principle of equality before the law. By virtue of this principle, the citizen has the right to sue the *imām* himself and oblige him to appear before the court in order to settle a dispute. The well-known story of the Bedouin who compelled the *imām* al-Khalīlī (1919–1953) to present himself to the court to judge a lawsuit concerning the sale of a camel is significant; the more so as the Bedouin in fact won his case.

Bayt al-māl *(public finance)*

The treasury of the *imāma* has three main sources of revenue. First source: the tax on exports of Omani products (dates, citrus, fish and livestock); this tax is the counterpart to the taxes levied on imports from India, Africa and Persia.

A second source stems from *al-zakāt* (religious tax), one of the five fundamental religious duties required by the Koran. *Zakāt* is often translated as 'legal alms' which must be understood as 'alms' demanded by law.[129] *Al-zakāt* is one of the fundamental aspects of the social philosophy of Islam; for the *Ibāḍis*, this duty is a response to the demand for social equality; its application is supervised by the *'ulamā'*.

As for the third source, it consists of a 'duty' tax on non-Muslim traders and non-Omani minorities. This differential fiscal device *vis-à-vis* foreign traders trading in Oman is not the outcome of discrimination, indeed it is the opposite, since the sum raised is equivalent to the taxes paid by Omanis in the countries of those traders. Yet again, the principles of justice and equality are present in commercial law as in Omani culture.

Similarly, supervision of expenditures connected with internal projects and reforms and their use is an attribute of the *imām*, indeed it is theoretically one of his chief preoccupations. But the *imām* cannot discharge this duty without seeking the counsel of the *ahl al-ḥall wal-'aqd*. And since this money belongs to the *bayt al-māl*, that is to say it constitutes the public property of the Muslims, the whole people, the *imām* may not dispose of it without submitting to precise monitoring. Any unjustified use of these funds outside the general interest is considered to be a sin and as such punishable by the *sharī'a*.

Al-jaysh *(the army)*

The *Ibāḍi* conception of the role of the army in the *imāma* system is worthy of mention. *Ibāḍis* have always disapproved of the existence of a professional army for fear that the *imāma* might exceed its traditional mission and that the elected *imām* might become a despot. Despite the frequent aggressions to which Oman has been subjected throughout her history, the *Ibāḍis* have always sought to preserve the peaceful nature of the *imāma* and hence the importance given in their system to the principle of temperance fostered by the *shūrā*. Here we see yet another way of applying the key principle of *shūrā*, guaranteeing the democratic values of the *Ibāḍi* system.

However, if war cannot be avoided, the *imām* asks the Omani tribes to take part in the defence of the *imāma*, whether against internal danger or external aggression. So an army is mobilised consisting of volunteers and enlisted men drawn from the sons of the tribes. To respond to the *imām*'s appeals, as leader of the army, is both a national obligation and a religious duty. This is how the Ibadhite constitution puts it: 'If the imam is well established in his imāma and he is attending to the right of his subjects, they must respond to his appeal and come to his aid if he invokes their help.'[130] In another article, the same constitution states that obedience to the imam is a duty. 'He who disobeys the imam commits a great sin'.[131]

External relations

A principle of doctrine, formulated in the Ibadhite constitution in the second half of the first century of the Hegira, indicates clearly the external policy of the *imāma*. It demands that the *imāma* respect the principle of moderation and reject that of *al-khurūj* (the principle of 'leaving'): Consequently it is impossible to attack or wage war on another party unless the *imāma* is the victim of aggression.

The external policy of the *imāma* has functioned throughout its history in three essential dimensions. The religious, doctrinal dimension and the dimensions of trade and politics. The last two may be linked. Traditionally it is on record, for example, that the political relations of Oman with the countries of the Gulf on the one hand, and with India on the other are concerned mainly with commercial and economic interests.

As for the doctrinal dimension, it is more to the fore in Oman's relations with East Africa and especially the region of Zanzibar and Tanzania, but it is not absent from relations with the countries of North Africa, and particularly Algeria, thanks to the existence of Ibadhite communities in those countries.

In fact, East Africa can be considered as a historical, political, doctrinal and even a national extension of Oman. As we shall see in the chapter on the sultanate of Oman and Zanzibar, this region has been under the direct rule of the Omani authorities ever since the time of the Yaʿrūbites in the middle of the seventeenth century. The *'ulamā'* of Oman have exercised direct supervision of the *Ibāḍi* communities in that region and considered them an integral part of the Ibadhite movement.

To come back to Ibadhism in North Africa, it undoubtedly also represents a doctrinal and cultural extension of the Ibadhism of Oman. But, because of the geographic factor, the link with Oman has been fairly limited. Nevertheless, the contact has been maintained by means of correspondence exchanged between the *'ulamā'* of the two countries and by visits of the North African *'ulamā'* to Oman, which continued in their eyes to stand as the ideal centre of the Ibadhite movement. Various *Ibāḍi 'ulamā'* from Algeria have stayed in the Nazwa region. Furthermore, it is the custom, when a new *imām* is elected in Oman, for the Omanis to write to their North African brothers to keep them abreast of the situation in the *imāma* and introduce the new *imām*.

At the beginning of modern history, new political and strategic factors were imposed on the external politics of Oman, such as the quasi direct conflicts with the western powers, first with Portugal, then with the Dutch and lastly with the British. This latter conflict was to colour Omani history for the last three centuries.

As for other regional relations, hostility towards the Persians often assumed a political dimension. With the Wahhābis, a hostile relationship developed on both doctrinal and political grounds.

Generally speaking, the *Ibāḍis* have made it a principle to limit cooperation with foreign forces and reliance on non-Muslim auxiliaries. Indeed, the *Ibāḍi 'ulamā'* are of the opinion that cooperation with foreign forces is acceptable provided that it is clearly defined and limited. But the *imām* does not have the right to decide on his own to resort to non-Muslims in his *imāma* or to accept their influence. If he does so, he must 'repent', otherwise he deserves to be moved aside or even fought against.[132]

These are the principles and ideas that underlie the *Ibāḍi* political system and are the basis of its originality. By studying the political history of Oman in the rest of this book, we shall be able to examine how the power and institutions of the *imāma* function.

2 The Portuguese period

1500–1650

The first colonial phase

The period from the fifteenth to the seventeenth century marks a phase of decline not to say almost total eclipse for Oman and the whole Gulf region. The remarkable strategic and commercial position that had brought success and prosperity to Oman was also a source of weakness when faced with Persian and European ambitions in the age of discoveries and new stakes in international trade. This was more as the *imāma* found itself enfeebled and atrophied at the end of a long process of disintegrating power. Having been powerless since 1154 due to the succession of usurper kings of the Banū Nabhān (al-Nabhāni), the *imāma* was only just beginning to recover in a limited part of the country, when the first Portuguese 'conquistadors' approached the Gulf region. And in the absence of the *imāma*, no one would then be able to prevent them carving up the country and setting in motion a long period of decline and political and economic stagnation. The period of colonial exploitation of the region had started and for nearly a hundred and fifty years, the Omanis would be obliged to look on helplessly at the colonial manipulations by Europeans in the region.

Historical outline

Ever since Antiquity, eastern and western trade had followed two main routes: that of the Red Sea and Egypt and that of the Gulf and al-Chām (greater Syria), both under Arab domination.[133] The Omanis and Yemenites operated in the Gulf and the Indian Ocean while Phoenician ships criss-crossed the Red Sea and the Mediterranean Basin. Their roles at that time were parallel and complementary.

Thanks to her fleet, Phoenicia (*al-Bunduqiya* in Arabic), a principle hub of ancient trade, was the obligatory intermediary between East and West. This monopoly had been steadily crumbling away throughout the Middle Ages, notably ahead of the advance of the Turks. And when the latter occupied Constantinople in 1452,[134] the historic commercial role of the Phoenicians was eclipsed; they lost their position and privileges in the East, and especially in India, for good. At the dawn of the sixteenth century, with the success of the Portuguese voyages of exploration and discovery, trade in silk and spices which were luxury goods in

Europe, passed into the hands of the Lusitanian navigators; the trade route was modified and the new history of international trade took another course.

The new configuration of world trade was not without its repercussions in the Gulf region. Yemenite and Omani supremacy was challenged by the activity of the Portuguese who were not slow to snatch local trade from the hands of the Arabs;[135] it remained under their control for nearly 200 years. So it is hardly surprising that the Portuguese intrusion should have been resented so bitterly and lastingly by the Omanis; they were the first victims of the blow struck by Vasco da Gama and his emulators not just against their commercial interests, but against their freedom and sovereignty.

But before considering the Portuguese domination and its impact, we must set the scene in which the Lusitanian intervention unfolded, and first of all the geo-economic facts.

The 'second' Hormuz was then flourishing, a small island constructed in 1300 at the entrance to the Gulf after the annihilation by Mongol invaders in the twelfth century of the state of ancient Hormuz on a neighbouring island. It formed an important link in East–West trade.[136] Despite its small area and complete lack of vital resources (vegetables and water), the island's population in the fifteenth century reached 40 000 inhabitants (Persians and Arabs), a considerable figure for that period. English specialists claim that its volume of trade at that time exceeded that of London or Amsterdam at their zenith.[137] Although too general, this comparison gives some idea of the strategic and commercial importance of Hormuz.

Oman at that time was living through a troubled period in its history, under the yoke of a usurping dynasty, which condemned the country to confusion and incursions by foreigners.[138] It is worth noting, too, that the history of Oman in the Middle Ages is somewhat obscure; even the main sources of reference, like *Tuḥfat al-A 'yān* by al-Sālmi or *Kāshef al-Ghama* by Azkaui fail to throw sufficient light on the events of that period. It is reasonable to suppose that the oppression practised against the *'ulamā'* of the time may have kept the chroniclers silent. During that period, Oman was subject to the kings of Banū Nabhān who had usurped power from the hands of the imamites and were to keep it over most of the country until the election of *imām* Nāṣer ibn Murshed al-Ya'rūbi in 1624. The reign of the Banū Nabhān dynasty lasted almost 500 years, a period described by Omani historians as a dark phase in their country's history, since the imamite religious dignitaries had to undergo terrible persecution; books were burnt, religious and teaching activities were annihilated. At the same time, the doctrinal laws that conformed to Ibadhite traditions were abolished and total, widespread anarchy was the result. Generally speaking, the Omanis were exposed to many types of oppression: land and property were confiscated, forcing some tribes to move away to the interior of the country or to flee altogether.[139]

In spite of everything, a few broad lines emerge from the general confusion of this period, revealing increasing mobilisation against the power of the Nabhāni. This opposition was at first held in check, then gained confidence from the election of the *imām* al-Hawari ibn Mālek in 1406 and, from the defeat of the Nabhāni kings in the interior of Oman, but failed to get the better of them completely. The resistance of the Nabhānite kings under pressure was concentrated around Bahla, which became their capital. After the death in 1435 of *imām* Mālek ibn 'Ali, whose name is always associated with the 'legitimist awakening', Oman was able to elect several *imāms*: Abū Ḥassan ibn Khamys (1435–1451), 'Umar ibn al-Khaṭṭāb (1451–1490) and lastly 'Umar al-Sharīf, Aḥmed ibn Muḥammad and Abū al-Ḥassan whose respective dates remain uncertain.[140]

The fact is that these last four *imāms*, belonging to the tribe of al-Yaḥmady, proved incapable of suppressing the rebellious tribes, reunifying Oman and restoring stability. But they did manage to mitigate the evils of the Nabhānite period and preserve the first signs of a return to legitimacy. It was only with the election of *imām* Muḥamad ibn Isma'īl in 1500 that Oman was able once more to enjoy some kind of stability in the interior.

On the eve of the arrival of the Portuguese, the map of Oman, excluding internal partitions which we shall deal with later, showed several distinct geo-political areas: the *imāma* in the interior of the country, the last Nabhānite kings, concentrated in the Bahla region and as for the coast, it was still under the sway of the king of Hormuz with two deputies, one in the coastal town of Qalaḥat and the other in Muscat.

The Silk route

For about half a century, the Portuguese had been undertaking voyages of exploration looking for a sea route which would enable them to bypass the Turkish intermediary (or enemy) and reach India, its silk, spices and minerals, the keys to the European market, without firing a shot. None of these efforts would bear fruit until the reign of Dom João (1481–1495).[141]

No one could then foresee that these campaigns of exploration, aimed initially at opening up a trade route would signal a new era in the colonial exploitation of the East.

In July 1497, Vasco da Gama left Lisbon, rounded the Cape of Good Hope, and then sailed slowly up the coast of Africa, from port to port, searching for a pilot who would guide him to India. At Malindi, an important port on the coast of modern Kenya and a centre of exchange for goods coming from India, the Red Sea and the Gulf, Vasco da Gama persuaded Aḥmed ibn Mājed from Julfār (Ra's al-Khaymah), the famous Arab navigator, to lead him to Calcutta, then to Goa in India, where they arrived in 1498.[142]

Thanks to Aḥmed ibn Mājed, who had seen genuine benefit in his contribution to contact the civilisations of the East that he knew and the West that he aspired to know and who could as yet not imagine the unexpected results of what he did, the first expedition of Vasco da Gama was crowned with success.[143]

When Vasco da Gama reached India, he ordered his men to buy everything they could get hold of in the way of spices and at double the price, to the amazement of the Indian and Arab traders. Back in Lisbon, Vasco sold his goods for sixty times the original price and covered the costs of his expedition six times over. And when the news of a final profit of 3000 per cent spread through the town, the same eastern adventure tempted many an amateur.[144] The success inspired king Manuel I to add the titles of *Lord of the conquest, navigation and trade of India, Ethiopia, Arabia and Persia* to his own. And the Pope gave his blessing to that title.

True, the first objective was of a commercial order but it was mixed with an undeniable spirit of crusade and 'reconquista' in Vasco da Gama, Alfonso de Albuquerque and their military chiefs. From the testimony of an eighteenth century Portuguese historian like João de Barros, it seems that their actions in that part of the world aimed at maximum devastation:

> By a special gift of God, Portugal had been granted the prerogative – and that is her true heritage – of winning the titles for his Crown thanks to conquests over the infidels, especially the Arabs who, as we said at the start, leaving the eastern regions where their homeland of Arabia lies, came all the way to our western countries. It seems that, after having allowed them to be the scourge of Spain and a punishment for her sins, destroying and devastating the lands and their inhabitants, God willed that, after so many centuries, the Portuguese should exercise their natural right in the same way, at sword point; and not only in sterile Arabia, where they destroyed towns, burned houses, carried women and children away captive, seized their property and their homeland, but in Persia too.[145]

These remarks need no comment. But if we add the commercial profit, which could be up to 3000 per cent of the purchase price in the East, we may well imagine how frantically the Portuguese hurled themselves on Indian, African and Omani towns and later on Hormuz and Bahrein.

In fact, the strategic prospect of building a Lusitanian empire only became clear after Albuquerque's visit to India in 1502–1503. A three-point plan then came to light: first to occupy Aden so as to guarantee Bāb al-Mandab and control shipping in the Red Sea; second to occupy Hormuz and the Omani ports of Qalaḥat, Qurayāt, Muscat, Khūr-Fakkān and Julfār and take control of trade in the Gulf; last to occupy Diu and Goa and extend Portuguese domination over all the regions of India.

In 1502, then, Vasco da Gama set out again for India at the head of a flotilla of five vessels. It was not long before the hostile nature of this expedition became clear; Vasco da Gama started by sinking any ship he encountered on his way. The Indian Ocean, which had been peaceful till then, was quickly transformed into a zone of conflict and piracy. Thus Vasco da Gama managed to dominate the coasts of India and complete the first stages of the Portuguese colonial plan. In 1505, Dom Francisco de Almeida was appointed governor general and king Dom Manuel of Portugal's viceroy in India.[146]

The Portuguese invasion

In 1508, another Portuguese fleet led by the celebrated sailor Alfonso de Albuquerque arrived in the Yemenite island of Saqatra, near the entrance to the

Gulf. The Portuguese believed a legend which told that Jesus had passed that spot when travelling to India. Maybe that was what made the Portuguese sailors use it as the starting point for their expeditions to India and the Gulf. It was there that Albuquerque made preparations for the second stage of his colonial plan in the Gulf region.

The offensive was launched on 10 August 1508 and in less than ten days four Omani towns were set on fire, sacked and occupied: Qalahat, Qurayāt, Muscat and Khūr-Fakkān.[147] The Portuguese troops had no compunction about behaving in the cruellest way then current and they tortured the conquered people savagely. The captives' noses and ears were cut off either as a joyful celebration of victory[148] or else as a punishment and to forestall any attempt of resistance.

In the course of that same month, Albuquerque continued his expedition against Hormuz; despite relatively limited means, but as a result of the widespread fear in the region, he was able to neutralise 40 Omani ships and sign a first agreement with the governor Sayf al-Dīn who was appointed king of Hormuz. By that agreement, freight was declared exempt from customs duties and the king undertook to pay an annual poll tax, no longer to the Persians but to the Portuguese.[149]

Subsequently, Albuquerque continued to carry out the Portuguese colonial programme elsewhere. In 1514 he led an expedition to Aden and tried in vain to occupy Massawa and close the Red Sea to Egyptian ships.[150] Wilson states that if the king of Portugal had been able to dominate Aden as he had Hormuz and Malga, and achieve complete mastery of those three straits, he might justifiably have accepted the title of master of the universe, following the example of Alexander the Great when he crossed Al-Jānz.[151] In a second expedition in 1515, the Portuguese admiral overcame the whole Gulf region and pushed on further: Mombasa, Malindi and a few other islands fell to him.

Altogether, in a few years of unequal struggle in which surprise and fear had played a major part, the Portuguese had taken control of a huge region, from the east coast of Africa to the west coasts of India. At the centre of this system, Oman and the gulf of Hormuz controlled all their traffic in the Gulf.

After 1542, when the governor of Hormuz was unable to pay the poll tax demanded, the Portuguese decided to appoint two 'supervisors' to collect customs duties. By this oppressive procedure, they became the veritable owners of Hormuz.[152]

They now had to circumvent Persian power and there too circumstances favoured their interests wonderfully: shah Ismail (1499–1542), who had made Tabriz in the north of the country into his capital, was more interested in that region than in the south. What is more, he attempted to fight the Ottomans, who crushed his army at the battle of Chaldoran in 1514 and occupied his capital for several years.[153]

Endangered by the Ottoman thrust in a region particularly close to his heart, the shah saw no alternative but to cede territory in the Gulf where he faced the Lusitanian colonisers. He even accepted the occupation of Hormuz and acknowledged his dependence on the king of Portugal.

How is this attitude of the shah towards a threat that seemed, all in all, at least as serious as the Turkish peril to be explained? In the words of the Portuguese historian João de Barros:

> The Portuguese were going to punish the Persians, a noble people, renowned for their ancient country, their arms and their civilisation, who had paid for the slight committed against Spain when they converted to the religion of those barbarous Arabs.[154]

In fact, shah Ismail found himself weakened politically by a doctrinal choice: he had been the first to make Shiism the official doctrine of his kingdom; hence the fierce hostility of the Ottoman empire towards him. By placing this doctrinal antagonism in the foreground, the two countries opened the way for the machinations of the Portuguese colonisers.[155]

Because of their religious zeal in the Islamic world, the Turks could have won the approbation and alliance of the shah of Persia and the Mogul emperor in India and kept the Europeans away from the Indian Ocean for many years. But Suleiman the Great had failed to understand the importance of mobilising his forces to that end.[156]

The Portuguese forces benefited from the tension between Ottomans and Safavites and equally from a local regional dissension: a new division – doctrinal, between Shiʿites and Sunnis – was added to the political and tribal dissensions that had weakened patriotic resistance to the Portuguese.[157]

Indeed, we may imagine that, if the Ibadhite movement in Oman and its *imāma* had not been marginalised by the reign of the Nabhānis, in other words, if Oman had been united, it could have stood up to Portuguese aggression. Why? Because, with the *imāma*, the Omanis had at their disposal a stable institution with which they could identify, capable of structuring resistance to the invasion. But also because war against the invader and bloodshed in defence of the *imāma* were a sacred matter for the *Ibāḍis* and a moral obligation which none felt able to evade.

So once the surprise and consternation were over, the peoples of the region soon rallied and the Portuguese had to deal with rebellious movements in 1519 and 1521. Then, on 30 November, 1522,[158] a general insurrection broke out. The Portuguese only managed to stifle it by appealing for reinforcements sent specially from India. But the Omani populations did not lay down their arms. The country was still a prey to uprisings and revolts. In particular, a new insurrection occurred in 1526 and lasted for a year,[159] but in vain. Oman would have to await the advent of the Yaʿrūbite *imāma*.

All these internal and external challenges obliged the Portuguese to reinforce their positions in Muscat – an important strategic point – and to transform that city into a substantial military stronghold at the entrance to the Gulf. In 1587, the Portuguese set about building two colossal fortresses at Muscat. The first was San Goa renamed by the Omanis *al-Jalāli*, and the second, al-Qobṭān, renamed *al-Mīrānī*.[160] They are still standing, perpetuating the memory of the occupiers of those days in Muscat.

A challenge to Portuguese domination

Meanwhile, with the signature of a peace accord between the Ottoman and Safavite states in 1555, the balance of political power in the Gulf region had been disrupted[161] with Persia giving up her claims on Mesopotamia and transferring her interest back south towards the Hormuz region. Then, with the advent of shah Abbas I (1586–1629), Persia received a strong boost, both internal and external, and was prepared to play an important regional role again.

The exclusive supremacy of the Portuguese, called into question by the Persian awakening at the end of the sixteenth century, was compromised at the dawn of the seventeenth century by the rise of rival European imperialisms. Great Britain and Holland would become the two chief protagonists in this new act on the Gulf stage.

Meanwhile, the Portuguese presence had done considerable harm to the country and its infrastructures; the Arab merchant fleet had suffered a fatal blow, reducing activities in the region to zero. These ravages spread to all the sectors linked with commerce.

Altogether, due to the permanent Portuguese domination of the sea lanes in the Gulf, the local culture of the nation had, so to speak, disintegrated so that when the English and Dutch arrived, the region was, more or less, ready for a new colonial stage, unable to offer the least resistance.

The British and Dutch phase

It was owing to contacts with Persia that the British set foot in the Gulf region. The first contact between Great Britain and Persia was established on the initiative of unofficial persons, notably the Briton Robert Charly. Then came the time of more official relations, of a firm convention and lastly an alliance between the two countries. And so the English managed to make a place in the sun for themselves, in the words of their own historians.

To start with, it was a question for them of asserting themselves over their Dutch competitors who in 1602 had set up their own Eastern Company, a rival to the East India Company, set up by the British by a law of 31 December 1600,[162] and operating in the areas of Indonesia and eastern India. The two companies promptly embarked on a bitter struggle over spheres of influence. The theatre of activities spread from the coasts of Indonesia and India as far as the Gulf. Later, thanks to the Persian–British alliance, the British company was able to take up a position in the port of Jask (Bandar Jask) lying about 150 km from Hormuz. The English thus scored the first point.

At the same time, Persian policy began to work indirectly and then directly for British interests. In 1602, shah Abbas I struck a first sharp blow at the Portuguese in the area of Bahrein. Later the shah expressed a wish for an alliance with the British. In about 1618, the British East India Company thus obtained exclusive rights for the purchase of every kind of Persian silk.[163] This monopoly, the first of its kind, gave an appreciable boost to trading relations between the two countries. The British presence in the Gulf increased.

The wind had turned and Portuguese supremacy was henceforth challenged by a series of interests. In 1610, shah Abbas decided to transform the area of Gamberun opposite the island of Hormuz into a major port, which he called Bandar Abbas.[164] This new port site restricted the influence of Hormuz, which affected Lusitanian commercial activity. The Portuguese reacted to this challenge by attacking Bandar Abbas which they occupied in 1612 and which remained under their domination until the Persians threw them out in 1615.

A first clash between British and Portuguese forces took place in 1612, followed by others in 1615. The Portuguese fleet was defeated off the coast of Surat, which allowed the English to garner other privileges in India. In 1613, they founded a branch of the East India Company in Surat.

Seeing Portuguese hegemony shaken, the Arab populations of the coast were able to start demonstrating their discontent and speculating on help from their Persian neighbour. And, indeed, the shah tried at first to take advantage of the movement; he cooperated with the inhabitants with the aim of driving the Portuguese out of the Julfār region.[165] But the 'allies of the inhabitants', the Persian forces, in fact became the new occupiers of the Arabian coast. Furthermore, in the climate of conciliation following the departure of the troops from Hormuz, an agreement was struck between the Persians and the Portuguese. The latter reoccupied the region and built a new fortress near the one that had been occupied by the Persian forces at Julfār.[166] The shah for his part kept a foothold on the coast. Finally, the disenchanted natives saw the occupation of their land reinforced not just by one but by two foreign powers.

None of the parties could leave things there. The Persians and the British concentrated first on getting rid of their Portuguese rivals in Hormuz. An accord was concluded between the shah and the East India Company with a view to joint military action against the Portuguese stronghold. This accord, also the first of its kind, stipulated, among other clauses, that in future the customs revenues from Hormuz be shared equally between the English and the Persians and that English trade be exempt from tax.[167]

British ambitions were now quite clear and, over and above commercial objectives, the English rulers were out to press their advantage in the region, to control its strategic points so as to ensure clear and lasting domination (in the event, for more than 300 years) over the East, its wealth and its lines of communication.

After investing in the Qishm region, the source of food and water supplies for Hormuz, the combined Persians and English troops laid siege to the place. On 21 April 1622, it fell into the hands of the Persian and English forces after the destruction of the town and the capitulation of the Portuguese. An agreement was reached to transport the remaining troops on English ships to their fortress at Muscat.[168]

The Portuguese domination of Hormuz was at an end, and with it the prosperity of the town, doomed henceforth to ruin and desolation. This abandonment was to benefit the port of Bandar Abbas, which became the main centre of the East India Company. Despite this harsh blow and the irreparable decline of their empire, the Portuguese contrived to maintain their positions around Oman for a while, notably in Muscat.

In the meantime, with the death of shah Abbas, Great Britain lost a friend and ally. Persia went through a period of relative withdrawal until the advent of Nāder Shah. The Dutch took advantage of this interval to push their colonial interests; they won a victory over the Portuguese in the Indian coastal region and strengthened their presence in Indonesia. The Dutch company founded Batavia (Jakarta) in 1619 and succeeded in driving the Portuguese from Malacca in 1641 and also from their best trading posts in India. Throughout the seventeenth century, this company enjoyed great prosperity and secured a monopoly of the spice trade with Indonesia.[169]

The Dutch collaboration with the English against the Portuguese fleet had resulted in Batavian privileges in Persia analogous to those enjoyed by the British. Following the example of the English company, the company from the Netherlands adopted Bandar Abbas as its headquarters and gradually, during the first half of the seventeenth century, Dutch commercial activity in the Gulf reached its peak. It even threatened to stifle British activity. All the import–export trade of Persia was in the hands of Dutch merchants, their ships sailed the region and had no hesitation in resorting to violence to secure their exclusive position in local commerce at the expense especially of English interests.

In the East, as in Europe, the naval and commercial powers of Great Britain and the United Provinces found their interests converging to such an extent that ultimate military confrontation became inevitable. In less than 20 years, from 1652 to 1667, four Anglo-Dutch conflicts broke out in Europe and in the colonial regions (in particular around Bandar Abbas in 1654).[170] Even though these wars brought no change in the position of the Netherlanders in the Gulf, they none the less allowed the British to establish the undisputed supremacy of their empire.

From the arrival of the French to the conclusion of colonial rivalries

The more belated irruption of French interests into the colonial game in the East modified the respective positions of the colonial powers for a while. By licence granted in 1664, Louis XIV in turn founded an East India Company, which was not slow to find its way to the Gulf region, and, like its English and Dutch counterparts, adopted Bandar Abbas as its headquarters.[171] The assertion of this new ambition opened yet again a period of conflict in the region.

Louis XIV, with an intention to first put an end to the commercial power of the Calvinists, opened hostilities in the Mediterranean and destroyed the fleet of the Hispano–Dutch coalition.[172] Seeing in that a chance to put a full stop to Dutch expansionism, Great Britain made an alliance with France initially. Then, once the defeat of the united Provinces was complete, the English switched alliances, following the pressure of English public opinion which was hostile to France, and signed a separate peace with Holland in 1674.[173]

By that alliance, the balance of power was again disturbed, as was the political game. The year 1688 saw an Anglo-Dutch alliance formed in Europe aimed at barring the way to French hegemony. Thereafter, the Low Countries adjusted their interests to those of their British partners even beyond the peace of Rijswijk, which put a brake on French ambitions (1697).[174]

Having conciliated Dutch power, the aim of the English, from the second half of the century, was to circumvent their weakened ex-rivals, the Portuguese, freed since 1640 from the tutelage of the Habsburgs in Spain.

> In 1661 ownership of the island of Bombay and its port was transferred to the British throne as part of the wedding present given by the Portuguese princess to her husband Charles II, king of England. In return, England undertook to protect the security of the Portuguese possessions in the islands of the East Indies.[175]

Allied successively, as her interest dictated, with the Persians, the French, the Dutch, and finally the Portuguese, Great Britain emerged as the only winner from this colonial wrestling match and 'diplomatic slalom', in which the whole future of her empire was at stake. Defeated at Hormuz, the Portuguese actually maintained a presence in Oman, but their colonial policy in that region as elsewhere would in future be in thrall to that of the English. The same held good for the Dutch whose colonial future, since the liquidation of their influence, was linked to that of Great Britain. Allies for a time (against the Low Countries), the French too had ultimately to yield to British pragmatism. In its eagerness to make preponderance on the continent of Europe its priority, the France of Louis XIV and then of Louis XV, would allow itself to be outstripped, notably in the East, by English imperial expansion. So, from the second half of the seventeenth century, Great Britain was in a strong enough position to lay the foundation of a lasting presence in the East, and in particular to organise her colonial space in the region. 'The English East India Company divided India into three geographical entities: the governments of Bengal, Madras and Bombay. Thus the Gulf region fell under the responsibility of the government of Bombay.'[176]

In other words, not only had the Gulf region entirely lost its sovereignty, but it was diluted politically in a composite whole with the minimum of cohesion from a historical, cultural and ethnic standpoint. The situation could not be more revealing of the state of mind that had inspired this colonial expansion and of the fate meted out to the peoples, their traditions, cultures and identities. It was the fate to which Oman was condemned henceforth, whether under the yoke of the Portuguese, the Persians or the English. And the idea of being one day lost and forgotten in that way has certainly much to do with the initiative of national awakening which, in Oman, would restore the *imāma* in the hands of the Ya'rūbites.

3 The example of the Ibadhi Islamic State in modern history

> Since no man has any natural authority over his follows, and since force alone bestows no right, all legitimate authority among men must be based on covenants.
>
> (Jean-Jacques Rousseau, Du contrat social)

The Yaʿrūbite state (1624–1741)

It was in the interests of *al-umma* and *al-waṭan*, in order to reunite the country and free it from foreign occupation, that an agreement was reached in 1624 between the two schools of Nazwa and al-Rustāq, as a result of which Nāṣer ibn Murshed al-Yaʿrūbi (1624–1649) was elected. Oman was then embarking on an exceptionally important phase in its modern history, one during which the *imāma* was reconstructed and the social unity of the country realised. Then Sulṭān ibn Sayf (1649–1688), a man of skill and rare strategy, succeeded Nāṣer ibn Murshed, liberated Oman, drove the Portuguese out of East Africa and built the 'Arab–African' state of Oman. This period saw the *Ibāḍi* model of an Islamic State take shape.

Towards the end of the seventeenth century, however, the Yaʿrūbite state began to move towards a dynastic system. The traditional practice of election to the *imāma* remained in force but, with the *imām*s always belonging to the same family, it forfeited its democratic content and gradually the tradition of election came to an end. This unique experiment was thus compromised from within and eventually ended in civil war.

Imām Nāṣer ibn Murshed al-Yaʿrūbi (1624–1649)

For some five centuries after the fall of the first *imāma* in the third century of the Hegira (AD ninth century) and under the reign of the Nabhānite kings, Omani society had departed from the model designed by its values, its Ibadhite culture, codes and traditions. It had experienced disruption and total anarchy, a long stretch strewn with national and moral setbacks and, to cap it all, the occupation of the coastal towns by the state of Hormuz towards the middle of the thirteenth century, followed later by the arrival of the Portuguese, who again occupied those regions, including Hormuz, in 1508.

Oman was then divided up into more than ten districts, provinces and regions, semi-independent from each other with autonomous governments: Mālek ibn Abil ʿArab at Rustāq, Sultan ibn Abīl ʿArab at Nakhal, Māneʿ ibn Sinān al-ʿUmairy at Semayl, ʿAli ibn Qāṭạn al-Hilāly at Semed-ash-shān and Moḥammad ibn Jufair at Ibri.[177] Likewise, six fortresses in six different regions came under the sway of various tribes, while, as we have seen, Muscat, Maṭraḥ, Suḥār, Ṣūr and Qurayāt were under Portuguese domination from 1508 and Julfār was under the dual sway of Portugal and Persia.

There seemed to be no prospect of unity in Oman. In order to save the country and put these trials behind it, the only solution consisted in setting out on the road to national unity and rallying around the Ibadhite movement, which would present its candidate, the man of consensus and national salvation, Nāṣer ibn Murshed al-Yaʿrūbi.

Thanks to the eminent Sheikh Khamīs ibn Saʿīd ash-Shakasy, Nāṣer ibn Murshed al-Yaʿrūbi was presented as candidate at the first traditional consultation among the *Ibāḍi ʿulamā'*. The meeting of *al-majlis al-ʿām* (the general assembly), bringing together 70 men from the elite of the *ʿulamā'* and Omani dignitaries, took place in the village of Kesra, in the region of al-Rustāq. It ended, exceptionally, in consensus on the name of the new candidate. And that is how Nāṣer ibn Murshed al-Yaʿrūbi, then aged about 21, was elected in 1624 and was told of the decision.[178]

It was not really possible for Nāṣer ibn Murshed, any more than for other *imāms*, to refuse this religious and patriotic duty. But, unusually, instead of having the conditions normally placed on the new *imām* imposed on him at the time of his *bayʿa*, (his allegiance), it was the *imām* who imposed on himself his sole condition: total loyalty. The *ʿulamā'* took the oath[179] and the *imām al-shirā'* was elected.[180]

> This election not only inaugurated a new dynasty but opened a new era in the history of Oman, in which the country advanced to a previously unknown pitch of prosperity and glory, while in Naser Bin Murshed it brought to the front a man of unusual sagacity and power, who was to rank as one of Oman's most famous princes.[181]

The new *imāma* had to tackle some truly historic tasks. All through the Nabhānite period, tribal spirit had become deeply rooted in society and had impregnated its culture. Moreover, the external Portuguese factor had come along to complete the collapse of internal cohesion. The mission of liberation was therefore only accomplished by rebuilding social cohesion and strengthening national unity.

During the first eight years of his reign, *imām* Nāṣer ibn Murshed, in a reasonably organised fashion, applied a steady, firm and strong policy *vis-à-vis* the rebellious tribes. He was rigorous in forcing both them and the purely formal petty kingdoms set up in the provinces and regions to submit. Tolerance and clemency towards his opponents went hand in hand with the *imām*'s firmness and this reinforced his spiritual position in the minds of the Omanis: 'By this practice, the imām's strength was further consolidated and his image as a man who was just and lenient towards the seditious spread throughout the country, with the result that they rallied round him.'[182]

The towns fell one after the other as if at that moment they were ready to wipe out forever all traces of the Nabhānite period and bring Oman out of the darkness in which it was languishing. This change was accompanied by the abolition of the 'feudal laws' which had been imposed by the tribes and the Omani kingdoms. So the revolution of the *imāma* completed a crucial stage in the process that would rescue the country from anarchy.

> This Prince proved to be one of the ablest and strongest rulers Oman ever had; he soon made himself master and tranquillised the interior and then turned his attention to the task of expelling the foreigners who held the coast forts and commanded the sea, with whom during his reign he was engaged in incessant warfare.[183]

The *imām* sent his army to the south to subdue Nāṣer ibn Qatn al-Hilāli. There, the imamite troops met the Banī Yās tribes, whose leader, Saqar ibn ʿIssa was killed. In trying to avenge him, his brother met the same fate.[184] And so the tribes of '*Sāḥel Oman*' were subdued. Thereafter, until al-Bū Sa ʿīdī came to power in the mid-eighteenth century, these tribes remained subject to the authority of the Yaʿrūbite state.[185]

Just the first eight years of the new *imāma* had sufficed to reunify Omani society and put an end to dispersal and disorientation. Society as a whole adhered to the new regime and ceased to be dominated by tribal spirit; Oman rediscovered herself and internal peace returned. The Omani people then prepared to free the coastal towns from the Portuguese yoke.

Liquidating the Portuguese presence

It is worth remembering that throughout this period, Anglo-Portuguese relations had been those of an alliance. Similarly, Perso-Portuguese relations were based on a good understanding. So the Omanis had to confront the Portuguese occupier relying only on their own forces. In the Julfār region, they actually had to fight both Portuguese and Persian troops at the same time.

The *imām* prepared an army and put ʿAli ibn Aḥmed in charge, supported by one of his close associates, al-Yaʿrūbi.[186] After two days of fighting, the imamite forces were victorious and threw both Portuguese and Persians out of the Julfār region (Ra's al-Khaymah) in August 1633. This was the first military victory against foreign forces.

One year later, in 1634, the region of Ṣūr and Qurayāt surrendered to the *imāma*.[187] Suḥār and Muscat remained subject to Portuguese troops. In 1644, the forces of the *imāma* embarked on intermittent wars with the Portuguese power but they were unable to break through the wall surrounding Muscat, which had been built by the Portuguese at the same time as the two fortresses of al-Mīrānī and al-Jalāli.

In 1648, the Omani troops under the command of Masʿūd ibn Ramadan and Khamis ibn Saʿīd set out on a new campaign to besiege and liberate Muscat. An encircling operation began on 16 August and lasted until 11 September, at the end of which the Omanis forced the Portuguese to accept the terms laid down by the *imām*. On 31 October 1648, an agreement was signed[188] containing five clauses, one of which dealt with the abolition of the law concerning the tax imposed by the Portuguese on the Omanis.

This was the first agreement concluded by a national force in the face of the colonisers. It was both a political and a moral victory for the Omanis. But the Portuguese did not give up; they asked their chief rulers in India for reinforcements. They were well aware, in fact, that if they lost their positions at Muscat, it would spell the end of all their positions in the Gulf region.

The conflict swung this way and that. It was no longer a struggle between colonial powers concerning zones of influence but between a rising national force and colonisers who were detested throughout the East. But the *imām* did not see the outcome of his liberating enterprise. In April 1649, after 26 years of government, Nāṣer ibn Murshed died, aged about 47, and was buried in the town of Nazwa.[189]

Imām Nāṣer's achievements were considerable. He had brought about the unification of Oman and wiped out five centuries of national bitterness. He had restored Omani dignity, re-established the traditions of the *imāma* and revived its heritage and prestige in the minds of the Omanis. He had laid the foundations and the main elements of the Yaʿrūbite state and it is thanks to him that Oman was able to approach modern history united and equipped with a spiritual message and a clear cultural and national identity.

Sulṭān ibn Sayf al-Yaʿrūbi (1649–1688)

On the very day of *imām* Nāṣer ibn Murshed's death, the *'ulamā'* held a general assembly to elect a new *imām*, in conformity with traditional procedures, and the consensus emerged on the person of Sulṭān ibn Sayf, a kinsman of the late *imām* and one of the military commanders. Sulṭān had participated in the earliest phase of the rebuilding of the Yaʿrūbite state. He was renowned for his wisdom and strength of purpose.

> To Sultan ibn Sayf I, who had succeeded his cousin Naser, fell the glory of this reconquest. A skilled strategist, he engaged in intense activity in the country while it was temporarily pacified (. . .) he equipped the country with a powerful navy which secured his victories over the Portuguese.[190]

The new *imām* was well aware of the missions he had to accomplish and of the abilities of the Omanis to do so. He was in a position to outline the future of the Omani state while taking advantage of the political legacy of the late *imām*. So Sulṭān ibn Sayf I's reign appeared to be a continuation of that of the founder of the Ya'rūbite state. This was the second stage in the *Ibāḍi* construction of the Islamic State in Oman.

But for the moment, the Portuguese had profited from Nāṣer ibn Murshed's death to renounce the agreement reached with the *imāma* and violate its articles, especially the abolition of the tax burden on the Omanis living on the coast. They had likewise resumed their exactions from the populations. The new *imām* responded unhesitatingly by declaring a war of liberation.

Sulṭān ibn Sayf personally supervised the military operations until, within a space of no more than six months, victory had been won. He forced the Portuguese governor general to hand the fortresses over to the Omani forces on 23 January 1650.[191]

In less than a year from the start of his reign, Sulṭān had triumphed, liberated Oman and completed the building of the Omani state. Thanks to this phase, Oman had regained its position as the most powerful maritime state on the Indian Ocean, extending its power and influence from the Gulf to East Africa.

The *imām* was not content with this victory and he set about hounding the Portuguese outside the frontiers of Oman. At the same time, the Omani and Arab communities of East Africa had asked the *imām* to free them from Lusitanian domination.

> They pursued the invaders by sea in a series of battles and even attacked them in their East African possessions. The fall of Mombasa in 1665 set the seal on the Portuguese capitulation and the end of more than a hundred and fifty years hegemony over the Gulf, the Arabian Sea and the Indian Ocean.[192]

Sulṭān ibn Sayf won another victory over the Portuguese by liberating the islands of Kilwa, Bata, Zanzibar and Mombasa and placing them under Omani authority. There, he appointed Omani personalities to administer the affairs of the islands of Zanzibar, Pemba and Mombassa. This whole area became officially part of the state of Oman.

During this period commercial and cultural relations between Oman and Africa were strengthened, as was the Arab presence in East Africa. From then on, the Omani community played a major role in the management of the economy and trade in that region. Omani culture was dominant, even though Swāḥili remained the most widely spoken language and the use of Arabic was limited to an elite of religious dignitaries and a few men in government and commerce.[193]

Later, in 1670, the Omanis led an offensive against the 'Diu' region near the gulf of Bombay, one of the centres of Portuguese colonisation. Then, in 1674, the Omanis attacked the 'Bessin' region, another Lusitanian colony.[194] These blows disturbed the balance established by the Portuguese in the coastal regions of India and reduced their influence for a time.[195] In honour of the Omani victories, the *imām* undertook the building of the famous fortress of Nazwa, financed by some of the booty brought back by the Omani forces from the battle of Diu; this enterprise lasted more than twelve years and was one of the milestones in the patriotic history of Oman.

For Oman, this period marked a development and renaissance in every field, economic, social and cultural. Thanks to a stronger merchant fleet, trade was thriving and Muscat replaced Hormuz and again became the most important place commercially and the transit port for the whole of the Gulf. Agricultural production, too, reached its highest level.

Oman also experienced a notable rebirth in the pedagogical and cultural fields. Men of religion and *Ibāḍi 'ulamā'* were the driving force. But the chief credit for this renewal is due to the climate of freedom that Oman was beginning to enjoy under the *imāma*.

Sulṭān ibn Sayf helped to prolong this flowering and took a particular interest in strengthening the institutions of the *imāma*. He kept a continuous and detailed watch on the judges and *wālis*, who in turn played a considerable role in administering the various regions of the *imāma*.

Altogether, in addition to the rediscovery of its identity, a genuine reconstruction of the state of Oman and of Omani society took shape under the aegis of its two re-founding *imāms*. It is fair to say that if Oman rediscovered itself in the days of Nāṣer ibn Murshed, with *imām* Sulṭān ibn Sayf I it was able to realise a large measure of its potential. The Ibadhite model of an Islamic state had therefore been built when *imām* Sulṭān ibn Sayf I passed away in 1688, his mission completed.

The controversial election of Bel'arab ibn Sulṭān (1688–1711)

After the death of *imām* Sulṭān, his son Bel'arab ibn Sulṭān was elected by a consensus, as a man endowed with all the qualities required for the post, who even had such a reputation for liberality and generosity that he was known as 'the father of the Arabs'. He continued the work undertaken by his predecessors. It was he who was credited in particular with creating official teaching establishments and offering every facility to students, including boarding and lodging. Later these schools trained an elite of judges and men of letters, including the famous poet Rashed ibn Khamis al-Habsy.

Fundamentally, there was nothing wrong with the election of Bel'arab ibn Sulṭān, no violation of the *dustūr* or *Ibāḍi* customs, especially as the newly elected *imām* had been very close to most of the great developments and achievements of his father's reign. He had even contributed to them personally.

But because of his position as a son of the *imām*, and despite his legitimacy (in the absence of any article in the constitution prohibiting the election of an *imām*'s son), this election marked the start of the change in the nature of the *imāma* in modern history. It was the precedent for and the beginning of a new tradition in the *Ibāḍi* political culture of Oman. Moreover, this decision opened the way to ambitions and claims to power. In short, we may not unreasonably conclude that from this moment on, the spiritual power of the *imām* was compromised and his function was transformed into that of an authority liable to be overthrown by force of arms.

> In losing the democratic condition, the election also, for the first time, lost its true value (…). If, at the beginning of the reign of the Ya'rubite imams, the election was a source of strength, its absence became a weak point in their final reign.[196]

The succession of subsequent 'elections' confirmed that a first flaw had appeared in the Ibadhite traditions. Seven *imāms* belonging to the same family succeeded to power, but the last ones did not enjoy complete legitimacy. Sayf ibn Sulṭān II was re-elected three, and perhaps four times, in 1718, 1722 and 1728, and even so did not acquire the required legitimacy. It fell to him to conclude the Ya'rūbite experiment in a tragic and regrettable way. He humiliated his homeland, even asking the Persians for help in a desperate attempt to consolidate his illegitimate *imāma*.

Once the 'dynastic' breach was operating in the name of elective sovereignty, it inaugurated a different kind of conflict. Sayf ibn Sulṭān challenged the authority of his brother Bel'arab and the pair embarked on a bloody war. Bel'arab, the legitimate *imām*, died after a reign of seven years.[197]

Sayf ibn Sulṭān I (1692–1711) managed to win over a group of tribes who paid him allegiance, although the *'ulamā'* of the Ibadhite movement had denied it him and considered him to be a usurper. But for fear of the reprisals of Sayf ibn Ṣulṭān, renowned for his cruelty, the *'ulamā'* formulated no open objection.

As a consequence, the investiture had completely lost its elective element; it ceased to be an effective practice and became more a matter of ceremonial formalities instigated by the tribal chiefs so as to impose their own candidates. The Omanis were obliged to obey, under pain of unleashing a civil war.

Be that as it may, *imām* Sayf ibn Sulṭān I had been the leader of great initiatives in both internal and external affairs. Externally, the power of Oman was increasingly consolidated under his reign and the merchant fleet was strengthened. He had also been able to send 3000 men to East Africa in 1696 to retake the island of Mombasa, which had fallen into the hands of the Portuguese, and bring it under the influence of Oman.[198]

> By the start of the eighteenth century, the Yarubite imams ruled a state whose political influence extended throughout the lower Persian Gulf, as well as to the coasts of East Africa and southern Arabia in the west and to the coastal approaches of the Indus valley in the east. The economic influence of this state reached out from the shores of the Gulf into interior Iran, Iraq and Arabia; at its western limits this influence extended to the central African lakes and in the east it touched the Ganges.[199]

Internally, he is credited with great developments in the agricultural economy, introducing new plants not previously grown in Oman, the most important being saffron and coffee. Finally, he set about reforming and structuring the irrigation.[200]

Whatever taint of illegitimacy may have sullied his election, Sayf ibn Sulṭān I remains a remarkable ruler, the last in date of the outstanding personalities of the Ya'rūbite state. He certainly did not consider himself a *'ālim* but he was nevertheless a first class statesman. The other criticism that could have been made of him was that he had become the greatest trader and the greatest landowner in Oman. He owned scores of slaves, which, admittedly, was acceptable in those days. But his life style did not offer the best possible model for his spiritual position among the Omanis, especially as the contrast with the image of Nāṣer ibn Murshed, an austere man, was still very present in their minds.

All in all, the material balance sheet for this period is by no means negative, but it is clear that the material development of the state and society was not matched on the spiritual plane. By losing its moral and spiritual dimension, the *imāma* had shed part of its content and was no longer really able to justify its existence as an institution.

The fact is that on 16 October 1711, *imām* Sayf ibn Sulṭān died and his son Sulṭān ibn Sayf II was elected and invested as *imām*.

Historians have reviewed the question of the election of the new *imām*, but they have given no details concerning the position of the *'ulamā'* of the Ibadhite movement in that election. Either the *imām* had the benefit of consensus, or else this omission is explained by a lack of sympathy towards the *imām* on the part of the Omani historians. This is a plausible hypothesis, given that the Omani historians have deliberately neglected the historiography of a regime that was illegitimate in their eyes, and which they called the regime of the *'jabābirah' imām*s ('unconstitutional rulers'), thereby condemning it to oblivion.

That said, Sulṭān ibn Sayf, was, like his father, known for his strong personality. The Omani historians have clearly criticised his waste and misuse of public funds. He spent the entire fortune bequeathed by his father and borrowed a great deal from the mosques and *al-awqāf* (property in mortemain).[201] Yet the Omanis did not protest against him, perhaps because of the fear he inspired.[202]

During this period, Oman succeeded in liberating Bahrein from the Persians, and the Omanis occupied places on the Persian coast: Qishm, Larak and Hormuz. So the country finally established its domination of the Gulf region, which would last till the nineteenth century.

The decline of the Yaʿrūbite state

On the death of Sulṭān ibn Sayf II, Oman entered a fresh phase of violent power struggle. Although legitimate, the election of Bel'arab ibn Sulṭān (1688–1711) had given the *imāma* system a hereditary character. Yet a historian who is also a legal expert, al-Sālmī, confirms that, even under the reign of the last Yaʿrūbites, the *imām* did not automatically inherit power but assumed it after the allegiance and election by *'ahl al-ḥall wal-'aqd'*.[203]

Whatever may be the case, the germ of 'this hereditary tradition' would, in the absence of an accepted successor, provoke a bitter power struggle and cause the political and tribal situation in the country to explode.

Sulṭān ibn Sayf II left several sons, the eldest, Sayf, being twelve years old. Although he was a minor, a group of tribes attached to the Yaʿrūbite family presented his candidature to the *imāma* in succession to his father. Once more, this kind of procedure was basically the outcome of a dynastic mechanism, which now had nothing to do with the system of the doctrinal and spiritual *imāma*.

In this exceptional circumstance, *ahl al-ḥall wal-'aqd* strongly opposed this candidature, which threatened to change the spirit of their institutions and traditions. We should remember that the *dustūr*, the Ibadhite constitution is categorical on this point: 'The imāma of a minor is unacceptable since he would be barred from sovereignty at prayers. How, then, could a minor become imam…?[204] And how could one who has undergone neither judgement nor punishment judge and punish others?'[205]

Faced with this constitutional and political crisis, it was the duty of the *'ulamā'* to resolve the matter; on the suggestion of sheikh 'Ādi ibn Sulaymān, they presented another candidate from the same family, Muhanna ibn Ṣulṭān, Sayf's uncle. By an unaccustomed expedient of the *'ulamā'* and a separate and exclusive agreement, the election of Muhanna ibn Sulṭān as the new *imām* took place in the citadel at Nazwa in May 1719.[206]

This election did not, however, obtain tribal consensus, nor a majority that would ensure the success of the attempt. Undoubtedly this rapid procedure was a relative departure from the customary electoral procedure. But the chief question is still to know whether it was possible to obtain tribal consensus in such circumstances. Certainly not. That makes the position of the *ahl al-ḥall wal-'aqd* understandable and we may judge this exceptional procedure to have been necessary.

However, it is possible to say that in view of the method apparently followed in this election, *ahl al-ḥall wal-'aqd* had ceased to be the principal actors on the political stage in Oman. They had, up to a point, yielded the levers of power to the tribes. We shall see later that the *'ulamā'* will end up no longer enjoying final decision-making in the country. It is clear that decision had already ceased to depend on *shūrā* (consultation) and *ijmā'* (consensus), but was more a matter of strength. Thus, before a year had passed, Ya'rūb ibn Bel'arab, a kinsman of Muhanna, led an offensive against the new *imām* at Rustāq and forced him to renounce the *imāma*.[207]

Before giving up, Muhanna had asked Ya'rūb for protection, which had been granted. But after his accession to power, Ya'rūb renegued on his commitment and put Muhanna in prison in chains.[208] This action led to an outburst of hatred, a reversion to clan mentality and ultimately to a climate of extreme violence.

In a precedent unique in Omani history, Ya'rūb set himself up as the guardian of Sayf ibn Sulṭān until he should reach the age of reason and become the future *imām*. This precedent was debatable and was contested doctrinally and constitutionally.

Thus the guardian Ya'rūb ibn Bel'arab, lured by power, abandoned paternalism and gradually managed to persuade some of the *'ulamā'* to grant him the *imāma*. The Omani historian ibn Ruzayq was able to say that the judge 'Ādi ibn Sulaymān had granted him pardon for his actions and for the murder of Muhanna. Ya'rūb thus obtained *al-bay'a* in the end. What Ibn Ruzayq and other Omani historians have failed to explain is why and how. They have been content to report that Ya'rūb had regretted his actions and so had been pardoned. In the light of this decision, then, the murder of Muhanna was *licit*[209] and so 'acceptable'.

On reflection, it is difficult to imagine how this allegiance found sufficient support in *Ibāḍi* legislation, especially as the man who granted allegiance to Ya'rūb and made the murder of *imām* Muhanna 'licit' was none other than the qāḍī 'Ādi ibn Sulaymān, the very one who had granted allegiance to Muhanna.

So another view of things is essential; it was to avoid bloodshed and in a spirit of conciliation that this eminent ʿālim accepted the nomination of Yaʿrūb ibn Bel'arab.

But the inhabitants of al-Rustāq did not accept the *imāma* of Yaʿrūb and demanded that Sayf be maintained in office. They appeared before one of the most influential tribal personalities, Bal'aʿrab ibn Nāṣer, the maternal uncle of Sayf. Bal'aʿrab ibn Nāṣer in turn made preparations, allied himself with the Banī Hanāh tribe and rescinded the confiscation of its possessions imposed by the first Yaʿrūbite *imām*, Nāṣer ibn Murshed. He also allowed him to resort to arms, which had previously been prohibited.[210]

Bal'aʿrab ibn Nāṣer launched a savage war against Yaʿrūb which lasted a whole year. In consideration of the war and under further pressure from some of the tribes, Yaʿrūb finally ceded the post to Sayf, who was imposed as *imām* in 1722 without having yet reached the age of eighteen. In return, Sayf took his conquering uncle to be his guardian and gave him the official title of 'State chargé d'affaires',[211] an exceptional post with exceptional status.

But Yaʿrūb had not abdicated completely: he resumed hostilities against his new adversaries and died the same year. As for the qāḍī ʿĀdi ibn Sulaymān, who had supported him, he was finally crucified with Sulaymān ibn Khalfān and his followers in the al-Rustāq region.[212] And Oman entered a period of decline and chaos.

The civil war (1718–1737)

An attempt to preserve the lost peace by submitting to the authority of the tribes and by the spirit of reconciliation failed to calm things: instead, conflict flared up between Bal'aʿrab ibn Nāser and the Ghafirite tribes who did not accept the *fait accompli* and denied the uncle guardian his title of 'State chargé d'affaires'. In the absence of a firm and stable central power, the social equilibrium was disrupted and Oman was sucked into a ferocious civil war which caused the country to regress into a state of anarchy very like the one preceding the advent of Nāṣer ibn Murshed in 1624. The tribes rose up, led by Khalaf ibn Mubarak, 'the sheikh of the Banī Hanāh, and Muḥammad ibn Nāṣer, the sheikh of the Banī Ghāfir. Two factions were born (Hināwi-Ghāfiri) and the tribes of the country rallied to their banner'.[213]

There were no accurate estimates by the Omanis of the number of victims sacrificed in that war. However, the report from the chevalier Podery, who was staying in Bandar Abbas, to cardinal Dubois, the French secretary of state, on 26 September 1723, mentions:

> The civil wars in Muscat are still going on between the two imams, Seif, the son of Sultan, and Yareb, the son of Boulareb. There have been more than forty thousand dead on each side in the two years they have been at war.[214]

This war in a sense was the death knell of the *imāma* system. As often happens in a state of vacuum and conflict, the Omanis regrouped around their tribes, which began to play an increasing political role at the expense of the *imāma*, social unity and internal peace. This war finally robbed the post of *imām* of its spiritual content.

> The duration of the conflict as well as its character profoundly altered the place and role of the imama in the life of Oman. It debased the office by making it a trophy to be won by force of arms and it brought into contempt the theological qualifications normally required of a successful candidate.[215]

To put an end to the bloodshed and save Oman from complete destruction, leading figures from the *'ulamā'* agreed to present a personality from outside the Ya'rūbite family, Muḥammad ibn Nāṣer al-Ghāfiri, as candidate and, in spite of his reluctance, he was elected in 1724.[216]

For the first time for just about a hundred years, this election removed the *imāma*, provisionally, from the hands of the Ya'rūbites. Several Omanis saw in this change a hope of getting Oman out of the crisis. But once again the election did not fulfil the hopes raised. In reaction, the Banī Riyam tribes in Jabal-al-Akhḍar (the Green Mountain) and the Banī Bū 'Ali in Jalan met together and formed a broad front against the new *imām*.

Muḥsmmad ibn Naṣer al-Ghāfiri in fact proved to be a competent man. He confronted the rebel tribes and imposed his authority on them. 'But, by an irony of fate, the two adversaries who had been enemies for five years, were both killed in the same battle'.[217] That was at Suḥār in 1728.

On the death of Muḥammad ibn Nāṣer, the tribe of Banū Ghafir confirmed the re-election of Sayf ibn Ṣulṭān, took him to Nazwa, the *Ibāḍi* capital, and asked, as a special case, that his allegiance be proclaimed. But Sayf's *imāma* did not last long since, because of his private life, as the *Ibāḍi* historians put it, he was isolated by the *'ulamā'*.[218]

The Persian invasion (1737–1741)

Sayf and the rest of his allies, the Banī Rawāḥa tribes, impugned these innovations in their turn and had some clashes with the new *imām* and his supporters.Unable to extricate himself, Sayf made the mistake of asking the aid of Nāder Shah who could never have dreamed of a better opportunity to extend Persian influence via the Gulf right up to the coasts of Oman.

In 1739, Nāder Shah invaded Oman with thirty ships and a large number of ships.[219] The landing took place in the coastal regions of Khur Fakkan, then the forces infiltrated and were deployed in the coastal towns of Oman, as far as Nazwa, which had to suffer the exactions of the invaders.

However, the presence of Persians on Omani territory temporarily transformed the internal conflict into one of secondary importance and the national struggle against the Persians came to the forefront. Despite their differences, the Omanis put up a strong resistance to the enemy, which helped to reunify the Omani house and quench a civil war that had lasted nearly twenty years.

Sayf had realised belatedly that his own interests were of no account to the Persians and finally, under pressure from certain tribes, he chose to give up the *imāma* in favour of Bal'a'rab ibn Ḥamyār. Thanks to this reconciliation, the Omanis succeeded in freeing most of the regions from the hands of the Persians, with the exception of Suḥār, administered by Aḥmed ibn Sa'īd al-Bū Sa'īdī.[220]

To restore the situation and find some kind of entente, the princpal tribes – Banī Ghāfir from al-Dhāhira and Wadi Semayl from al-Mu'ādel – joined with a group of *'ulamā'* and decided to offer the *imāma* to another man, Sulṭān ibn Murshed al-Ya'rūbi: his allegiance took place in 1738. For the first time since the civil war, this allegiance obtained a large majority and was the result of an understanding between the two opposing camps, al-Ghafiri and al-Hanāwi.

This agreement had in effect helped bring about the unity of the country. However, despite the refusal of the *'ulamā'* and the majority of the Omanis, Sayf persevered in his futile determination to recover the *imāma*. He helped to open old wounds and prepared the tribes who were attached to him to fight the new *imām*. What is more, he repeated his request for help from the shah, who forthwith hastened to send him considerable forces.

In September 1740 three Persian expeditions took place, supported by 6000 soldiers and commanded by Mirza Muḥammad Taqi Khan. They set sail from Bushehr and landed at Julfār about a month later. On his arrival, Taqi Khan built a fortress and harried the al-Hawla tribe who dominated the region of Khasab and had rallied to the cause of Sulṭān ibn Murshed.[221]

Imām Sulṭān ibn Murshed made the question of liberating Oman his overriding priority. Throughout his reign he tried to resist the Persians and engaged in battles against them. It is said that he wrote the final page of the Ya'rūbite state[222] and he died fighting in 1740. His death marked the end of the Ya'rūbite era.

Meanwhile, Sayf ibn Sulṭān, who was the prime cause of the civil war and had allied himself with the Persians against his own people, disappointed in his aspirations, decided to retire to al-Rustāq where he died. Omani historians did not even record the date of his death, which may have occurred around 1740.

The end of the Persian presence

In 1728, a meeting took place between Sayf ibn Sulṭān II and Aḥmed ibn Sa'īd al-Bū Sa'īdī, who had been appointed first *wāli* in the coastal region of Suḥār, one of the most important for trade.

Aḥmed ibn Sa'īd's distinguished and ambitious personality soon won him a reputation. He was to play an active part, not just in Suḥār but in the whole of Oman. This very soon gave rise to anxiety on the part of Sayf ibn Sulṭān, who promptly led desperate attempts to get rid of him, all to no avail. Aḥmed eclipsed Sayf swiftly and completely in the game of politics. This gave him a favourable opportunity to play a prominent role in Omani history.

Meanwhile, Persian forces had occupied Muscat and some of the coastal areas including Suḥār. They were met with resistance from the Omanis and especially in the Suḥār region, under the control of Aḥmed ibn Sa'īd. The resistance went on for seven months without a break and Aḥmed ibn Saʿīd lost 3000 men.[223] But his actions exhausted the Persian forces and the two camps entered into negotiations. An agreement was reached, by which the Persian troops were to withdraw from the Suḥār and Birka areas, leaving them to Aḥmed ibn Saʿīd's forces. But Muscat was to remain under Persian domination and Aḥmed had to pay an annual poll tax to Nāder Shah.[224]

The acceptance of this agreement, which did not involve the complete liberation of Oman, was merely a delaying tactic by Aḥmed ibn Saʿīd. He soon came to Birka as its liberator and appointed Khalfān ibn Muḥammad of al-Bū Saʿīdi as *wāli*.[225] From then on his aim was to stifle Persian activity by depriving Muscat of its economic role. He succeeded in having all maritime and commercial lines diverted to Birka, so enriching the liberated port and marginalising Persian-controlled Muscat.

This economic warfare considerably weakened the Persian positions. The invasion forces soon found themselves unable to continue with the occupation of Muscat. Worse still, the death of Sayf ibn Sulṭān further destabilised their position and the colonial dreams of Nāder Shah collapsed; the Persians decided on a swift withdrawal from Muscat. But what they had in mind was simply to fall back while sowing discord, which would favour their return: they resolved to hand Muscat over to the allies of Sayf and not to Aḥmed ibn Saʿīd. 'So the Persians sent a kinsman of Sayf, Majed ibn Sultan, to the shah to ask for his authority to hand Muscat over to him'[226] But Aḥmed ibn Saʿīd, who wanted to deal a knockout blow to the Persians, seized the opportunity to meet cunning with cunning.

> He intercepted the reply and used it to deceive the Persians, who handed Muscat over to him, and he put on a lavish leaving party for them at Birka; the party ended in a general massacre; any who escaped were piled into ships and, as soon as they were out to sea, the crews set fire to the ships and swam away.[227]

So 1741 saw the end of the Persian presence in Oman. That did not mean simply a victory over the invader. Once again it had only been possible to surmount this period of trial through a surge of national feeling: it was a victory of unity over dissension and of the will to re-establish an *imāma*, which, even without claiming to revive the prosperity and brilliance of the first phase of the Yaʿrūbite pre-eminence, nevertheless still represented a national political ideal for the Omanis.

4 Al-Bū Saʿīdi's state

The origin of the sultanate system

Transition from the *imāma* system to the sultanate system

Omani–French relations and Great Britain

The modern history of Oman can be divided into two closely linked stages: the first, the *imāma* system, which ended with the Yaʿrūbite state during the civil war of 1728–1737; the second, the sultanate system, which began with the reign of *imām* Aḥmed ibn Saʿīd (1741–1783). It was during this reign that the first implicit separation between the two political systems began to come to light. Yet the Ibadhite movement would continue to put its stamp on the history of the interior of the country, and the *Ibāḍi* culture would still impregnate the country as a whole.

Meanwhile the diplomatic landscape had been somewhat modified. In France, the Revolution and then the Empire were looking for a reorientation of their external policy. Contacts took place with a view to establish friendly relations between Oman and France. Napoloeon's expedition to Egypt in 1798–1799 constituted a threat to the entire British colonial system in the East. So for England nothing was more urgent than to try and plug the gap by signing a first treaty with Oman. Nevertheless, France continued to maintain relations with the Omanis, so throwing its weight on to the politico-colonial chequer board in the region.

Imām Aḥmed ibn Saʿīd al-Bū Saʿīdi (1741–1783)

Aḥmed ibn Saʿīd,[228] the founder of the al-Bū Saʿīdī state, had come on to the political scene, as we have seen earlier, when he was occupying the office of *wāli* for Sayf ibn Sulṭān II. However, by his contribution to national resistance and his leadership of it in the Suḥār region, his name was associated with liberation from the Persian presence. Seasoned by those grim years, he was the man to rescue Oman from her state of civil war, restore her to her regional place in the Afro-Asian and maritime system and make a decisive contribution to the shaping of her modern history, a history of the sultanate as opposed to the *imāma* system.

But in spite of the political and national credibility enjoyed by Aḥmed, his accession to power was not a foregone conclusion. The consolidation of his position required violent conflict because, on the one hand, traces of the civil war (1718–1737) were still present, and on the other, his regime lacked the required consensus, a prime condition for stability. One of the main factors that unleashed the civil war had been precisely the absence of that consensus.

First of all, Aḥmed had to remove his direct rival, Bal'a'rab ibn Ḥamyār, believed to have been elected twice at al-Rustāq, once before the death of Sayf ibn Sulṭān II and a second time after it. Probably Bal'a'rab had offered himself again as candidate for the *imāma* after Sayf's death, in conformity with his first allegiance ceremony. The question has not been resolved by Omani historians and is still shrouded in uncertainty. It is a fact that certain of the *'ulamā'* on principle adopted a negative attitude towards his second candidature.

Moreover, there is a report that Bal'a'rab hesitated to offer his candidature a second time, but that he changed his mind after being assured of the support of al-Qawāsim. And, in fact, when Bal'a'rab confronted his adversary Aḥmed ibn Sa'īd, he was at the head of 5000 men.[229] Such a large number is undoubtedly testimony to the active participation of al-Qawāsim in the political reality in Oman. Whatever the truth of the matter, it did not prevent Aḥmed emerging victorious from the battle, in which Bal'a'rab was killed. After which, Aḥmed gathered together the tribes who had followed him, asked for their approval and was granted the *imāma*.

The question of this *bay'a* is still a matter of controversy among historians. They have reservations on two points. The first concerns the lack of credibility of the two men who granted him the allegiance, and this provoked an absence of consensus from the *'ulamā'*. The second has to do with the absence of tribal consensus. In other words, national division was the result of the absence of consensus of the *'ulamā'* on one side and a civil war on the other.

Al-Sālmī referred to the objections of certain *'ulamā'* concerning this allegiance and concluded that *al-bay'a* was held without consulting the Muslims (the term 'Muslims' here means the *'ulamā'* and also includes the people of the country). The two men who pronounced the allegiance, Ḥabib ibn Sālem al-Bū Sa'īdi and ibn 'Arīq, are not among those who commit the Muslims to an act of allegiance, still less as it was concluded after a '*fitnah*' (discord).[230]

This thesis tends to demonstrate that Ḥabib ibn Sālem and ibn 'Arīq did not figure among the *'ulamā'*, in other words, they did not constitute a religious reference and consequently could not enjoy the power conferred by *Ibāḍi* law, that is to say derived from the constitution. So their decision was not bound to commit the *'ulamā'* or *'ahl al-bilād'*, the people of the country (the citizens). According to the Ibadhite constitution, to be legitimate the *bay'a* must have the approval of a minimum of six *'ālims*; this is a fundamental condition. That may be the reason why the *Ibāḍi 'ulamā'* did not commit themselves in this *bay'a* and why it was not generally accepted by the people.

In the opinion of the British historian Lorimer, Aḥmed's election to the *imāma* at al-Rustāq was apparently a carefully orchestrated affair. But doubt exists as to whether he was elected by consensus. The presence of certain Ghafirite tribes who later opposed it indicates that he acceded to the *imāma* thanks to the allegiance of the Hanawites, to whom the al-Bū Sa'īdī tribe belonged.[231]

For his part, al-ʿAqād observed that credit was due to Aḥmed for liberating Oman and that is why he obtained the allegiance for the *imāma* in 1741.[232]

In addition to his initial comments, al-Sālmī indicates that sheikh Saʿīd bin Aḥmed al-Kindi (one of the most celebrated of the *'ulamā'* and of historians) had spoken with Aḥmed about the *imāma* and that the majority of the people had attributed it to him.[233] So he was appointed *imām* in the traditional manner.

Whatever the facts, it is certain that Aḥmed ibn Saʿīd had not obtained the required consensus. However, he was deemed to be a special case. With his qualities as a statesman, he took advantage of his credit nationally and politically to accede to power, to the *imāma*. That is how, contrary to custom, he was able to make tradition obey policy and not the reverse. Besides, his ambition led him to be more a political ruler than a spiritual leader.

Oman in the reign of Aḥmed ibn Saʿīd

Aḥmed had no lack of political sense and more than once during his long reign (1741–1783), during which there was no shortage of troublesome factors, he had to make use of it. In the interior, his reign could be divided into two phases. The first saw the birth of antagonism with the hostile Ghafirite tribes. The second was marked by the revolt of his two sons, Sayf and Sulṭān at the end of his reign.

After putting an end to his differences with Bal'aʿrab ibn Ḥamyār, he had to confront another adversary, Nāṣer ibn Muḥammad, the chief of the Ghafirites;[234] his own son-in-law, a clever and politically prudent man, plotted against Aḥmed. When the latter got wind of what was being planned, he raised a colossal army of 30 000 men and the clash took place in the al-Dhāhira region. Despite his huge force, Aḥmed was beaten by his opponent. The tribes incorporated into Aḥmed's great army had been forced into it by the *imām*, hence their resentment and ineffectiveness against the troops fielded by Nāṣer. Aḥmed learned from his defeat and manoeuvred to limit its consequences and to be reconciled with his opponent: 'Ahmed allowed Naser ibn Muhammad almost total independence with purely formal recognition of the central power.'[235]

Whatever his methods of governing, great credit is due to Aḥmed for having managed to defuse the civil war and rid Oman during his reign of the attitudes and crises that went with it. He also developed the administrative system of the country. He built a naval and a commercial fleet and strengthened the position of his realm as a regional force in the Indian Ocean and the Gulf. He even tried to extend Oman's possessions in the area of East Africa that had been controlled by the Yaʿrūbite state before the civil war. However, while the governors of the islands of Zanzibar, Pemba and Bata proclaimed their allegiance to the power of Muscat, the al-Mazrūʿi family that governed Mombasa refused to recognise Aḥmed's sovereignty.[236]

Elsewhere, in the field of external relations proper, with the renewed power of Oman, the spectre of colonial subjection tended to recede. In spite of the moderate orientations of *imām* Aḥmed ibn *Saʿīd*'s policies, and more especially at the time of the boom in trade and the opening of Oman to the outside world, there were no special or official relations with Great Britain. The *imām* even refused a request from the East India Company to establish a branch in Muscat.[237] The *Ibāḍis* considered Aḥmed's firm attitude to colonial hegemony as one of his merits.

In the Indian Ocean, the new *imām* tended to play the French card, notably in his relations with Mauritius (île de France), with La Réunion (île Bourbon) and with India, more particularly with Tipu, the chief of the land of Mysore, a noted adversary of Great Britain. We shall return to this in more detail later.

Once traditional Omani influence had been re-established in the Gulf region, the Ottoman sultan asked Oman for an alliance in his conflict with Persia, which had blockaded Basra (1775–1776). *Imām* Aḥmed then took the initiative and sent a naval force of ten ships carrying 10 000 men. His son Hilāl was at the head of the expedition.[238] The Omanis were decisive winners in the clashes that followed and they raised the blockade of Basra. Thus they won another victory over their Persian neighbour and at the same time strengthened their relations with the Ottoman state. As a mark of his gratitude, the Ottoman sultan granted the sovereigns of Oman a pension that was still being paid at the end of the nineteenth century.[239]

A little later, as an expression of the specific nature of Omani–Indian friendship, *imām* Aḥmed sent the ship *al-Raḥmānī*, which had led the battle of Chat al-'Arab against the Persians, as a present to Sulṭān Tipu in Mysore.

In the new system of alliances of the restored power in Oman, relations with Mysore were further strengthened and an office was founded for a political representative in, Muscat and given the name of '*House of Deputies*'.[240]

Altogether, the enhanced influence of the *imāma* had, in a few years, made Oman a place of importance on the regional scene and, beyond the continued colonial presence ready to pounce on any weakness, had consolidated the country's traditional alliances.

Externally strong, the regime was nonetheless exposed to threats of destabilisation in its internal affairs. The two sons of the *imām*, Sayf and Sulṭān, initiated two attempted uprisings against their father.

In February 1781, the two brothers set out to occupy Birka and assassinated the *imām*'s *wāli*. The *imām* promptly retook Birka and pardoned his two sons. But a second revolt took place in December of the same year. Sayf and Sulṭān occupied the two fortresses of al-Jalāli, near their father's residence, and al-Mīrānī in Muscat, where they locked up their brother *Sa'īd*. The *imām* launched a huge counter offensive to retake the latter fortress and set *Sa'īd* free. At that juncture, ibn Raḥmah, one of the al-Qawāsim sheikhs of Julfār, took advantage of the confusion and set out to occupy al-Rustāq. *Imām* Aḥmed once more managed to restore the situation, raised the siege of the two fortresses, again pardoned his sons and recovered al-Rustāq, now abandoned by ibn Raḥmah.[241]

Some historians have justified Sayf and Sulṭān's revolt as a protest against the favour shown by their father to their brother Sa'īd, the child of a different mother. There is no doubt that it was the motive, but the role of Qawāsim, opponents of Aḥmed, who had no hesitation in supporting his sons' revolt against him, should not be underestimated.[242]

In addition to the convulsions that shook the interior and the considerable strengthening he brought about in external affairs, the long reign of Aḥmed ibn Saʿīd (about 39 years) also saw changes and new tendencies appearing in Omani society. This reign did not merely forge a new vision of a political system; above all it helped to lay the foundations of a new political, national and cultural identity.

For various reasons and in the first place because of the *imām*'s strong personality and his political and economic role, the era of Aḥmed ibn Saʿīd was considered as a transitional stage from an *imāma* to a sultanate system.

Sheltered by this new type of power, what non-Omani historians are wont to call the moderate wing of the *Ibāḍis* was able to develop. Its characteristic was a desire for moderation in applying certain *Ibāḍi* laws and doctrinal codes. These moderate tendencies gradually became one of the aspects of Omani culture in the coastal region in contrast to the lands of the interior that clung to so-called 'conservative' positions.

The advent of Aḥmed marked the beginning of a change in the power structure. Having departed from the traditional model of the *imāma*, he no longer relied just on the *'ulamā'*. He preferred to surround himself with kinsmen and sons for consultation and also for running the affairs of the *imāma*. He appointed *wālis* and *qāḍīs* without referring to the *'ulamā'*; still less did he seek their approval. The *'urf* (custom) of political power, along with social tradition, underwent inevitable and progressive change.

As a corollary, the Ibadhite movement found itself gradually isolated in the political arena, which necessarily restricted its influence on the historical process in modern Oman, although the movement remained preponderant in the interior of the country.

At the same time, a large and influential trading class grew up in this period of peace and security and brought Oman to a commercial and economic peak. This new group would in turn lay the foundations of the future political regime.

One of the principal questions emerging from this context of renewal had to do with the evolution and future of the tribal system. The answer could be only dimly perceived. Some tribes had, in fact, been strengthened by the long civil war, which had ended by creating an opposition to certain *imāms*, and they had found in the new regime an alternative that suited their clan interests, flouting the traditional demands of the political system of the *imāma*.

On the other hand, the tribes had often given strength to the *imāma* system and had, in the course of time, provided the country with many scholars, judges and *imāms*. The importance of the tribes lay, in some respects, in the fact that they had supplied symbols, models and outstanding personalities to the history and culture of Oman. Yet this interesting fact, peculiar to Omani society, must not conceal an even more striking reality, that of repeated tribal divergence in the absence of a strong *imām*; this contributed to the retreat from applying the principle of *al-shūra*, the weakening of the *imāma* system, its deviations and even its destruction.

In order to train his sons for accession to power, Aḥmed conferred on them the title of *'sayyids'* which had nothing whatever to do with the surname *'al-Sādah'*, given to descendants of the Prophet; it simply meant 'the masters'. There again, the succession question was a central stake in the game of the durability of the regime. All these elements were to give Omani history a new orientation. For they would contribute to the sidelining the Ibadhite movement, and its influence on political power would be marginalised.

Division: the Oman of the interior and the Oman of the Coast (Muscat)

The period following the death of Aḥmed ibn Saʿīd in 1783 determined the course of modern Omani history. A new national political map was to be established, and later a new national political culture taking in two systems, that of the *imāma* and that of the *sayyids*; the latter would be known later by the name of sultanate.

After the death of Aḥmed ibn Saʿīd, his fourth son, Saʿīd was elected *imām*. Hilāl, the eldest son, the most popular with the Omanis, had lost his sight as a young man; he left for India to undergo treatment and died there. The second son, Sulṭān and the third one, Sayf, were no longer acceptable to the Omanis after the way they had defied their father. Sulṭān, however, was later called on to play a historic role.

In fact, Aḥmed's succession was not really settled at his death; Saʿīd had not obtained the *imāma*. The Omani historian al-Sayyābi maintains that Saʿīd appointed himself *imām* without obtaining the *bay'a* of the *ahl al-ḥall wal-'aqd*.[243] History does not tell us what title Saʿīd bore after his father's death. Hence the question: was it as a successor or with the exceptional agreement of the *'ulamā'* that he acceded to power?[244] Either way, it confers no legitimacy on him.

For his part, al-Sālmī answers the question as follows: Saʿīd had appointed himself *imām* and Abū Nabhān addressed him by that title.[245] We know that Abū Nabhān was one of the most eminent *'ulamā'* of that period. All the same, Saʿīd's *imāma* was unconstitutional because it was obtained without the required consensus of the *'ulamā'* and without approval.

In any case, the new ruler, Saʿīd ibn Aḥmed did not turn out to be a statesman, particularly as Oman was going through an important stage in her development at the time. In fact, even in his father's reign, Saʿīd had not been accepted by the Omanis, notably when his father had entrusted him with certain official missions.

Besides, Saʿīd was not above reproach and one of the chief complaints against him later was that he gave huge powers to his son Ḥamad, who represented him in the coastal region; in other words, he was already exercising the authority of a governor simply by virtue of the fact that he belonged to the family of al-Bū Saʿīdi.

In 1792, nine years after the start of his reign, his two brothers, Qays and Sulṭān rose against him and Saʿīd was obliged to hand over power to his son Ḥamad ibn Saʿīd, who had a strong personality and had at an early age shown aspirations to power.

Hence the silence of the sources on that period; the *'ulamā'* of the Ibadhite movement had been progressively marginalised and their role, both as historiographers and as a political counterweight had suffered.

We do not know the position of the *'ulamā'* at that time. It is quite certain that *'imām'* Sa'īd had not renounced his title of *'imām'*, it was just political power that he ceded to his son, *al-sayyid* Ḥamad. If Sa'īd kept his title of 'official *imām*' and remained at al-Rustāq, his son Ḥamad, now the effective wielder of power took the historic decision to move his political capital to Muscat.

This strategic decision had an appreciable effect on the subsequent development of Omani history. Not only did it sanction the first structural separation between the political system and the religious system, but it also directly exposed the new capital on the coast, indeed the whole of the country, to foreign political, military and cultural influence, chiefly British. So Oman had two capitals: Nazwa, the traditional capital, the religious and spiritual centre of the interior, and Muscat, the commercial and political capital on the coast.

We must also, in Bondarevsky's view, see this measure as a first success for the British East India Company which, in spite of the absence of official relations between Oman and Great Britain, managed thus to place a marker in Oman. The transfer of the capital to Muscat was, in fact, decided on the suggestion of the Indian trader Ram Chandar Raadji, an agent of the East India Company in Muscat.[246]

Ḥamad ibn Sa'īd's reign, although a turning point, did not last long; the new ruler died in the year when he officially came to power. Consequently the power struggle resumed between the 'official *imām*', Sa'īd, alone in al-Rustāq and his two brothers, Qays and Sulṭān. But Sa'īd found no opportunity to regain dominion over the country, whereas Sulṭān, with his strong personality, began to be seen as the designated substitute and a competent statesman.

At the meeting between the inheritors of power in the little port of Birka, an agreement was reached over the division of Oman, containing three main points. Sa'īd, the official *imām*, remained in Rustāq and Sulṭān seized power in the Muscat region. Qays, for his part, took Suḥār, an area near the straits of Hormuz as his centre of power. Thus in 1793 and with the collaboration of the British, the Islamic state of Oman, which had existed for more than a thousand years as a unit, left the political stage.[247]

This agreement did not just represent the start of a new political and cultural history, it meant above all a gradual negation of the tradition of the *imāma*. Oman lived through a period of political and cultural disturbances and change. Muscat emerged with a new political, cultural and strategic configuration, in short, with a new national identity.

The geographical environment in turn played an important part in strengthening the new socio-political formula in Oman. The country found itself 'divided' on a long-term basis into two quasi 'separate' or more precisely delineated zones, despite the absence of geographic frontiers. The Ibadhite movement remained established in the interior with Nazwa or al-Rustāq as its capital. The sultans controlled the coastal region, which encompassed Ṣūr, Suḥār, Ja'lān, Muscat, Maṭraḥ and the coast of al-Bāṭina. And they made Muscat their definitive capital.

A decisive relationship undoubtedly exists between the geographical environment and the nature of the political system. Gradually this division tended to crystallise.

Just as the coast now moved towards openness, just as, of necessity, it espoused external conditions and matched its interests to those of its new partners, so the interior, for its part, had to suffer isolation and still clung to conservative values. Consequently, a cultural rift opened up between these two regions. Great Britain was implicated in that rift and tended later to transform it into a genuine national, political and cultural partition.

Franco-Omani relations from the age of enlightenment to the expedition to Egypt

As a maritime force in the region, Oman was historically the ally and supplier of the islands of Mauritius (île de France) and La Réunion (île Bourbon) in the southern corner of the Indian Ocean, and was also a historical and traditional ally of India. It was normal that this geopolitical equation needed to be completed and that Oman should also become the ally of France to the east of Africa and the Indian Ocean, especially as Great Britain was beginning to appear as a danger threatening Oman, India and all the countries of the Gulf.

However, France awoke quite belatedly to this equation. She started to become really aware of the consequences during the Revolutionary period, in 1796 and then under the Consulate in 1803, sending representatives to Oman. Yet, due to circumstances outside the control of the two camps, these endeavours to form a firm alliance, which might have pushed the history of the region in a different direction, foundered, although the relationship between the two countries was maintained at a high level.

The permanent warfare between France and Great Britain, and especially the Seven Years War (1756–1763) had repercussions on maritime activity and trade in general in the region. Franco-British antagonism had put Oman in a very uncomfortable position. As the French position *vis-à-vis* England weakened, that of Oman as a regional power was also restricted. When, in contrast, the French position strengthened against Great Britain, the Omani position also gained.

France had a representative in Basra since 1755 and set up a consulate there in 1765. At about the same time a French catholic bishop appeared in Baghdad and also functioned as French consul. With the revolution, or at least in 1796–1797, the French representative had ceased to be a cleric; his title was 'emissary for external relations', much the same as a consul.[248]

In fact, direct Omani–French contacts go back to the earlier phase of Aḥmed ibn Saʿīd. Although relations between the two countries did not start under the most favourable auspices, *imām* Aḥmed, from the beginning of his reign, stressed the importance of his friendship with France. In contrast, he refused to have any contact with Great Britain.

During the Seven Years War, in 1759, admiral d'Estaing's fleet seized a vessel belonging to Muscat, the *Manoudy*[249] (perhaps *al-Maḥmūdy*) in the Gulf. Aḥmed made an official protest but France did not seem to respond. The same thing happened in 1781. The French navy confiscated another Omani ship, *al-Ṣalāḥi*, in an operation of bloodthirsty piracy during which the Omani captain and several sailors were killed. Aḥmed again protested to the French authorities and demanded compensation. More than that, he resolved to place an embargo on cereals for the French colonies.

These protests were echoed by M. de Souillac, the governor of île de France and by M. Rousseau, the French consul in Bagdad. These two officials pressed Aḥmed's claims with the French authorities and decided to urge them to pay the damages he was seeking.

Moreover, the officials in île de France tried to set the aggression and piracy committed against the Omani ships and set them in a legal and non-political context. Oman's right was acknowledged and in their report to the central power, the French officials adopted Rousseau's point of view; they asserted the value of Omani–French friendship and asked that a consulate be opened at Muscat.

> France fitted out Venus, under the command of Rosily for a voyage the purpose of which was scientific. He came to Muscat; the imam told him of further grievances, protesting his friendship for the French and offering them a trading post in Muscat, something he had refused to England.[250]

This initiative on Aḥmed's part underlines the importance of Omani–French relations and the *imām*'s need to find a new alliance that would neutralise British influence. And yet Louis XVI's government was slow to react to this overture. The delay was contrary to the interests of both countries, particularly at a time when the British presence in the Indian Ocean was being further consolidated.

> It was only four years later that M. de Souillac's successor as governor of ile de France, the Comte de Coudray, would be able to buy a vessel to replace [al-Salahi], captured nine years earlier. This vessel did not reach its destination until March 10th 1790; it was handed over amid great pomp.[251]

In fact the ship did not reach Muscat in the lifetime of *imām* Aḥmed ibn Sa'īd, but in the days of his son Sa'īd, who was no less aware of its value to Oman in renewing the friendship between the two countries.

Meanwhile, with *sayyid* Sulṭān ibn Aḥmed's arrival in power in 1792, Muscat began to be restored to the place in the region that it had enjoyed in the reign of his father. *Sayyid* Sulṭān led two great and successful military and political operations. He occupied the Gwader area (part of modern Pakistan) and at the same time launched a sea-borne expedition against the sheikhs of the Arabian Ma`an tribe, living in the two strategic islands of Hormuz and Qishm. Then in 1794, he again demanded to rent the port of Bandar Abbas from the new ruler of Persia, Agha Muḥammad. Commenting on these acquisitions and advances, the Russian historian Bondarevsky stresses that they were realised thanks to the support of the British East India Company.[252]

There was undoubtedly cooperation between Sulṭān and the East India Company. But there is no proof that the politico-military successes of Oman were permitted or even fostered by the English, as Bondarevsky seems to imply. Besides, Sulṭān ibn Aḥmed was far from being on good terms with Great Britain and that state of affairs did not improve, even after the signature of the Omani–British treaty of 1798, to which we shall allude later.

On the other side of the Gulf, France had ambitious political aims. The revolutionary government sent two naturalists of repute, Bruguière and Olivier, on a mission to Turkey, al-Chām (Syria), Egypt and Persia. Their journey lasted five years, from 1793 to 1798. In addition to the scientific material they collected, this campaign enabled them to prepare for Napoleon Bonaparte's expedition to Egypt in 1798.[253]

Also on the agenda was the creation of an alliance of the Ottoman state and Persia with France against Russia, the traditional adversary of the two Islamic states and a member at that time of the coalition of European monarchies against the French Revolution.[254]

On 4 February 1796,[255] the Committee of Public Safety created a consulate in Muscat and appointed citizen Beauchamp to run it; he had been chosen as coadjutor by his uncle Dom Miroudot du Bourg, the bishop of Baghdad. 'By his efforts, zeal and activities, Citizen Beauchamp will justify the government's choice and make every effort to ensure that the expenses of the new consulate are useful to the Republic'.[256] Beauchamp also had a reputation as a man of learning, a traveller and an astronomer.

The importance of this mission is reflected in the instructions given to citizen Beauchamp in the memorandum handed to him, as well as by the eminent personality of the emissary. His mission was at once political, strategic, economic and cultural. The memorandum entrusted the French representative with the task of studying the manners and customs of the Omani people, described as the 'premier people in the world'. Indeed, the text reveals the broad outlines of French policy and her long term strategic aims in the region.

> French establishments in Muscat would moreover be exceedingly useful to our colonies of ile de France and Réunion; they would gain new means of subsistence, which they often lack in time of war, as this war has proved. The islands were almost reduced to famine in 1794 and they would not have had that experience if we had had an agent in Muscat at the time'.[257]

The second instructions concerned information about the political forces in the Arab region and the Indian situation, notably about British forces:

> Citizen Beauchamp must not forget that he has been placed in Muscat with a view to keeping the government informed about the political situation of the powers in Hindustan, and about all English operations in those lands and the surrounding seas. Nothing of that must escape his notice and attention; he must be meticulous in conveying to the government everything of interest that he may learn.[258]

The same memorandum laid down that citizen Beauchamp should also make every effort to serve science and literature. He should likewise try to find precious manuscripts for the Bibliothèque nationale in Paris. The memorandum also enjoined the emissary to study Arab horses and the diseases that might affect them, as well as methods of treatment in use by the Arabs.[259]

But things did not go as planned. Citizen Beauchamp was re-directed at the last moment and never arrived at his posting. Rather than have him go directly to his post, he was charged with reconnoitring various routes in Asia Minor. When Bonaparte arrived in Egypt, he found Beauchamp sick, with no resources and brought there by countless adventures.[260] According to al-Aqād, Beauchamp could have justified having failed to continue his mission by the anti-French feeling in the Arab and Islamic countries as a result of Napoleon's expedition.[261]

So ended the first attempt to establish firm Franco-Omani relations. Subsequently Napoleon Bonaparte's expedition came along to change all the political and strategic, not to say historical circumstances in the area.

Napoleon Bonaparte's expedition to Egypt in 1798

The French expedition to Egypt marked the beginning of a new phase and changed the historical process of the whole of the region, including the Indian Ocean and the Gulf. The balance of power was modified, but Great Britain, whose interests were at first threatened, succeeded in surmounting the ordeal.

General Bonaparte, who had perceived, among other things, the special importance of Oman, sent a letter after his arrival in Egypt, to the sultan of Muscat; in it he reaffirmed the old Franco-Omani friendship and assured the sultan that the presence of French forces in Egypt would not interfere with Omani shipping and trade to Suez.

> To the imam of Muscat:
>
> I am writing this letter to inform you of what you have no doubt already learned, the arrival of the French army in Egypt. As you have always been our friend, you must be convinced of my desire to protect all the vessels of your nation that you commit to sailing to Suez, where they will find protection for their trade. I ask you also to send this letter on to Tipu Sahib by the first transport to India.[262]

The English intercepted this letter, which only reached *sayyid* Sulṭān at the end of a year. In the course of that year, then, Great Britain attempted to thwart Omani–French contacts. She even aimed to neutralise Oman as an influential power in the region.

The treaty of 1798 and its extensions

Throughout the period of the French revolution, England lived in fear of a possible alliance between France, Oman and Mysore (a region of India opposed to

English influence). In practice, and because of the traditional friendship between the parties concerned (France being represented by the two islands of île de France and La Réunion), this alliance got under way. As such, it led in the medium- to long-term to the hampering of British colonial projects in the region of the Indian Ocean, the Indian sub-continent and eastern Asia. This was what Great Britain wished to avoid at all costs.

Meanwhile, a wave of indignation against France swept the Arab and Islamic countries: this was one of the consequences of Napoleon Bonaparte's expedition to Egypt. England was only waiting for the opportunity and took advantage of it to turn the situation in her favour. One of her first initiatives was to establish contacts and send active and important diplomatic and political missions into the area, including Persia, Jeddah and Oman.

It is worth noting that until then the aim of British policy had been to avoid expansion or military intervention in the area, so that the British company would not get involved in expenses, the returns from which would be uncertain. However, this policy changed with the arrival of the marquess of Wellesley in April 1798. This man was one of the apostles of an expansionist policy, unrestricted by purely financial considerations. It was at his instigation that the government of Bombay reconsidered its policy in the Gulf.[263]

In response to these British initiatives, Mahdi ʿAli Khan charged one of the representatives of the East India Company in Bushehr, a Persian national, to contact *al-sayyid* Sulṭān ibn Aḥmed and try to conclude an agreement with him. Contrary to all expectations, the emissary succeeded after ten days of talks in convincing *al-sayyid* Sulṭān of the need for a first agreement with Great Britain; it was signed on 12 October 1798.

The treaty contained seven clauses, bearing principally on the neutralisation of Oman and the interruption of Omani–French relations, in particular by withdrawing the offer of an office for the French agency in Muscat and the facilities granted to French and Dutch ships at war with England. More than that, the last paragraph of the second article demanded: 'that the friend of one become the friend of the other and his enemy will be our enemy'. The seventh and final article had as a corollary the granting of military facilities to the British navy in the port (Gambaron) of Bandar Abbas, in Persia, which had been under the authority of Muscat since *al-sayyid* Sulṭān, as we have already seen.[264]

Bearing in mind the circumstances under which it had been signed, this treaty was an outstanding success for British policy. Moreover, it was the first treaty between an Arab country and Great Britain. It would give a kind of 'legal' cover to the British esence in the region. Duncan, the governor of Bombay, could write to Wellesley, the governor-general of India: 'With this agreement, Mahdi ʿAli Khan obtained more than we were hoping for.'[265]

This document crowned with success a whole process of expansion, dreamed of by the Portuguese and completed with more success by the English, as al-Naqib observed. In fact, between 1688 and 1839, Great Britain had succeeded in carrying out the grand imperialist design previously conceived by the Portuguese, who failed in their attempts. In 1688, the English had snatched control of the straits of Hormuz from Holland and taken charge of eastern trade with China and the islands of the East Indies. They dislodged the Dutch from their positions in the Gulf in 1765 and succeeded in settling in Muscat in 1798. Thus they dominated trade by controlling the straits of Hormuz. The phases in this great design, conceived by Alfonso de Albuquerque in 1513 had finally been completed one by one.[266]

This survey shows clearly the point reached by British domination of the shipping lanes in the Indian Ocean and the chief eastern ports as well as the extent of their subsequent seizure of trade with the East. And it gives an indication of the actual causes behind the signature of the treaty by *al-sayyid* Sulṭān ibn Aḥmed.

Moreover, the general political attitude was hostile to France and had won over some of the Arab and Islamic states to the idea of opening up, albeit hesitantly, in the direction of English influence. Thus the Shereef of Mecca had welcomed the British representative, Wilson, in Jeddah and received from him the letter sent by Napoleon Bonaparte to Sulṭān ibn Aḥmed and Tipu Sahib, and intercepted by the English.[267]

As for Oman, this treaty that was so restricting seemed, against all expectations, to have hardly any effect on her policy. If, however, it had been applied to the letter, it would gradually have diminished independent political decision-making in Oman as a state and would certainly have limited her role as a traditional power in the region. As it happened, however, Oman preserved the independence of her political and strategic decision making. The country even kept her commitment to relations established previously with the islands of île de France and La Réunion.

In fact, *al-sayyid* Sulṭān soon sought to be rid of the burden of this agreement. The British historian Wilson reports that Sulṭān refused categorically to authorise the setting up of a British office in Muscat on the pretext that it would suck him into a war with the French and the Dutch. And although at the outset he had accepted the designation of a British ambassador in Muscat, he withdrew his consent.[268]

For her part, England had no intention of allowing the treaty with Oman to remain a dead letter. So the government of India took the initiative of sending the famous emissary captain John Malcolm to meet *al-sayyid* Sulṭān once more and remind him of his obligations under the 1798 agreement.

Al-sayyid Sulṭān had no wish to receive the British emissary. So he left Muscat on board his private ship for the island of Qishm lying roughly at the entrance to the Gulf. Malcolm did not hesitate to overtake Sulṭān on board his boat and use threats to oblige him to sign a new agreement, consolidating the treaty of 1798. The British emissary was at pains to remind him that the French had been almost completely driven out of India and to stress the superiority of England over all the other states. He even threatened Sulṭān with closure of the Indian ports to Omani ships. By these means, he obtained his signature[269] on an agreement with two points (January 1800): the first reaffirmed the commitment of 1798, calling it a 'fixed and full force';[270] the second article appointed Dr Bogle as British political agent. As a surgeon, he became Sulṭān's personal doctor.

'His profession will enhance his influence and he will have the ear of the prince.'[271] Narrating this diplomatic campaign, Sir J. Malcolm's biographer ends with this sally: 'We really owe our Indian empire to trade and the medical profession'.[272]

This was Great Britain's second decisive strategic success in less than two years. This political and 'medical' emissary did indeed play an important political role and influence the personal position of *sayyid* Sulṭān. He caused a reversal of his policy towards the French. Yet his stay in the country was brief; he died there at the end of 1800.[273]

The challenge to the treaty of 1798 and the emergence of the Wahhābis[274]

At the beginning of 1801, a conflict that had broken out between the Wahhābis and the pasha of Baghdad on the one hand, and between the Wahhābis and the Omanis on the other intensified. The Omanis began to seek support from their new allies, the English. But, in the hope of remaining on good terms with the nascent Wahhābi movement, the English did not respond to their appeal. Thereafter the Wahhābi question became a permanent fixture in the history of Oman.

This passive attitude on the part of Great Britain towards her Omani allies implicitly annulled the validity of the treaty of 1798. Oman had found an opportunity to get rid of this burdensome commitment and reactivate Omani–French relations. France, in turn, was ready to give an immediate response, notes A. Auzoux in an article that appeared in 1910:

> The (French) privateers had captured three vessels from Muscat, the Ahmedié, the Mustapha and the Phidelem. Magallon (the governor of île de France) refused to recognise the validity of the seizures. He charged the lieutenant in command of the Chateauville to bring back the three ships captured, in his opinion, in violation of the rights of the people, so as to restore them to the prince whom he hoped to make his ally.[275]

M. Laffite returned the ships with the official apologies of the governor of île de France. More than that, in response to the request of Sulṭān ibn Aḥmed, the French despatched part of their fleet to help him in his war against the Wahhābis and al-ʿUṭub *Al-sayyid* Sulṭān ibn Aḥmed expressed his gratitude at once in these terms:

> By this note, we have the pleasure of informing you of the arrival of our friend M. Laffite... and also of the gifts you were so generous as to send us; it is impossible to express to you our joy at their arrival, and above all at the troops you had the goodness to send us. We received them with open arms and will always feel bound to consider them as our brothers and our friends.[276]

The French naval forces spent about a year and a half under the command of the Omani authorities. They helped Sulṭān ibn Aḥmed to strike a severe blow at the forces of al-'Uṭub and the Wahhābis and, in 1801, to occupy the islands of Bahrein, of which Sulṭān made his son Sālem governor. Omani–French relations were not just restored, they appeared henceforth in the best possible light.

The lieutenant in command of the Chateauville, who was the inseparable companion of Sulṭān for fifteen months, testifies to this: 'During my stay in Muscat, I received distinguished treatment and all my expenses. When I left, the prince instructed me to tell the general that he offered him his services for supplying the colonies.'[277]

Naturally, Great Britain did not look favourably on this turn of events. Omani–British relations at that time were in a state of extreme tension. By way of reprisal, England took steps, using severe economic pressures, to strangle the Omani economy and perhaps ultimately to weaken Sulṭān ibn Aḥmed's position. The government of India arranged to annul both the privileges granted to Oman after the signing of the treaty of 1798 and also the commercial exchanges between Oman and India.[278]

In actual fact, the privileges enjoyed by Omanis and Indians dated from before the signature of the treaty with England. They were among the terms of an Omani–Indian relationship that had seen the light well before Great Britain's seizure of the east.

In reply to these retaliatory measures by Britain, *al-sayyid* Sulṭān took the initiative of sending his representative sheikh 'Ali, called the ambassador of Oman by historians, to M. Magallon, the governor of île de France. This sheikh was known for his hostility to England and his favourable attitude to the consolidation of Franco–Omani relations.

In a letter to the minister of the Navy dated 19 February 1803, Magallon indicates the importance of this visit:

> The political objective is very important, even for the interests of this prince, to be kept secret and to solicit the friendship and protection of the French Republic. It seems that the prince has many grievances against the English government.[279]

Naturally Magallon was very pleased with the Omani initiative. But establishing a common strategy against the British threat took time. An effective initiative was only adopted two years after Sulṭān's request, in 1803, when the First Consul,[280] aware of the regional importance of Oman, had decided to send his emissary Cavaignac as French consul in Oman. But it was not a good choice; Cavaignac had neither the subtlety nor the finesse necessary for such a mission.[281]

Moreover, the arrival of Cavaignac in October 1803 coincided with the end of the peace of Amiens and the resumption of hostilities between France and England. Sulṭān ibn Aḥmed could then only apologise for having received the mission, for fear that Great Britain would exploit the terms of the treaty of 1798 against Oman, especially the fifth article which required the neutrality of Muscat in the event of war between France and England. For in that case England could suspend the export of the main foodstuffs like Indian rice to Oman, that is to say decree an economic blockade of the country.

So Khalfān, a personal emissary from Sulṭān ibn Aḥmed, left to receive the French mission and explain his government's new situation to Cavaignac:

> It would have been desirable that you came in time of peace. The sultan would have welcomed you eagerly; but [at present] the English would hold it against my master if he admitted you, since war has been declared between you. We have twenty big ships in their ports in Bengal or on the Malabar coast; there is no doubt that they would seize them as soon as they learned of it.[282]

So this second attempt failed. But the failure did not affect the nature of relations between Oman and France. Cavaignac showed understanding for the critical situation of the Omani government and its difficult neutrality.

In 1804, the regional fighting between the Wahhābis and Oman resumed. This time, Sulṭān ibn Aḥmed went to seek support from the pasha of Baghdad, another adversary of the Wahhābis. But in vain. On his way, in Muscat, he came up against the fleet of al-Qawāsim, powerful allies of the Wahhābis and they barred his way. And, in a naval battle not far from Lingeh, Sulṭān ibn Aḥmed al-Bū Sa'īd lost his life (1804).

The Wahhābi question

Following the fundamentalist call by Muḥammad ibn 'Abdel Wahhāb in the second half of the eighteenth century, the Wahhābi movement was born at Najd, in the middle of the Arabian Peninsula. In about forty years, this movement, which emir ibn Sa'ūd adopted as doctrine, managed to unite the tribes in that region and construct the first Saudi state (1793–1818).

The second phase saw its expansion in the region and the spread of the Wahhābi doctrine in several neighbouring lands. Oman itself was shaken by a violent doctrinal and political conflict. The Wahhābi movement, which described itself as 'unifying', had no qualms about using any and every means to impose its doctrine and extend its influence and, according to al-'Aqād, the Saudis themselves confirm this. Wahhābi historians (like Ben Becher) have indeed told of Saudi attacks against the wealthy towns of the Gulf and Iraq and described the rich booty from these raids in a spirit of pride.[283]

We shall not examine here the question of doctrinal differences between Ibadhism, a specific school of thought that arose in the first Islamic state with millennial traditions, and Wahhābism, a recent sect. That lies outside the scope of this book. But we shall set out the political aspect of the latter movement in the region, its role and influence, especially in Oman and the Julfār area, which had recently come to be called '*Sāḥel Oman*'.

In the context of this expansion, some of the tribes in the *'Sāḥel Oman'* region, like the Na'aym, Banī Ka'b and the Banī Jatab embraced the Wahhābi doctrine towards the end of the eighteenth century. Because of the presence of those tribes in the Buraymi oasis, one of the largest Omani agglomerations on the borders of the Saudi state, Wahhābi influence cast its shadow over the history of that region and then of Oman.[284] A Wahhābi force led by the ruler al-Ḥarīq then seized the Buraymi oasis; its fortresses and the al-Na'aym and al-Dhawahir populations were overrun. In the eighteen years that followed, the Wahhābis used the oasis as a base from which to attack Oman and they levied a poll tax on the al-Bū Sa'īdi sultans.[285]

The historian al-Sālmī reports that the advent of Muṭlaq al-Muṭayri (the Wahhābi ruler leading attacks against Oman) was a 'scourge and a calamity. He called the Muslims *mushrikīn* (polytheists) and killed all who did not adopt his doctrine. He forced the Omani rulers to pay the poll tax'.[286]

With the conversion of al-Qawāsim, the maritime power in the region of Ra's al-Khaymah and al-Sharijah, to the Wahhābi doctrine towards the end of the eighteenth century, the Wahhābi state just about reached its zenith. Later, when the Banī Bū 'Ali tribes had embraced the Wahhābi dogma at the beginning of the nineteenth century, the movement was able to infiltrate as far as Ja'lān in the al-Sharqiya region in the east of Oman.

From the beginning of the nineteenth century, as we shall see in the course of our survey of Omani political history, the active Wahhābi influence would weigh very heavily on the development of Oman, prompting permanent interventions in her internal affairs, particularly at the time of the revolution of *imām* 'Azzān in 1869–1871, and with the al-Buraymi question in the middle of the twentieth century.

Sa'īd ibn Sulṭān al-Bū Sa'īdi (1806–1856)

In the two years that followed the death in 1804 of Sulṭān ibn Aḥmed, Oman once again entered on a bitter power struggle that set the minor sons of *al-sayyid* Sulṭān, Sālem and Sa'īd against their cousins Qays and Badr. Thanks to Wahhābi influence, which had infiltrated the family, and after a bloody war, Badr was triumphant. But the Wahhābis imposed an agreement on the new government requiring payment of an annual poll tax amounting to 50 000 dollars (so-called Maria Theresa dollars) to their capital, al-Dar'iyya. To see that the agreement was honoured, the Wahhābis posted 400 Saudi cavalrymen at Birka.[287] But Badr did not hold his position very long; he succumbed to a new family power struggle in which Sa'īd came out on top.

Sa'īd ibn Sulṭān, then aged seventeen, assumed power in 1806 and held it for half a century, till his death in 1856. The first *sayyid* of Oman was then given the title of Sultan and later he was called 'the Great'.[288] Powerful and ambitious, he strengthened the system and institution of the sultanate that Oman was to know almost continuously down to our own day.

From the time of his arrival, Sa'īd tried to avoid conflict with the Wahhābis and prepared to renew the poll tax. This did not make the Saudis change their attitudes and desires *vis-à-vis* Oman. For a century and a half, their relations with Oman were marked by intermittent tension and violence. Kajare observes:

> He [Saʿīd] had the two great European powers, France and England against him; the latter because she was courting the good will of the Wahhābis and fostered their ambition, and the former because of the failure of Cavaignac's mission in 1802.[289]

The new sultan, genuinely fascinated by Napoleon, was well aware of the importance of his country's relations with France. Like his father Sulṭān and his grandfather *imām* Aḥmed, he was always open to the idea of strengthening friendly relations and traditional cooperation with France. He wanted his country to follow France's reasoning; particularly as Great Britain's attitude to the Omani–Wahhābi conflict ran counter to Omani interests. But it was the aim of the British to wreck these overtures of the new Omani government and in July 1806, the English frigate *Concord* captured in the port of Muscat a French ship, the Vigilant.[290]

This misdeed provoked a general outcry among the French and the Omanis. Saʿīd swiftly seized the initiative and sent General Decaen, who had succeeded M. Magallon as governor of île de France, a message in these terms:

> Your Excellency must certainly be aware of the effrontery and arrogance of the English nation as well as of its power in India. The conduct of this English frigate has so outraged us that we have sent one of our ships to Bombay with letters for the general concerning this affair and we hope, with God's help, to succeed in delivering the French ship from the hands of her enemies.[291]

The sultan was not content with that; he sent the French authorities a sum of money by way of compensation. And, anxious to show both how deeply he regretted the incident, and also his devotion to France, he wrote somewhat extravagantly:

'We hope Your Excellency will deign to consider our country as belonging to you and always ready to obey you.'[292]

Fortunately, General Decaen did not take this exaggerated Arabian praise literally; instead, despite the sultan's attitude, he seized his ship and his emissary and attempted to take advantage of the situation. He asked the sultan to send him a representative with full powers. So Saʿīd despatched Mājed ibn Khalfān and endowed him with the requisite political and juridical powers. This emissary was one of the most eminent personalities in Oman. In July 1807, he signed an important agreement with Decaen, containing four points which, in short 'authorised natives of Muscat to go to the ports of the British adversary and even in a neutral port and... stipulated Oman's obligation to receive a French agent'.[293]

Just as this agreement suited French strategy, by the same token it served Omani intentions, which aimed more and more pointedly at finding a formula for cooperation or even an alliance between Oman and France. Even so, the Omanis considered the agreement, as an aid to relations between the two countries, to be belated and coming in difficult circumstances. It foundered on a legal defect.

'The treaty of 1807 was not ratified by the imperial government on the pretext that it was contrary to maritime law, established by the decrees of 1806 and 1807 on the Continental System (1808).'[294]

Like other important projects, this one was adjourned. Time was pressing, especially as the balance of power in the Indian Ocean was clearly to the advantage of Great Britain. And in fact, in the years that followed, she imposed a severe blockade on île de France. In spite of the historic role played by the Omanis and their potential capacity to break the economic blockade of the island and save the population from famine, in December 1810, île de France fell to the English, and was renamed Mauritius.

Omani–French friendship, several times proclaimed and reaffirmed, could have modified the balance of power in the region and thwarted British supremacy. Ill-served by the central royal, revolutionary and then imperial power, this friendship was in fact no more than a relationship between Oman and the French islands of île de France and La Réunion. A half-measure, that, in the long run, merely led to a strengthening of British colonial power and provided it with a new strategic base.

But with the eclipse of French friendship, Oman also saw the waning of an alternative relationship that might have allowed her to guarantee her sovereignty in the face of English imperialist expansion and the increasing influence of the Wahhābis. The French withdrawal left the new sultanate system quite alone to face the new threats to the integrity of Oman.

5 *'Sāḥel Oman'*[295]

The common history (1750–1850)

Historically the Julfār region, sometimes called 'al-Sir' and generally '*Sāḥel Oman*', corresponds to a part lying in the north west of Oman. From the second half of the eighteenth century, it witnessed the emergence of particular ethnic and political formations. Later, when the region had a confrontation with England, she renamed it the 'Pirate Coast'. But when she had subjugated it by force, and after the tribes had signed the Maritime Truce in 1853, England renamed it the 'Trucial Coast'. While examining in this chapter how the historical and national identity of the region and its independent political frontiers were formed, we shall try also to throw some light on the distinctive features of the common history of Oman and '*Sāḥel Oman*'.

A historical reminder

This region of many names, each with its own historical significance, stretches for 500 km along the south coast of the Gulf, from the Musandam peninsula, north-east of the town of Ra's al-Khaymah, to Qatar. It also has 75 km of coast on the gulf of Oman.[296]

With the appearance of the al-Bū Saʿīdi dynasty in the middle of the eighteenth century, two ethno-political entities appeared at the same time on 'the coast'. The first, the confederation of the Banī Yās tribe and its allies, constituted a land force dominated by the al-Nahayān family and settled first in al-Dhafrah then on the island of Abu Dhabi. The second, al-Qawāsim, an important naval force, had as its main centre the town of Ra's al-Khaymah.[297]

If we look closely at this historical phenomenon, we see that it was after the fall of the Yaʿrūbite *imāma* and the long Omani civil war that followed it (1718–1737) that these entities appeared and that tribal particularisms, held in check in the days of the *imāma*, revived. Fostered by this re-awakening, tribal loyalties (Ghafirite and Hanawite) intervened to stir up two centrifugal socio-ethnic forces in the history of Oman and '*Sāḥel Oman*'.

The most important of the Omani geo-political mutations had started then in that region. Two parallel entities emerged: first the al-Bū Saʿīdi dynasty in Oman and then al-Qawāsim and Banī Yās in the region of '*Sāḥel Oman*'. This new reality was to have a geo-political dimension and put an end to the former historic frontiers, replacing them in practice with new, independent political boundaries.

Al-Qawāsim

Al-Qawāsim had played a telling role quite soon in the history of '*Sāḥel Oman*' still more in that of Oman and especially in the history of the Gulf region itself. An ancestor, the great Qasim, had come and settled at Julfār in the seventeenth century. Through him, the town became the main settlement of al-Qawāsim and was renamed Ra's al-Khaymah (head of the tent).[298]

However, historians are still debating two questions: the origins of al-Qawāsim and the date of their arrival in Julfār. The British historian Kelly thinks that al-Qawāsim formed a branch of Banī Ghāfir that had emigrated from Najd, in the centre of the Arabian Peninsula, to Oman around the seventeenth century.[299] According to the Egyptian historian Nawfal, on the other hand, they were Arab tribes whose origins went back to ʿAdnan and whose initial home was Sāmerrā' in Iraq. They settled in their new homeland in the first half of the seventeenth century or thereabouts.[300]

But if it is difficult to define their origins, it is possible to be specific about the date of their arrival. And that is of some interest in determining when the presence and role of al-Qawāsim started in the area. In 1633, when Julfār was freed from Persian and Portuguese occupation, the historiographers made no mention of the name al-Qawāsim alongside that of Aḥmed ibn ʿAli, the war leader of the Yaʿrūbite *imām*, Nāṣer ibn Murshed. And yet it seems likely that these Qawāsim occupied the area before the date put forward by Nawfal: 1723. They did indeed make a sizeable contribution at the time of the Omani civil war, from 1723 on. They also played a considerable part in the Omani war of liberation against the Persians (1737–1741). So there are grounds for thinking that the arrival of al-Qawāsim occurred after Julfār had been liberated from the Persians in 1633 but before the Omani civil war (1718–1737).

Ra's al-Khaymah and Muscat

The geopolitical reshaping of this region during the eighteenth century was marked by conflict between two main forces, al-Qawāsim and al-Bū Saʿīdi. And this antagonism found expression in a series of tribal and doctrinal fields. The latter in particular revealed a sharp contrast between the 'Ghafirite' and Sunni Qawāsim (before they adopted the Wahhābi doctrine) and al-Bū Saʿīdi 'Hanawites' and *Ibāḍis*.

During the Omani civil war (1718–1737), al-Qawāsim aligned themselves with the chief of the Ghawāfir, Muḥammad ibn Nāṣer al-Ghāfiri, while the other side was led by the chief of the *Hanāwi*, Khalfān ibn Muḥammad al-Hanai. In 1723, so five years after the start of the civil war, sheikh Raḥmah ibn Maṭar al-Qāsīmī (1722–1760) intervened with a force of 6500 men, most of whom belonged to the 'Shaḥūḥ'[301] from Ruʿūs al-Jibāl (mountain tops).[302]

Following the death of the Ghafirite chief Muḥammad ibn Nāṣer, al-Qawāsim returned to their initial positions at Ra'ʿs al-Khaymah. After the arrival of the Persian expedition in Oman in 1737, the Omanis put an end to their quarrels so as to confront the Persians; al-Qawāsim then sided with the coalition of Omani tribes who were waging the war of national liberation. They joined forces with Aḥmed ibn Saʿīd who was besieging the Persian troops at Suḥār and helped him prevail. Then al-Qawāsim set about the Persians in their own land, at the port of Bandar Abbas on the Persian coast.[303]

Thanks to this war, the Omani people rediscovered their unity, but it was short-lived. In fact, this was the last time the tribes reunited and the population of '*Sāḥel Oman*' affirmed their solidarity with the rest of the tribes. As soon as Oman was liberated in 1741, tribal reconciliation was called into question and national unity fragmented. Although the civil war was over and a spirit of solidarity had taken its place at first, Hanawite and Ghafirite tribal loyalties soon got the upper hand and the question of the *imāma*, which had been suspended, was again on the agenda.

As we saw in Chapter 4, Bal'aʿrab ibn Ḥamyār reappeared on the political scene after the liberation of the country and that was thanks to the support of al-Qawāsim, who wanted to restore the Yaʿrūbite state for his benefit.

Despite this strong opposition, Aḥmed ibn Saʿīd al-Bū Saʿīdi managed to defeat the candidate of the Qawāsim and the Ghafirite faction, Bal'aʿrab ibn Ḥamyār, who died; Aḥmed took political power in Oman but, of course, he could not obtain the allegiance of al-Qawāsim, nor could he fully impose his authority over them. Thereafter they preserved some kind of autonomy in the area of Ra's al-Khaymah.

And so the political frontiers of '*Sāḥel Oman*' began to be drawn while the power of Ra's al-Khaymah was starting to grow. It is worth noting here that the area had not committed itself to a separatist process until after the fall of the Yaʿrūbite state, which had, in turn, contributed to the emergence of the al-Bū Saʿīdi entity in Oman. In other words, the appearance of the '*Sāḥel Oman*' region went hand in hand with the emergence of al-Bū Saʿīdi. The region had already ceased to be controlled by Muscat, that is to say be under the dominion of al-Bū Saʿīdi, particularly after the death of *imām* Aḥmed ibn Saʿīd (1741–1783), whereas it was still totally subject to the Yaʿrūbite *imāma* (1624–1741).

However, because of tribal links, some of the Hanawite tribes from the '*Sāḥel Oman*' region (Banī Yās and al-Bū Falāsa) maintained their customary and traditional relations with the al-Bū Saʿīdi in Oman until quite recently.

And because geography often determines policy, this new geopolitical fact demanded politico-military sanction. In 1758–1759, the first so-called Yaʿrūbite revolts against *imām* Aḥmed took place, first at Ṣūr and Jaʿlān, in the Sharqiya region, then a rebellion of al-Qawāsim flared up at Ra's al-Khaymah. *Imām* Aḥmed despatched a fleet there, which succeeded in quelling the uprisings and putting an end to them provisionally.[304]

But this controversy was bound to continue; so when *imām* Aḥmed Ibn Saʿīd's sons rose against their father in 1787, al-Qawāsim, at their request, supported the revolt. And the episode was repeated later, after the death of *imām* Aḥmed and the nomination of his son Sa'īd as his successor; Sayf and Sulṭān again asked al-Qawāsim to back them, this time against their brother.

Despite appearances, this was not a personal dispute but much more the concrete expression of a geopolitical antagonism. Uḷtān ibn Aḥmed had taken power in Muscat (1793–1804), having twice relied on the support of al-Qawāsim, against his father and against his brother Sa'īd, he found himself in conflict with his former allies, that is to say Ra's al-Khaymah, who intended to take advantage of the power struggle in Oman to achieve independence. Sulṭān ibn Aḥmed met his death in 1804 in a naval battle that ranged him against al-Qawāsim. But the struggle between Muscat, the seat of the central power, and Ra's al-Khaymah, the seat of the leading separatist force, would continue until the latter fell into the hands of the British in 1820.

The struggle between al-Qawāsim and Great Britain

Though al-Qawāsim had been a first class naval power throughout that period (estimated at 750 ships and 18 000 sailors), their military prowess on land left much to be desired. Despite the domination they had acquired over most of the Ghafirite tribes in the '*Sāḥel Oman*' region, they could not hold out for long against the pressure from the Wahhābis who had allied themselves with al-Na'ym, another tribe in the area. With the help of their allies, the Wahhābis launched two offensives against al-Qawāsim at Ra's al-Khaymah towards the end of the eighteenth century. After a first assault had failed, 4000 men, led by Muṭlaq al-Muṭayri, succeeded in encircling the town of Ra's al-Khaymah.[305] The besieged city soon capitulated and the chief of al-Qawāsim, Saqar ibn Rached al-Qāsīmī (1722–1760) was made subject to Wahhābi authority.

Following this defeat, al-Qawāsim had to adopt the Wahhābi doctrine which they had initially strongly opposed. Their surrender brought the Wahhābi state to its zenith. But it is worth recording that the population of the Ra's al-Khaymah area did not, even so, change the Sunni doctrines that were current among them (*al-Ḥanbalī* and *al-Māliki*). They preserved them down to our own day.

But far from languishing in that situation, al-Qawāsim gained a political trump card by their conversion to the Wahhābi doctrine. Their alliance with the Wahhābi force, which was in the ascendant in the area, shored up their position against al-Bū Sa'īdi in Muscat, traditional adversaries of the Wahhābis. Similarly, their sovereignty over '*Sāḥel Oman*' was reinforced. On the other hand, the fact of having embraced Wahhābism did not strengthen them in the long run against the British colonial threat.

The gradual assertion of the commercial and military power of al-Qawāsim and its dependencies was in fact beginning to give offence to the English in the area. During the second half of the eighteenth century, the fleet of al-Qawāsim had finally reached second rank in the Gulf, after that of Muscat. It was continually developing. At the dawn of the nineteenth century, it numbered 63 ships of substantial tonnage, 810 smaller vessels and between 18 000 and 25 000 sailors and crewmen.[306]

So al-Qawāsim constituted an economic and commercial competitor to the British fleet; they were even frustrating the policy of English colonial hegemony in the Gulf region.

First confrontations with the British

In 1805, the English made an alliance with Badr, then sultan of Muscat, who was seeking to retake the port of Bandar Abbas from the Qawāsim, who had occupied it by means of a naval expedition on the death of Sulṭān ibn Aḥmed. The Qawāsim were defeated by the allies; a treaty followed between England and al-Qawāsim, which called for peace between the East India Company on the one hand and Sulṭān ibn Saqr al-Qāsīmī and all his subjects on the other.

It is worth noting that Great Britain apparently forced no concessions on the Qawāsim, despite their military defeat. Quite the opposite, the treaty basically acknowledged the existence, sovereignty and sea power of the Qawāsim. This sudden benevolence on the part of the English was obviously not entirely disinterested. For them the whole point was to gain time in the area while they transferred the bulk of their forces to the struggle against France in Europe, which had recently flared up again.

Political diplomacy in the region was affected by this unexpected treaty, behind which the Wahhābis suspected at first a reversal of the position of the Qawāsim towards Great Britian. Consequently, the Wahhābi power resolved to get rid of the chief of the Qawāsim, Sulṭān ibn Saqr. In 1808 he was ordered by Sa'ūd to Dar'iyya, the capital of the Wahhābis, to be reprimanded for having flouted Wahhābi principles, and was replaced by his cousin, Ḥussein ibn 'Ali (1808–1814), and then by Ḥassan ibn Raḥmah until the English expedition of 1819–1820.[307]

In spite of Wahhābi mistrust, Great Britain had viewed its treaty with the Qawāsim merely as a delaying tactic. The clash between the two maritime powers in the area was inevitable since the presence of English naval and merchant vessels could not fail to be detrimental to the activity of the local fleet.

The Qawāsim had no alternative but to reinforce their position in the region and prepare for the eventuality of armed conflict. As a sign of their resentment of the unjustified presence of the British, they seized the English ship *Minerva*. Then, in 1809, they took it into their head to demand that the British government in Bombay pay transit dues for the safe passage of English vessels in Gulf waters.[308]

Their intention was to assert their sovereignty and the independence of the Arab merchant fleet in the Gulf. Great Britain saw it as a challenge to her interests and decided to launch an expedition against Ra's al-Khaymah. In so doing she had no qualms about calling the Qawāsim 'pirates' and even '*enemies of humanity*'. A pretext for the expedition having been found, Ra's al-Khaymah was shelled mercilessly by British heavy artillery. And, according to Bondarevsky, fifty Arab ships that were in the port, the only means of survival for the local population, were set on fire. After that, the 'humanitarian' mission crossed the

Gulf and set fire to the port of Lingeh, controlled at that time by Ra's al-Khaymah.[309]

The way the population of Ra's al-Khaymah defended itself filled the British with admiration and amazement if we are to believe the testimony of Smith, one of their officers: 'It is impossible to imagine greater determination on the part of our enemies [al-Qawāsim]. We have been faced with fierce resistance: they had decided to defend their bastions to the last man'.[310]

This episode deserves our close attention for it sets out clearly the terms of the relationship between the coloniser and the colonised. Indeed, in the present instance, the ruling power, with no counterweight in the region because of France's withdrawal, uses the resources of law unilaterally. Thus the seizure of the *Minerva* an act of sovereignty and a warning shot against the restraints on Arab interests imposed by the wrongful presence of the English, is arbitrarily interpreted as an 'act of piracy' and a *casus belli.*

Now piracy only came into the area with the Portuguese sailors once they had conquered and occupied Oman and other places on the Gulf (1508–1650). The practice had previously been foreign to the region.

In any case, it is difficult to talk of piracy when a whole country is marking its rejection of a foreign presence. It then becomes more a matter of national defence. The Russian historian Bondarevsky places the question in a more precise political context and asserts that this defence was in fact one of the ways of fighting against the British colonisers who had deprived the local population of vital resources, closely linked with the sea.[311] So it was not an act of piracy but a legitimate exercise of national sovereignty, a national duty.

Besides, when the forces of al-Qawāsim seized the English ship, the sailors cleaned her, purified her and treated her with incense before conducting her to Ra's al-Khaymah as spoils of war. This practice is known as the 'perfume ritual'; the purification of the ship is thought to free it from 'European impurity', to use Bondarevsky's expression. The same historian adds that throughout the history of piracy over thousands of years, no example of a similar ritual exists. This is a sign that it cannot be seen as an act of piracy but rather of purification, in both the literal and the figurative sense of the word, of removing the contamination from foreign and 'heretical' colinisers.[312]

It is significant, too, that, after taking possession of the ship, the sailors of al-Qawāsim arrested the captain's wife among the prisoners. Mrs Taylor subsequently testified that 'they had shown her the greatest respect'[313], an attitude in striking contrast to the way genuine pirates were accustomed to treat female passengers.

A final contradiction: Great Britain had not hesitated to sign various agreements and treaties with al-Qawāsim previously; can 'the protectors of civilisation' possibly negotiate or sign treaties with pirates?[314]

Diplomatically, this operation was exceedingly well prepared: Great Britain was careful to circumvent the Wahhābis before the expedition to Ra's al-Khaymah in 1809. In a letter addressed to the rulers in al-Darʿiyya, the English informed them that the aim of their expedition was to strike a blow at 'local piracy'.

On receiving this letter, the *'ulamā'* of al-Dar'iyya held a meeting, during which 'they decided that since the English were people of the book, jihad was not a duty for them'.[315] The politicians accepted the opinion of the *'ulamā'* and as a result they redefined their policy towards the British.

It is paradoxical that the Wahhābis should have adopted such an attitude after having attacked al-Qawāsim and taken their leader prisoner on the pretext that he had concluded a separate non-aggression pact with the East India Company in 1805, as stated earlier.

Undoubtedly it was the new political context in the region that explains this *volte-face* by the Wahhābis; Great Britain had then just eclipsed the French rival in the Indian Ocean (the fall of île de France in 1810). At the same time, British forces had succeeded in stifling the nationalist movements in India. So Great Britain had no other obstacle to her ambitions in the region, but al-Qawāsim and Ra's al-Khaymah. Conscious of the new balance of power, the Wahhābis had no hesitation in changing their position, to the detriment of their ally al-Qawāsim.

But sheikh Sulṭān ibn Saqr, the previous ruler of Ra's al-Khaymah, who had been deposed and imprisoned in 1808, had managed to escape meanwhile from al-Dar'iyya. Muḥammad 'Ali gave him asylum in Egypt and sent him to Oman to prepare an alliance with the sultan of Muscat against the Wahhābis. This Egyptian initiative was well received in Muscat.[316]

The English use of force had revived the politico-military activity of the regional powers. Thus the sultan of Oman led two consecutive expeditions against Ra's al-Khaymah, the first in 1813 and the second in 1814. Both failed from a military point of view but helped nevertheless to restore Muscat's new ally, sheikh Sulṭān ibn Saqr al-Qāsīmī, the former governor of Ra's al-Khaymah, now installed in the governorship of the al-Sharjah region. Thus the two towns of Ra's al-Khaymah and al-Sharjah were both subjects of the al-Qawāsim family, although politically they were independent of each other and fairly autonomous.

The two expeditions of 1816–1819 and the fall of Ra's al-Khaymah

The establishment of indisputable English supremacy in the region was still coming up against the resistance of the Qawāsim. So in 1816, British naval forces led a third expedition against Ra's al-Khaymah in the hope of administering the *coup de grâce*, but this campaign ended in total failure. Contrary to what the English authorities anticipated, the result of the expedition was to strengthen the power of al-Qawāsim in the region. The British did not disarm but they were now convinced that they would not be able to bring their colonial plans in the region to fruition so long as the Arab fleet at Ra's al-Khaymah was not completely destroyed.

It is not just the capacity of the population to defend itself against determined aggressors; it is also their ability to reconstruct their fleet and to make the town of Ra's al-Khaymah rise from its ruins after each devastating expedition.

After the failure of the 1816 expedition, and for a period of about three years, the government of British-India redoubled its initiatives and preparations with the aim of finishing once and for all with al-Qawāsim, its last adversary in the region, and with the town of Ra's al-Khaymah, the beacon of resistance to colonial intrusion. Bearing in mind the resistance offered so far, English diplomacy intended to leave no stone unturned; as to alliances, the Ottoman State, Persia and Muscat were approached and the Egyptian Pasha was also contacted. The shah of Persia displayed a wish to take part alongside British forces in a campaign against the forces of al-Qawāsim on the Persian coast, seizing the occasion to drive the Arabs out for good. The most eagerly-awaited decision was that of Muscat, so far largely opposed to English interests but keen to return Ra's al-Khaymah to Oman. The sultan gave his unqualified agreement to the coalition arranged by the British and even made ready to play a leading part in it.

On 2 December, 1819, the British fleet set sail for Ra's al-Khaymah, accompanied by two warships from Muscat with *al-sayyid* Saʿīd himself, escorted by 600 men recruited from Omani tribes, on board.[317] This was the most imposing naval force ever assembled in the Gulf. The government of British India had appointed General Keir to head an expeditionary corps of more than 3500 officers and men.[318]

The siege of Ra's al-Khaymah began on 3rd December. After six days of fierce resistance and bitter fighting, the town fell to the allies and the majority of the population was exterminated. Two hundred and two Arab ships were burned, mostly fishing boats and merchant vessels.[319]

With the taking of Ra's al-Khaymah, half a century of resistance to western colonial power vanished. The last bolt holding back British pressure in the Gulf gave way. The '*Sāḥel Oman*' region no longer formed an obstacle to colonial hegemony. Moreover, the English succeeded in capturing the chief of al-Qawāsim, sheikh Ḥassan ibn Raḥmah, and some prominent people of the region.

In 1820, Great Britain imposed on the coastal governors (sheikhs) – sheikh Shakhbūṭ ibn Thiban, representing Abū-Dhabi, and, from Dubai, Muḥammad bin Hazzaʿ bin Zaʿal[320] – the so-called 'victorious' treaty, officially entitled a 'preliminary undertaking', which was to prepare the way for the signing of a definitive 'general treaty'. Ḥassan ibn Raḥmah signed the preliminaries in the name of the government of Ra's al-Khaymah. But it should be noted that on the copy signed by the government of Ra's al-Khaymah, a supplementary article (Article 1) was added, requiring 'that the town of Ra's al-Khaymah be in the hands of the British government',[321] in other words imposing the direct submission of the population of Ra's al-Khaymah to the British authorities in India.

Sheikh Sulṭān ibn Saqr, the governor of al-Sharjah, signed a similar undertaking but it contained exceptional articles concerning the capitulation of al-Qawāsim and their auxiliaries to the British authorities in the al-Sharjah region. Fortresses, ships and cannons at al-Sharjah, ʿAjmān and Umm-al-Qaywain were also to be handed over to General Keir.

The 'preliminary undertaking' included a subtle appendix, which in fact constituted the most important text of the whole undertaking. It stipulated: 'By this undertaking, the state of hostility between the General and Sulṭān ibn Saqr is dissipated but [and this is the most important part], in this particular instance, their ships [al-Qawāsim's] are prohibited from going to sea'.[322]

The aim of this additional article was strategic. It made the economic blockade a fundamental point of British strategy. The shipping rights of al-Qawāsim's vessels, here presented as just an appendix, were from the outset the actual point at issue and the cause of the war. A permanent blockade clearly meant that the fate of the region was sealed and that henceforth it was inseparable from that of Great Britain.

The general treaty with the Arab sheikhs (1820) and its fallout

On the ruins of Ra's al-Khaymah, General Keir once more summoned the sheikhs of the coast and required them to sign a definitive treaty. It was known as a 'general treaty with the Arab tribes of the Gulf'.[323]

Without going into details, we note that this treaty established the sovereignty of Great Britain over the region, its population and its rulers. And on the pretext of fighting piracy, as mentioned in the first article, Great Britain granted herself the right to monitor merchant shipping in the whole of the Gulf region. Similarly, British power was authorised to intervene in the internal affairs of the tribes in order to settle differences between them. In short, Great Britain became the high legislative and executive authority in the region. Not to mince words, the fall of Ra's al-Khaymah opened an era of unreserved hegemony for the British colonial power in the Gulf region.

Yet the government of British India found fault with it; General Keir was criticised for his 'lack of firmness in dealing with the population of Sāḥel Oman'. He was blamed for having freed Ḥassan ibn Raḥmah and Ḥassan ibn ʿAli and for not having specified the number of ships the tribes could own, nor the maximum capacity of those ships.[324] The general had no difficulty in defending both his own position and the terms of the treaty to the government of India. What followed amply demonstrated that the conditions of British domination were in fact harsh and exacting for the region.

This treaty marked an important stage in the establishment of British protection over the northern coast of Oman on the Gulf, which was thereafter officially called 'the Pirate Coast' on British maps and then on maps in the rest of Europe.[325] The destruction of Ra's al-Khaymah and the annihilation of the Arab fleet were to have particularly unfortunate consequences in the history of the region.

First of all, in the geopolitical field, this treaty officially fixed the independent frontiers of '*Sāḥel Oman*', giving them de facto recognition. As for the sultan of Oman, who had put all his political and military weight into taking part in the expedition of 1819 alongside Great Britain, his ambitions were not realised. After the fall of Ra's al-Khaymah, the sultan had to return to Oman, deal with his internal affairs and leave those of the '*Sāḥel*' in the hands of Great Britain alone.

More materially, the harsh blow struck at the Arab fleet of al-Qawāsim had ended in the collapse of the local economy, which relied chiefly on external trade and had known remarkable development in the second half of the eighteenth century; in comparison, the other resources, traditional fishing and pearl fishing, seemed puny. Over and above the closure of the Arab trading links from the Gulf to India, Africa and vice versa, it meant ongoing economic encirclement of the region. Finally, the draconian conditions of the 'general treaty' gravely compromised economic reliance on fishing activities and local trade, because small vessels were also targetted by the application of the ban. All these difficulties arising from the text of 1820 would have a dire effect on the life of the local population for a century and a half.

This economic collapse was not without repercussions on social evolution; it hampered the subsequent natural development of society. With commercial, economic and semi-industrial activities (for example, ship building and maintenance) obliterated, a large section of the active or productive population found itself stranded. Consequently the emergence of a 'middle class', a necessary process in social development, was bound to come to nothing. So the movement of continuity and evolution, which reshapes society and contributes both to the formation of social homogeneity and to national and cultural identity, was disrupted over a long period of time.

In the absence of natural economic development, the separate commitments agreed with the tribes crystallised the tribal landscape and fostered dispersal. With no unified central and national framework for the region, Great Britain insinuated herself into the role of supreme central power and the small, scattered tribal groups were transformed into semi-political forces, unable to survive as semi-independent socio-political units except through their connection with the British presence.

All Great Britain had to do now was to maintain the situation she had created and built up with the formula of 'British protectorates', the only official political identity in the region until recent times. Alongside tribal culture, the only alternative was a culture of 'follow my leader' in relation to Great Britain and within the framework of the protectorates.

Later developments in Oman and '*Sāḥel Oman*' until the protectorate regime

In Oman

For Oman, the precedent of the sultan's participation in an expedition against Ra's al-Khaymah was bound to have political repercussions on the internal situation in the country, especially as Muscat had obtained none of the anticipated benefits from that 'unnatural alliance' with the English. After the ill-advised expedition, the sultan returned empty handed, while the region fell definitively under the direct control of the English.

At the beginning of the 1820s, the Ja'lān region in the east experienced a large-scale armed uprising as a protest against the sultan's attitude towards Ra's al-Khaymah. This rebellion brought together various tribes from the area, with the tribe of al-Bū 'Ali, of Wahhābi obedience, at their head. In order to deal with it, the sultan asked England for support, which was refused.

An accident embroiled Great Britain's in the war after all. One of the English ships fell into the hands of al-Bū ʿAli. An emissary was despatched to demand an explanation of the action and he died on the journey.[326]

In fact, the crushing of al-Bū ʿAli's uprising was beginning to interest the English as much as the sultan, if not more so. Two expeditions were launched against the rebels and the sultan took part only in the first. He almost lost his life trying to help one of the British officers.[327]

Great Britain could not stop at a defeat that affected her position and her military prestige. The government of British India decided to humble the rebels, got all its forces together and prepared for a new, so-called 'punitive expedition'. In order to avoid yet another reverse, the governor of Bombay assembled an expeditionary corps of almost 3000 men, of which 1263 were Europeans and 1686 Indians. The command was entrusted to Colonel Smith.[328]

At the beginning of February 1821, the British troops clashed with the forces of Jaʿlān; the balance of forces favoured the English. Losses on both sides were heavy but the action ended in total defeat for Jaʿlān. Out of the total men captured, 150 were from the al-Sharqiya area, including 59 from al-Bū ʿAli's tribe. Members of the council of the East India Company let it be known that al-Bū ʿAli's tribes had at least won general admiration for the heroic defence of their lands and inhabitants.[329] A few of the rulers among the captives were exiled to India and ended their days there.

The uprising had revealed an internal political crisis that was to become one of the permanent features of Omani society and find almost continuous expression. But, at the same time, this episode improved relations between Muscat and Great Britain, which had gone through a 'cold' phase after the fall of Ra's al-Khaymah. This 'warming' enabled England to consolidate what she had gained by signing a series of undertakings with the sultan, focussing, among other things, on limiting the slave trade.

Oman had indeed concluded a first agreement with Great Britain in 1820, by which dealing in slaves was considered as an act of piracy. Chronologically, this text coincided with England's engagement alongside the sultan in suppressing the Jaʿlān uprising. Emerging victorious from that war in 1822, England signed a second agreement with the sultan that focussed on banning the export of slaves to any British or European possessions, and even their transport in Arab ships to European possessions. The text provided for the appointment of a British official to supervise the application of the agreement in *al-sayyid* Saʿīd's possessions in East Africa.[330]

There is no need to stress the extent to which the application of these undertakings concerning the slave trade might hamper the economic activities of the countries on the Gulf. Indeed, British ships thereafter engaged in policing activities and intercepted Arab ships, searching them and confiscating their cargo if slaves were discovered. This point will be dealt with more directly in Chapter 6.

In 'Sāḥel Oman'

For the region of '*Sāḥel Oman*', this form of economic blockade promptly led to a deterioration in the economic and social climate. Furthermore, tribal differences grew deeper due to the crisis, more particularly between the Banī Yās and the Qawāsim. These differences in turn led to conflict, setting Ghafirites against Hanawites; this had already been a problem in the Omani civil war (1718–1737).

This state of affairs only accentuated the economic stagnation; pearl fishing which, following the collapse of commercial activity had, together with fishing, become a major resource, was seriously affected. The quality of life suffered considerably and this was one of the main reasons for the 'maritime truce' that was signed on 11 May 1835.

The parties to the conflict had recourse to Great Britain to resolve their differences. Sheikhs from the region, or their representatives, held a meeting with the British vice-president at Bushehr, and in 1836 a first agreement, called a truce, between the tribes was signed. At first it only dealt with a period corresponding to the pearl fishing season, that is to say duration of six months. It was renewed the following year and then proclaimed annually renewable, in agreement with the resident general, until 1842. The government in Bombay then proposed that the truce commitment be made definitive.[331]

But what did the British actually gain politically from this commitment? The government in Bombay won the right to oversee the operation of the truce, which, by the same token, justified their playing a military role in the region; and second, it gave their presence a legitimacy that suited their strategy.

In 1839, likewise, Great Britain signed a first agreement with Sulṭān ibn Saqr, the chief of al-Qawāsim, at al-Sharjah, relating to the banning of the import of slaves. Other tribal rulers had done the same.

A political reading of this whole question reveals that this other agreement also served British interests in the sense that it officially sanctioned yet again the right of the British fleet to monitor, restrict, not to say hamper all that was left of Arab maritime trade.

The agreement for perpetual maritime peace of 1853

In line with the logic of Great Britain's plans to date, and in harmony with her strategy, the agreement for perpetual maritime peace with the tribes was entered into in 1853; it was also called the '*perpetual truce*'. One of its articles required that England supervise its application among the Arab tribes. And so once again we see the British presence established as guarantor of tribal equilibrium in the region; her insistence on maintaining this type of presence became one of the permanent features of her strategy.

According to al-ʿAqād, the 1853 agreement must be seen as the end of a period in the history of '*Sāḥel Oman*'. The treaty did not only prevent clashes at sea, it tended to further the preservation of the *status quo*, knowing that some of the really tiny sheikhdoms would have difficulty sustaining themselves as political units. On the other hand, this agreement allowed Great Britain to rise to the rank of permanent arbiter, forcing sheikhdoms whose ships had been guilty of aggression, or whose attitude in purely political affairs did not suit them, to make compensation.[332]

Moreover, at the time of what was called the preliminary undertaking in 1820, after the fall of Ra's al-Khaymah, 'Ajmān and Umm-al-Qaywain did not sign it, as those territories were under the authority of al-Qawāsim. But later, in an effort to chip away at the power of al-Qawāsim, Great Britain separated the two towns and emphasised the separation by connecting them with the signature of the '*general agreement with the Arab tribes*'.

While condemning the Gulf States to division and dependence, the 1853 treaty at least had the merit in their eyes of abolishing the ignominious name of '*Pirate Coast*' which England had given the zone at the beginning of her quarrel with al-Qawāsim; it was renamed '*the Trucial Coast*'. This new appellation was more in keeping with the region's situation *vis-à-vis* Great Britain. It remained in force officially throughout the British colonial period, more particularly in the administrative vocabulary of the Indian government, while the name '*Sāḥel Oman*' remained in popular usage until the sixties of the twentieth century.

The 1892 undertaking concerning territorial concessions

In 1892, England imposed a new undertaking on the region, known by the name of the 'banning undertaking';[333] among other things it obliged the sheikhs to guarantee and bind themselves, their heirs and successors, never to cede, sell or mortgage or otherwise allow their territories to be occupied except to the British government. The friends of the English would be the friends of the sheikhs and the enemies of the English would be their enemies. In return, Great Britain undertook to protect the region from foreign interference.

This undertaking needs no comment. An analogous undertaking would be signed with Oman in 1891, in the reign of sultan Fayṣal ibn Turki (1888–1913). But this was only after Great Britain had threatened to proclaim official British protection for Oman and after Zanzibar had been separated from Oman in 1861. We shall return to this later.

In this way the Arab coast was transformed into British protectorates. In a hundred and fifty years of occupation, Great Britain had succeeded in completely isolating the region and depriving it of any commercial and cultural contact with the outside world.

The coast had to live through harsh economic poverty, social isolation and cultural atrophy. To give some idea of what was happening, we note that, until the middle of the twentieth century, it had no elementary school and no hospital. And that is just one example among many of its complete destitution. This situation would change hardly at all until oil exports began and the United Arab Emirates was formed in 1971.

Conclusion of Part I

A certain number of experiences and political lessons emerge from a study of this part of the book. The *imāma* system had been patiently built up, based on a constitution and on original Ibadhite codes, but it was not invulnerable. It did not exclude the risk of internal destabilisation, as first happened with the fall of the *imāma* of al-Ṣalṭ ibn Mālek in the third century of the Hegira (AD ninth century) and then with the drift of the Ya'rūbite State (1624–1741) and the fall of the *imāma* system, ending in a crisis of national unity, the emergence of clan loyalties and a series of long and exhausting civil wars.

Despite this vulnerability and the dissensions that might flow from it, for the Omanis the *imāma* system remained a point of reference and a political ideal of equilibrium and unity, based on the principle of *al-shūrā* and *al-ijmā'*, in other words on wholly original democratic values. As long as they were possessed of a particle of sovereignty, the Omanis always aspired to recreate conditions of respect for the Ibadhite system.

On the other hand, the fall of the *imāma* and the divisions that followed it always led to geographical partition. After the fall of the *imāma* of al-Ṣalṭ, Oman split into monarchies and semi-independent provinces. Similarly, following the fall of the Ya'rūbite state, in a short while two new entities had been formed. Furthermore, any weakening of the *imāma* exposed the country to external aggression. So, after the fall of the *imāma* of al-Ṣalṭ, the Portuguese faced no structured resistance and as a result succeeded in occupying the coasts of Oman for a century and a half.

So it is not by chance that, after the disappearance of the *Ibāḍi* Ya'rūbite state and the decline of the country, the history of Oman was no longer just a history of the Ibadhite movement. The abandonment of the *imāma* amounted for the country to a severance and to the formation of a duality in the national and cultural identity all through the modern period.

Was the end of the Ibadhite model in Oman irreversible? In the light of past experience it certainly was not, for until then Ibadhism had always been, as it were, the country's loadstone. But the geopolitical circumstances had been profoundly modified. Great Britain was now playing a major role in the whole of that region and had an interest in maintaining weakness and divisions.

A number of factors such as the withdrawal of France and the fall of India, Oman's historic ally, into the hands of the British, as well as the English domination over the ports and sea lanes in the East and the Indian Ocean, effectively marginalised the Omani fleet and progressively weakened the country as a regional force. Lastly, the collapse of the fleet of al-Qawāsim and the destruction of Ra's al-Khaymah by the British struck a fatal blow to economic, social and cultural development, not just in the region of Oman and '*Sāḥel Oman*', but throughout the Gulf.

British power set as little store as possible on the accumulated culture and political experience of these countries, particularly of Oman, the heir of a thousand year old Ibadhite tradition; she imposed on the whole region, and especially on the area of '*Sāḥel Oman*' not just structures and interests that were foreign to them but also a particularly harsh colonial history.

Part II

From the colonial challenge to the imamate response

From the dismantling of the Omani empire to the present day

> The destinies of the Gulf countries were decided thousands of miles away from their owners.
>
> (Lord Salisbury (1830–1903) British Prime Minister)

After realising its main objectives in a first phase (from the late eighteenth to the mid-nineteenth centuries) Great Britain's strategy for the second colonial phase, a global one this time, tended towards splitting the Omani–African state and separating Zanzibar from Oman (1861).

The subjugation of Oman was one of the *sine qua non* conditions for completing the reinforcement of British positions in the Gulf region and ensuring control of the route to India. But with the increase in British influence in Oman, the deterioration of the economy reached a critical stage; only the *imāma* alternative still offered a way out of this impasse. And so, in 1869, the Ibadhite movement, which was closely following developments in the country and was fully aware of the implications, took the decision to proclaim revolution.

It is highly significant of the strength and popularity of the imamite movement that the Omani capital should have fallen after just one month, provisionally ending the sultanate system. ʿAzzān bin Qays, one of the leaders of the revolution (1869–1871), was then elected *imām* and the Ibadhite movement succeeded in restoring the *imāma* system after a break of about half a century. But in the end, England would succeed in stifling ʿAzzān's *imāma* economically and overthrowing it.

Sultan Turki (1871–1888), who re-established the system of the sultanate for his own benefit, would be unable to solve Oman's problems. His reign and that of his successor, his son Fayṣal (1888–1913), were marked by tribal disturbances, economic downturn and the increase of British influence.

So in 1913, the Ibadhite movement would again proclaim revolution. Just as in 1869–1871, this revolution would be led with such burning intensity that, had it not been faced with an active British defence, the regime of the sultanate would have been overthrown. In the end, the imamites would be obliged to sign the famous treaty of al-Sīb (1920), by which Oman would be divided into two distinct parts: the '*imāma* of Oman' and the 'sultanate of Muscat'.

This partition was to remain in force until quite recently and during all that time the country would live in a state of stagnation and total paralysis. With the region's entry into the era of oil production, renewed conflict between Great Britain and the symbols of the *imāma* was inevitable.

Although Oman embarked on a new phase in her political development with the uprising of 1955–1964 and the Omani question managed to find a place on the international stage within the framework of the worldwide liberation movement, the uprising itself would achieve nothing of importance at the time. It would, however, help to affirm and revive national political awareness in Oman and mark a historic turning point. But, curiously, Oman and her cause were to remain largely unrecognised.

6 The Omani–African state (1650–1860)

The sultanates

The sultanate of Oman and Zanzibar

Linked from the outset to the Arab–Omani-Islamic communities of East Africa (the Zanzibar coast), the Omani–Ya'rūbite state only began really cultivating that link after its liberation from the Portuguese yoke at the beginning of the seventeenth century. Having now become the second centre of economic interest for the powers in Oman, the Swāḥili coast came gradually to be seen as an extension of Oman until, in the nineteenth century, it became the true centre of wealth of the Omani state, now threatened with strangulation by British expansion. The sultan of Muscat even moved his capital to Zanzibar. This chapter considers how the Omani–African relationship developed up to the separation from Zanzibar in the second half of the nineteenth century.

Omani–African links till the end of the eighteenth century

The region of East Africa encompasses a collection of islands and coastal towns, among them the most important being Zanzibar, Pemba, Kilwa and Mombasa. It is this coastal stretch, some 1500 km long, that is called the Zanzibar region

The Arabian and notably the Omani presence in this region goes back to the second century of the Hegira (ninth century), although contacts existed well before that date. However, the start of a noteworthy and official Omani presence dates only from the second half of the seveneenth century.

There can be no doubt that the early contacts were motivated by commercial considerations; but alongside these were motives of a politico-religious nature. With the fall of the state of the Islamic caliphate in the second half of the first century of the Hegira, and as a result of internal religious disputes, certain Arab tribes and communities felt constrained to leave the Baṣra region, then a great Islamic and cultural centre, and seek refuge in Oman, Bahrein and the Arabian peninsula. Later a number of these communities emigrated towards the east African area.

To be more precise, it was after the fall of the first *imāma* in Oman, that of al-Jalanda ibn Mas'ūd (AH 135/AD 751), under the agression of the Abbassids, and after the subsequent bloody repression of the *'ulamā'*, that Omani migration to the region was stepped up. The Omanis succeeded in establishing Arab emirates in the area. The al-Ḥārthi tribe built two towns there, Mogadishu (Mogadiscio) and Brava, around AD 924.[334]

Well away from the internal squabbles of the Arab–Islamic state and thanks to the richness of the region, these emirates as a whole enjoyed great political stability and a flourishing economy for more than seven centuries, until the arrival of the Portuguese.

It was only in 1501, when Albuquerque arrived on his way to conquer the East that this erstwhile peaceful region entered a period of violence and tension, and local prosperity came to an abrupt halt. It was fruitless for the inhabitants to take up arms against the invader; they were manifestly outclassed by Lusitanian military power and the terror it installed in the whole of the area. So much so that, according to Western travellers, the theatre of the crusading wars shifted in the sixteenth century from the Mediterranean to the Indian Ocean.[335]

The East African region thus came to be completely dominated by the Portuguese. According to al-Qāsīmī, the population of Zanzibar recognised Lusitanian authority over the island and had to agree to pay the occupier an annual poll tax. Subsequently, the Portuguese seized the coastal towns and ruined their trade. The result was the dramatic impoverishment of the whole region, from which it was destined never to recover.[336]

C. Le Cour Grandmaison has traced the stages of the Omani presence. As she sees it, Omani expansion on the Swāḥili coast developed in three stages: in the first it was driven by the restored political unity of Oman; in the second, internal unity fractured and Oman's troubles affected her African possessions; finally, in the third, the winning faction in Oman enhanced its authority in East Africa. That period of the greatest florescence of the Omani presence on the East coast and it reached its peak in the mid- to late-nineteenth century.[337]

In the seventeenth century, following the liberation of Oman, *imām* Sulṭān ibn Sayf I (1649–1688) responded to a request from the Omani community in Africa and undertook to rid their territory of the Portuguese occupier. By that intervention, the Omani presence in the region was strengthened and thereafter Oman was to play a predominant political role there. More than that, the whole eastern face of Africa was henceforth deemed to be officially a dependency of Oman.

Imām Sulṭān ibn Sayf I, the liberator of those lands, had appointed prominent Omanis as *wālis*, so as to be in direct control of the affairs of the islands of Zanzibar, Pemba and Mombasa; the latter was comparable to Zanzibar in strategic and economic importance and the Omani family of al-Mazrūʿi was placed at its head. An Omani–African state had come into being.

The Yaʿrūbite state was keen to consolidate commercial and cultural links with its African branch and it is notable that it affirmed the Islamic *Ibāḍi* laws there. Nevertheless, the land preserved its distinctive character: the mixture of Arab and African blood had created a cultural duality, Omani–*Ibāḍi* and African, and also a particular socio-ethnic type, later known by the term '*Sawāḥili*'. Moreover the use of the Arab language had been restricted to the '*ulamā'* and the elites, while Swāḥili had remained the dominant tongue.

During the Omani civil war (1718–1737), official links between Oman and the East African region, that is to say between the *wālis* and their central government, were broken. Yet, although the *wālis* enjoyed traditional conditions of autonomy, this did not at first create a state of separation, even though the effects of the civil war were felt in the African part as well. It was with the deterioration of the situation in Oman towards the end of the civil war, and the collapse of the Ya'rūbite state (1741), that Sayf ibn Sulṭān II al-Ya'rūbi had to designate Sheikh Muḥammad ibn 'Uthmān al-Mazrū'i as *wāli* of the town of Mombasa and grant him almost complete authority over the island in return for the payment of an annual tax. This unaccustomed arrangement paved the way to an ambiguous situation concerning the status of the island.

When *imām* Aḥmed ibn Sa'īd al-Bū Sa'īd (1741–1783) came to power, the *wālis* of all the islands in the East African area gave their approval and proclaimed their loyalty to the new *imām*, with the exception of the *wāli* of Mombasa, al-Mazrū'i, who contested Aḥmed's authority and stopped paying the annual tax to Oman.

In the face of this separatist challenge, *imām* Aḥmed had no hesitation in taking stern measures. His forces tried several times in vain to retake the town of Mombasa and in the end its status remained vague until the advent of sultan Sa'īd ibn Sulṭān (1806–1856).

The period of Sa'īd ibn Sulṭān

In the first half of the nineteenth century, Sulṭān Sa'īd began to show a special interest in the island of Zanzibar. Among other achievements, he fostered the introduction of cloves, imported from the island of Mauritius in 1818, and their cultivation. This soon became the chief source of wealth in the area and made Zanzibar the first worldwide exporter of cloves.[338]

This success was accompanied by a significant migration of Omani traders, who settled semi-permanently in East Africa. Clove growing spread and increased meanwhile and the number of trees on Zanzibar Island reached one million.[339] While the strategic and economic position of the area gained in importance, the Omani presence too was considerably reinforced.[340]

Ever since 1830, the sultan had been spending more time in Zanzibar than in Muscat and then he made it his African capital.

> He only took up residence in Zanzibar after 1837 and in seven years the town became the seat of a flourishing trade. (...) Business in the port of Zanzibar, taking imports and exports together, in 1843 reached a figure of 1 200 000 Spanish piastres or more than 6 000 000 francs.[341]

Zanzibar had actually become the chief preoccupation of the Omani state, to the detriment of its Asiatic capital, Muscat. This interest in the African region was won at the expense of Oman, which was beginning to be neglected and gradually to lose both its political and its economic importance. From a very different, geopolitical angle, however, Muscat would continue to lie at the centre of British strategic preoccupations.

The sultan's arrival in the region and his establishment in Zanzibar had not been all plain sailing. He had to face strong opposition from the rulers of the Mombasa region, the Mazrūʿi, the very ones who had rejected the power of the al-Bū Saʿīdis and refused to pay the annual tax. The sultan was obliged to lead several expeditions against these rebels.

The subjugation of Mombasa was by no means secure. Once more in the hands of the Mazrūʿi, the town opposed the sultan's enterprises in 1834. It was only on his fourth journey to East Africa (from November 1836 to September 1839) that Saʿīd succeeded in gaining definitive possession of the town, capturing its masters, the Mazrūʿi, and putting them to death.[342]

And so the necessary repossession of a zone that had become economically vital to Oman was finally achieved. After that, a redefinition of the diplomatic balance in the region became the order of the day. From his new platform in Zanzibar, the sultan intensified relations with Great Britain as well as with France and, indeed, the United States. Certain Omani ships even started to fly the French flag,[343] notably those belonging to the al-Sharqiya, Ṣūr and Jaʿlan regions. It is worthwhile recording this fact straight away, as it was to be the origin of a crisis between France and England that was taken to the court in The Hague in 1904.

Zanzibar the Linch Pin: sequence of Omani-Franco-British relations

As has been described earlier, the British asserted their hold on the Gulf region at the beginning of the nineteenth century. This development had its repercussions on the African branch of the Omani state. The sultan, anxious to keep room to manoeuvre in spite of the burdensome presence of the English, made discreet moves towards a rapprochement with France, which, having obtained the return of île Bourbon in the treaty of Paris (1814), was now back in the Indian Ocean.[344] The hope of an alternative to British hegemony determined the sultan to reactivate, as far as possible, the traditional alliance with the French possessions in the region.

The authorities of île Bourbon signed two orders, on 1 April 1822 and 11 May 1829, laying down the conditions for a commercial agreement with the *imāma* (sultanate). But it was not until 1837 that France obtained the right to instal a consular agent in Muscat and in 1844, under a treaty of trade and friendship, a consul in Zanzibar.[345]

England could not look favourably on the Franco-Omani rapprochement, which might raise questions about the 1798 agreement; she considered that 'this commitment would, in the long run, draw England into a war with France.'[346]

According to Kajare, in 1840, *al-sayyid* Saʿīd, still fearful of British ambition and aware that the position of Muscat did not give the guarantees of independence he wanted, resolved to draw closer to the African coast.[347] 'The situation was more acute when, in 1840, *al-sayyid* Saʿīd had, on the advice of French agents, transferred his capital to Zanzibar, so as to be more independent of English power and nearer to the possessions of his friend, France.'[348]

In his search for new counterweights to English domination, the sultan had also turned to American diplomacy: he signed the first agreement with the United States of America in 1833. For the Americans, it was their second agreement with an Arab country (a first one having been signed with the monarchy of Morocco). And the American emissary, Roberts, declared on this occasion that he was happy to see that the United States had made friends with one of the powers in Asia, the one that was proud to possess a larger fleet than the United States. In fact it numbered no fewer than seventy-five ships.[349]

In 1839, France signalled her wish to develop relations with Oman and send an official emissary in the hope of concluding a treaty analogous to the one Muscat had signed with the United States in 1833.

In spite of tensions between Oman and the English, the sultan judged it advisable to consult them; he sent two letters to the government of British India, asking its opinion of French intentions and what he should decide concerning France. The reply naturally recommended that he should not enter into any agreement with France. And the government of India did not omit to remind the sultan on this occasion of the terms of the treaty of 1798.[350]

A copy of the instructions given by M. de Hiel, the governor of Bourbon, to M. Page, a captain of corvette in command of *La Favorite*, and dated 31 August 1841, indicates that France sent her emissary, Captain Guillain, to hold talks with the sultan about installing M. Noel as French consular agent in Zanzibar and M. Ben Calfaun in the same capacity at Muscat. M. de Hiel added:

> Since M. Guillain's journey to Muscat, a new circumstance may have further alienated the Imam's good will. He has sent me a totally unfounded complaint against France's occupation of the island of Nossi-Bé, which he claims belongs to him and I have had to dismiss it.[351]

M. de Hiel explained that if the sultan should mention the subject of the island of Nossi-Bé or the question of Mayotte in future talks, French policy must be clear and firm.

> I acknowledge to no power rights over Madagascar and its dependencies which might be such as to take precedence over those of France, and as for the islands, I consider them as independent countries, each free to give itself to the power that can best ensure the welfare of its inhabitants.[352]

In fact, contrary to all expectations, the subject of the islands was not mentioned and, once the sultan had been reassured about the French position concerning the independence and sovereignty of Muscat and Zanzibar, his attitude changed radically.

In 1844, a Franco-Omani treaty was signed, and ratified on 4 February 1846. Article 5 of this convention formally recognised the reciprocal rights of the contracting parties to appoint consuls and consular agents in their respective states. From then on, France maintained agents in both Muscat and Zanzibar.[353]

This treaty certainly represented an important benefit for both countries even though its signing came very belatedly. Whatever the case, it accentuates the rivalry between France and Great Britain in this zone. Certain of its articles will be discussed later in connection with sultan Fayṣal ibn Turki (1888–1913).

In Paris, the *Journal des débats* summed up the tenor of the text:

> The treaty with the sultan is conceived in a liberal spirit which does honour to the intelligence and good will of that prince. In future, the French will be wholly at liberty to enter, reside, trade and circulate in his states; they will enjoy all the immunities which are, or may in future be granted to the subjects of the most favoured nations.

The newspaper added: 'The sultan has also given orders that the 5-franc piece, which to date has suffered huge depreciation in his domains, shall in future be accepted in all the markets at its real value.'[354]

These significant developments in the political history of Oman caused dissensions both between Britain and Oman, and between France and Britain. Thus in 1854, France sent Captain Fristal to sultan Saʿīd to obtain an agreement to purchase the Kuria Muria islands but, under pressure from England, the sultan had to refuse the request and the islands were presented as a gift to Queen Victoria in 1854.[355]

At the same time, faced with the economic prosperity experienced by East Africa since 1840 (even after *al-sayyid* Saʿīd) and up till 1870, Oman's role as a maritime power had been appreciably reduced, to a point where the Omani 'metropolis' was no longer capable of defending its national sovereignty. Kelly notes that in 1856 the number of Oman's maritime vessels had sunk to five and even these were not all able to put to sea; the sultan no longer had any naval officers or seamen.[356] Blighted by the British hold on its historic centre, the Omani state now survived, paradoxically, only in its African dimension. Its rulers had soon understood this, as witness the transfer of the capital to Zanzibar. But how long could the haven of prosperity in East Africa hold out against English colonial ambitions?

The question of the slave trade

Despite the appeals and encouragement of Islam for the freeing of slaves, the trade continued to be buoyant in this region. It formed an important resource for the Swāḥili coast, while representing a less than glorious page in its history. That said, the British intention to put an end to this activity arose in the first place from a politico-strategic design. And that is why it is as well to view Great Britain's 'abolitionist' policy with considerable circumspection.

Since the eighteenth century and the creation of the French Society of Friends of the Blacks [Société française des Amis des Noirs], opinion had been gradually being sensitised to the anti-slavery cause. The credit for espousing it with sincerity goes to certain European religious and even political thinkers who wanted to put an end to an inhuman practice. But the British rulers saw in this noble and humanitarian cause first and foremost a welcome legal and moral cover for the development of their colonial strategy, after the so-called drive against 'piracy'.

Was it not in fact a paradox to see Great Britain, which had devoted more than two centuries to colonial interventions and intimidation of the peoples in the region, destroying their economy and civilisation while waving the banner of the human rights?

By the terms of the two agreements signed by England, first in 1820, then after the end of the Jaʿlān uprising in 1822,[357] the slave trade was effectively banned; she implemented legal and military procedures that struck hard at the expansion of Arab trade. British ships in fact took to policing activities, intercepting Arab boats, searching them and confiscating their cargoes when they discovered them to be transporting slaves.

In reality, these confiscation procedures were not restricted to vessels actually conveying slaves, they also affected certain merchant ships and this gave rise to protests to the government of British India, which always dodged its responsibility for what was happening.

Arab merchant vessels were no longer free to navigate in safety. The discontent of the Omanis finally put pressure on the sultan, who in turn set about finding a way out of the crisis through the development of his relations with France, despite great initial hesitation. Hence the conclusion of the Omani–French agreement of friendship in 1844, about which Great Britain launched a veritable outcry.

To regain control of the situation, British power endeavoured to bring about the signing of a third agreement banning the slave trade, but this time in the region of Zanzibar, the heart of Omani economic and political sovereignty. Needless to point out that, in the event, slavery was only a pretext for intervention in a zone resistant to British influence.

The slave trade was an important source of revenue for the sultan. Agreeing to such a treaty amounted in the long run to cutting himself off from his food supplies. That is why he first laid down four conditions:

1 Annexation of Bahrein and its possessions, on condition that Great Britain undertook to guarantee the reign there of *al-sayyid* Saʿīd.
2 Non-interference by Great Britain in the operations transferring slaves from the interior of Africa to Zanzibar.
3 *Al-sayyid* Saʿīd not to be held responsible for infringements of the law banning the export of slaves if they occur without his knowledge.

Another point was added and, according to Kelly, considered as the fourth 'condition':

4 'We hope and pray that the British government will cherish our two sons, al-sayyid Khalid and al-sayyid Thuwayni.'[358]

Two main points emerge from these conditions. First of all, the question of the annexation of Bahrein to Oman. This region, the object of a long-standing ambition on the part of the sultan, did not yet constitute a strategic site for Great Britain. Hence the notion that she would not, in theory, prevent it being handed over to the sultan. But the context might render the decision tricky: it ran counter to the interests of both the Persians and the Wahhābis, the Iranians because of their ambitions in the region of Bahrein and the Wahhābis because of their doctrinal and historic divergence from Oman, as well as their alliance with the al-ʿUṭub tribes that governed Bahrein. Great Britain had no desire to damage relations with her friends the Persians, nor with her potential allies, the Wahhābis, considered to be the future great power in the region.

The most important point, in fact, had to do with the fourth condition laid down by the sultan, whereby he hoped that Great Britain 'would show consideration towards his two sons al-seyid Khalid and al-seyid Thuwayni'. Great Britain could wish for nothing better. Indeed, she interpreted this condition as a request from the sultan that the British government should *guarantee* the succession of his two sons to power, one in Muscat and the other in Zanzibar, in other words, preparing the partition of the sultanate: the separation of Muscat and Zanzibar. That is to say the end of the Arab–African state. From the British point of view, this condition set the seal on the sultan's political '*testament*', a testament that suited the interests of Great Britain to perfection and that she would be all the more careful to see executed.

Hence the relatively casual way in which she overlooked the other conditions laid down by Saʿīd. So shortly afterwards she obliged him to sign the agreement. Kajare tells that immediately following the treaty between France and the sultan of Muscat, England succeeded in concluding an agreement with the sultan, dated 2 October 1845, an agreement couched in these terms:

> I – The sultan of Muscat undertakes to prohibit, subject to the severest penalties, the export of slaves from his possessions in Africa.
>
> II – He also undertakes to prohibit the import of slaves of African origin into his possessions in Asia and to use his influence with all the chiefs of Arabia to the same end.
>
> III – He grants to the warships of her Britannic Majesty and to those of the India Company permission to board and to confiscate any vessels, whether they be the property of His Highness the Sultan or of his subjects, which are engaged in the slave trade, with the sole exception of those transporting slaves between his various possessions in Africa, that is between latitude 1° 57′ and 9° 2′ south, including Zanzibar, Pemba, etc.
>
> IV – This agreement will take effect on January 1st 1847.
>
> Concluded in Zanzibar 2nd October 1845.[359]

As it stood, the tone of this agreement aroused misgivings which the official British historian, Kelly, was bound to note: how had sultan Saʿīd been able to accept the terms of the 1845 agreement? In his view, the reasons remain hazy and a mystery.[360]

Actually, the reasons were not so hazy, especially for a historian like Kelly; the British riposte to the sultan was a reaction to the rapprochement between Oman and France in the context of the convention of 1844.

However, this agreement, by which England hoped to counterbalance the French treaty of 17 November 1844 through an extension of her control over all the vessels of the sultan and his subjects, failed to have the results she expected because of the attitude of France.[361] So the role of France with regard to her Omani friends became increasingly vital for the protection of Oman and Zanzibar.

From the separation of Zanzibar to the Franco-English declaration of March 1862

On the death of *al-sayyid* Sa'īd, which occurred on 30 October 1856 in the course of a voyage from Muscat to Zanzibar, Thūwayni

> the third of the sons of the late sultan,[362] declared himself sole heir to power in Oman. By the same token, he was heir to all its dependencies; for the unity of the Empire remained intact, his father having divided only the administration and not the sovereignty which, as in the past, had to continue to belong to the sultan of the Asiatic metropolis.[363]

Yet circumstances militated against this principle of unicity. Indeed, immediately after the death of his father, Mājed, with the support of some notables, proclaimed himself sultan of Zanzibar. This quite clearly signified the secession of the African part of Oman.

Thūwayni, for his part, refused to accept Mājed's decision; he sent Muḥammad ibn Sālem as emissary to Zanzibar and the emissary succeeded in brokering an amicable agreement between the two brothers: Mājed consented to pay Thūwayni dues of 40 000 crowns, reflecting the sum previously set aside by his father for the Muscat budget.[364] But this solution settled nothing as far as the status of the Zanzibar branch was concerned. Thūwayni saw the tribute paid as a sign of Zanzibar's dependence, but Mājed had a quite different understanding of the matter. A year later, he stopped paying his contribution, thereby annulling the agreement.

Thūwayni, plagued by internal and regional crises, was unable to react to his brother's decision until a year had elapsed. He is then believed to have assembled some fifteen thousand men and set sail for Zanzibar, only to be stopped a few miles from Muscat by the English fleet, which, by virtue of the sovereignty of the seas that it had arrogated to itself, sent *sayyid* Thūwayni's ships back to port.[365] The Zanzibar question was entering a decisive phase.

Constrained by these new circumstances, sultan Thūwayni accepted the mediation and arbitration of the viceroy, but claimed his right to reservations, which Great Britain in turn categorically rejected. In the end she obtained a pre-agreement, drawn up by Thūwayni, by which he undertook to accept the decision of the arbitration without prior conditions. In a letter dated 21 September 1859, Thūwayni wrote:

> I, the under signed, Seyid Thuwayni, declare that the high government of India having requested that I take no action against Zanzibar, I have abstained in deference to its desire, in order to submit all my grievances against my brother Majed to the government, through the kind intervention of Colonel Russell. And now, whatever may be the decision of H.E. the governor general in his arbitration between me and my brother Majed I shall submit to it, come what may. Firmly resolved to submit to his decision, whatever it may be.[366]

In other words, Thūwayni rashly signed a kind of blank cheque on his own fate and that of Oman. *Sayyid* Mājed, in turn, a prisoner of his own logic, his limited vision and his personal interests, asked England to be his 'advocate' against his brother and against Oman.

> I have passed the settlement of the said disagreement and the appeasement of the said discord to His Lordship the Governor General, Viceroy of Her Most High Majesty in the government of India. And whatever may be the decision of the said governor, I accept it and consent to all his arbitration on my part.[367]

The arbiter, as it happened, was both judge and litigant. In the same spirit as the agreement for the sharing of Oman between the three brothers, Saʿīd, Sulṭān and Qays, signed at Birka in 1793, Great Britain continued the work of dismantling even dismembering the Omani state.[368] The separation of the African part of Oman from the Arab part entered this strategic procedure as the most logical next stage.

All that remained was for this procedure to be given a legal format so as to keep up appearances on an international level, *vis-à-vis* the colonial competitors, in this case the French. So the famous letter was brought out, written by *al-sayyid* Saʿīd at the time of the negotiations for the treaty of October 1845, containing the recommendation: 'We hope and pray that Great Britain will cherish our two sons al-sayed Khalid and al-sayed Thuwayni.' Great Britain claimed to consider this letter as a 'testament' of sultan Saʿīd. Even accepting it as such, the letter most certainly did not indicate that the sultan had wished the Omani state to be divided between the two brothers after his death.

In truth, this 'testament' contained nothing that could authorise Great Britain to dispose of the empire of *al-sayyid* Saʿīd legally or juridically. But at this stage of her colonial development, Great Britain hardly felt it necessary to justify her acts and decisions. She interpreted this 'testament' in accordance with her political and strategic interests and charged General Coghlan to see to the execution of the 'testament', in other words to put into effect a plan determined long beforehand.

The 'Arbitration': General Coghlan's report and its consequences

The report sent by the commission representing the government of India and chaired by Coghlan insisted on the need for partition on the basis of the following points:

1. Maintaining security. It was said in the report that, despite the veneration he enjoyed, Saʿīd was incapable of controlling the mob and internal tensions in the sultanate, and that every time he left for Zanzibar an insurrection broke out in Oman. When he went back to restore order, it was the whole of Africa that was then exposed to upheavals.
2. Under Saʿīd's rule, the Arab colonies were the only centres of the slave trade. But now the large towns were more important than Oman.
3. The fight against slavery would be facilitated by the separation.
4. Recognition of the new state by the great powers, especially France, was already achieved, thanks to Mājed's action.
5. It was in Great Britain's interest – and that was the all-important point – to prevent a strong empire being built up on the Indian Ocean.

More than that, the report concluded that for the policy of partition to bear fruit, it should be accompanied by the maintenance of dual control by Britain: the Asiatic part would receive financial aid guaranteed by Great Britain, while the African part would be indebted for its independence to that same Great Britain.[369]

The British government promised at the same time to settle 'equitably' the disagreement between the two brothers, who were thus forced to accept the arbitration of the Viceroy of India. Lord Canning decided that the sultans of Zanzibar should pay the sultans of Muscat an annual sum of 40 000 écus,[370] about 80 000 Indian rupees, but that would carry no implication of dependence or vassalage.

The text of the arbitration stipulated very clearly that the annual payment in no way implied Zanzibar's dependence on Muscat but rather that Oman abandoned and totally gave up her claim. It also guaranteed the non-interference of Oman in the affairs of Zanzibar. Consequently, the two parties to this arbitration were politically separated. Thereupon Great Britain gave each of the two brothers, Thūwayni and Mājed, the title of sultan.

It is obvious that such a mortgage imposed on the future of their homeland by heirs, now promoted heads of state at the cost of the dismemberment of their empire, and by the self-interested policy of a foreign power, could not pass without considerable repercussions. A long controversy raged between the representatives of the parties concerned around the legal, juridical and even religious basis for the partition. The question was to know precisely whether the late sultan had or had not the right, from the point of view of *al-sharī'a* to divide the 'Omani empire'.

But the fundamental question lay in the fact that the partition had obeyed not the testament of the sultan, but only the strategic demands of Great Britain.

> The arbitration was not voluntary, as is usual, but imposed on the two parties. It was Great Britain who 'intervened', in her own interest, between the claimants to the succession of sayyid Saʿīd and imposed on them an obligation to accept her mediation and at the same time to submit to the results of that mediation[371]

It was an enormous success for English colonial policy. The partition was considered to be a triumph equivalent in importance to the colonisation of India.[372] According to Pelly, the British resident in the Gulf, quoted by Landen, only the introduction of modern maritime routes in the region equalled this separation in importance.[373]

The American historian Landen very strangely describes this decision as a 'solution', although he does add that the solution imposed by the government of India was worse than the actual problem. This partition split up a united state that had been known as the 'first maritime power', dismantled both its economy and its political unity and contributed to the weakening of its commercial maritime activity.

If the Birka agreement of 1793 had divided Oman and put an end to its unified *imāma*, this latest separation definitively ousted her from the political scene,[374] ruining her position as a strong and influential sultanate. The state of Oman, stifled by British colonial tutelage, would gradually be reduced to the rank of a poor emirate, isolated from the world by its ambiguous status as a state that had been colonised unofficially.

As a last comment on the nature and scope of this arbitration that would weigh so heavily on the destinies of the ex-empire of Oman, we quote Kajare's disillusioned remark at the end of his analysis:

> Although it had been given the name of arbitration, it is neither an arbitration in the true sense, nor a mediation that we find here, but an intervention. A very curious intervention moreover, which cast off the usual, rather brutal and arbitrary forms of intervention in order to invest itself with a juridical character, at least in appearance.[375]

A subtle distinction, it is true, but one that deceived nobody at the time, certainly not French diplomacy which saw this alleged arbitration as nothing more than a stitch-up which could not go unanswered.

The Franco-English declaration of March 1862

French protests against the British 'arbitration' unleashed a new diplomatic crisis which Great Britain proposed to pacify by making sure that the two rival powers formally undertook to respect Zanzibar's independence. But France, shown to be powerless in the arbitration affair, meant to go further, and the agreement concerned the sultanate of Muscat as well. The 'dual accord', signed on 10 March 1862, stated that the two governments, French and English, each undertook to respect the independence of the two authorities, in Muscat and in Zanzibar.

> Taking into consideration the importance of maintaining the independence of His Highness the sultan of Muscat and His Highness the sultan of Zanzibar [France and Great Britain]...have thought it right to engage reciprocally to respect the independence of these Sovereigns.[376]

The declaration of the dual accord, which looked like a simple political proclamation, was nevertheless crucial for the course of Oman's political history. The declaration was intended to prevent the decision on the official protection of Oman by Great Britain, that is to say the declaration of the official colonisation of Oman.

Lorimer makes the following comment:

> This manifesto attracted no interest or attention from any one at the time of its signature, for the government of India knew nothing about it until 1871. Yet such an undertaking had restricted the room for manoeuvre of the signatories.[377]

In fact, as far as France was concerned, it was not a restriction but rather a stroke of fortune for her foreign policy. England, on the other hand, felt shackled by the accord, but she would infringe it insistently and repeatedly. Overall, she remained the chief beneficiary of this development in the age-old game of diplomacy, both in the Gulf region and in the Indian Ocean and East Africa.

Kelly recalls in this connection that no state had managed to exercise full and complete domination of the sea routes in the Gulf from the Abbassid caliphate down to our own day, except in two periods: the age of the Portuguese (sixteenth and seventeenth centuries) and the zenith of British colonial power (nineteenth century).[378]

And, far from her hegemony in the waters of the Gulf being circumscribed, Great Britain had been able to pursue her advantage as far as the eastern face of Africa, stalking the last vestiges of an Omani prosperity whose influence might ultimately have damaged British interests. Furthermore, by working for a definitive partition of the Omani–African state, Great Britain had made sure she could guarantee the political weakness of the once great Oman. This separation, in fact, had severe repercussions on the evolution of the Asian section of the former Omani state.

7 The revolution of *imām* ʿAzzān ibn Qays al-Bū Saʿīdi (1869–1871)

Oman after the separation from Zanzibar

While Great Britain was attending to the maintenance and reinforcement of her presence in the region, the history of Oman was shaken by turmoil and dissension which no one at the time could have suspected would give way to an unprecedented recovery. In the depths of the economic stagnation and bankruptcy of the political regime, the *Ibāḍi* ideal was more alive than ever. So much so that it would be no exaggeration to say that, through all its ordeals, Oman survived as a nation, thanks to the alternative offered by the Ibadhite dream. So, when a small group of respected and determined personalities had undertaken to revive the dream, the *Ibāḍi imāma* enjoyed a dazzling success, the scale of which amazed all observers, starting with the British. All the old demons that had been plaguing Oman for decades caved in and withdrew before the reawakened authority of an *imāma* held in high esteem by all; tribal squabbles, the spirit of clan and faction, foreign intrusion were so many scourges for which the restored *imāma* brought rapid and uncontested remedies.

This restoration of order and the boost to the economy that followed commanded respect. British officials started to discover, or rather to glimpse the resources of a civilisation for which they had always refused even to spare a glance. Disconcerted, and caught between their admiration and their interests, they were even about to let their political line falter. Yet it was on that line that a political destiny for Oman, henceforth condemned to paradox, would still hang; for any genuine influence of an independent *imāma* must inevitably come up against the question of official British recognition.

New developments in British policy

In order to understand the scope of the *imāma* better, we must take a step back and look again at the development of Oman and the countries of the Gulf after the separation from Zanzibar. For Oman, this period marked a phase of historic decline that would lead the country to political, economic and moral bankruptcy. Certainly there was some development, but only in the sense that the whole Gulf region was carried along into a more advanced and active phase of British colonisation. One of the features of this development was the introduction of postal and telegraph lines into the Gulf. They would play an effective role, first and foremost, in consolidating the seizure by the British. Indeed, even through its decline, Oman again became the main focus of a British strategy that was another historic burden it was obliged to shoulder.

In 1858, parallel and important changes took place in India in the fields of politics and administration. The former East India Company had, by a decree of the government of India in 1858, dissolved its board of management. Henceforth the supreme ruling authority belonged to the minister of state for Indian affairs, who was a member of the British cabinet and bore the title of 'Viceroy of India'. This minister was assisted in his task by a cabinet of ministers for India with members drawn from officials living in that country.[379]

Similarly there were movements of personnel among the political and military officials in office in the Gulf region. In 1861 British representation was raised to the rank of that in Zanzibar. An officer named Bensly was appointed political resident in Muscat but his stay was brief. He was replaced by Major Grant, who only remained in office for a year himself. In 1861, Major Herbert Desbrew succeeded him while Colonel Lewis Pelly was appointed political resident general for the Gulf at Bushehr.[380] These developments on the British side heralded a crucial turning point in the history of the Gulf and notably that of Oman.

Thūwayni ibn Sa'īd (1856–1866)

Such a critical period required a ruler of calibre, combining a certain number of conditions for the exercise of his power: firstly, national unity and the support of the *Ibāḍi 'ulamā'*; secondly, a clear-cut attitude to Great Britain.

Not having received the support of the *'ulamā'*, Thūwayni could not fulfil the first condition. And having close links with Great Britain in that his regime depended on her for political and material support, he could not satisfy the second condition either. The future for Oman looked more than ever like a dead end.

The real crisis for the nation certainly had to do with the separation of Zanzibar and Oman, which had direct and immediate consequences on the economic and social situation, even affecting the sultanate system itself. For the Omanis, the separation from Zanzibar meant at that time an authoritarian partition of the family, the tribe and even of the economy, history and future of Oman, in short the dismemberment of the State, of the 'homeland'. So it can be said that, after the separation of the African part, the history of Oman was one of continuous decline.

This is particularly noticeable in economic matters: following the partition, the majority of traders moved to the African part, which was more prosperous. Capital that had sustained the national economy left Oman. The agricultural and commercial sectors suffered severely. The whole economy of Oman reeled under the blow.

Even the social structure was hit; ushering in a period of imbalance. Internal crises became more acute. Omani society was standing on the threshold of a genuine catastrophe, which, from the dawn of the twentieth century and with the help of Great Britain, would assume tragic dimensions, and last for more than a century.

This crisis did not spare the al-Bū Saʿīdi family itself. Once the two branches of the family, the Arab and the African, were separated, the four brothers resorted to arms to settle their differences. In the African part, *sayyid* Mājed was faced with a fairly general uprising led by the African branches of the al-Ḥarth tribe, which denounced the decision to separate Zanzibar. Moreover Mājed's brother Barghash, supported by France, came into conflict with him. Mājed was indebted to help from the English in putting an end to these two rebellions. In the Omani part, *sayyid* Turki, a younger brother of Thūwayni, also contested the decision to split up and rebelled against his brother in 1861. In a desperate move, Turki tried to separate the Suḥār region, where he was governor, from the power of Muscat, but in vain. Here too, the English helped the sultan to crush this attempt. Later, Thūwayni, by an act of treachery, captured Turki and put him in prison.[381] In 1862, Turki obtained his freedom on certain conditions, which reduced him to silence.

Qays ibn ʿAzzān, governor of the town of al-Rustāq, a traditional centre of the Ibadhite movement which enjoyed a kind of autonomy, launched another challenge to Thūwayni's authority. Qays belonged to the second branch of the al-Bū Saʿīdi family. But above all he was considered to be a man of the Ibadhite movement, that is, a supporter of the *imāma* system, and he enjoyed the respect of the *'ulamā'* and of the populations of the interior of Oman.

In a parallel move, the al-Saʿd tribe from the al-Bāṭina region also rebelled against the power of Muscat. It asked Qays to bring the region under his authority. But, in a battle against the governor of that region, Hilāl, both Qays and his adversary were killed.[382]

Sultan Thūwayni had hardly put an end to this conflict when he found himself facing yet another challenge, even more serious this time. Quite clearly all these tensions were not merely tribal; they weighed heavily on the whole field of national politics. Thūwayni's new adversary, ʿAzzān, who had become governor of al-Rustāq after the death of his father Qays, proved to be an even more formidable and charismatic personality. Moreover, ʿAzzān was the bearer of a historic alternative.

The two parties came into conflict several times over a period of two years with no significant result. Sultan Thūwayni was preparing to attack the town of al-Rustāq when, in this warlike climate, al-Sudayri, the Saudi military chief whose troops were occupying al-Buraimi, sent forces in the direction of the belligerents, led by ʿAbd al-'Aziz ibn Muṭlaq, who had entered Oman disguising his pretensions in order to pose as an intermediary between the two warring parties.[383]

Sultan Thūwayni was afraid the Wahhābis might seize this opportunity to meddle once more in Omani affairs, so he abandoned his plan of action. But his backtracking did not alter Muṭlaq's intentions and he headed for the al-Sharqiya region in order to join forces with his allies, the al-Bū Wahabeh and al-Bū ʿAli tribes.

In 1865, these two tribes supported by the Wahhābi forces launched violent and devastating raids against the sultan's troops in the region and also, according to

Lorimer, against the Indian minority living in the town of Ṣūr. The British powers then decided to intervene: Colonel Pelly, the political resident in the Gulf, sent a warning to the Wahhābi prince demanding written apologies and compensation for the damage done.[384]

Receiving no response in this matter from the Wahhābis, he appealed, with the backing of the British authorities in India, to maritime units and ordered them into action against the ports of al-Qatif and al-Dammām, while another British force was attacking the allies of the Wahhābis in the Omani region of al-Sharqiya.

Finally on 20 February 1866, Pelly received a letter from the Wahhābite emir 'Abd Allāh, who had just acceded to power after the death of his father Fayṣal, notifying him of the Wahhābis' commitment not to harass or attack the Arab tribes that had agreements with Great Britain, especially Oman, provided that the latter discharged the *zakāt* (payment) imposed.[385] The British government undertook in return to see that payment was made and so became a kind of surety for the fulfilment of the accord.

Thanks to Colonel Pelly and indeed to this new conflict, the strategy of Great Britain was able to start scoring points in the region again. Thereafter her habitual interventions in fact became part of the political equation and balance in the region and almost acceptable to the warring parties. Did not the very text of the Wahhābi reply to Colonel Pelly mean implicitly that Great Britain was considered to be the official representative of Oman in the Gulf?

Sultan Thūwayni for his part tried to take advantage of the Wahhābi retreat to solve the problems stemming from their presence and notably the question of al-Buraimi, a zone then occupied by the Wahhābis. Ṣāleḥ ibn 'Ali al-Ḥārthi, a powerful ally of the sultan, gathered together a certain number of tribes opposed to Wahhābi influence in order to support Thūwayni in a show of national unity. At the same time, the sultan had, with the idea of confronting his adversaries, prepared a strong-armed force and given the command to his son Sālem. It is worth noting too, that *sayyid* Turki, now reconciled with his brother, came to his aid.

However, it was foreordained that Thūwayni's sultanate should bear the mark of chaos and decline. For the Wahhābis on their part had hatched a plot and succeeded in involving Thūwayni's son Sālem, who was at that time governor of the town of Suḥār. Instead of leading his father's army against the Wahhābis, Sālem himself came and assassinated his father while he slept.[386]

Sālem ibn Thūwayni (1866–1868)

The patricide that had brought about the advent of Sālem was reason enough to isolate him in his palace in Muscat until his fall. Nevertheless Sālem had the support of the Ghafirite tribes, allies of the Wahhābis, and for two years the Omanis lived through one of the unhappiest and bitterest periods in their history.

Great Britain's attitude, at least to start with, consisted in refusing to recognise Sālem as sultan of Oman. Colonel Pelly, according to al-Sālmī, went to Muscat to ask Sālem to relinquish power. Quite clearly, Sālem rejected this suggestion (or order) after which Pelly left Muscat while making his disappointment very plain.[387]

Unfortunately al-Sālmī does not tell us the name of the successor in whose favour Sālem was asked to abdicate.

In fact the first challenge to Sālem's authority was made by his uncle, *sayyid* Turki. Although Great Britain had not yet recognised Sālem's power and was engaged in seeking an alternative at the time, curiously, she took a firm stand against *sayyid* Turki's endeavours. She compelled him to do nothing against Sālem and even exiled him. Why this hard line if at heart she disapproved of Sālem's accession? The only real explanation we can suggest has to do with the fact that Turki had previously declared himself opposed to the English decision to separate Zanzibar from Oman in 1861, and that since then he had always fought for reunification. So it is understandable that Great Britain was not keen to back a rebellion led by such a ruler.

Sālem's first concern was to obtain recognition of his power by the British authorities. The political landscape had changed somewhat; Pelly, formerly fiercely opposed to recognition, paid an official visit to Muscat and presented Sālem with his government's official recognition of him as sultan of Oman. And in 1867, a British consulate was opened in Muscat.[388]

Furthermore the subsidy paid by Zanzibar having been suspended by sultan Mājed after Sālem came to power, Great Britain, in her role as 'intermediary', asked Mājed to resume payment. According to Lorimer, Great Britain took this line primarily to ensure that there was no direct contact between the two parties.[389]

The revolution of ʿAzzān ibn Qays (1869–1871)

The Ibadhi Nahḍa

All the conditions required to unleash a revolution were already present, but Sālem's coming to power had hastened things. The general situation had deteriorated to the point where Oman had no alternative to a revolution leading to real recovery. There was now no salvation for the country other than in the spirit of the *imāma*.

However, in the eyes of the imamites, the march on Muscat amounted only to a first step towards *al-Nahḍa*, the *Ibāḍi* renaissance. And Wilkinson notes that it is very difficult to date the modern renaissance of Ibadhism, which had, in fact, never really faded. What had faded was the *imāma* itself but on that point the *Ibāḍi ʿulamā'* had no illusions. The kind of *imāma* with which they had had dealings in recent centuries at least had never been very 'pure'.[390]

Heading *al-Nahḍa* movement beside a group of Ibāḍi *ʿulamā'* were four main personalities: the eminent *ʿālim* Saʿīd ibn Khalfān al-Khalīlī, *al-ʿālim* Muḥammad ibn Sālim al-Gharbī, the famous Ṣāleḥ ibn al-Ḥārthi and ʿAzzān ibn Qays, the *imām* in waiting. The imamites were determined to construct a more solid *imāma* and secure themselves against any deviation or backsliding.

In September 1869, they carried out their plan to attack Muscat on two fronts. ʿAzzān progressed towards the capital, passing through al-Rustāq, and on the way he took the coastal town of Birka. In the neighbourhood of Muscat, the two bodies of troops, those of 'Azzān and those of al-Ḥārthi, were to join forces for the final assault. However, before embarking on this decisive move, the *'ulamā'* left a last chance for clemency: they asked sultan Sālem to repent. Sure of English support, Sālem refused the offer.[391] So, on 29 September, 'Azzān took Maṭraḥ, a town bordering Muscat, and at the beginning of October the capital fell. On 12 October, with the permission of the imamites, Sālem was able to leave on a British ship and reach Bandar Abbas; he was never to see Oman again.[392]

At the start of hostilities, the English had attempted to save Sālem's regime, using their naval forces to prevent the advance of 'Azzān's troops on Muscat. But the rapid crumbling of Sālem's regime disconcerted them. They could only yield to *imām* 'Azzān and accept the *fait accompli.*

So, after being in existence for more than ninety years, the sultanate system collapsed without any one really wanting to save it in the end. Sālem's failure meant first and foremost the failure of a system that had neither credibility nor traditional legitimacy and entirely lacked popular support. At the very moment when great politico-strategic and economic changes were taking place in the region, the system proved completely incapable of ruling the country.

Landen writes that any one looking through the events of this historic period can easily ascertain that the rulers of this dynasty were not capable of understanding the kind of morass in which they were mired. For such events could not be controlled by any ruler. British interference and economic and maritime transformations in the Indian Ocean may have been among the chief causes of this collapse.[393]

Landen's opinion is not unfounded. And yet the main causes of the crisis were really elsewhere, within Oman itself and not outside it. In this respect, Wilkinson advances a point of view that seems closer to reality:

> The Omanis . . . understood perfectly well that such vicissitudes were in large measure 'ultra vires'. What mattered was whether they were doing their best to protect Omani interests or whether they showed themselves weak to the increasing demands of the British and their subjects, or even actually to be working against their own people.[394]

On the subject of the victory of the imamites, Landen makes the following remarks:

> The conservatives' victory in 1868, then, was due to the attractiveness of their programme to many in Oman, dedicated leadership from the conservative religious class, the presence in the conservative camp of respectable 'legitimate' leaders from the Qays branch of the royal house, the adherence of . . . tribal leaders' to the conservative cause (after 1867) and finally the growing weakness and inefficiency in the camp of the moderate sultans.[395]

The fact remains that, despite their tribal components, the forces of the revolutionary imamites had displayed remarkable discipline. Their final offensive at Maṭraḥ and at Muscat had caused no damage to persons or property among the Omani inhabitants or the Indian minorities. Al-Sālmī reports that in his address to the army before the final assault, ʿAzzān ibn Qays gave the soldiers strict orders forbidding them to touch the property and possessions of the populations. On the other hand, he authorised them to confiscate anything they might find in the sultan's palace.[396]

It is worth noting that the Ibadhite movement, in an exceptional departure from custom, had not this time elected the *imām* before declaring the revolution; they did so only after the victory. A general assembly, composed of the *'ulamā'*, the leaders of the revolution and the chiefs of the tribes who had supported it, was then to be held for the first time in Muscat.

The eminent *ʿālim* Saʿīd ibn Khalfān al-Khalīlī presided over the assembly. In line with the Ibadhite constitution and traditions, and with the support of Ṣāleḥ ibn ʿAli al-Ḥārthi, he presented ʿAzzān ibn Qays as candidate for the post of *imām*. The *'ulamā'*, in turn, gave their consensus, and approval unreservedly; thus all the required conditions for the legitimacy of the election came together. The *imām*, who enjoyed all the qualities necessary for his office, belonged to the al-Bū Saʿīdi family, a significant feature of this period and this election: Under these leaders, the *Nahḍa* began to find political substance in alliance with the Qays branch which had pretensions both to the titular succession the Imama of Ahmed ibn *Sa'īd* and to regaining the patrimonye of Suhar and Rustaq'.[397]

Following the normal procedure, the *'ulamā'* proclaimed the *bay'a*. However, 'Azzān's *bay'a* was that of an *imām da'īf*, in other words 'weak'. Because, according to the Ibadhite constitution, an *imām* who is not a *'ālim* cannot be given the *bay'a* of al-*shirā'*. So *imām* ʿAzzān would in future be obliged by the Ibadhite constitution and tradition, to refer to the *majlis al-shūrā*, the upper council, before taking any decision whatsoever. His *bay'a* indicated these rules exactly:

> We have decided to make you our imam and the imam of all the people so that you may defend them and on condition that you take no decision, nor pronounce any judgement, nor put any decision into effect without having taken the opinion of the Muslims and without having received their approval.[398]

In any case, it is important to note that the conditions of this *bay'a* did not reduce the validity of the *imām*'s position; on the contrary it enhanced it, and the *imāma* system as well, for the procedure of recourse to the *majlis al-shūrā* was vital to ensure that the principle of consensus and of power sharing was applied. It is all these practices together that make up the foundation and the value of the Omani democratic tradition.

The formation of the government

ʿAzzān's arrival in power did not mean a change just in the person of the ruler but in the nature and basis of power itself. The new *imām*'s accession marked an important stage by abolishing the hereditary system and its culture, but it also represented as it were a change of course in the history of Oman. For the *al-Nahḍa* rulers, linking up with *Ibāḍi* history was also linking up with the future. It was no small challenge.

The *majlis al-shūrā* was composed of leaders of the revolution. In it was concentrated the consultative and supreme executive authority. Alongside the *imām*, who was at once the president of the government, the head of the army and the person responsible for the *bayt al-māl*, were three historic personalities, the first of whom was Sa'īd ibn Khalfān al-Khalīlī. Al-Khalīlī was the theoretician and organiser of the revolution, its legal and legislative reference, the chief of the *qāḍīs*: he was the supreme moral authority and father of the revolution. He was also to occupy the post of governor of the capital, Muscat, during the period of the *imāma*, Modelling himself on his forebears, al-Khalīlī had been working since his youth to build an *imāma* similar to that of al-Jalanda ibn Mas'ūd (second/eighth century), or to those of al-Ṣalt ibn Mālek and Nāṣer ibn Murshed in the seventeenth century. He had toiled tirelessly to bring into being the *Ibāḍi* design for the building of an Islamic society.

Ṣāleḥ ibn 'Ali al-Ḥārthi, the ruler of the al-Ḥarth tribe, was the second historic personality. A former pupil of sheikh al-Khalīlī, he had committed himself to serving the revolution from the outset. He was part of 'Azzān's government, but his influence on political decision-making was limited.

A third personality was *al-'ālim* Muḥammad ibn Sālim al-Gharibi, an influential member of the al-Sa'd tribe on the coast of al-Batina. Still others played a far from negligible role within the government, men like Ibrahim ibn Qays, the brother of the *imām*, who had military responsibilities, and Hilāl ibn Sa'īd al-Bū Sa'īdi.

This group of rulers was inspired by the *Ibāḍi* model of the Islamic state: the *imāma*. The moral strength, charisma, conviction and solidarity of these few personalities would set a rare stamp on the new regime.

From the government programme to the first stages of al-Nahḍa

The programme of 'Azzān's *imāma* revolved around four main points.

The first thing was to abolish the independent power of the tribes opposed to the *imāma* system, by bringing them under the new central government; to put an end to the state of anarchy and re-establish *Ibāḍi* laws; to appoint new *qāḍīs* and *wālis*. All these objectives were vital for the reunification of Omani society in the framework of *al-Nahḍa*.

Second it was important to liberate the al-Buraimi region from the Wahhābis occupation and end their influence in Oman once and for all.

The third objective was ending British influence and domination and annulling the undertakings and accords imposed on Oman during the sultanate. Instead, an attempt would be made to get Great Britain to recognise 'Azzān's *imāma* while reasserting unreservedly the independence and sovereignty of Oman.

The fourth and last phase of this programme was the retaking of Zanzibar and placing the questions of Gwader and Bandar Abbas, which had been under the control of Oman before the revolution, on the agenda.

But first of all, and in line with custom, the *'ulamā'* of Oman wrote a letter to their *Ibāḍi* brothers in North Africa in which they informed them of their coming to power; in order, they claimed, to put an end to the state of oppression, violation of the sacred, flouting of Islamic laws and supremacy of the uneducated, and to re-establish a state of justice and equality under the protection of the restored *imāma*. By this missive, they also presented their new *imām*.[399]

Internally, the first measure was the rigorous and immediate implementation of the first point of the programme. 'Azzān's government had soon put an end to the state of anarchy reigning in the country, particularly in the big towns, and re-instated *Ibāḍi* laws. New *qāḍīs* and *wālis* were appointed in the regions under the authority of the *imāma*. The government also decided to confiscate the goods and property of the ex-sultan, these goods being considered an integral part of the *bayt al-māl*. The *'ulamā'* authorised this by a precedent going back to the fifteenth century, that of *imām* 'Umar ibn al-Khaṭṭāb al-Yaḥmadi (1451–1490); he had decreed, under *Ibāḍi* laws, the confiscation of the possessions of the Nabhānite kings.[400]

On the tribal level, although 'Azzān's *imāma* had enjoyed the unreserved support of the Hanawite tribes as well as the backing, al-Sālmī says that some of the rulers of the Ghafirite tribes, who were traditionally anti-*imāma*, had opposed the new power.

So *imām* 'Azzān attacked tribal opposition relentlessly. He even went so far as to apply the severe measures implemented by *imām* Nāṣer ibn Murshed two and a half centuries earlier to put an end to secessionist tribal power.

In this way, Omani unity was achieved in the context of the *imāma* (with the exception of '*Sāḥel Oman*'). It was the first great objective attained by *imām* 'Azzān in his first year in power. Lorimer makes this comment: The crushing success of Azzan ibn Qays shows clearly that this man had a moral strength and firmness long unknown in the government of Oman.[401]

Landen, for his part, stresses the importance of the first gain: the total subjection of the country, which very few men in power had managed to achieve before.[402]

Pelly notes on this subject; 'the tenacity with which the de facto government of Muscat insisted on the principle of centralisation against feudalism is quite remarkable'.[403]

Ibrahim ibn Qays, the *imām*'s brother, made a notable contribution to the realisation of this first objective; carrying out the plans drawn up by the *imāma*, he led several missions against the Ghafirite tribes under al-Jabri in the Izki region and then subdued the tribe of al-Bū 'Ali in the region of Ja'lān.[404] From then on, the way was open for new developments in the *Ibāḍi* programme.

The question of the al-Buraimi oasis

During the Wahhābi expansion in the nineteenth century, the oasis of al-Buraimi had fallen under their influence. The influence was consolidated after the tribe of al-Na'yim espoused Wahhābism.[405] Wahhābi occupation was irksome; the election of *imām* 'Azzān offered a chance to shake off the yoke. So their ruler, Muḥammad ibn 'Ali asked 'Azzān for help to drive out the Wahhābis. And the *imām*, who asked nothing better, declared war on them.[406]

On 18 January 1869, after four days of a vigorous offensive, al-Buraimi was liberated. 'Azzān immediately took radical steps to eliminate all traces of Wahhābi influence. The Wahhābi laws imposed on the region were abolished, *qāḍīs* and *wālis* were appointed from among the population. The *imām* then had to return the goods and property confiscated by the Wahhābis to their original owners.

Once again 'Azzān had scored, taking over as a strong, but loyal and just ruler. Kelly notes, incidentally, that the *imām*'s success against the Wahhābis helped him to win the trust and approval of the local citizens who had lived for a number of years as a prey to the arrogance of the Wahhhabis and in constant fear of their attacks.[407]

So in its first year, the *imāma* had scored five historic successes: first the reunification of Omani society, the abolition of tribal power, the achievement of internal peace and stability, then the liberation of al-Buraimi and lastly the restoration of the *imāma* system. A British document summed it up as follows:

> The height and extent of the imama's power over Oman reached its peak in the late autumn of 1869. This rule was one of the strongest ever attempted in Omani history. Few rulers in Omani history could boast, (as 'Azzān ibn Qays could) that their realms included the coastal provinces as well as the main inland tribal areas.[408]

Returning victorious from al-Buraimi, the *imām* passed through the region of '*Sāḥel Oman*' The visit chimed in with a twofold plan: first, it recalled the historic links between the two regions and their common interest; second it marginalised the Wahhābi influence there. And in fact, after driving the Wahhābis out of al-Buraimi, *imām* 'Azzān signed a mutual defence pact against the Wahhābis with Zāyed ibn Khalīfah I, the chief of the Banī Yās tribes at Abu Dhabi.[409]

The imāma *and Great Britain; external relations*

At the same time as the *imām* was taking steps to settle the tribal question and reassert the *imāma* system in the interior, he started parallel moves in external affairs notably the very thorny matter of relations with Great Britain. Lorimer characterised the attitude of the colonial power to the *imāma* of 'Azzān thus: 'Great Britain was at first more indignant over the fact of 'Azzan's seizure of power than she had been over the power of the patricide'.[410]

What really alarmed Great Britain was precisely the fact that the new ruler was an elected *imām*, enjoying considerable legitimacy and popularity. He belonged to the Ibadhite movement whose thinking laid the foundations of the independence and national sovereignty (*al-waṭan*) of Oman, and had been doing so ever since it came into being some thousand years earlier, even before Great Britain was aware of the concepts of sovereignty and nationhood.

Worse still, the *imāma*'s national programme aimed to render null and void among other things, all the undertakings and accords imposed on Oman by Great Britain. The programme also had as objectives the annulment of the British decision to separate Zanzibar from Oman in 1861 and the reunification of the two parts. These were the real reasons for Great Britain's indignation.

All the same, the *imām* acted like a statesman in his dealings with Great Britain: he sent an Omani delegation to India to study the conditions of Omani–British relations and try to give them a new basis, founded on a principle of equality and reciprocity. The ultimate aim of this mission was to obtain British recognition. But it was fruitless as Great Britain did not react favourably to the Omani initiative and the delegation returned empty handed.

Worse still, Great Britain did all she could to stifle ʿAzzān's young *imāma* and bring about the failure of this experiment in reconstruction. Among other things, when Nāṣer ibn Thūwayni, the son of the late sultan Thūwayni, had brought down *imām* ʿAzzān's governor in Gwader and seized power, Great Britain immediately backed the *coup d'état*[411] and gave him the solace of official recognition. On the other hand, when *imām* ʿAzzān had made a show of sending a warship to try and restore the situation in Gwader, the British resident in Muscat prevented him.[412]

Moreover, this was not the only biased attitude adopted by Great Britain towards the policy of the *imām*; the British also persuaded the Persian authorities to annul the contracts signed with Oman in Thūwayni's reign concerning in particular the renting of the port of Bandar Abbas. They also prevented the *imām* from extending his authority over the port. Two questions, the governorship of Gwader and control of Bandar Abbas, came in the hands of the English rulers, so many trump cards by means of which they could put pressure on the *imām*'s government.

But that was not their only weapon; Great Britain could operate the economic and commercial levers as she chose. She did not rest till she had deprived Omani merchant ships of their regular activities on the two routes to India and East Africa. She also used the pretext of the presence of Indian communities in Muscat and Maṭraḥ to infiltrate the internal politics of Oman in the guise of protecting minorities subject to her crown.

British recognition and the Wahhābi question

In October 1869, the government of British India decided to send Colonel Pelly to Muscat to study the internal situation in the *imāma*. At the time *imām* ʿAzzān was engaged in settling his differences with the al-Bū ʿAli tribe in the al-Sharqiya area. Official British reports indicate that the outcome of this dispute would determine British recognition of the power of the *imām*. Indeed, Pelly wrote that if *imām* ʿAzzān emerged victorious from the armed confrontation with this tribe; he would have consolidated his position considerably and would wield a power over the territory of Muscat firmer than any other.[413]

What in fact delayed Great Britain's final decision, apart from the worrying affirmation of the *imāma* system, was the Wahhābi question. Lorimer tells us that official recognition of 'Azzān would have resulted on the one hand in arousing Wahhābi annoyance with Great Britain, and on the other in reinforcing 'Azzān's power with regard to his adversaries.[414] Great Britain assuredly did not want this.

So, after ascertaining that the *imāma* was sound, Pelly began studying the situation of the Indian minority in an attempt to detect any possible negative effects of the *Ibāḍi* measures and laws. But contrary to the reports of Desbrew, the British resident in Muscat, who was fiercely hostile to *imām* 'Azzān and his government, Pelly found that the minorities were experiencing no oppression or discrimination, either religious or ethnic, and that, on the contrary, they were enjoying all the privileges of traditional Omani hospitality and generosity.

It goes without saying that Omani–Indian relations were as old as the hills. Under both the *imāma* system and the sultanate, Indian minorities and others had lived in peace and security in Oman. And in fact it was only since Great Britain had become established in the region and imposed herself as 'intermediary' that the climate of good understanding between the Indian and Omani peoples had been affected.

Meanwhile, on his return from al-Buraimi, 'Azzān wrote a letter to Pelly on 19 August 1869 in which he pointed out the complete success of his campaign, crowned by the liberation of al-Buraimi.

> I have returned to Muscat after having captured Buraymi. We had fighting for four days... The people of Buraymi and those parts were thus relieved of the oppression of the Wahhabis. I restored to the people what the Wahhabis had forcibly taken from them, such as landed estates and they are much pleased at the defeat of the Wahhābis and praise God for it. They are now in peace.[415]

The *imām* finished his letter by asking Pelly to look favourably on the question of recognition of his *imāma*. He added that he was awaiting a decision.

'Azzān had won the respect and admiration of Colonel Pelly to such an extent that, with a letter replying to the *imām*, Pelly wrote this curt note to Desbrew: 'I have the honour to request you will be so good as to cause [this letter] to be delivered to Syad Azan in a polite manner and inform me of your having done so.'[416]

Pelly promised *imām* 'Azzān that he would present his request to the government and give it his backing. Indeed, on 18 April, he wrote a report to the authorities in which he asked for recognition of 'Azzān's government but he accompanied this request with the following reservations: 'Recognition would probably be considered to imply restoration of Gwader and the other outlying Muscat territories: also perhaps our good offices in respect to a release of the Bandar Abbas districts and... would secure to him the Zanzibar subsidy'.[417]

To these points he should have added the prospect of a beneficial effect on the economic situation and in particular on commercial activity. Such an effect was the more predictable as agricultural production had started to show a marked improvement during the period.

In another report dated 20 November 1869, Pelly indicated that at present and until the recognition of 'Azzān's government was accomplished; the *imām* was freed from all his obligations under the accords with Great Britain. But the British government in India did not accept the opinion of its resident in the Gulf and sent this reply:

> The treaties in which the British government is directly a contracting party with the Muscat state must be held to be in full force, notwithstanding any changes in the internal constitution of the Muscat Government or in the person of the Ruler. It is impossible that our treaties can be considered in abeyance while we have continuously maintained a Resident Agent at Muscat and insisted on the rights and privileges that are secured to us by these treaties.[418]

This was the language of colonialist logic but for the *Ibāḍis* in particular it could have no validity. How could undertakings imposed on the sultans have been continued by elected *imāms*? How can anyone imagine an *imāma* fighting for its freedom and yet accepting undertakings of a colonial nature? In any case, although ʿAzzān's government had not declared its official position regarding the undertakings in question, in practice it considered them to be null and void.

At the beginning of the year 1870, the government of the *imāma* was strong enough from its internal successes to be completely in control of the political scene in the region. So Great Britain really had little choice but to draw back and reassess her general attitude to the *imāma*. In another letter dated 12 February 1870, Colonel Pelly wrote quite strongly to his own government, asking it to give him all the necessary authority to grant official recognition to the government of ʿAzzān ibn Qays.[419]

These important developments and the growing power of the *imāma* had provoked lively discussion within the British government in London. So a note was sent to the British government in India in which the authorities in London admitted that they could not make up their mind and were unable to take a clear political stance in relation to ʿAzzān's government. The British authorities were now in a state of indecision in this affair, as the terms of this note bear witness:

> We feel so forcibly the difficulties in which we shall be placed by a recognition of the de facto government of Muscat without a definite intimation of the views of Her Majesty's Government as to the policy to be adopted in future towards that state, that we earnestly solicit an early decision on the various points...
>
> First whether the recognition of ʿAzzan ibn Qays is to be accompanied by a declaration of our future policy towards Muscat and an intimation of our intention to maintain all existing treaties and engagements with the Muscat State; or if Her Majesty's Government are not prepared to maintain all former treaties and engagements, it is necessary that we should know which of them it is prepared to abandon and which to maintain.
>
> Secondly whether the payment of the Zanzibar subsidy is to be enforced; and if not enforced, whether we are to inform the Ruler of Muscat that we

> should interfere to prevent a recurrence of that state things which existed when Lord Canning intervened to mediate between Muscat and Zanzibar; and, in the event of hostilities being threatened, as they were, whether we should send an armed force to prevent the Ruler of Muscat from enforcting that to which he doubtless considers he has an indefeasible right?.[420]

The three other points raised related to the questions of Gwader and Bandar Abbas; they implicitly acknowledged the authority of Oman over those regions. Altogether, this note demonstrated unequivocally an appreciable retreat in the British position: they no longer looked on prior undertakings and the question of Zanzibar as non-negotiable.

Even while the British government in India was hesitant and totally disorientated in its attitude, 'Azzān's government was continuing to notch up successes in external policy. On 12 March 1870, a French ship arrived in Muscat; its commander was bearing his government's official recognition of the *imāma* of 'Azzān. Immediately afterwards a Dutch ship also came to bring its country's recognition of the Omani government.[421]

These two recognitions alarmed Great Britain; she realised, moreover, that the opening of the Suez Canal in 1869 would alter the political situation in the Gulf in favour of 'Azzān's *imāma*. As a result, the British government in India ordered Colonel Pelly to hasten to grant his government's official recognition to the *imāma*. Both political and diplomatic success were within the grasp of 'Azzān's *imāma*, which was on the point of making the British Empire accept the independence and sovereignty of Oman.

The watershed of 1870 and the fall of the *imām*

Again it was the Wahhābi question that was to change the course of events drastically in the region and hinder British recognition. The British government in India was informed that the Wahhābis were preparing a large-scale offensive against al-Buraimi and that Sālem, the ex-sultan, would be taking part. In fact, the Wahhābis sent a threatening letter to *imām* 'Azzān, who took no notice but prepared for the eventuality of an attack.

However, neither the attack nor British recognition came about. At that very moment, events took a radical turn. *Sayyid* Turki ibn Sa'īd finally convinced the British government of his ability to overthrow 'Azzān's *imāma* and asked for English aid. Great Britain agreed to help him on condition that he would give up definitively his notions of uniting with Zanzibar. Having secured this commitment on the part of Turki, Great Britain gave him her material and moral backing as well as the support of his brother, sultan Mājed of Zanzibar.

Elsewhere, in the field of internal affairs, the Ghafirite tribes were more than ready to support a 'counter revolution' to overthrow the *imāma*, as was the tribe of al-Bū 'Ali in al-Sharqiya. And even amongst the Hanawite tribes, there were some who opposed certain measures demanded by the *imāma* and were ready to support *sayyid* Turki.

In May 1870, Turki ibn Saʿīd went to the *'Sāḥel Oman'* area and attempted to win the moral and political support of the rulers of the local tribes. He failed because the sheikh of Abu Dhabi, Zāyed ibn Khalīfah I was loyal to ʿAzzān and had asked the other sheikhs not to support Turki's venture. A second attempt by the latter however ended in success. The sheikhs all agreed to support him, with the exception of Zāyed ibn Khalīfah I who, with good reason, feared that the departure of *imām* ʿAzzān would leave the door wide open to Wahhābi aggression; he refused and stuck to his position.

Thus Turki garnered all the conditions necessary for the success of his mission: the good will of the Ghafirite tribes, the support of the sheikhs of the *'Sāḥel Oman'* and of the Wahhābis who wanted to be avenged on the *imām*, financial and political aid from Zanzibar and lastly the crucial backing of Great Britain.

In September 1870, Turki came down to the region of Khūr-Fakkān and headed for al-Buraimi where he joined the tribes of Banī Jetab and a few tribes from al-Naʿyim, the ruler of al-Naʿyim having, like Zāyed ibn Khalīfah, refused to join in the venture. Even so, Turki was able to assemble some 4000 men.[422] And on 12 October 1870, his army clashed with ʿAzzān's men in the Dank area. In that battle, the *imām*'s army suffered its first major defeat.

A little later, towards the end of 1870, the army of Sayf ibn Sulaymān al-Bū Saʿīdi, another ally of Turki, set off to meet the army of *imām* ʿAzzān. There followed a long battle which, on 30 January 1871 saw the death of the *imām* and of his adversary. It was not long before the *imāma* itself foundered. Turki won the ensuing battles against the *imāma* and entered the capital victorious. He was not to win the peace.

Although the *imāma* and its symbol had fallen, al-Khalīlī, together with his son and followers continued to hold out in a citadel in Muscat. The firm determination of the imamites to continue the struggle inspired him to ask Ibrahim ibn Qays, the late *imām*'s brother, to agree to succeed him. Ibrahim did not feel up to the task; he declined the offer and retired with his followers to the interior of Oman.

Turki's army tried in vain to bend the will of *al-ʿālim* al-Khalīlī who had devoted his whole life to his convictions and to the Ibadhite ideals. A few tribal rulers then tried to play the part of mediators but al-Khalīlī challenged them all, accusing them of having betrayed the *imāma*. However, in a symbolic gesture, he accepted the official mediation of Colonel Pelly and the British resident in Muscat, Major Way, who had replaced Desbrew. The result was an accord between al-Khalīlī and Turki which was signed by the representatives of the two parties in the consulate of Great Britain in Muscat. This accord was officially supervised by Pelly and Way; it stipulated nine points, including these, concerning the position of al-Khalīlī:

> 1. That I should not be answerable for having entered into the [service of the late] Government and for the changes that had taken place affecting persons and property during the reign of that Government.

> 2. That I should reside where I like and that he (Sayyid Turki) should protect me from molestation and from any person who might bring charges against me, and that I in turn should not countenance or encourage or put up any enemies against him or entertain any ill intentions towards him.

In a final point, al-Khalīlī asked that the rulers of the Ghafirite tribes and those of the Hanawites should not intercept or disturb his friends or his kinsmen, ʿAbd Allāh ibn Sulaymān ibn Ḥamūdeh, Sayf ibn ʿAli, Ḥamad ibn Khalīfah, Najm ibn Muḥammad and others.[423]

Pelly took care to add a paragraph to this accord, in which he indicated that Great Britain would not be responsible for implementing it. However the official involvement of Great Britain in this affair cannot be denied and if Colonel Pelly extricated himself politically, he was at least morally responsible. After all, it was only on the word and moral commitment of Pelly and Way that the sheikh had decided to come down from the fortress in which he had taken refuge.

But this accord was neither observed nor respected. A month after al-Khalīlī had agreed to leave the fortress, a plot was hatched against him and his son; he was accused of having contacts with Ibrahim ibn Qays and inciting him to revolt. Sheikh al-Khalīlī was summoned to an audience by sultan Turki who, according to al-Sālmī, informed him of his anger and claimed that he had formerly made him [Turki] 'leave our homeland', etc. The sheikh replied: 'All we did was to apply *al-sharīà*'. After this the sultan ordered him and his son to be clapped in irons and taken to the prison of al-Jalāli[424] (a fortress built by the Portuguese in the sixteenth century). The next day, 16 February 1871, the death of al-Khalīlī was announced and, that of his son Muhʿammad[425] on 17.

Major Way, who had orchestrated and supervised the negotiations and won the trust of sheikh al-Khalīlī, opened an official enquiry into the mysterious deaths of the *ʿālim* and his son. The official British documents establish that both the sheikh and his son had been ill-treated and beaten to death and had then been buried in the fortress of al-Mīrānī.[426]

However the official reply of the Omanis to Way was that the deaths of al-Khalīlī and his son were due to 'diarrhoea and fright'! The major, who knew the truth, was shattered by this reply; the burden of this new responsibility drove him to commit suicide by shooting himself.[427]

Reflections on the fall of the imāma

Great Britain had in fact succeeded in causing the second great Omani revolution in modern history to fail. Thus the *Ibāḍi* project for an Islamic State (after that of the Yaʿrūbites) was aborted and the dream of the majority of the Omanis was shattered once more.

Historically this leads to a question that deserves attention. What was the real reason that led Great Britain to hamper the course of Omani history and the development of its civilisation?

It would be demeaning to see nothing but strictly colonial interests behind their reasoning. They are certainly important, but not sufficiently to account for the colonial power's total ignorance of the history, culture, values and civilisation of this region and particularly of Oman. Badger, a politician and man of the Church, who was close to these events, was also a member of Coghlan's committee that decided on the separation of Zanzibar, and the translator of a book by ibn Ruzayq, *The Imams and the sayyids*; he provides this unequivocal testimony to that ignorance:

> It is remarkable and by no means creditable to the British Government in India that notwithstanding our intimate political and commercial relations with Oman for the last century, we know actually less of that country than we do of the Lake districts of Central Africa.[428]

Wilkinson in turn was to underline the inability or unwillingness of the English to grasp and accept the reality of the region and its culture: 'The first was the inability or unwillingness of the Indian government and its agents in the Gulf to countenance, or indeed comprehend, any local viewpoint that did not coincide with their own'.[429]

But Badger and then Pelly, two important personalities, express points of view which follow the same lines as the theme of this chapter and, better still, reinforce one of our main hypotheses, namely that Great Britain's aim was to disrupt Omani history and destroy the country's civilisation. Badger asserts that:

> Azzan was as eligible for sovereignty as any of his rivals and he had unquestionably shown evidence of much greater political sense and military valour, a combination of qualities essential for anyone claiming to maintain some kind of order among the turbulent tribes of Oman.[430]

Pelly, with commendable clearsightedness, went further in his analysis; he had realised that ʿAzzān's *imāma* could have guided Omani society to a remarkable level of unity. Once again, although he was a natural political adversary of ʿAzzān, Pelly did not disguise his admiration and respect for this *imām* and his work,

> It appears to me that, whatever may be the personal feelings of the parties as toward Syud Azzan's Government or towards aspirants to power from the Syud Saeed's dynasty, the main question that underlies these feelings is that of centralisation versus feudality. Under the Syud Saeed branch, every Chief, and more particularly the warlike Chiefs of the interior and south, were respected and their authority little interfered with.
>
> But the Government of Azzan-Khalīlī has been an attempt to cripple the independent power of the Chiefs and supplant them by local governors or deputies of the central power [...] Considered from a European point of view, precedents might be found for similar attempts made successfully. But it is open to doubt whether such a policy would be permanently practicable amongst the Arabs.[431]

And in another letter Pelly sums up the life of the *imām*: 'Azzān, he said, lived as a hero and died as a hero.[432] But in fact the main reason for the fall of 'Azzān ibn Qays was the absence of British recognition.

There were assuredly economic aspects involved in that recognition, or rather non-recognition. Great Britain had closed the Indian and African ports to Omani trade and that had caused economic stagnation in the country. This situation, which lasted for more than two years, forced traders to leave the country and left Muscat with no commercial activity at all.

Lorimer sums up the reasons for the fall of *imām* 'Azzān in these words:

> If the British government had not refused to recognise him officially, and if he had not then lost the support of Zanzibar, and if on the other hand the government of India had not freed his enemy Turki, Azzān would have been able to overcome all his difficulties; he would have been able to set up a kingdom for a while in Oman with a high level of organisation and efficiency.[433]

In spite of its failure, this experiment provides both a history lesson and an important precedent because, apart from its successes in the internal political field, the *imāma* had been able to make Great Britain step back and halt her progressive annexations. It could even have forced the colonial power to recognise the independence and sovereignty of Oman, and certainly the legitimacy of its government.

Turki ibn Sa'īd (1871–1888)

The advent of Turki ibn Sa'īd was important only because it set the seal on the re-establishment of the sultanate system. On the other hand, for Oman, his arrival marked the start of a long period of civil war, which outlasted his reign and those of his successors. This was also Pelly's view: according to him the death of 'Azzān opened the way for Turki, but it also rendered stability virtually impossible.[434] And as Wilkinson has it 'With the terrible death of the imam and of his éminence grise, Sa'īd ibn Khalfan al-Khalili, a pitiless war broke out, similar to the one eleven centuries earlier between the Ibadhite movement and Julanda.'[435]

Ṣāleḥ ibn 'Ali al-Ḥārthi, the third personality in 'Azzān's *imāma*, had escaped al-Khalīlī's fate and went on leading vigorous attacks against Muscat. Similarly Ibrahim ibn Qays, although he had withdrawn into the interior of Oman, constantly launched raids against Turki's forces. Turki had, with the aid of Great Britain, succeeded in overthrowing the *imāma*, but he could not master the internal situation for all that. And British aid proved powerless in this instance.

Besides, Great Britain had taken her time before publishing her recognition of Turki's government. The tragic death of sheikh al-Khalīlī and his son, together with the suicide of Major Way had made her reluctant: her recognition was only made official on 16 June 1871.[436] The recognition proved totally useless in the affairs of the interior. On the advice of Major Ross, the new political resident in Muscat, Great Britain declared her official protection of the towns of Muscat and

Maṭraḥ. She could not in any case extend that protection to the whole of Oman; the common Franco-British declaration of 1862 prohibited it.[437]

Major Ross, then, was authorised to announce the protection officially, indicating that Great Britain had decided for specific reasons to support Turki's position against any aggression against him throughout his lifetime, but on condition that he ruled Oman in a manner acceptable to the government of India.[438]

Later, the British government in India went further in its support of the al-Bū Saʿīdi family in Muscat. It declared unequivocally that:

> His Excellency in council would also gladly see the Muscat throne perpetuated in that family, with which the British government has had such intimate relations since the beginning of the present century. To secure results so desirable, the Government of India is willing to exert all the moral influence at its command.[439]

At the same time, in 1871–1872, sultan Turki had tried to make contact with the sultan of Zanzibar, Bargash, who had come to power after the death of his brother Mājed, that is to say at the same time as sultan Turki himself; he wanted to obtain the restitution of the subsidy from Zanzibar. But, to avoid the renewal of close political and family links between the two parties and between the two brothers, Great Britain intervened again and insisted that the subsidy be paid through her intermediary. In 1880, Turki, faithful to Omani–African unity and the idea of Greater Oman, made a brave attempt to short circuit British tutelage by proposing that his brother Bargash become sultan of both Zanzibar and Oman. In other words, Turki was prepared to give up his post in order to restore Omani–African unity in spite of the English.[440]

Lorimer, who refers briefly to this important fact, makes no further comment. Indeed it is obvious that Great Britain killed this plan off before it could bear fruit. For it is impossible to imagine that sultan Turki could then have completely forgotten or abandoned an idea so dear to him, just as it is difficult to imagine that this generous offer by Turki was not well received by Bargash. On the contrary, the sultan of Zanzibar must have seen it as an unexpected opportunity to reconstruct the great sultanate to his benefit, and to reign, like his father, Saʿīd ibn Sulṭān (1804–1856), over a reunited Oman and Zanzibar. Division, even dismemberment was decidedly the lot reserved for the restored dynasty of the sultans. Any alternative greatness was henceforth prohibited by an unrivalled and unrestrained British domination.

As proof of this dismantling of Omani power, the Wahhābis seized the opportunity of Turki's advent, which, by the way, they had supported, to strengthen their influence in the al-Buraimi oasis. Thus Oman found itself a country with no political structure and no civic peace. It was torn by civil war, which again fostered the clan spirit and tribalism. It was subject directly to British power, and so England became the official representative of Oman. This annexation would be confirmed in the period of Fayṣal ibn Turki.

8 Oman between independence and dependence

> What I value is my independence.
> As long as I live, Great Britain
> shall not interfere in my State
> (Sultan Fayṣal, 1891)

Sultan Fayṣal ibn Turki (1888–1913)

The reign of Fayṣal ibn Turki was marked by the Anglo-French conflict and the sultan's struggle for his country's independence. Having been forced to abandon the project of annexing Muscat and Maṭraḥ, having failed in her project of direct protection contested by France, Great Britain imposed the famous 'engagement concerning the transfer of territories' of 1891. Oman was then transformed into an unofficial colony. In 1899, Fayṣal provided France with a coal depot. Great Britain protested violently and the question resulted in an acute crisis, known as the 'Muscat crisis'; it was followed by litigation over the question of the French flag being flown by Omani ships in 1905, the whole business being taken to arbitration at the international court in The Hague. But it was also a period of rifts and acute conflicts in the interior; they had been unleashed at the fall of ʿAzzān's *imāma* in 1871 and carried on during Fayṣal's sultanate until the revolution of 1913–1920.

Fayṣal's dilemma

Fayṣal, unlike the sultans who preceded him, is not much written about by the historians; he adopted patriotic positions and tried to demonstrate a firm stance in relation to Great Britain. For their part, the government of India, led by Lord Curzon, and the British government under Lord Salisbury, saw this attitude as the unacceptable challenge of a 'petty prince', whom they had preferred to his elder brother Muḥammad and who should never have forgotten that he owed his advancement to them.

But Fayṣal rejected the notion that his reign was simply an extension of that of his father Turki. He still hoped to become the ruler of a unified, independent state, freed from all foreign influence. Fayṣal was particularly angered by England's domination over government politics in Muscat, a domination for which he could see no valid reason.[441]

The young sultan, who had come to power at the age of twenty-four, did not aim solely to build an independent sultanate. He was also influenced up to a point by the *Ibāḍi* model for an Islamic state, the *imāma*. He even gave himself the title of *imām*. It was he who instructed a ʿālim, ʿAbd Allāh bin Ḥumayd Nūr al-Dīn al-Sālmī to write the history of Oman, Tuḥfat al-Aʿyān bi Sīrat ahl ʿUman.

Yet the Ibadhite movement, which, after the fall of ʿAzzān, had entered the traditional phase of al-kitmān (dissimulation) did not, for all that, accept sultan Fayṣal. His tendency to favour the *imāma* system and his firm opposition to Great Britain's policy did not redeem him in the eyes of the *Ibāḍi ʿulamāʾ*. So Fayṣal had to face on one side the mistrust of his people and the conflicts endlessly breaking out against him, and on the other the change in the attitude of the English, who now wanted to have him replaced.

In any case, the root of the question was still the actual status of Oman. In theory, and by virtue of the Anglo-French declaration of 1862, Oman was considered to be an independent state, and it was on that fact that Fayṣal's anti-British attitudes were founded. But, following the fall of the *imāma* of ʿAzzān ibn Qays in 1871, British influence had reached a point that left no room for the exercise of any kind of independence or sovereignty.

The Ottavi report of 1894

In 1894, *Monsieur* Ottavi, the new French vice consul, arrived in Muscat. An active, clever man, he soon won the friendship and trust of the sultan and played an outstanding role in defending the interests of his country, taking advantage of the climate of intense discord then existing between the sultan and Great Britain. At the same time he supported the sultan's independent tendencies. However, his skills, together probably with the lack of modern means of communication, often prompted him to intervene in the internal affairs of Oman without necessarily referring to his supervising ministry. Anyway, he was instrumental in causing British policy in Oman and the Gulf no end of trouble.

On 19 January 1895, he sent his ministry in Paris an important political report in which he painted an exact and detailed picture of the political situation in Oman and the Gulf region. He reminded it of the way Britain had extended her domination over all the international lines to India and how the latter was preparing to become a centre of gravity, comparable to what Rome had been, to which, the proverb tells us, 'all roads led' 'The trade route from Basra to Alexandretta and from Muscat to Cyprus must belong to us, said the English, because it is one of the routes to India.'

Ottavi took advantage of the situation to ask his government to adopt measures aimed at putting a stop to British influence, which was beginning to dominate all the old shipping routes linking the nations of the Gulf. It should be remembered that these routes had been in constant use since the Babylonian period.

Oman was the central point of the report. She also had to be the pivot of the French policy in the Gulf region and the Indian Ocean. Ottavi asserted:

> Instead of letting England go on being the arbiter of the destinies of Oman and the small sultanates of the Persian Gulf, instead of considering that she has the exclusive duty to defend the rights of humanity against barbarism, instead of abandoning the monopoly of trade and shipping in these parts to her, we could perhaps in Oman assume the half of the condominium that was granted us in the conventions of 1862 and 1890.[442]

In addition to the value of the details and descriptions in which it abounds, the tone of this excellent report heralds the change in France's traditional attitude to Oman. Oman was no longer a regional power and a respected ally of France. She had become a 'cake' to be shared with England. Thus France too revealed a colonial temptation regarding her traditional and historic ally. Through the intermediary of M.Ottavi, she would attempt with all possible determination to impose herself on the lands of Oman as an equal partner with England. But it would be in vain.

The internal situation

In the meantime, Fayṣal had to face one of the most serious challenges to his power when, in 1895, the Hanawite tribes, supporters of the *imāma* system, led a general uprising which roused the whole of Oman. This movement hardened still more after Ṣāleḥ ibn ʿAli, chief of the al-Ḥārthi tribe, broke his allegiance to the sultan and joined the insurrection. In February 1895, most of the regions around Muscat fell. The capital was encircled and in the course of one attack, the sultan came close to losing his life.

In March an important conversation took place between the British political representative and Muhṣein ibn ʿUmar, one of the leaders of the uprising, accompanied by a sheikh of al-Ḥārthi. The two local rulers set out their motives for the uprising and called it a 'social movement' aimed at the overthrow of the sultan, which they said everyone wanted; the aim was to set up a strong leader who would command the respect of the whole country. On this occasion the two representatives personally expressed the wish of the sheikhs of the al-Ḥārthi tribe to place the sultanate of Oman under Ḥumayd ibn Thūwayni, the sultan of Zanzibar. If this solution proved impractical, they wanted to have one of ʿAzzan's sons in charge of Oman.[443] England asked for time to study these proposals.

In spite of the important contribution to the uprising made by Ḥamud and Saʿūd, the sons of *imām* ʿAzzān, and of Saʿūd's attempts to lead it, the Ibadhite movement, following the fall of its two historic chiefs, ʿAzzān ibn Qays and al-Khalīlī, was not in a position to accept responsibility for the insurrection on his behalf. It was not yet ready.

In March 1895, the British political resident came personally to meet Ṣāleḥ ibn ʿAli al-Ḥārthi to inform him of the final reply of the Government of India to the proposals of the representatives of the uprising. Great Britain let it be known that the reunification of Oman and Zanzibar was out of the question and that, furthermore, the possessions of British nationals must in all cases be respected under pain of retaliation.

And yet Great Britain did not ask the al-Ḥārthi tribes to put an end to the uprising. She even rejected the sultan's request for aid to resist it. In fact, the British authorities had resolved, after deliberation, to let the crisis rage on and take advantage of it to advance their interests on several points. Three political alternatives were under consideration:

1 To annex t Maṭraḥ o the British possessions and indemnify the sultan.
2 To proclaim British protection over the whole of Oman.
3 An ultimatum to the great sheikhs of Oman, proclaiming that, whatever the disagreements between themselves and the sultan, the British government, in order to defend its general interests in Oman, would not accept any attack on Muscat or Matraḥ.[444]

The first point amounted to a colonial bluff that was doomed to failure or at least to be particularly 'hard to swallow', even for the British Empire. The second point was dismissed: France would not accept it. It was provisionally decided to implement the third point, which consisted in appealing to the tribal chiefs in Oman to spare Muscat and Maṭraḥ in their attacks.[445]

It seemed, when all was said and done, as though Great Britain, for a variety of political reasons, was not seriously worried by this uprising, so long as Muscat and Maṭraḥ were spared. Paradoxically, the weakening of the sultan might even serve the interests of the colonial power.

At first, some of the leaders of the uprising had indeed attempted to keep Great Britain out of the conflict. Most of the tribes had kept their word and spared British interests and also the possessions of Indian and English nationals. But when certain leaders of al-Ḥārthi had started making concessions to England and negotiating with her, the rising burst all bounds and lurched into violence and destruction.

The British consul in Muscat, Whyte, even wrote a letter to the sultan, holding him responsible for the destruction and demanding compensation for the losses. He also asked him to raise a tax on the tribes of the interior. In his letter to the sultan, the consul specified: 'Your Majesty is urged to inform the tribes concerned that the tax is the result of British insistence.'[446] In other words it was Great Britain who was openly taking Omani affairs in hand and becoming not just the arbiter but the supreme authority: the tribes were to recognise her as such.

Finally, however, the uprising ended in a 'non-aggression agreement', signed by the two belligerents, Ṣāleḥ ibn ʿAli al-Ḥārthi and sultan Fayṣal, with Great Britain as intermediary. In his report, Ottavi indicated that the sultan had paid a sum of 17 000 écus in exchange for the departure of the tribes from Muscat, and he concluded that 'Fayṣal thus remains sultan but is none the less defeated'.[447] By this agreement, Fayṣal found his influence much reduced, in fact, and his power no longer extended beyond the territory of Muscat and Maṭraḥ. The situation was still ready to explode again.

Compensation for Zanzibar

Great Britain had previously offered financial aid estimated at 80 000 Indian rupees to the sultan's government as indemnity for the sum the government of Zanzibar was supposed to pay by the terms of the convention of partition imposed in 1861. As we know, she had suspended this aid on the accession of *imām* ʿAzzān to power in 1868 and re-instated it only after his fall, with the advent of sultan Turki, but this time in the context of well-defined policies.

Lorimer notes that the British governments in London and India shared the payment of this aid equitably and that they gave Turki to understand at the time that they would go on paying the indemnity as long as the sultan remained true to the prevailing treaty obligations and kept up his friendship with England.[448]

But the truth is quite different from what the official English historian Lorimer reports. For it was not from her own budget nor that of the Government of India but rather from Zanzibar's income that Great Britain levied the sum to be paid. French diplomatic archives confirm this:

> Let it be quite clear: it is Zanzibar that is paying the sum to Muscat. If England, which has now taken Zanzibar over and inherits the obligations of the sultanate, pays this sum, she does so, or must do so with the resources of Zanzibar and not from the Indian budget.[449]

In fact, Great Britain had inserted a clause on subvention from Zanzibar to Muscat in order to get the planned partition of the Omani–African state passed in 1861. On that basis, and by means of threats, she had been able to overcome the protests of Thūwayni, who had of course not accepted the decision, but he had no other choice.

If the British government later claimed to be attending to the recovery of the 'aid' or 'indemnity', and insisted that it was being paid through its own intervention, it did so with the aim of severing all official links between Oman and Zanzibar. Once that objective had been achieved, it stated that it held the aid to be derisory, although at the time it amounted to a quarter of the sultan's budget. Thus England was able to open up a pretext for her subsequent influence, indeed interventions, in the internal affairs of Oman. And the country found itself a victim twice over, first of the actual partition and second of the results of that partition, the loss of its independence and sovereignty.

Ottavi had perceived the paradox of a situation that he summed up as follows:

> The assured revenues of the sultan seem to be little more that 600 000 francs, the recognition of the British government accounts for a quarter [...] so Oman is considered by England to be a vassal of India [...]. Muscat is treated as a dependency of Calcutta and the sultan of Oman as a rajah in the pay of the Empress of India.[450]

In 1890, Great Britain finally proclaimed protection of Zanzibar. So Zanzibar was officially transformed into a British colony and the breach between the two parties was consummated. Oman was obliged to conduct the fight with Great Britain alone and at a disadvantage. What was at stake for the country? To steer a future between independence and colonial hegemony.

The 1891 engagement concerning the transfer of territories

In his efforts to reduce British influence and his fear that Oman might suffer the same fate as Zanzibar, Fayṣal tried to strengthen relations with France. This choice was essential in order to create some approach to equilibrium in the field of external relations. So, for the first time, he received a representative of Russia, a country allied to France, in Muscat, with a mission to restore Omani–Russian relations.

Although the political results were modest and limited, these contacts in themselves represented a new challenge to the supremacy of England, who immediately set about thwarting the plan.

At that time, the British government had it in mind to take measures to guarantee no infiltration of foreign influences into Oman. It is probable that the British government would have proclaimed Oman a protectorate under the British crown but for the Anglo-French common declaration of 1862, which precluded that possibility. The British government resorted to another solution: in 1891 it prepared an engagement which, when imposed on the sultan of Oman, obliged him and his successors to grant no privileges and to neither sell nor concede any part of his territory to any foreign power other than England.[451] In order to camouflage this engagement, known politically by the name of 'secret prohibition engagement', Great Britain at the same time signed a solemn trading accord with the sultan and announced it publicly.

This secret engagement is considered to be one of the most compromising and perilous documents Oman had signed in her history. It is particularly difficult to imagine why any government or independent sultan should have consented to such an agreement except in circumstances of coercion.

The secret report of the French Ministry of Foreign Affairs – we refer to it for the first time – reveals and clarifies the reasons that constrained the sultan to sign this agreement. On 4 February 1895, the sultan Fayṣal showed exceptional confidence in Mr Ottavi. After admitting in secret the tyranny practised by Anglo-Indian agents on his country, the sultan allowed him to read the text of a secret convention, signed by Colonel Ross, the English resident in Bandar Bushehr, on 20 March 1891. The report adds that the sultan had not concealed from M. Ottavi that he had signed under duress and he confirmed:

> But I set store by my independence. As long as I live, Great Britain shall not lay a finger on my State.
>
> If I wanted to be protected, I should certainly not appeal to the English government. I have learnt from the lesson of Zanzibar. I signed under duress. I was abandoned.[452]

That, then, is what impelled the sultan to accept the unacceptable, for in other respects he was quite categorical *vis-à-vis* Great Britain. However, the validity of Fayṣal's assessment of his independence may be disputed, even though it was founded on his eagerness to protect Oman from British sway, at least officially. For the moral and political weight of this engagement leaves no room, not even hypothetically, for the independence or sovereignty of either Oman or the person of its sultan. This engagement would have been a political defeat for Fayṣal's hopes of independence.

In another report to the Ministry of Foreign Affairs in Paris, M. Ottavi summed up the status of Oman following this convention in these terms: 'After such a treaty, the independence of Muscat is nothing but a fiction.'[453] On the general situation in the Gulf, he concluded: 'The Persian Gulf now is just an English lake, with the disguised possession, Muscat, at the entrance to the acknowledged possession, Bahrein, towards the centre.'[454]

This agreement of 1891 unquestionably constituted Great Britain's greatest victory in the region, after the first treaty of 1798 and then the separation from Zanzibar in 1861. It was first and foremost the logical complement of British policy and its crowning glory. After the 1891 watershed, Oman was no longer an independent, sovereign country, however strong the sultan's will to resist might be.

Lord Curzon, the viceroy of India had previously explained with precision the British position on the Omani question. He left no doubt on the subject in an article in the Times in 1892, a translation of which was published in *the Journal des Débats* in Paris in 1899.

> Oman may rightly be considered to be a British dependency; we give its chief a subsidy. We dictate its policy; we must not tolerate any foreign intervention. Personally, I have little doubt that the day will soon come when we shall see the Union Jack fluttering on the ramparts of Muscat.[455]

These remarks need no comment. Yet events did not unfold as the English had hoped or even expected. And the oppressive agreement that had been imposed on him did not divert Fayṣal from his attitude, still hostile to Great Britain. The first expression of the sultan's discontent following the British manoeuvrings for power can be seen when he disclosed the secret engagement of 1891 to the French vice consul, Ottavi. Moreover, in 1893, Fayṣal provided the French government with a permanent residence for its consulate. Significantly, it was one of the finest houses in Muscat, later called *Bayt Faransa* (the French house) by the Omanis. Another sign: the sultan did not respond to British moves pressing him to forbid Omani traders to fly French flags in the al-Sharqiya, Ṣūr and Jaʿlān regions. Without disarming, Fayṣal used what little latitude remained in his power to signal at every opportunity his disapproval of British pretensions.

The Muscat crisis

True to his own reasoning and political convictions, the sultan then took his most striking measures. On 20 November 1898, *the Jounal des Débats* announced that

Muscat had authorised France to establish a coal depot at Jeseh (five miles south east of Muscat). It added that Great Britain was known to have presented a protest.[456]

Indeed, Great Britain considered this favour as a severe blow to her interests and a slight to her reputation in the region. The political agitation that followed led to a very real crisis in the region. This affair, in which French Foreign Affairs Ministers, the Home office and the India Office, French and British agents in the Gulf and the viceroy of India, Lord Curzon, were all actively involved, became 'the Muscat incident'. The English did not win a decisive victory but the incident illustrated the imperialist policy practised by Great Britain in the Gulf.[457]

Lord Curzon, one of the fiercest upholders of British colonial expansionism, wrote a letter to Lord George Hamilton, the secretary of state for India, on 12 January 1899, telling him that he had given Major Fagan, the political resident in Muscat, orders to ask the sultan to explain his actions. And if the truth of the story was confirmed, the major was to inform the sultan that his act would be considered as a breach of the treaty of 1891 and that the British government would not tolerate it. At the same time, Lord Curzon despatched colonel Meade, the British resident in the Gulf, to Muscat to undertake a complete revision of British relations with the sultan. He recommended:

> Supposing the sultan to show a conciliatory temper, Meade would, of course, approach him in the same spirit, but if he proves refractory and if his recent attitude is, as seems likely, indicative of a settled policy of antagonism to ourselves, a much stiffer attitude on Meade's part would be required.

And Curzon went further,

> I am looking into the question of our annual subsidy to the sultan and I am glad to find that it is dependent on his good behaviour and fulfilment of treaty engagements. The threat to diminish this may turn out to be a very useful weapon and would probably bring him to his knees at once.[458]

This letter is an eloquent résumé of the colonial mentality and designs; the more so as Curzon, one of the linchpins of the imperial system, was certainly not inclined to understand the sultan's attitude, still less the legitimacy of his claims for national sovereignty. Fayṣal's position having been confirmed, England did not hesitate to interrupt payment of the subsidy in order to make him give way, thereby helping to plunge Oman still further into economic crisis. Ottavi, who witnessed these events, wrote a report to his minister containing these questions:

> why do the English consuls in Muscat make play of this subsidy to exact all the concessions they want from the sovereign of Oman? Why do the Anglo-Indians, at the slightest opposition from the sultan to their wishes, threaten to deprive him of revenue to which he is entitled by virtue of a verdict passed by the viceroy of India himself in arbitration?[459]

To accept the British view, in other words consent to the view that the sultan, by his attitude, was violating the secret treaty of 1891, meant accepting the juridical and moral validity of that engagement and its political and international legality. But that treaty had been imposed on Muscat under threat, represented an attack on the national sovereignty of Oman and, on an international level, proved the more unacceptable in both form and content in that it also contravened the joint Franco-British proclamation of 1862. Did not Lord Hamilton himself declare: 'The (secrete) arrangement of 1891 was inconsistent with the Proclamation of 1862'?[460]

In fact, from a purely juridical point of view, the sultan's decision to grant France a coal depot conformed with Article XVII of the Franco-Omani treaty of friendship of 1844, which stated: 'The French will be entitled to make depots or stores of provisions of what kind soever at Zanzibar or any other points in the States of H.H. the sultan of Muscat.'[461]

So Fayṣal was fully aware of the implications of granting the authorisation and thereby honouring his commitments to France. But the decision was only a limited attempt to exercise the sovereignty of his country.

In the letter quoted earlier, Hamilton confirmed that in international law France was justified in setting up this depot and that it was impossible to deny it to her. The official British attitude, however, took no account of Hamilton's proper point of view. It was based more on Curzon's analysis, which gave a rather specious interpretation of articles in the treaty in question. Thus of article XVII: '[the French] means French persons, not the French government'. For as he still saw it, the obtaining of a coal depot by France was the result of an 'intrigue' and fraught with strategic perils.[462]

Not only did Curzon not recognise the independence and integrity of the sultan and his country but also he made it Abundantly clear that he intended to confine him to a position of servility. Thus, referring to Meade's visit to Muscat: 'I think this may afford a good opportunity for reading the Sultan a sharp lesson and teaching him his proper place',[463] which meant in plain terms that the sultan must behave obediently again.

It is certainly worth noting that these letters exchanged between Curzon in India and Hamilton in London – who was actually expressing the views of the prime minister, Lord Salisbury – showed less than complete agreement between the two men responsible for the question of the famous coal depot. However, more important than this informal difference of opinion was the firm formal agreement of the two personages on the need to replace sultan Fayṣal. On this point Curzon declared: 'We shall not permit this petty Chief to defy us.' And he added:

> The 1862 Agreement, as I read it, guarantees the independence of his throne but not his personal occupation of it [...] and there is a loyal brother in the palace who is reported to us by Meade as a not unsuitable successor, should any such be required.[464]

To which Hamilton replied: 'I entirely agree with you that we cannot allow this petty potentate to defy us.'[465]

Later, Curzon changed his mind on the subject of the sultan's brother who was living in the palace with Fayṣal himself:

> From a number of reports I gather that the brother at Muscat is no good for our purposes being dull, weak and stupid; and that if we require to run another candidate, it will have to be the uncle from Bombay.[466]

It is surprising, in fact, that Curzon could have arrived at such an interpretation, because the declaration in question, which affirmed that France and Great Britain had deemed it right to make a reciprocal engagement to respect the independence of the sultan of Muscat and the sultan of Zanzibar, was quite unambiguous.[467]

The British Foreign Minister spoke the same language and confirmed Curzon's point of view since, according to him, and after the juridical commission of the ministry had spoken, it must be considered that the proclamation of 1862 'guarantees the independence of the territory and not the individual upon the throne'.[468]

So, after a first tortuous reading of article XVII of the Franco-Omani treaty, the two British government organs, in India and in London, got away with another tortuous reading of this proclamation which literally and with no possible equivocation demanded the independence of the sultan and of his country. Obviously, there could not be total independence of the country without the total independence of the ruler of the country.

A policy of violence

In February 1899 on the orders of Lord Curzon, Meade, the political resident in Bushehr presented the sultan with a memorandum containing several British demands, the first of which was aimed at the withdrawal of the grant of a coal depot to the French; the aim of the second was to exclude sheikh ʿAbdel ʿAziz al-Rewiḥī, a national figure hostile to British influence, who had occupied the post of minister and adviser to the sultan.[469]

Sensitive to British pressure, the sultan declared his readiness to accept most of the points, including the dismissal of his minister, but he refused to yield on the question of the coal depot because he did not see it as a regional concession or as an infringement of the agreement of 1891. He asked the British authorities to give him time to think about it.

The British rejected this proposition and replied in a threatening and alarming tone that the 'period of flexibility and indulgence was over'. He was given a 24-hour ultimatum in which to change his position. The sultan was not slow to respond: on 13 February, he announced in a letter to the political representative that he had decided to cancel the 'privilege' of the coal depot. According to Lorimer, he even went further, requesting British protection for fear of French reactions,[470] although this cannot be confirmed.

All the British demands were thus met in practice, in both the political and the strategic fields. But the colonial claims were not about to stop there. Immediately afterwards, the ship *Eclipse* arrived in Muscat from Bombay with Admiral Douglas, the chief of the Indian naval units, on board. He was preceded by the ship *de Brest*. The aim of this show of strength was to make Fayṣal capitulate and strike a decisive and definitive blow at French influence in Oman and in the Gulf.

On 15 February, Meade sent an ultimatum to the sultan requiring him to abolish the French 'privilege' publicly at a general conference and to draft an official dispatch to that effect. With hardly any hesitation, the sultan acceded to these new demands. He informed Ottavi, the French vice-consul, of his decision to abolish the 'privileges' conceded to France. But that was not enough for the British. They insisted that the sultan be put on board Admiral Douglas' ship. Meanwhile the second vessel, Eclipse, prepared to set fire to the palace and the town's defences.[471]

Curzon, who at the time enjoyed the full support of the British government, wanted to push his advantage to the limit in order to assert his government's interests and put an end to the remotest chance of revolt on the part of the sultan. It was also an opportunity not to be missed to teach other Gulf chiefs a salutary lesson.

On 16 February, the sultan felt constrained to yield to Curzon's demands; he went aboard the admiral's vessel and declared his unconditional compliance with all the British demands. The next day Douglas paid a visit to Fayṣal and apparently presented him with the formula of a speech the sultan was to make that very day to a general conference at which all the notabilities of Muscat would be present. The sultan also proclaimed the withdrawal of the concessions granted to France and renewed 'close and friendly' relations with Great Britain.[472]

This event was greeted with dismay by the Omanis, including the opponents of the sultan, and also among the populations of the Gulf. On an international level, it met with the sharpest reactions and criticisms. Many newspapers, particularly Indian and French, denounced the arrogance displayed by the viceroy of India, Lord Curzon, whose behaviour basically differed very little from that of the Portuguese Alfonso de Albuquerque at the beginning of the sixteenth century.

For his part, the Prime Minister, Salisbury, expressed his embarrassment over the behaviour of Curzon and his subordinates, not, paradoxically, in connection with the pressure put on Fayṣal to embark in a British warship, but rather with the pressure that had obliged the ruler of Oman to renegue publicly on his engagements with France, a fact that, in his words, would damage Great Britain's reputation and was about to undermine Anglo-French relations. Lord Curzon replied to his government's protests by unhesitatingly asserting:

> We had recourse to force because the Indian people, the people of the Arab Gulf and oriental peoples generally do not understand any other language. Imperial prestige is the chief factor in the external policy of the government of British India, and it has had a great influence on the minds of the Gulf Arabs and was of more use than Monsieur Delcassé's speech to the French National Assembly.[473]

The writer of such a letter, full of racist remarks, held a high position in the British system of government and was actually viceroy of India: the colonialist in all his glory. Ignorance apart, this letter throws light on some essential points: first, the underlying colonial thinking is fundamentally contemptuous of the values, cultures and civilisations of the Indian and Arab peoples; second, it sums up the principles of British colonial policy in the region over almost a century and a half.

Elsewhere Curzon attempted to justify his action by alleging that:

> Though Muscat is in theory an independent state... it reminds me a little of the semi-French kingdom of Cambodia... but over which, nevertheless, the French Government exercise an absolutely predominant control and in which they would tolerate no interference.[474]

With these developments, British influence had reached its peak. The sultan was ordered to refer to the British political resident in Muscat before making any decision whatsoever, whether in internal matters or those of external relations. The powers of the British political resident in Muscat became greater than those of the sultan himself. Oman was completely integrated into the British colonial sphere of influence. So ended the designs for independence and any ambition Fayṣal might have cherished to maintain a sovereign state. But Admiral Douglas, who was 'an English gentleman' nevertheless did not omit to mention that 'he was favourably impressed by the Sultan, who bore himself, under trying circumstances with great dignity'.[475]

This new situation also put an end to the Omani–French special relationship. France ceased to treat Muscat as the nucleus of a semi-independent state, relatively emancipated from British influence. She no longer contemplated neutralising Oman, nor, following Ottavi's proposals, sharing influence in the country with Great Britain.

France did indeed continue to adhere to the joint declaration of 1862, which was supposed to prevent England claiming official protection of Oman in the future. However, apart from a few official protests before the French National Assembly, the 'Omani crisis' had no really negative repercussions on Franco-British relations; quite the opposite, it seems to have encouraged the two states to further dialogue, notably on the previously thorny topic of 'colonial frontiers', which were best approached now in a politico-juridical framework. From another angle, it was no longer advisable for France, in the midst of an internal political crisis, to adopt an intransigent attitude in the colonial field.

Paradoxically, after this English takeover that was so damaging to Oman and sultan Fayṣal and to French interests, Great Britain granted France a coaling station in the area of Hadramawt, not far from Omani territories. And Great Britain brazenly sent an official message to the sultan, indicating that there was no longer any problem about France obtaining this depot as long as the British authorities signalled their intentions or their agreement on the matter.

In spite of all these developments that redounded to her advantage, Great Britain continued to discuss the possibility of replacing the sultan. On 3 March 1899, after three weeks of the 'Muscat crisis', Hamilton wrote to Curzon: 'I will endeavour to get the consent of the government to giving you the necessary authority to apply further pressure to the Sultan and if necessary to depose him.'[476]

The question of the French flags

In the spirit of her traditional relations with Oman, reaffirmed in the accord of 1844, France had, as an exception, granted official documents and French flags to some Omani merchant ships (about forty).

The aim of this politically very weighty decision was to guarantee the safety of the vessels against any harassment on the part of the British fleet, which did indeed systematically impede the movements of Arab ships on the pretext of suppressing the trade in black slaves.

The activity of British patrols against this trade had dealt a severe blow to the Arab dhows and boutres.[477] Boarded and diverted on the slightest suspicion of slaving, they were burnt if they had been persuaded to carry slaves. The American consul in Zanzibar, Mr Webb, affirmed that 71 Arab ships had been destroyed in that way by English patrols in 1868 and 1869. It was the ruin of the ancient system on which the power of Oman and Zanzibar had been based. Arab shipping took refuge in part under the French flag. These Frenchify Arab sailors found their numbers increasing considerably since 1873, from about 10 at that date to 23 in 1891 and 44 in 1896.[478]

Unlike the law of 9 June 1845, which gave French status to the ships of her colonies and was passed after the colonisation of Nossi-Bé and Mayotte in 1841 and 1843, this practice did not place Omani ships under the direct influence of France. 'This concession of the French flag is not an arbitrary act. There is no absence of rules, just different rules.'[479]

It was an exceptional decision in an exceptional case. Besides, sultan Fayṣal had nothing against such a measure that he saw as a service to the Omanis. '. . . The sovereign of the country raised no objection to protection being extended to the owners, captains and crews of the dhows since, by fostering trade, this protection contributed to the country's wealth'.[480]

It is perfectly logical that Fayṣal saw it rather as an expression of his independence or his non-capitulation to British influence. Moreover we should not overlook the fact that this measure represented a victory against British hegemony in the region. As proof of this, Great Britain was unable to accept the situation. She accused France of protecting the slave trade and of a kind of interference in Omani affairs.

In fact some of the British complaints about the slave trade were not unfounded; the al-Sharqiya region had a reputation for this activity at the time. But according to Kajare, France had obtained guarantees to avoid Abūse of her flag, which was granted only under certain conditions.[481]

In 1900, unconfirmed reports say that Ottavi had tried to declare French protection for the region of Ṣūr. This irritated Cox, the British political representative in Muscat. As a reaction and in the same year, he took the sultan with him on an official visit to the port of Ṣūr. On that visit, Fayṣal demanded that the

French documents be replaced by those of the sultanate of Muscat, and the same for the flags.

This stance aroused strong reactions on the part of the French government, against Muscat this time and not against England. The French ambassador in London, Monsieur Cambon, sent a letter to his foreign minister, Delcassé, who was enthusiastic about the improvement in his country's relations with Great Britain. He expressed his dissatisfaction over this event, by which, rumour had it, the sultan wanted to disturb Anglo-French relations. Cambon suggested to his government that France should receive compensation from the sultan.

He also added that he had met the British prime minister, Salisbury, who had instanced insufficient information on the subject and concluded: 'What can you expect? We are paying the sultan of Muscat and he imagines that by acting in that way he is creating a claim to our recognition and showing us that he is really earning his money.'[482]

Cambon's own picture of the sultan was not very different from the British colonial view: he had no hesitation in stigmatising Fayṣal's attitude, yet before the Muscat crisis and through all the years of his reign he had displayed his firm intention to consolidate and improve Omani–French relations. His efforts had even formed one of the principal reasons for his differences with Great Britain. But Cambon was unaware, or chose to be unaware of that past. Concerning sultan Fayṣal, the friend of France, he could find nothing better to say than 'He is an Arab and I know of no other Arab among all the great chiefs who cannot be bought'.[483]

There we have French diplomacy's opinion of the Arabs. Yet the French archives – and Mr Cambon could hardly have been unaware of them – established that Fayṣal had previously countered the insistence of Great Britain on halting the use of the French flags. In reality, the desertion of the sultan at that point in time seemed to the French diplomacy as a very small sacrifice in return for Franco-British rapprochement.

The Hague tribunal

When Great Britain had brought the Boer War to an end in 1903 and the first signs appeared of a Franco-British entente, which was crowned by the 'act of friendship' of 1904, an accord concluded on 13 October 1904 was used to refer the disagreement over the French flags to the court in The Hague. On 28 January 1905, the president of the French Republic published the following declaration:

> A compromise having been signed in London on October 13th 1904 between France and the United Kingdom of Great Britain and Ireland, and the ratifications of that act having been exchanged in London on January 18th 1905, the said compromise, the terms of which follow, will be put into full and complete operation:
>
> Whereas the French government and that of His Britannic Majesty have held it to be right, by the declaration of March 10th 1862, 'to undertake reciprocally to respect the independence of H.M. the sultan of Muscat'.[484]

According to the statement by the president of the Republic, certain difficulties had been noticed further to flying French flags by dhows belonging to citizens of Oman, for which reason it had been decided to have recourse to official international arbitration. Therefore the two camps agreed on the nomination of Victor Emmanuel as a neutral arbiter *vis-à-vis* the two countries, Great Britain and France, and on that of a supreme arbiter alongside the king of Italy. Then the governments of the French Republic and His Britannic Majesty nominated the members of the tribunal.[485]

No differences occurred between the two states concerning the members of the tribunal nor the dates of the meetings which were postponed more than once. On the other hand, a dispute broke out between France and Great Britain when the latter brought before the tribunal a memorandum in the name of the English government and the sultanate of Muscat. By this move, Great Britain expected to achieve two objectives. The first, to present an official complaint, in the name of Oman, asserting that the fact of flying French flags on Omani boats was nothing but an undesirable interference and amounted to an infringement of Omani sovereignty. The second, to reinforce the official representation of Oman.

France protested against this memorandum and her ambassador in London, M. Cambon, sent the British government a letter in which he explained:

> Such a document would lead in the end to making the British government the advocate and legal guardian of the independent sultan of Muscat and my government would find it impossible to accept such a claim. The sultan of Muscat is in no way entitled to intervene in litigation exclusively concerned with the interpretation of the Franco-English declaration of March 10th 1862. He was not a contracting party to that declaration nor to the arbitration compromise of October 13th 1904.

Cambon concluded his letter in these terms:

> I am therefore charged by my government to present you with an observation on this subject and to declare to Your Lordship that we cannot accept the introduction of the sultan of Muscat into the discussion that is to take place before the arbitration tribunal in The Hague.[486]

The essential question was still to know who was the principle party, the party concerned and the object of the dispute before the court. Was it Oman? In theory, the party concerned by the declaration of March 1862 was indeed Oman. The objective of the declaration was respect for the independence of Muscat on the part of Great Britain and France, that is to say, non-interference in her internal and external affairs or with her national sovereignty. The special committee for Oman at the United Nations Organisation would note later on this point:

> The significance of the Declaration was not only in its respect for the independence of Muscat and Oman but also in the manner in which two majort powers recorded that independence as a fact and as something which it was important to preserve.[487]

The role of the Hague tribunal was not to determine the right of the country concerned in the context of respect for its independence and sovereignty, but rather to determine the 'legality' of colonial influence and hegemony, whether British or French so as to confer international legitimacy on it. As for Oman, it was not expected to take any further interest in its fate.

Great Britain did not insist strongly on this point; on the other hand she despatched Major Cox, then the political resident in Bushehr, to the sultan in Muscat to work out with him the sequence of events. The British authorities expected this visit to carry weight in the workings of the tribunal in The Hague and to strengthen their position. Following this move, the sultan sent a letter to the French consul in Muscat, in which he raised the tone to inform him:

> The question of the flags is currently being examined by the arbitration court in The Hague and the British government is my representative at that tribunal. Consequently this affair is within the competence of the English government and concerns it. There is no need to explain this.[488]

France very much suspected that sultan Fayṣal had yet again been coerced into writing this letter; moreover, the French vice-consul in Muscat sent an account to his minister: 'Secret: the sultan has informed me in great confidence that he has been compelled to make this protest'.[489]

Vice-consul Ottavi then drafted a report in which, based on information from persons close to the sultan, he announced Major Cox's visit and the methods he had used to persuade the sultan to be represented directly by Great Britain: 'That is why (...) for fear of upsetting his formidable protectors, he [Fayṣal] replied favourably to the invitation he was sent.'[490]

But these disagreements did not disturb the process of arbitration undertaken by the two powers, both intent on resolving this dispute by the path of international justice. And the judgement of the Hague tribunal was as follows:

It was incumbent on the Omanis to comply with the judicial power of the sultan in all cases. As to the central question of flying the French flags, the judgement made a distinction between two groups: ships that had obtained the privilege before 1892 could carry on flying French flags; those that had acquired it after that date lost it. The year 1892 was chosen because it corresponded to the date on which the modification of the Brussels system concerning inspections at sea and the fight against the slave trade had been decided. It was further decided that ships flying the French flag, even in the territorial waters of Muscat, could not be opposed. The judgement also prohibited the transfer of the privilege of French nationality from one owner to another, even if it was his heir, a privilege the Omani ships had enjoyed until then. In other words this text doomed French colours to disappear from Oman in fairly short order.[491]

So Great Britain had won the day 'juridically' in her efforts to 'legitimise' her influence in Oman. But in reality she had imposed herself on the land well before the verdict was pronounced in The Hague. And Lorimer confirms this:

> As to the French intrigues in Oman, the English brought them to naught by the decisive operation in Muscat, and in fact the affair of the French flags in Oman was settled even before an arbitration commission found in favour of the British at The Hague.[492]

But if we are prepared to look not just at the juridical value of this judgement, which is open to all kinds of interpretation and criticism, and if we leave aside the number of points scored by the British at the expense of France, the political, historical and strategic content lies fairly and squarely in the fact that Great Britain, by this verdict, had acquired international 'legitimacy' as the official representative of Oman in external affairs and as the guardian of Muscat. It was a 'colonial legitimacy' and the real loser in this litigation was the party concerned: Oman.

French flags vanished from Omani ships soon after this convention and, by the same token, the influence of France became progressively less.

Fayṣal and the question of abdication

There is nothing more indicative of the gravity of the general situation in Oman than the spectacle of the sultan seeking to stand down. After all the insults and disappointments inflicted on him by England, Fayṣal decided to abdicate in favour of his son Taymūr.

The sultan informed the political agent in Muscat of his intention: 'For some time I have been thinking seriously of handing over the reins of government.'[493] When the English agent asked him if this decision was motivated by illness or age, the sultan replied that it was neither of those but rather the incessant problems he encountered with the tribes, on the one hand and financial difficulties on the other.

These were certainly obvious causes, but not such as to incite Fayṣal to abdicate. The British political agent was not deceived; he tried to get to the bottom of the true reasons for his decision. In the report he wrote for the Government of India, he concluded:

> It appears to me that the situation is really as follows: Seyyid Feisal, as he frankly states, is weary of the many worries of the difficult and artificial situation in which he is placed – a Sultan in name only.

And he added: 'He desires to avoid before his people and for his own self-respect the appearance of ignominiously throwing in his hand and giving the government of the country into the hands of the British.'[494]

As we can see, the report reveals a thorough knowledge of local realities: the forces motivating the sultan's decision are well analysed, but there are others that are not acknowledged. As the political agent had in fact himself testified in his correspondence, the sultan had considered abdicating immediately after the incident of the French flags. But that was just the straw that broke the camel's back. The determining phase – not mentioned in the British diplomatic documents – was the humiliation the English inflicted on Fayṣal over the question of the coal depot in 1898. They had forced him then to board the British admiral's ship, the better to emphasise the capitulation of the power of Muscat to Great Britain.

Besides, it is significant that the political agent made no attempt to make the sultan go back on his decision; he was now more interested to know whether, in the event of his son Taymūr coming to power, the political situation in Muscat would be comparable to that in Zanzibar, that is, completely subject to English authority. To this, Fayṣal replied in the affirmative.

Be that as it may, Great Britain deemed the moment to be inopportune for the sultan to leave power while his son was still very young, and she persuaded him to stay on, knowing full well that he was so weakened that he would offer neither a challenge nor any opposition to British influence in his country. Great Britain had finally reduced him to the status of a ruler without ambition, without ideals and without power.

But more than that, the activities linked with the arms trade, which was traditional in the country, soon became the target for a new colonial campaign. The claim to fight against that trade provided a new pretext to interfere in the activities of Omani merchant ships.

The settlement of this question gave rise to much bargaining between France and Great Britain at a time when the frontiers between the two empires were being firmly drawn as part of a great colonial realignment. According to Le Cour Grandmaison, arms trafficking in the Gulf increased considerably from 1907. The Franco-British entente cordiale, signed in 1904, required the agreement of France if the traffic were to cease. Attempts at exchanges between colonial powers were made: the arms trade in the Gulf against the territory of Gambia in West Africa, a British enclave in the French colony of Senegal.[495]

Although he had the firmest intentions regarding the sovereignty and independence of his country, sultan Fayṣal none the less saw Oman sinking into an alarming state of dilapidation and dependence. In spite of himself, his whole reign was marked by compromise. The situation was repugnant to him.

The sultan remained completely isolated, subject to every kind of pressure and manipulation. Abandoned by everyone against the background of the Entente Cordiale and Anglo-French reconciliation in the face of Germany, Fayṣal could see no other recourse than to abdicate. Even that favour was denied to him: Great Britain condemned him to preside to the end over the rout of his moribund state. And that painful ordeal brings us to the threshold of the revolution of 1913–1920, which would determine the modern fate of Oman.

9 The sultanate of Muscat and the *imāma* of Oman

> Liberty is not achieved without blood and tears. Fear is the curse of life and to doubt victory is defeat.
>
> (al-ʿālim al-Sālmī (1868–1914))

The Ibadhite Revolution of 1913–1920

The arbitration in the dispute over the French flags at the court in The Hague having concluded in her favour in 1904, Great Britain was able to make good the 'international legitimacy' of her influence in Oman and put an end to the French alternative. By the same token, the argument of the fight against the slave trade was no longer of use to British strategy. The slogan of the succeeding period was the struggle against the arms trade: a fresh pretext for tightening control of shipping in the region. But basically it was a matter of stressing her domination there, the better to integrate the region into British imperial strategy throughout the Orient. And to that end, rather than officially declaring the British protectorate over the regimes then in place, it was preferable to keep them weak and divided and in a state of vassalage in relation to the colonial power manoeuvring in the wings. This was the 'British lake', a stagnant sheet of water from every point of view.

The threat of a loss of a national and cultural identity and the increasing disrepute surrounding the regime of the sultans left no alternative but insurrection for Omanis conscious of their decline; the Omani *Nahḍa* was to trouble the waters of the British lake from 1913 to 1920. However, emerging victorious from the First World War, the colonial power would impose a new partition on the country, separating the *Ibāḍi imāma* in the interior from the sultanate on the coast. This status quo, unsatisfactory all round, would only help to isolate the country, delaying its economic development and political maturity.

'The British lake' and the challenge of the Ibadhite movement

Since Balfour's arrival at the Foreign Office in June 1902, the British government had shown a greater interest in the Gulf region and in Iraq. He tried to implement a clearer, more precise policy. He was convinced that, in order to strengthen Great Britain's presence in India and eastern Asia, it was necessary to reinforce her positions in the Gulf. After defining this strategy, the Foreign Minister decided to create special committees (the Bunsen committees) to make a closer study of the new state of affairs in the region. These committees were also charged with drawing a new geopolitical map.

In 1903, Lord Curzon set out on an official visit to several of the Gulf countries, including Oman and the 'coast of Oman', then called the 'Trucial coast'. The aim of the historic visit of this 'victorious man' was, in fact, to proclaim officially the end of French influence and the now indisputably exclusive nature of British influence. In a famous speech at al-Sharjah in November 1903 in the presence of the governors of the 'Trucial coast', Curzon was to announce:

> You have not lost your independence; on the contrary, we have safeguarded it and it will now be more firmly guaranteed than ever. We shall keep the peace in the waters of the Gulf, and for that, British supremacy must remained unchallenged.[496]

We know that the reality was quite different. Witness these remarks by the British Prime Minister, Lord Salisbury, who unhesitatingly proclaimed: '... questions affecting these destinies would be decided many thousands of miles from the Gulf.'[497] This was an admission of the system of colonial dependence, while at the same time categorically denying Lord Curzon's remarks and summing up the steadfast policy that would determine the course of history in the Gulf countries.

The fact remains that Lord Curzon's visit was not devoid of ulterior motives of a military complexion. He was also concerned to look into the establishment of military bases and this would prove to be fraught with political, demographic and cultural consequences for the region. In particular, it was Arab national and cultural identity that was at stake. For Landen, the fact of imposing British domination in the Gulf by force entailed the intention to set an essentially British and Indian stamp on the region. The subsequent history of the Gulf countries has merely confirmed this analysis and later influenced the way events unfolded when accelerated by the discovery of oil.[498]

Thus the socio-politico-cultural map of the Gulf countries today appears to be merely the fruit of British policy at the start of the century. The stakes were well chosen. It was a question of weakening the social structure and undermining Arab cultural identity, the better to impose total colonial domination.

Just how far should the colonial hold on the region be pushed? The question was still being debated in the British Foreign Office at the end of the First World War.

Bondarevsky states that, during the war, the Bunsen committee had initiated discussion of certain projects aimed at creating an Arab caliphate, which would include the whole of the Arabian peninsula and all the areas of the Gulf with Arab populations. But this idea had met with opposition from Grant, the head of the foreign department of the British colonial administration in India, and from Hirtzel, the influential head of the political department at the India Office. In their report these officials stressed that Great Britain did not want a unified Arabia, but rather a weak, divided Arabia, split into countless tiny principalities under British suzerainty and with no possibility of uniting against her.[499]

With the end of the First World War, Great Britain again found herself with absolute mastery in the region. The other shore of the Gulf, the Persian shore, had experienced a struggle for influence between Russia and Great Britain which was to end, between 1907 and 1917, with the partition of Iran into three zones: the Russians in the north, the English in the south and a neutral region in the centre. However, after the Bolshevik revolution in October 1917, this partition was modified and Iran fell completely into the hands of the British. Meanwhile, on the Arabian shore of the Gulf, the situation would remain quasi static for almost a century and a half. So the dream of Curzon and Salisbury came to pass and the region had gained its still famous nickname of the 'British lake'.

Elsewhere, the British seizure of the African ports on one side and the Indian ports in eastern Asia on the other, as well as the domination of the shipping routes in the Indian Ocean and the Gulf, had paralysed what was left of the Omani fleet, and its dilapidated state was depicted by the British historian Kelly: 'The once powerful Al-Said navy fleet was now reduced to a few hulks rotting at their moorings.'[500]

This description is enough to give us a clear impression, not only of the now non-existent commercial activity but also of the economic situation as a whole and even the lifestyle of the Omanis. Naturally, in the absence of commercial activity, agricultural production was declining. The export of dates, an important arm of the national economy was reduced to nothing. Omani society was in a state approaching asphyxiation. In the words of the British resident himself, Wingate, Oman's contact with external civilisation was reduced to one boat a week.[501] Before the arrival of the British, a century earlier, the Omani ports sheltered hundreds of ships.

Clearly, this is why sultan Fayṣal had to hand over almost all his country's affairs to the British authorities. Landen even reports that he gave up one of his major prerogatives, the day-to-day supervision of the country's affairs, to the British political resident in Muscat, Major Wingate, and that in return he received 650 000 Indian rupees, which were supposed to enable him to pay his debts.[502]

The twilight of the Omani state, which had begun in the middle of the nineteenth century after the separation from Zanzibar (1861), became, towards the end of sultan Fayṣal's reign (1888–1913) a darkness in which Oman would continue to be plunged during a century and a half. It was the slow agony of a country and of a people.

But sooner or later, from the stagnant waters of the 'British lake', currents would resurface and would be all the deeper and stronger because they had been repressed and because they appeared to be the only hope of reversing the process of decomposition in the country. This would be the Omani *al-Nahḍa*.

The movement of **al-Nahḍa** *(renaissance) in Oman*

For the third time in the modern history of Oman, as had been the case on the eve of Nāṣer ibn Murshed's revolution in the seventeenth century and before

'Azzān ibn Qays', revolution in the nineteenth century, the only hope of checking this collapse and saving the nation consisted in rallying the Omanis round the Ibadhite movement and attempting to rebuild the *imāma*. It was in that spirit that the Omani *al-Nahḍa* was undertaken.

The *al-Nahḍa* leadership regrouped fourteen *'ulamā'* and tribal chiefs and [Nūr al-Dīn] 'Abd Allāh al-Sālmī appeared as guide. These rulers named their movement 'the movement of the Omani al-Nahḍa' a term that testified to the wealth of hopes vested in the Ibadhite movement. Yet, although the *al-Nahḍa* movement had seemed capable of realisation forty years earlier, it is hard to see how it could still be possible after the reinforcement of the British presence in Oman.

[Abū Bashir] Muḥammad al-Sālmī, the son, who was the historian of this revolution and one of its leaders, reports that his father, 'Abd Allāh al-Sālmī, who had close links with sultan Fayṣal, asked the sultan to change his attitude to the British. This move by al-Sālmī has to be understood as a tradition among the *Ibāḍis*: a warning by the *'ulamā'* prior to declaring a forthcoming revolution. But Fayṣal, who had lost all hope of independence, ignored the gesture.

'Abd Allāh al-Sālmī, who had lost his sight at the age of sixteen but was not really handicapped by his infirmity (he has produced remarkable literary and juridical work), then started to prepare the revolution with all the conviction and strength of mind he was capable of, constantly repeating his famous slogan: 'Liberty is not achieved without blood and tears. Fear is the curse of life and doubt in victory is defeat.'[503]

In the manner of *al-'ālim* Sa'īd bin Khalfān al-Khalīlī at the time of 'Azzān's revolution and inspired by his example, al-Sālmī played the part of guide, unifier and spiritual father of this *Nahḍa*. Hence his nickname of father of the 'Omani *Nahḍa* of the twentieth century'.

Moreover, al-Sālmī envisaged the spread of this *Nahḍa* in the Arab world through the *Ibāḍi 'ulamā'*. Indeed, according to Wilkinson, a form of pan-Ibadhism was developing as well, in the sense that the Ibadhite communities were starting to show much greater interaction with each other and to develop a common approach.[504]

So al-Sālmī had decided to make the pilgrimage to Mecca and take advantage of it to contact the Ibadhite *'ulamā'* from Algeria and Tunisia, notably Muḥammad bin Yusuf Aṭfayyish. He was hoping to inform them of the imminence of the Omani revolution and garner their moral and material support. In fact this period was marked by the spread of *Ibāḍi* literature and saw the development of co-operation with the *'ulamā'* of the Maghreb and the Mashreq, tightening links so as to ensure support for the *Ibāḍi* project in Oman.

But in view of the gravity of the internal situation in Oman, al-Sālmī was unable to undertake his journey; instead, he set out on a tour in the interior of Oman so as to contact the rulers of the tribes and prepare them for revolution. Very diplomatically, his first visit was to the 'prince of the green mountain', Sheikh Ḥamir bin Nāṣer al-Nabhāni, the Ghafirite chief of Tanuf, a historic town close to Nazwa. This visit was particularly significant because the Ghafirite tribes had not played a very important part during the *imāma* of 'Azzān ibn Qays

(1869–1871), who had tended to favour the Hanawites; the absence of support from the Ghafirite tribes had been one of the main causes of the fall of that *imāma*. Al-Sālmī, who understood the tribal mentality, was intent on eliminating this imbalance by a gesture that al-Nabhāni was not slow to appreciate. A parallel move consisted in reactivating the links with the Hanawite tribes. Indeed, al-Sālmī had made contact with their famous chief, ʿIssa bin Ṣāleḥ al-Ḥārthi, who had been hesitant about giving his support to the future *imāma*.

The imāma *of Sālem bin Rashed al-Kharūsi (1913–1919)*

In 1913, a group of *ʿulamāʾ* and tribal chiefs met in the town of Tanuf. This gathering had just one purpose: the election of an *imām*. And so ʿAbd Allāh al-Sālmī proposed the candidacy of *al-ʿalim Sālim bin* Rashed al-Kharūsi. But al-Kharūsi, who was not expecting this proposal, attempted to excuse himself: 'I came to give my bay ʿa rather than to receive it'.[505] However, he had no right to refuse this candidacy, nor, from a doctrinal point of view or in the eyes of tradition, was it in his power to do so. To refuse the possibility of being elected was to refuse the trust that the *ʿulamāʾ* had invested in him. Added to which, such a refusal might also divide the ranks of the Muslims.[506]

Al-Kharūsi had no choice but to accept this *bayʿa*. He came from a family which had produced *ʿulamāʾ*, *ʿqāḍīs* and *imāms* throughout Omani history. So the *bayʿa* took place in the *al-Sharīa* mosque in the same town of Tanuf, according to the traditional forms. All the *ʿulamāʾ* and some of the tribal chiefs took part. *Al-ʿālim* bin Khamīs bin Masʿūd al-Māliki and *al-ʿālim* ʿAbd Allāh bin Muḥammad bin Ruzayq al-Azkāwi were charged with reading the *bayʿa* and supervising the ensuing measures.[507] This *bayʿa* was one of *al-ḍuhūr*.[508] The new *imāma* was proclaimed and Nazwa, the *Ibāḍi* spiritual centre, was declared its capital.

The programme of al-Kharūsi's *imāma* consisted of four points: to put an end to the system of the sultanate; to put an end to the presence and influence of the British; to work toward the unification of the country and last, the restoration of the *imāma* over the whole of the country. In fact, in modern history, all the *Ibāḍi imāmas* had almost identical programmes; they differed only in time and context.

About a month after this *bayʿa*, Sheikh ʿIssa bin Ṣāleḥ al-Ḥārthi, accompanied by some chiefs of the Hanawite tribes, arrived in Tanuf, a region under the Ghafirite tribes, and gave the new *imām* his approval. It is thanks to al-Sālmī and al-Kharūsi that, after fifty years, an agreement could be reached between the two chiefs of the hostile Ghafirite and Hanawite tribes. And so the revolution was assured of one of the most important conditions for its success: its unity. Omani society seemed thus to have regained its unity even before the *imāma* was established. This revolution had the benefit of conditions that had been absent in the days of ʿAzzān ibn Qays.

Curiously, after giving his *bayʿa*, ʿIssa bin Ṣāleḥ al-Ḥārthi proposed mediation between the *imām* and sultan Fayṣal. According to Muḥammad al-Sālmī, this totally unexpected proposal could have spread despondency among the imamites at a time when the revolution was only just beginning. But it was categorically rejected both in form and content by the *'ulamā'*. What is more, it aroused both indignation and amazement.

In line with tradition, *imām* al-Kharūsi sent an official letter meanwhile to sultan Fayṣal, notifying him of the setting up of the *imāma* and asking him to put an end to British influence and to apply the Islamic laws of *al-sharī'a* in the country. In other words, asking him to withdraw from power. At the same time the *imām* sent emissaries and letters to the tribal chiefs all over the country to inform them of the establishment of the *imāma* and obtain their approval. The majority of the chiefs responded positively and gave him their *bay'a*. In a short while, almost all the main towns had assured the *imām* of their loyalty; just a few towns still influenced by the power of Muscat refused.

In a summary of the situation, the British annual report notes that the uprising of the tribes in Oman under the leadership of the 'so-called *imām* of Tanuf' Sālem bin Rashed al-Kharūsi had eclipsed all the other events in the tribal history of Oman for the year in question. This uprising could be laid fairly and squarely at the door of the preaching of the principal *Ibāḍi* sheikh, ʿAbd Allāh bin Ḥumayd al-Sālmī.[509]

There was evidence of general support for the *imām*, especially in the towns, which, one after the other, had given him their approval. This gave the British cause for alarm, the more so as figures close to the sultan, like Sayf bin Sulṭān al-Bū Saʿīdi and his brother Hamud had sought refuge with the *imām* and offered him their *bay'a*, even asking him to forgive them.[510]

'On the 2nd July 1913, Major Murphy of the Intelligence Department arrived from Bushehr to study the situation with a view to making arrangements, should necessity arise, for landing British troops for the defence of Maṭraḥ and Muscat. On 6th July, His Highness the Sultan appealed to the political agent for assistance.'[511]

But these measures did not seriously hamper the progress of the imamite forces. And about two months after the *imāma* was declared the Izki region fell to them, followed by the al-'Awabi region and their *wālis* came and sided with the *imām*. Finally, in August 1913, the strategic region of Samayl fell into the hands of the imamites. This radically changed the balance of power in favour of the *imāma*: since then the authority of the sultan was restricted just to Muscat, Maṭraḥ and a few nearby coastal towns. Almost the whole of the country was now under the authority of the *imāma*. In order for it once more to become the historic reality of the Omanis just one last stage remained: the liberation of the capital.

Faced with this situation, Great Britain realised that the fall of Muscat would mean the end of her influence in Oman; she regrouped her forces round the town, determined to save her last bastion. Furthermore the British resident in Muscat sent a warning and threatening letter to the *imām*, who was engaged in preparing his final assault.

The *imām* replied:

> You know very well that the affairs of Oman have always belonged to the ʿulamā'. And if the king [the sultan] clashed with the 'ulamā', he would be removed from power in the Islamic state . . . rejected by the Muslims . . . Fayṣal was found to be at odds with the Ibadhi code and he refused to stand down.

> You must stop importuning the Muslims and you must not attack us. God will help us against those who attack us.[512]

At this juncture, on 4 October 1913, sultan Fayṣal died. So ended a reign of twenty-five years, as stormy as it was difficult for what Landen this 'unhappy' ruler. On 8 October, Fayṣal's son, Taymūr, then aged 17, was enthroned as the new sultan.

It is worth reporting the opinion of the British on the subject of the late sultan Fayṣal. In a letter dated 1 January 1914, to his superior, the British historian Lorimer, who was political resident in the Gulf at Bushehr, Major Ronx, then the British resident in Muscat, wrote:

> A much abused man while he lived, Syud Faisal bin Turki has, in many quarters, been deeply regretted since his death. He was undoubtedly a weak ruler but his pleasant genial manners and accessibility had won him some popularity. He never wanted personal courage and was undoubtedly kindly and humane.[513]

The testimony is certainly very accurate but rather belated. Because in spite of all these qualities, the English had not treated Fayṣal as they should. As for the claim that he was weak, it was certainly more due to British pressure, which had succeeded in breaking his will, than to his own temperament.

Another authorised opinion of him deserves mention here that of the *Ibāḍi 'ulamā'*. Although they considered Fayṣal to be a ruler rejected by the Omanis, al-Sālmī, the moral authority in the country, described him as an honourable, wise and courageous man.[514]

Like his father, the young sultan Taymūr came to power when his country was once more plunged in a grave and prolonged internal crisis. But his fate was probably even more dramatic than his father's for he would have to face a revolution that would last seven years and determine the modern history of his country. This revolution was to be the longest in the Arab history of the period. The economic situation of the sultanate was deteriorating rapidly, the state treasury was empty and the unpaid soldiers were demoralised to the point of threatening to join the imamites.

The British authorities understood something of the new sultan's situation:

> Syud Taymur has inherited a throne in which his power extends only so far as the guns of British ships can reach . . . Cut off from the Arab tribes by a rebellion that was in force before he came into his own, living in a capital of which the population consists mainly of British subjects, Baluchis and negroes, and in which there are no leaders of Arab opinion.[515]

As for his character and personal traits, the report continues:

> On the other hand, he gives promise of good judgement and is possessed of sound common sense – when he is left to himself – which, with maturity should make him a better ruler than either his grandfather or his father, provided that he is left with something to rule.[516]

The question was precisely to know to what extent Great Britain would leave the new sultan something to rule and with what margin of responsibility and freedom; his father and grandfather had known more constraints than independence.

Meanwhile, in January 1914, the *imāma* lost one of its most eminent spiritual chiefs, the leader of its Nahḍa, sheikh [Nūr al-Dīn] ʿAbd Allāh al-Sālmī. In him, Oman also lost a great historian, described by the Russian Bondarevsky as the father of Omani history. Although he died at the age of only forty, his short life had been remarkably fruitful. He left some twenty volumes dealing with the *fiqh* (Islamic law) or with literature, including two on the history of Oman. His life was marked by unremitting struggle in the service of Oman, its freedom and the *Ibāḍi* cause. With him, the revolution mourned its first great loss; his absence would be felt particularly in political decision-making and the direction and even the outcome of the revolution. Al-Sālmī was not replaced until 1915: the leaders of the *imāma* then elected *al-ʿālim* ʿAmer bin Khamīs al-Māliki to the post of 'director of the affairs of the *imāma*', a hitherto unknown title.

The First World War and the imāma *on trial*

Sultan Taymūr, urged on by England which was then preoccupied with the First World War, attempted at first to enter into serious negotiations with the imamites. It proved fruitless. Sheikh Ḥamdan bin Zāyed al-Bū Falaḥ, the governor of Abu Dhabi. Then offered himself as an intermediary between the sultan and the *imām*. On 9 December 1914, a meeting took place between the *imām*'s representative, ʿIssa bin Ṣāleḥ al-Ḥārthi, and sheikh Ḥamdan bin Zāyed in the al-Sīb region about 70 km from Muscat, which was to become the permanent site of all future negotiations. Ḥamdan succeeded in persuading al-Ḥārthi to accompany him to the sultan in Muscat to settle the preliminaries of a possible accord. Despite initial hesitations by the leaders of the *imāma*, a new interview was agreed on for the negotiation of this accord.

At the time of the meeting with the sultan in Muscat, an eight-point proposal was worked out; it was to be presented to the *imām* in the hope of winning his consent. Among these points it was envisaged that the *imām* would not move outside the limits of his present territory and that he hand over the fortresses of Bidbid and Samayl to the sultan; that the sultan should give up nothing of his claim to the 'kingdom of Oman' in favour of the Engish; that the sultan should not shelter any malefactor trying to escape from the justice of the *imāma* and that he show no unfriendly intentions toward the *imāma*. A fifth point stipulated that the sultan must administer justice according to Islamic *sharīʿa*, and refrain from all oppression. Finally it was proposed that customs duties imposed by Muscat on the export of dates and agricultural produce should not exceed 5 per cent of their value and that imports destined for the *imāma* should not be subject to examination by the authorities in Muscat.[517]

Most of the points of this accord were favourable to the *imāma*, yet the *imām* rejected them. On the first point, he declared that the Samayl region had been 'liberated', that henceforth it was part of the territory of the Muslims (the people), and that as such it could not be handed over to the *jabābira* (unconstitutional rulers). So this first attempt ended in failure. But the negotiation had scored a success for the *imāma* which was now recognised as a reality to be reckoned with.

However, an interview of sheikhs 'Issa bin Ṣāleḥ and Ḥamdan bin Zāyed in Muscat had sparked a dispute among the *'ulamā'*. For the English were then trying to circumvent al-Ḥārthi in order to sow discord between the Ghafirites and the Hanawites in the hope of driving a wedge between the revolutionary leaders. In fact, al-Ḥārthi had been very well received in Muscat, where he had even received certain gifts from the sultan. The British report interpreted this as the germ of an attempt to detach the Hanawite tribes from the *imāma*.

In parallel with these negotiations, military confrontation between the two parties was fierce. In 1914, the imamites had launched a first attack on the capital but without winning a significant victory. In January 1915, they returned to the attack, this time with 3000 men, but in vain. Their lack of military experience when faced with well equipped British and Indian soldiers caused the loss of 350 men as against seven dead and fifteen wounded in the ranks of the British.[518]

Moreover in January *imām* al-Kharūsi received a letter from the British consul in Muscat, Colonel Robert Arthur Edward Baine, who addressed him as 'sheikh' and not as *'imām'*, so marking the English determination to avoid recognising the *imāma* as an independent entity:

> Peace is one of the primary pillars of the Sharī'a of God (…) I wish to advise you that you should not delay informing us fully about your intentions regarding this matter, so that we can understand whether there is a serious problem that requires a solution. I look forward to your reply.[519]

In August 1915, a first official meeting between the imamites and the British took place at al-Sīb. Al-Ḥārthi and the *imām*'s *qāḍī*, sheikh Sa'īd bin Nāṣer represented the *imāma*. Baine led the British delegation. The aim of this interview was to study the new set up, the *imām*'s proposals and the latest proposals from Muscat.

This meeting might have brought the two parties to the threshold of an accord but Baine insisted that the imamite forces had to withdraw from the strategic region of Samayl. Al-Ḥārthi almost accepted, but Sa'īd bin Nāṣer rejected this condition categorically and the negotiations broke down. Great Britain, being well aware of the economic situation and of the conditions of life in the territory of the *imāma*, therefore resolved to apply a policy with three facets: first to subject the interior of the country to an economic blockade, then to play the tribal card and lastly to gain time. Later, Major Cox, who replaced Baine, sent a letter to the Government of India, in which he explained: 'This line of action was intended to await the early death of the imam, so as then to come to a financial reconciliation with Hamyar.'[520]

This last sentence seems to suggest that the English were setting up a plan to assassinate the *imām*, who was neither ill nor old. So just why should they expect him to die?

However that may be, the general situation was continuing to deteriorate, especially in the interior of Oman, which was beginning to suffer from the economic blockade. Time was decidedly on the side of the English strategy. In this difficult period, however, the Omanis closed ranks round their *imāma*. Figures close to the sultan even joined the *imām*.

To increase pressure on the *imāma* and following the advice of the British resident, the sultan raised taxation on agricultural produce from the interior: from 5 to 25 per cent on dates and up to 50 per cent on pomegranates. This decision had major consequences in the long term. The English were, indeed, well aware that 'it is on the export of their famous dates and pomegranates that the Omanis exist'.[521]

As predicted, this measure paralysed the economy and the commercial activity of the *imāma*: it was the start of a period of strangulation for the Omanis. Inflation became more pronounced; there was a shortage of money and in 1918 Muscat had to ban the movement of funds out of the country, which only aggravated the situation. Referring to a British report, Landen estimated that the losses then suffered by the Omanis far exceeded the mortality from the outbreak of cholera in 1818–1819 (20 000 victims).[522] To cap it all, the trade deficit had reached a sum of approximately 300 000 sterling; as for the Indian traders in muscat, they had shut up shop and left the country.[523]

The new British strategy (1919)

During three years, there were no significant changes in the general situation of the country. Great Britain had however started to put into action her post-war policy, just after her victory in the First World War.

As far as Muscat was concerned, one of the facets of this policy was a project for reforming the administration and maintaining security so as to strengthen the system of the sultanate, which was already weakened by a revolution that would soon enter its seventh year.

Early in 1919, Great Britain set about finalising a solution with a settlement that would be likely to be accepted by the leaders of the *imāma*. More important still, she was ready to make concessions in favour of the *imāma* and appeared to be disposed to recognise the *imām* as a moral authority in the country. A report confirms this:

> The situation was discussed with considerable frankness by both sides. The proposal of the Political Agent that the Sultan should be the temporal and the imam the spiritual head was, however, immediately negatived by the Omani Chiefs. It was realised that a settlement on the basis of the status quo was the only possible solution, the Omanis ruling their country and the Sultan his, with freedom of travel and intercourse and a guarantee on the part of both sides against attack.[524]

So Great Britain made up her mind to bring about the splitting of Oman with no reference anywhere to the opinion of the sultan. All that is known is that he made it plain later that he was certainly not in favour of such a solution. But it was not in his power to change or influence a decision, even though it concerned the future of his own country.

Regarding Franco-Omani relations, which now existed only in form (especially after the decision of the Hague tribunal in 1904), on 24 February 1919, France sent M. Lecoutour to fill the post of consul held by M. Jeannier who had died on 23 September 1918 after eight years' service in Muscat. He had in fact been all but forgotten.

The new consul, like his predecessor, enjoyed no attributions and it could be said that his presence in Muscat was virtually useless. After obtaining an audience to present his letters of accreditation to the sultan, he wrote an important report describing the ruler's difficult situation:

> He spoke to me of France in particularly friendly terms (...) I had no difficulty in the course of the conversations I had with His Highness in discerning that the sultan was far from satisfied with the political situation in Muscat, which is more precarious than ever.

And in another paragraph the consul added:

> It seemed to me that His Highness saw in my arrival in Muscat a token of his security from the point of view of maintaining his independence, but, in the absence of instructions from Your Excellency, I avoided replying to certain tendentious questions from His Highness and I remained absolutely reserved, as I was bound to under the circumstances.[525]

The tenor of this report confirms shall at least that the sultan had understood perfectly well that his country had fallen definitively into the hands of Great Britain and that he himself was sultan only in name. But what Taymūr appeared to be unaware of was that the Franco-British alliance during the war had changed the balance of power and the politico-strategic position. Besides, at that stage, colonial France no longer looked on Oman as an independent state, as had been the case during the Revolution and then under Napoleon I. And the sultan, who had realised it only belatedly, it seems, was trying even so to find some way out of his sultanate's historic impasse.

Meanwhile, following the rejection of the new British proposals by the leaders of the *imāma*, Major Haworth had sent a letter in May 1919 to the *imām* inviting him to reopen negotiations. The tone of the letter contained a veiled threat. It was the language of a colonialist and a conqueror. On account of its importance, it is worth quoting several paragraphs at length:

> As you know, and thanks to God, Great Britain and her allies have been victorious over the enemy, who has surrendered. We are today occupying Germany, Austria, Bulgaria and Turkey. Germany has surrendered its fleet and most of her ships are in our custody in England. The situation in Germany itself is one of confusion and famine. We have also occupied

> Istanbul from the Turks; and, as you know, Baghdad has been in our hands for quite some time now.

The text goes on to spell out plans and policies for the Arab countries:

> We are now installing in Baghdad and Basra an Arab government; we shall put the whole of Iraq under an Arab government and will not permit the Turks to rule it any more. Our friend and ally Al-Sharif Hussein, in the Hijaz has become very strong and has been named as the king of the Hijjaz. According to the conditions of the truce which we have granted the Turks, the city of Al Madina al-Monawara is now in the hands of the King of Al-Hijaz. In the Yemen also, Saïd Pasha has surrendered and he is now a prisoner in our hands. (...) I am writing you now these lines to advise you of our wish to help form an Arab government in all the Arab lands to rule according to their own traditions.[526]

Concerning the relations between Great Britain and Muscat more particularly, the letter indicated that an unstable situation in Muscat had obliged the British government in 1895 to notify the tribal rulers that she would support the sultan. To that end, Haworth wrote, we supported Turki, and after him Fayṣal and at present we shall support Taymūr. And he held out the threat:

> We have 500 000 trained soldiers who have now terminated their operations in Iraq and we have no need for them there. A few thousand of them would have sufficed to occupy the whole of Oman had we wished to harm you.[527]

Haworth added in conclusion that Great Britain controlled the coastline and could at any time impose high duties on merchandise 'destined for or coming from your country and you could do nothing to stop us'. Then he ends with these words:

> You also know that the control of the seas is in our hands. So, if you imagine that you can become our enemy, then we shall not permit anything such as rice, wheat or clothing to be sold to you and will not permit you to sell your dates, knowing that all your trade is with our countries.[528]

As can be seen, Major Haworth's line of argument spared no kind of threat in order to achieve his ends, including that of outright war and even the possibility of starving the population if necessary. Everything was in place to bring the *imāma* to its knees.

In August 1919, Major Wingate, who had just finished his mission in India and was on his way to take up a new one in Iraq, was ordered to change his destination and travel with all haste to Muscat to occupy the post of consul and general political resident. It seems this decision was taken after hearing news that sultan Taymūr bin Fayṣal, was in fact intending to step down, or, more accurately, to abdicate. The man best qualified to deal with such a crisis was Major Wingate, an experienced soldier and politician. Indeed, since the revolution of 1913, Great Britain had changed her political residents and consuls in Muscat fifteen times. In 1916 alone she had transferred eight.

As soon as he had arrived, Major Wingate had contacted the leaders of the *imāma* and asked for an interview with al-Ḥārthi. Wingate was well informed about the situation in Oman; he knew that the revolution, about to enter its seventh year, was having to face a dramatic economic crisis. And even if the *Ibāḍi* *'ulamā'* and their disciples, armed with their moral conviction and enthusiasm for the *Ibāḍi* alternative, could still put up with such a situation, it was very unlikely that the rest of the population could endure it for very long. In a case like that, it was customary for the tribal question once more to become a deciding factor. Wingate wanted to play the Hanawite card; they were led by al-Ḥārthi, whose interests appeared to be starting to diverge from those of the ongoing revolution.

The report of the French consul Lecoutour on 18 May 1919 indicates that, for his part, sheikh 'Issa bin Ṣāleḥ al-Ḥārthi intended to finish with Bedouin resistance once and for all and establish his undisputed authority at the same time as that of the sultan in Oman.[529] 'Bedouin resistance' here meant the imamite revolution.

Moreover, the English did not have to wait much longer for the death of the *imām*. In 1919, just after the signing of the treaty of al-Sīb, *imām* Sālem bin Rashed al-Kharūsi was killed. The assassin was a Bedouin fugitive who had dodged the justice of the *imāma* and belonged to the Hanawite tribes of al-Wahāyibah, dwellers in the territory of the sultan. The death of this *imām* meant the end of a life of struggle crowned by seven years at the head of the revolution. Al-Kharūsi had been the leader of the third *Ibāḍi* revolution, the longest in modern history. It was named 'the revolution of *imām* al-Kharūsi'.

The leaders of the *imāma* tried in vain to capture the assassin. They asked the authorities in Muscat for his extradition but of course to no avail. The English documents, incidentally, give no details on this point, and merely state: 'As the murderer had by this time escaped to Trucial Oman, nothing (...) could be done and the affair died down.'[530]

Of course, the region of '*Sāḥel Oman*' was directly under the control of the British authority and that is why the author of the report thought the affair had died down. This statement amounts to an admission of responsibility.

But the revolution had not only lost a great *imām*; another figure of importance, sheikh Ḥamyār bin Nāṣer al-Nabhāni, died about the same time, probably in April 1920. He was the chief of the Ghafirite grouping and the military head of the revolution from the start. The British political resident, delighted by the news of his death, wrote cynically '... the gods had fought against the Imam by removing sheikh Hamyar bin Naser al-Nabhani'.[531]

In this exceptional case, the son of the latter sheikh. Sulaymān bin Ḥamyār, aged fourteen, replaced him. But both his age and his personality proved a handicap to the unity of his tribes and, obviously, to the unity of the revolution. The death of his father aroused discord among the Ghafirites and this would be reflected in the progress of the revolution.

The *imāma* of Muḥammad bin ʿAbdullah al-khalīlī (1919–1954)

Immediately after the death of al-Kharūsi, the *'ulamā'* elected *al-'ālim* Muḥammad ʿAbdullah al-khalīlī as their new *imām*. *Al-'ālim* ʿAmer bin Khamīs al-Māliki, the head of the *qāḍīs* of the *imāma* had presented the new *imām* and *al-'ālim* Mājed bin Khamis al-ʿAbri, a former soldier of ʿAzzān's revolution, seconded him, then the other *'ulamā'* gave their approval. The new *imām* was one of the grandsons of the famous *'ālim* Saʿīd bin Khalfān al-Khalīlī, the guiding light of the *imāma* of ʿAzzān ibn Qays (1869–1871).

Al-khalīlī was a remarkable and capable man but nevertheless, the disappearance of *imām* al-Kharūsi had been deeply felt amongst the leaders of the *imāma*. For al-Kharūsi embodied the symbol of national unity, especially since the revolution had entered its critical phase. So al-Ḥārthi and bin Ḥamyār, the chiefs of the tribes, soon made clear their differences, not to say discordancy, with the new *imām*. It seemed as if two political lines were emerging: that of the *'ulamā'*, who favoured the continuation of the revolution and that of the tribes who could no longer see any point in it and were seeking a compromise.

At this juncture, in March 1919, sultan Taymūr decided to visit India. The journey was described as official. However, the sultan had his reasons for deciding to leave his country at that decisive moment, reasons that would only be revealed later. Major Wingate accompanied him. Before his departure, the sultan had charged the *wāli* of Maṭraḥ, Muḥammad bin Ḥamad bin Nāṣer, with the affairs of the country and Captain Mac Collum received the duties of minister. He was the first British minister in the country and in fact it was he who was really responsible for its affairs.

The treaty of al-Sīb (1920)

As soon as he got back, Wingate decided, with the consent of the new minister, to step up the economic pressure on the *imāma* with the aim of forcing it to accept his conditions, that is to say, his new policy, still unofficial. He himself reports on this subject:

> There appeared to be one method by which the Omanis could be brought to see reason. They had to export their dates to live. If the export of their dates could be made impossible, or at least very costly, and they could not retaliate, then they might be preparsed to meet me and to talk for a reasonable settlement.[532]

In other words the imamites would be constrained to negotiate. For these reasons, Wingate decided to return to India and get an official mandate from the sultan. In fact he contrived to be delegated total power 'I succeeded in persuading him to give me carte blanche',[533] he notes on this point.

So he put taxes on dates from the territories of the *imāma* at an unheard of rate of 50 per cent. This measure, coinciding with a structural change inside the *imāma*, upset the political balance. After a series of correspondances, the *imām* decided to open negotiations to find a settlement in order, he said, to spare the Omani people and the country tragedies and disasters.

In September 1920 the two parties met at al-Sīb. The Omani delegation was made up of several eminent *'ulamā'*, including al-Kindi, one of Oman's theologians. Al-Ḥārthi, who was in charge of the external affairs of the *imāma*, was the head of the delegation. Wingate, who at the same time represented sultan Taymūr, led the British delegation.

After two long days of bargaining, the two parties reached an agreement in principle on the terms by which the two belligerants should cease all meddling in each other's affairs. As a consequence, Wingate agreed to reduce the duties on the export of dates from the *imāma*. However, the negotiations came up against a basic problem raised by the English. Wingate rejected the demand of the Omani delegation, which wanted the final treaty to be signed by both the sultan and the *imām* of the Muslims. Wingate gave his reasons thus:

> This was fatal, and I knew that I could not possibly agree to it on behalf of the sultan, because it would mean that the sultan acknowledged another ruler, and a ruler who was already an elected spiritual leader and admitted temporal representative of the tribes. From that acknowledgement it was only one step further for spiritual leadership and temporal representation of the tribes to develop into a claim for the spiritual and temporal leadership of all Oman.[534]

The problem was very real. But, curiously, an analogous solution had already been contemplated by the English, namely that the sultan should be the temporal governor and the *imām* the religious, spiritual and moral authority in the unified country. This solution had been very important in its time. Remember that the imām himself had rejected this English proposal. But if the apparently much weakened revolution had not sufficient weight to impose its will, it is clear, on the other hand, that Wingate's game made no sense. Let us see how he tried to manoeuvre in this negotiation. He tells the story himself:

> Ehtisham whispered to me in English: 'Tell them the story of the Prophet and his negotiations with the people of Mecca'(...). So I told them the story, which of course they knew. The Prophet at Hadaibiyah had negotiated an agreement with the people of Mecca and had then attempted to sign the agreement as between the people of Mecca and 'Mohammed, the Prophet of God'. The delegates from Mecca had pointed out very reasonably that if Mohammed was the Prophet of God, there was no object in signing a peace with him in that capacity. How could the Prophet of God be a party to an agreement with mere mortals? The Prophet saw the point and his part in the agreement was as 'Mohammed, son of Abdullah'.

Wingate adds that after these conversations the sheikhs ended by smiling. The word *imām*, therefore, was not used in the text of the agreement, which was a simple statement of the conditions arrived at between the government of the sultan and ʿIssa bin Ṣāleḥ, the representative of the tribes of Oman.[535]

This solution, which seemed to Wingate to be a brilliant politico-legalistic trick, would nevertheless not really have the outcome anticipated by the English. But meanwhile, the treaty was to be definitively ratified by the sultan and by the *imām*, which would confirm the separation and independence of the two parties: sultanate and *imāma*.

On 25 September, the two parties in question arrived at a final formula for the treaty, afterwards known as the treaty of al-Sīb, which put an end to the revolution. The text follows:

> Treaty of al-Sīb, 1920
>
> In the name of God, the Compassionate, the Merciful.
>
> This is the peace agreed upon between the Government of sultan Taymūr ibn Fayṣal, and sheikh ʿIsa ibn Salih bin ʿAli, on behalf of the people of Oman, whose names are signed hereto, through the mediation of Mr. Wingate, I, C.S., political agent and consul for Great Britain in Muscat, who is empowered by his Government in this respect and to be an intermediary between the two parties. Of the conditions set forth below, four pertain to the governemnt of the sultanand to the people of Oman; those concerning the people of Oman are:
>
> Firstly: not more than 5% shall be taken from goods, coming from Oman to Muscat or Matraḥ, or Sur, or the rest of the towns on the coast.
>
> Secondly: all the people of Oman shall enjoy security and freedom in all the towns on the coast.
>
> Thirdly: All restrictions upon everyone entering and leaving Muscat and Matraḥ and all the coastal towns shall be lifted.
>
> Fourthly: the Government of the Sultan shall not grant asylum to any criminal fleeing from the justice of the people of Oman. It shall return him to them if they request it to do so and shall not interfere in their internal affairs.
>
> The four conditions pertaining to the Government of the Sultan are the following:
>
> Firstly: all the tribes and sheikhs shall be at peace with the Sultan. They shall not attack the towns of the coast nor interfere in his Government.
>
> Secondly: all those going to Oman on lawful business and for commercial affairs shall be free. There shall be no restrictions on their commerce and they shall enjoy security.
>
> Thirdly: they shall expel and grant no asylum to any wrongdoer or criminal fleeing to them.
>
> Fourthly: the claims of merchants and others against the people of Oman shall be heard and decided on the basis of justice, according to the law of Islam. Written and signed in the town of Sib on 11 Muharram of the year 1339 of the Hegira (September 25th 1920).

> In my capacity as deputy for the imam Muslimin Mohammed bin Abdullah al-Khailiī, I declare that I have accepted the conditions laid down therein by virtue of an authorisation from the imam al-Musliiīn.
>
> Written by 'Issa bin Saleh and Suleiman bin Himyar in their handwriting'.[536]

The imām had sent a copy for ratification. It was returned to Wingate on 7 October 1920 with this note from the imām: 'I have completed what Sheikh Issa bin Saleh has done on my behalf regarding these provisions. Certified by Imam al-Muslimin Muhammad bin Abdullah [al-Khalili] in his own handwriting.'[537]

Another copy had to be ratified by the sultan, while he was staying in India; it was sent back to Wingate in Muscat on 18 October of the same year. It is known that Taymūr was not in complete agreement with the solution adopted. But he found no fault with it.

So, after seven years of war, the revolution of 1913 ended with an official division of Oman into two quasi independent entities: the *imāma* of Oman in the interior, and the sultanate of Muscat on the coast. Wingate makes this comment on the outcome of this treaty: 'The Omanis have attained in their own eyes complete independence and practically they are correct, though the Sultan may assert that they only have home rule.'[538]

Be that as it may, with this treaty orchestrated and imposed by the English, the two systems recognised each other. From now on, Oman had two historic realities. And although they had only accepted the two powers of these systems as 'semi-independent', the English tacitly recognised their independence.

But this treaty contained serious legal defects: it did not define the territory of the two parties and no clause broached the question of external relations. A territorial limit, although vague, was nevertheless recognised in a so-called traditional way; in effect about 75 per cent of the territories were under the authority of the *imāma* at the time of the signing of the treaty. Despite its shortcomings, the treaty of al-Sīb was to remain a historic treaty; it would lead to a very lively politico-juridical debate at the United Nations in the 1960s.

There is reason to believe, in fact, that the fuzziness surrounding the demarcation of the two entities was not due to Wingate's negligence; we have here, on the contrary, a vacuum purposely preserved by him for later use. In a strategic analysis of the formulation of this treaty, Wingate explains that the more development there was in the coastal region, the more the interior would be isolated. Thus the *imāma* would no longer pose a future threat to the sultanate. So it was clear that British strategy now aimed at isolating the Ibadhite movement in the interior.

Yet according to Wilkinson, Wingate 'had no illusions as to what he had achieved'. Wilkinson refers to the report written by Wingate himself on 20 October 1920, in which he expresses himself unambiguously:

> Our interest was conceived only in relation to ourselves, it paid no attention to the particular political and social conditions of the country and its rulers. By bribing the sultans to get them to apply unpopular measures that

> benefited nobody but us, and by allowing them to rule badly and unopposed, it did more to alienate the interior and prevent the sultans re-establishing their authority than all the rest put together.[539]

This is the confession of a pillar of colonial politics and the only real author of the treaty, a confession that only confirms our analysis: this treaty, which was supposed to put an end to the Omani revolution under British arbitration, was actually organising a fragmented status quo favourable only to the interests of the colonial power.

The abdication of Sultan Taymūr bin Fayṣal and the isolation of the imāma

Sultan Taymūr's visit to India in March 1920, six months before the signing of the treaty of al-Sīb, was not a 'normal official visit', it was more like voluntary exile, an emigration of opposition, a kind of rejection, not just of his throne but of a country that was no longer his. For as soon as he arrived in India, Taymūr made a verbal request to the British government to be allowed to abdicate. After a reign of only seven years, the sultan was about to carry out an act that his father had wished to accomplish, but from which he was dissuaded, perhaps under duress. This phenomenon of the local rulers' disgust with power, incidentally hirtherto almost unheard of, was repeated in Oman from father to son, due to the English presence.

Such a decision was undoubtedly tantamount to accusing Great Britain of total responsibility for the situation and dramatic fate of Oman. This gesture of repudiation, painful for a sultan, pointed unequivocally to the historic culpability of the colonial power. The news, kept secret incidentally until today, had none the less shocked the British authority in India, in London and elsewhere, an authority generally known for its restraint and *sang froid*. Faced with this unexpected situation at a critical time for Oman, the English, perhaps for the first time, were at a loss as to what to do, particularly as the lawful heir of sultan Taymūr, his son Saʿīd, was only 11 years old.

Great Britain did not take the sultan's decision to abdicate seriously at first and was content initially to reply to Taymūr that there was no objection to his staying in India another three months before returning to Muscat in June. Such was Great Britain's hold over the sultan that she dared to decide for him how long he should stay in India and even the date of his return to Muscat. Yet a vast amount of correspondance, reports and official discussions between the British residents in Muscat, Bushehr and Bagdad had been exchanged meanwhile with the British government in India on one side and the Home Office of London on the other. The British officials were trying to answer the question: 'what should our policy be in the event of abdication?' It was a very real dilemma.

Anxious not to be outstripped by events, Wingate composed a detailed report dated 28 April 1920, in which he tried to outline future British policy in the region. This text was sent to the 'civil commissioner' in Baghdad. It started with this appraisal of the personality of Taymūr:

> He inherited his father's absurd ideas about his position and his independence, largely the result of the Anglo-French position in Muscat. Tired of the whole affair and especially of Muscat, he has however now definitely abandoned these ideas and thrown himself unreservedly on our mercy.[540]

As for the policy to pursue, the report envisaged first, the need to form a provisional government to replace the sultan during the minority of his son, Sa'īd, and manage the internal and external affairs of Oman. Wingate viewed this provisional government as a council of regency, which would consist of three or five members, including a British counsellor, invested with the power of veto, to whom the council would have to refer for all major decisions.

Oddly enough, Wingate saw no negative effects from a possible abdication, since, in his view, the sultan was by no means popular. He suggested, on the other hand, that the education of Sa'īd, the future sultan, be taken seriously.[541] But as to the rest, Wingate attached little importance to the profound motives for the sultan's abdication; he made no allusion to his difficulty in enduring the situation in Oman nor did he refer to the fact that the title of sultan had been deprived of all political and practical content.

Yet the situation in Oman had become truly catastrophic, to such an extent that the capital had been emptied of its Omani inhabitants, who had decided to leave their houses and possessions and emigrate. The sultan remained there alone with a few close associates exercising government over foreign communities. How could anyone fail to understand his scruples about continuing to reign under those conditions?

The French commander of the sloop *Altaïr*, which arrived in Muscat on 20 May 1920, sent this description of the state of the Omani capital in a report to Paris:

> It is well known that Oman has long been subject to English pressure, but what is now becoming clear is that this pressure is taking the form of a complete clamp down on the sultan and his country. He is the shadow of a sovereign, with no money, no army, no authority more than a few kilometres away from the sea.[542]

Immediately on arriving in Bombay, the sultan had contacted the French consul, who wrote a report for Paris on 16 March 1921: 'He has just arrived in Bombay and once disembarked, he came to see me and invited me to dinner (...) He wants more than ever to go to France on one of our warships'.[543]

There is no denying that the sultan was in despair and was looking vainly for some way out, so as to avoid being seized by the English. As the French consul reports, the sultan had underlined in their conversation the special nature of the relationship between their two countries: 'He told me that in Algeria (Mzab) and Tunisia (Djerba) there are many Ibadhites whose supreme head corresponded with him on religious questions and that this was a further link between France and Oman'.[544]

The consul took the opportunity to state that he was in favour of French support for this young sultan, who was, he felt, open to western ideas; in his eyes, Muscat was still important to France.

But in a letter to the French consul in Bombay dated 16 April 1921, the Foreign Minister replied that he could see no reason to justify a move towards bringing the sultan of Muscat to France.[545] In the meantime, in fact, on 19 June 1920, before the sultan contacted the French consul in Bombay, France had decided to leave her ally Great Britain a free hand to manage her affairs in Muscat. She closed her consulate and the building, which was a gift from sultan Fayṣal to France, had been reallocated to the English. But Taymūr apparently knew nothing of these developments.

During this time, British officials in India had never stopped trying to persuade the sultan to go back on his decision, but to no avail. So they began to exert pressure. For example, they forbade the sultan to buy a house in India, then they informed him that if he stayed on in that country his allowances would be cut from 10 000 to 5000 Indian rupees. And maybe one day he would be entitled to nothing.

On 17 July 1920 that is at the end of the three months the English had given him to stay in India, the sultan sent a letter to Wingate in which he excused himself, for health reasons, from returning to Muscat.

> Now I am in the hands of a doctor and therefore inform Government of the cause of the delay In the second place it is not a secret a doctor's treatment must take time and I have a medical certificate to this effect.[546]

The English had no option. In a telegram to his opposite number in Bushehr, the British consul in Muscat commented on an ironic and spiteful note: 'An independent ruler with a medical certificate is difficult to move.'[547]

England had to start re-assessing the sultan's situation and looking for an alternative compatible with her strategy. The under-secretary for Foreign Affairs of the British government in India had worked out three scenarios:

> 1) He [the sultan] may be allowed to abdicate, and his small son may be put in his place with a Council of Regency.
>
> 2) He may not be permitted to abdicate, but he may be allowed to exist, openly for reasons of health, largely as an absentee ruler, residing as a matter of form a certain number of months in the year in his country.
>
> 3) He may be forced to go back and to stay in his country practically permanently.[548]

The under-secretary added, however, that it was difficult to contemplate applying the third solution to an independent sultan. It is interesting that Great Britain, which had already been dominating almost all the country's affairs and influencing its fate for a long time, persisted in wanting to maintain the illusion of the sultan's independence.

The fact remains that the British government in India, before coming to a final decision, asked the sultan to give orders for the formation of a 'council of ministers'. This council would wield administrative power not only during the sultan's absence but also, if need be, in his presence in Muscat. According to this same British instruction, the sultan could preserve the supreme decisions concerning his state and his dynasty.

In fact, on 8 September 1920, the sultan sent a letter to Muḥammad bin Aḥmed bin Nāṣer, his chargé d'affaires in Muscat, in which he announced:

> I have decided to create a Majlis al-Vizarat (Council of Ministers) for conducting my Government which should meet twice a week, and have appointed four persons for the purpose charged with the responsibility of the good government of my State, excluding (from their jurisdiction) certain (class of) affairs which I will indicate on my arrival in Maskat in November next. I now desire that you shall carry out my order stated above. The Council will consist of my brother Nadir, Muḥammad bin Ahmed, the Vali of Matraḥ, sheikh Rashid bin Aziz and Haj Zubair bin Ali. My brother Nadir will be the President of the Council, but he will have no special authority (independent of the Council) except with the concurrence of all the four persons, each of whom will have equal vote. In certain important matters the representative of the British Government at Maskat should be consulted.[549]

This was the first decision of the kind taken by a sultan in the recent history of the country. But even so it had not solved the problem of the abdication. A memo from the secretary of the Political and Foreign Affairs department of the government of India, sent on 6 October 1920 to the political resident in the Gulf, at Bushehr, contained the final decision of the British government on the subject of the sultan. It categorically rejected the idea of abdication. The argument: it was contrary to the policy of Great Britain to recognise the reign of a minor while his father was still alive. And he added the following strange consideration:

> In the case of the Sultanate of Muscat, it (the abdication) is particularly objectionable because the Sultan is supposed always to be elected by his subjects. The present ruler is the only one who has succeeded without at least the formality of an election. This request must therefore be refused.[550]

One can only say that all this is absurd and not worth lingering over. But let us look more closely. What did the British officials mean when they objected that the sultan was considered to have been elected by his subjects? Had sultans ever been elected? The sultanate was purely hereditary. The elective system applied only to the *imāms*.

In any case, the British government in India had decided in the end that it was imperative for the sultan to reside in his country for at least four months of the year. While he was in his country he would receive revenue of 10 000 rupees a month, whereas he would receive only 5000 while staying the other eight months in India. But Taymūr completely ignored this decision.

Faced with this predicament, Great Britain had to step up the pressure again in order to bend the sultan's will. She informed him that she had decided to cut his allowances to only 2000 rupees a month and that the annual indemnity for the loss of the arms trade, amounting to 10 000 rupees a year, would be suspended. But all these attempts at intimidation failed to make the sultan yield an inch. And the English had to admit that no threat seemed to make the slightest impression on *sayyid* Taymūr, who declared: 'I have only a few years to live and wish to end my days in peace.'[551]

So Taymūr stayed in India. But even in that exile, he had to maintain the illusion of power, as the British dictated. In 1923, he was forced to issue the following declaration:

> We shall not exploit the oil that may be discovered at any point in our territories whatever, and we shall not grant permission for its exploitation without consulting the political agent in Muscat and without the approval of the High Government of India.[552]

In June 1929, that is ten years after his arrival in India, the sultan decided to return to Muscat and to step down the following year in favour of whoever the English might nominate.[553] At the time his son Sa ʿīd was about 20 years old, so he had come of age and had already started to take the chair in the council of ministers, a sign that he would be the future sultan.

A British report finally admitted that the real reasons that had driven the sultan to leave his country and strive so relentlessly to abdicate were his indignation at the practices of the British agents in Muscat and, in particular of Majors Haworth and Wingate. 'He feels that it is the British policy that has landed him in this predicament'.[554] The same report says that is why the sultan had decided to wash his hands of the affairs of his own country.

Only once ever did Taymūr return to his country. On 17 November 1931, with the consent of the British officials, he sent an official letter to the resident in Buchire announcing that he was stepping down in favour of his son.

> [W]e have from today, taken off our hand from all ruling rights, and we have made our successor our son Saiyid Saeed bin Saiyid Taymur . . . We leave it to him to direct the policy of the state and to administer the government and we have advised him to consult the Political Agent in Muscat in important matters.[555]

The British resident informed Saʿīd of his father's decision to abdicate and of his own enthronement. On 10 February 1932 the new sultan replied to the political resident in Bushehr: 'I acknowledge with pleasure the receipt of your honoured letter dated 9th January 1932, in which you informed me that my father had abdicated from the throne of his State and has appointed me as his successor'.[556]

It is of note that Great Britain took charge of all the details concerning the abdication as well as the enthronement. What is more, she drafted the formulae for the letter of abdication from Taymūr and then for the letter from the new sultan to the political resident in the Gulf and so on. She also informed the foreign countries concerned in this event. So on 10 February 1932, Saʿīd bin Taymūr officially acceded to power. He was about 20 years old. He had been educated at the school of the princes of Mayo, in the province of Ajmere in India for five years. He had also spent a period of 'training' in Iraq, under the guidance of Bertin Thomas, a member of the council of ministers in Muscat, and known later for his traveller's tales from the region.

In fact, ex-sultan Taymūr had wanted his son to go and study in Egypt with Muḥammad Rashid Reda, who was a celebrated figure in the Arab renaissance movement and a notorious anti-colonialist. But the English must surely have opposed it for fear that the future sultan might be influenced by Arab nationalist thought.

Unlike his father and grandfather, the young sultan proved docile *vis-à-vis* the English; on his arrival, he immediately carried out the order to dissolve the council of ministers that had been formed in his father's absence. Moreover, the British gave the new sultan to understand that he would not need a council of ministers but only two ministers, one for the Treasury and the other for Justice. They appointed Captain Alban, an Englishman, as minister of Defence and the Treasury, and sheikh Zubair as minister of Justice. Such was the government of the new sultan Saʿīd.

For its part, the *imāma* had formed a government in the interior of Oman. Following tradition, it had appointed *wālis* and *qāḍīs* in all the towns in its territory. But for a multitude of reasons, the *imāma* had gradually turned in on itself. This phenomenon stood in ever greater contrast with the rather rapid development of the Gulf region. Thus the Omani renaissance of al-Sālmī, al-Kharūsi, al-Kindi and their friends, the twentieth century *Ibāḍi* renaissance, found itself so-to-speak 'encircled' by the events of that century.

In the final analysis, Great Britain had succeeded in carrying through two strategies: the first was to bring about the isolation of the *imāma* in the interior, the second to work towards the 'recovery' and 'strengthening' of the sultanate. Thus Oman was permanently divided into two quasi-independent parts. But the sultanate too would turn in on itself and would gradually find itself almost totally cut off from the world once again. According to a British journalist, Oman would become the 'Tibet' of the Arab Peninsula.

Yet towards the 1950s, Great Britain, in line with the development of her oil strategy, would attack the *imāma* in the interior in order to put an end to its political system. This, in return, provoked the uprising of 1955–1964 and so would contribute, partly in spite of herself, to the writing of the final chapter in the modern history of Oman.

10 The revolution of 1955–1964

Towards the end of colonial partition and chaos

Si donc le peuple promet simplement d'obéir, il se dissout par cet acte, il perd sa qualité de peuple.

(Jean-Jacques Rousseau, Du Contrat Social)

The end of the imamite system

The separation of the *imāma* of Oman from the sultanate of Muscat continued to be within the limits of what had been agreed in the treaty of al-Sīb in 1920, that is to say in a state of 'truce'. Precarious as it was, this state of things was accepted as 'semi-natural'. There were no serious contacts between the rulers of the two entities but from the point of view of the populations there was no severance, other than a different allegiance. However, the *status quo* that Great Britain had created seemed no longer favourable to her strategy since the advent of the oil era in the region. The need for change was becoming imperative.

Even so, the period 1930–1970 was the worst the country encountered, and more particularly the coast and the region of Muscat, had to live through in modern history. Sultan Saʿīd bin Taymūr, who came to the throne when Oman was in fact heading for decline, did not just lack any interest in the development of his country, he opposed any kind of progress. He heaped despotic laws on his people, making Oman the land of prohibitions. Great Britain could not wish for a better sultan to set Oman sliding into oblivion, if not to remove it from history altogether.

It is in this context of apparent vacuum that in 1955, an uprising was unleashed which starts a new page in recent Omani history and leads us to the end of this work. Before that, we must pause at a crisis which is, as it were, a prelude to the uprising.

Al-Buraimi; the oil conflict and its consequences

The question of the al-Buraimi oasis, which had been in abeyance for more than a century, resurfaced in the 1930s with the raising of the international oil stakes. This region, made up of 9 villages (6 in Abu Dhabi and 3 in Oman), had been a permanent bone of contention ever since the appearance of the state of Saudi Arabia in the second half of the eighteenth century. The state of continual tension frequently verged on war, either over boundaries or over doctrine. The new circumstances in the region often made it seem like an oil war.

In July 1933, Ibn Sa'ūd granted an oil concession to the Standard Oil Company of California in a fairly vast, vague area defined as 'the eastern part of our kingdom of Saudi Arabia within its frontiers'.[557] The lack of clarity and precision led the United States to ask Great Britain, as protector of Oman and Abu Dhabi, to indicate precisely the frontiers of the 'three interested parties'.

England based her response on what was called the 'eastern frontiers', which in reality designated the line known by the name of the 'blue line' demanded by the Anglo-Turkish convention of 1913–1914. This blue line was several hundred kilometres away from the al-Buraimi region. Saudi Arabia challenged this reply and the three parties, England, the United States and Saudi Arabia, embarked on discussions and correspondence on the subject, which lasted till the eve of the Second World War.

In 1949, the Arabian American Oil Company (Aramco) began prospecting for oil on the frontiers of the Abu Dhabi region. This provoked a dispute which ended later in an agreement, through the intervention of an arbitration commission. The only documents in existence for defining the frontiers were British plans. Saudi Arabia denied their validity and asked the commission to base its findings on tribal allegiances. But this solution could not be judged acceptable on an international level. First, it was ambiguous and variable; second, the territorial definition of a state could not be decided on the basis of tribal rather than state allegiances. In February 1952, a congress was convened at al-Dammām in Saudi Arabia in the presence of representatives of the United States and the ruler of Abu Dhabi and Qatar, accompanied by Sir Robert Hay, the English representative in the region. But this meeting produced no result.

The litigation, left in abeyance yet again, opened the way to new challenges among the parties present. In October 1952, Saudi Arabia, supported by Aramco, sent Turki bin 'Aṭaishān as their representative to Ḥamāssā, one of the villages of al-Buraimi and once there, he proclaimed himself governor.[558] Oman, backed by Great Britain, protested against this interference which it saw as undermining its sovereignty.

The outcome was that the forces of Oman and Abu Dhabi joined with the English 'livi' forces. It is reported, moreover, that *imām* Ghāleb agreed that his forces should join the coalition. These forces together encircled the Saudi forces at Ḥamāssā and cut off their ammunition supplies. This critical situation lasted until the end of 1954, when Saudi Arabia and Great Britain agreed that the crisis should be discussed in the framework of a kind of international conference.

A commission was formed, consisting of Cuba, Pakistan, Saudi Arabia and Great Britain. It was presided over by a Belgian judge. Once more, Oman was absent. The first sessions of this commission took place in Nice on 24 October 1955.[559] Three days later it ended in failure.

Meanwhile, Great Britain had been aware since the end of 1954 of the existence of oil in the region of al-Fahūd and, at the frontiers of the imamate, as that coincided with the election of *imām* Ghāleb bin 'Ali following the death of *imām* al-Khalīlī (1919–1954), she decided to change her strategy and settle the problem by force of arms. Her troops joined with those of the sultan to drive out the Saudi troops and return the region to the legitimate power of Oman. The decision to end the dispute by force was intended to transform the al-Buraimi region into a military base, capable of confronting developments in the new *imāma* and cutting communications with Saudi Arabia.

Saudi Arabia took the question to the Security Council of the United Nations, where nothing came of it. The al-Buraimi oasis was to remain a bone of contention between Oman and Abu Dhabi on the one hand and Saudi Arabia on the other, and would reverberate in Anglo-American relations. In fact, the question was not settled until the 1980s.

The revolution of 1955–1964

While the international stakes surrounding the al-Buraimi dispute were becoming clear, in 1954 a new *imām*, judge Ghāleb bin ʿAli al-Hana'i, aged 45, succeeded Muḥammad bin ʿAli ʿAbdullah al-khalīlī, who had died during the year. For Oman, as for the whole Gulf region, this period marked a turning point in recent history: the time was ripe for an unprecedented development in oil-producing activities. Radical changes were taking place; the balance of forces and the former political and strategic equations were being disrupted and even overturned.

All the societies in the Gulf were starting to experience rapid and profound changes on the political and economic, and then the socio-cultural planes; the exception was Oman which had to wait till the 1970s. In this context, the Gulf held centre stage in western, and especially British, strategy.

Contrary to what had been anticipated by Wingate, the architect of the al-Sīb treaty of 1920, who had predicted that after that treaty the *imāma* would turn in on itself, so hastening its end, the imamite state had stood fast. It had even remained internally cohesive, despite its isolation. As for the region of Muscat and the coastal fringe, not only had Great Britain failed to introduce any changes, she had opted to neglect it altogether.

At the dawn of the oil era, the presence of an *imāma* 'turned in on itself' in the region began to form an obstacle to the new British strategy. On that subject, the sultan disclosed to the political resident in Bahrein his intention to overthrow the *imāma* system and extend his sovereignty over the interior of Oman.[560]

Muscat on the one hand, supported by the British oil companies, and Saudi Arabia on the other, backed by the American company Aramco, formed the pivots of a new oil-fed tension. The new deal inclined Saudi Arabia to gamble on the *imāma* as a force capable of facing up to Muscat and hampering British projects. This might seem paradoxical in that Wahhābi Saudi Arabia was historically the doctrinal adversary of the *Ibāḍi imāma*. But now the oil stakes made Saudi power a first rate ally for the *imāma*.

The opinion of the English regarding this alliance reflected what was really at stake in the new deal: 'The Saudis, acting through the *imām*, could seriously interfere with our future oil operations. Already, Saudi money, agents and arms are entering Central Oman'.[561]

In 1953, Oman granted a concession to the Iraqi–British oil company, but prospecting on territories under the rule of the sultan (in accordance with the traditional frontier treaty between the sultanate and the *imāma*) failed to yield major results. In 1954, Great Britain gave orders for prospecting in the al-Fahūd region, inside the frontiers of the *imāma*. To do this, she made ready for any eventuality and formed a special army, paid for by the oil company and known as the force of the 'terrain of Muscat and Oman'.

Oil was indeed discovered in that region, but in limited quantities. The *imām*, who saw the enterprise as an infringement of the independence of internal Oman and of the sovereignty of the *imāma*, even as a breach of the 1920 treaty of al-Sīb, protested against this aggression and prepared for a military confrontation. Great Britain, having foreseen this reaction, decided to seize the opportunity to put an end once and for all to the *imāma* system in Oman and annex the region of the interior to the authority of the sultanate. At one blow, all the territories of Oman would be open to prospection.

At the end of 1954, British forces in association with those of the sultan occupied the town of 'Abri. Great Britain had declared war on the *imāma*. And in 1955, the British cabinet decided to use its air power in the area and occupy the capital of the *imāma*, Nazwa ('operation Nazwa').[562] In the face of these rising perils, the *imāma* published a manifesto condemning the invasion and calling on the Omanis to rally round the *imāma* and prepare to fight against the British aggressor.[563]

Great Britain aimed to administer a knockout blow to the *imāma* as well as to the *imām* himself. The king of Iraq, Nouri al-Sa'īd, one of Great Britain's faithful allies in the region and one of the few who had been informed of operation Nazwa, advised the colonial power to be sure to liquidate the person of *imām* Ghāleb:

> He hoped that Muscat would arrest the Imam and that we should then be finished with him. I took this to mean that he fears that if the Imam is allowed to make good his escape to Saudi Arabia, he will be a continual thorn in our flesh, just like Rashid 'Ali and the Mufti of Jerusalem in the past.[564]

The fact is that the British forces succeeded in striking the resistance of the imamites in their capital Nazwa and then in occupying the town. Yet this victory did not tilt the balance of the war; the Omanis rallied round the *imām*, national resistance was organised and they prepared for a long popular war.

Imām Ghāleb formed a committee of leaders of the uprising, composed notably of his brother Tāleb bin Ạli, sheikh Sulaymān bin Ḥamyār al-Nabhāni and Ṣāleḥ bin 'Issa al-Ḥārthi. The last two were grandsons of the leaders of al-Kharūsi's revolution (1913–1920).

These rulers made their headquarters at al-Jabal al-Akhḍar (the green mountain) in the centre of Oman and from there they conducted military operations without interruption throughout the years 1956–1958. But after intensive air raids (a method of warfare almost unknown to the Omanis until then) and almost 150 attacks on land, the forces of the insurrection suffered heavy losses in men and even in territory, for certain villages and small towns were totally destroyed, including the famous city of Tanuf.

In the end, early in 1959, British parachutists managed to occupy the area of Jabal al-Akhḍar and hold it. With the fall of this strategic zone, the *imām* was obliged to seek refuge in Saudi Arabia together with the leaders of the uprising. Popular resistance continued for several years. However the decision to leave the country was to be fatal for the leaders. In trying to save themselves physically they shattered their image in the minds of the imamites.

The political struggle: the Arab league

On a political level, since before the accession of the new *imām* in 1954, the *imāma* had been trying to build bridges between the interior of Oman and the Arab states. Ghāleb had sent a letter to the Arab League, formed in 1945, asking that Oman might officially join that organisation.

Then, because the tripartite aggression on the Suez Canal in 1956 was accompanied by an intensification of the military operations against the imamites in Oman, the Omani and Arab causes became closely linked. The role of the Arab League was widened and encompassed Oman and the region of the British protectorates, '*Sāḥel Oman*', even the whole of the Gulf. The Omani question had become a matter for the Arab League, whereas, according to an English report, 'the Sultan was one of the very few rulers in the whole area who welcomed action being taken against Egypt'.[565]

Meanwhile the colonial positions inherited from the nineteenth century were being eroded at great speed, finding less justification every day. In July 1957, the *Washington Post*, commenting on the events in Oman, noted that if 'in the past it was possible to crush any uprising by means of force and violence, the failure of the Anglo-French attack on Egypt had made it impossible for that policy – the policy of violence – to succeed in our day'.[566]

The wind had changed. Classic colonialism was living out its last days under the criticisms of international opinion; in that sense the commentary in the *Washington Post* had merely summarised the spirit of most of the international newspapers and periodicals, which had condemned the British aggressions in Oman. Opinion saw them as operations doomed to failure in the face of the rise of Arab nationalism. British public opinion actually protested strongly against its government's policy. A letter, sent to the British government by one citizen, was particularly stern in that regard:

> The immorality and miscalculation of the Suez adventure have been abundantly proved by events – is this appalling disregard for life be repeated (...) by intervention in a native squabble in the sacred interest of oil? Is human life to be always the last consideration with this Government? Will it never learn? Has it no conscience at all?'[567]

Such denunciations, actually emanating from British public opinion, found no echo in the government then in power. But the link had been established in people's consciences between the Suez expedition and the aggression in Oman and nationalist thought was strengthened by it, from Egypt to the countries of the Gulf. In both cases, the reverses on land were accompanied by a matching qualitative leap in political consciousness and thinking, not only among the militants in the nationalist movements but among the populations too. From then on the Omani struggle was linked with that of the Palestinians, the Algerians and others. The affirmation of nationalist and anti-colonialist movements was progressing, despite military setbacks, through the awakening of an Arab political consciousness.

In concrete terms, the Omani cause found substantial support within the Arab League. Sheikh Ibrahim Aṭfayyish, belonging to the family of the great '*ulamā*' from Mzāb in Algeria, played an active political role in favour of Oman. Known as 'the ambassador of the *imāma*' in Cairo, he used all his weight to gain membership of the Arab League for Oman, while denouncing British aggression. Similarly Saudi Arabia, looking to her own interests, adopted the cause of Oman within the Arab League. Egypt and Syria likewise adopted an attitude favourable to Oman. The support of these countries was not restricted to diplomatic positions: the Omani uprising found military and financial backing from them.

Although a certain number of these states were favourably disposed to it, affiliation of the Omani *imāma* to the League was not possible. The political commission of the Arab League studied the Omani dossier and then referred it to the council of the League. But most of the members had reservations when it came to the vote. Their hesitation was due to the exceptional position of the *imāma* and the ambiguity of its political status as an independent entity.

Meanwhile, Great Britain was trying to hinder acceptance of Omani membership by asking her allies to abstain in the matter. She was also seeking the intervention of the United States so as to get the Saudis to change their attitude.

The escalation of military operations (1956), however, led the Arab League to set up a tripartite commission to study the 'Omani question'. The commission's remit was to proceed to a study of the political and social situations in Oman and also in the '*Sāḥel Oman*'. This hitherto unheard of measure gave rise to real anxiety within the British government.

On 31 July 1956, the Arab League presented the sultan with a demand that he allow the commission to enter Oman. The sultan ignored the demand and Great Britain replied that the sultan did not generally speak for himself, usually asking some one to speak for him. In reality the situation was more extreme: 'The sultan does not recognise the Arab League and therefore does not intend to make any reply'.[568] At least, that is the version of the English.

This attitude of the sultan and the international condemnations directed at Great Britain, which had intensified military operations in the hope of putting a speedy end to the problem, prompted the Arab League, in August 1957, to request the Arab members of the United Nations to act together and ask for an urgent meeting of the Security Council; the British acts of aggression were described as 'a real threat to peace and security in the Middle East'. Moreover, although the Arab League had not accepted the *imāma* as a member, it decided, at its conference in Casablanca in 1960, to devote a regular budget to supporting the *imāma* in Oman.[569]

In the face of these developments, Great Britain attempted to bypass the international condemnations and internal and external pressures: she offered the rulers of the *imāma* direct negotiations. The imamites accepted without hesitation and in 1961 three meetings took place in Beirut between the representatives of the *imāma* and the British political resident in Bahrein, who at the same time represented sultan Sa'īd bin Taymūr. On that occasion, the delegation from the *imāma* presented three proposals:

- to return the situation in Oman to the *status quo ante* 1955;
- the British to set all their prisoners free;
- the British to pay an indemnity for all the destruction they had caused.

The British negotiators agreed to study these proposals and they, in turn, presented two proposals:

first, the *imām* must, before anything else, withdraw the complaint submitted to the United Nations;

second, hostilities must be suspended.

On the first point, the *imām*'s representatives responded with a rejection: the United Nations having been set up precisely to resolve political differences, the complaint would only be withdrawn when the problem was resolved. On the second point, the *imām*'s representatives objected that it was not possible as long as the British had not proved their good faith in desiring peace.

Furthermore, the British representatives had proposed that all the chiefs return with the refugees and live henceforth under the authority of the sultan and the British. The *imām*'s representatives replied that this was not a matter of individuals but of a national cause. So the meetings ended without any result.[570]

In 1964, five years after the departure of the rulers of Oman, the imamites and their supporters held a congress at al-Dammām in Saudi Arabia. A high council was set up, consisting of five members. Sulaymān bin Ḥamyār al-Nabhāni, Ṣāleḥ bin ʿIssa al-Ḥārthi, Taleb ʿAli al-Hana'i and Muḥammad bin ʿAbd Allāh al-Sālmī sat on this council with *imām* Ghāleb bin ʿAli in the chair. In its final statement, the congress demanded that the future State of Oman be managed by a collective government. This was an important step forward. Similarly, military, cultural and financial commissions were set up. The council sent Muḥammad bin Sālem al-Maʿamari as representative of 'the State of Oman' to Beirut and ʿAbd Allāh bin Ḥamed al-Ḥārthi as its representative in Algeria.[571]

Belated as it was, this step allowed the representation of a 'government of the State of Oman in exile', which took responsibility for supplying the uprising with arms and training Omani combatants in Egypt, Iraq and Syria, and provided study missions for hundreds of young Omanis in the Arab states and the states of eastern Europe, notably in the Soviet Union. But the belatedly constituted 'government in exile' was soon to be overtaken by events and had only an ephemeral existence.

The United Nations

The question of Oman was raised for the first time in the United Nations in August 1957, when the representatives of eleven Arab states, in a letter dated 13 August 1957, had asked for a meeting of the Security Council, in accordance with Article 35 of the charter, in order to examine 'the armed aggression of the United Kingdom of Great Britain and Northern Ireland against the independence, sovereignty and territorial integrity of the *imāma* of Oman'.[572]

It was Great Britain's fear that she would see the 'Omani question' or 'Omani cause' arrive before the United Nations and so be exposed to international questioning. Indeed, the Arab position was based on the idea that the 'Omani question' fell well within the framework of the principle of 'forces of national liberation and the right to self-determination'.

Great Britain protested against this position and rejected the claims of the Arab group, arguing from the fact that there was no independent sovereign State of Oman in existence and that the district of Oman formed part of the States of the sultanate of Muscat and Oman, whose sovereignty over the coastal regions of Muscat and the mountainous regions of Oman had been recognised in several international treaties.[573]

The dispute was presented on the widest scale, historical, geographical and juridical. The fate of both the imamites and the sultan were at stake. For the very question of the actual political existence of the two systems had been placed on the agenda. Later, this question would be tackled seriously when the terms of the 1920 treaty of al-Sīb were discussed.

However, despite the general understanding and the convergence of views of the delegates of the Arab states that the Omani cause was well founded, the question could not be put on the agenda of the Security Council in August 1957. France, Australia, Colombia and Cuba opposed it, while Iraq, Sweden, the Philippines and the Soviet Union voted in favour. The United States and China abstained.

However, the support of Iraq, Great Britain's ally, for such an agenda did not mean she approved of the Omani cause. Wishing to avoid embarrassing the Arab states on the one hand and Great Britain on the other, Iraq had previously made sure that her vote would have no effect on the final result; besides, she had previously indicated to Great Britain that her vote would have no influence on their special relationship.

China's abstention was motivated by inadequate knowledge of the cause; hence the Chinese suggestion of further study. As for the American abstention, the motives were totally different, but this abstention was as effective as a vote against. So, the required seven votes not having been assembled, the question could not be placed on an agenda. But Great Britain was afraid that the reservations of the United States could be interpreted as non-recognition of the unity of Muscat and

Oman and could prevent the re-opening of the American consulate in Muscat, which had been closed by the United States in the days of Taymūr bin Fayṣal (1913–1931).

In September 1957, a representative of the *imāma* arrived in New York to work together with the Arab delegations, towards getting the Omani cause on the agenda of the General Assembly of the United Nations. But the Arab community failed in this attempt and the question was adjourned until 1958, then 1959 and finally 1960. However, the attacks carried out on the ground by the British throughout 1959 prompted the Secretary General of the United Nations, Mr Dag Hammarskjöld to state: 'The Omani cause is not a problem that concerns the Arabs alone, but the whole of humanity because of the killings and destruction going on there.'[574]

In September 1960, ten Arab countries compiled a memo consisting of a draft resolution with the aim of inserting the question of Oman on to the agenda of the fifteenth session of the General Assembly. The demand was referred to the special political commission which studied it at the twenty-fifth and even at the 259th session.

At the 259th session, the representative of Indonesia presented a draft resolution signed by thirteen countries. Recalling its resolution 1514 (XV), 'Declaration on the granting of independence to colonial countries and peoples', the draft asked the General Assembly to recognise the right of the people of Oman to self-determination and independence. In the course of the same session, the commission was obliged, for lack of time, to defer examination of the Omani question to the sixteenth session.[575]

For that session, the *imām* sent a high delegation to the United Nations, consisting of Taleb bin ʿAli, the brother of the *imām*, sheikh Sulaymān bin Ḥamyār and Muḥammad Amīn ʿAbd Allāh.[576]

At the sixteenth session of the General Assembly, the special political commission examined the question of Oman from its 299th to its 306th session. Voting by nominal roll, it decided by 40 votes to 26, with 23 abstentions, to accede to a request for an audience, presented in the name of an Omani delegation. At the 300th session, Muḥammad Amīn ʿAbd Allāh, speaking before the commission, declared that Oman had enjoyed freedom and independence for centuries. He added that the independence had been confirmed, among others and most recently, by the treaty of al-Sīb in 1920. If the United Kingdom had interfered in Oman, it was because the Omani people had refused to give up its sovereignty and the country's resources in her favour.[577]

Great Britain and the United States: from latent war to shared influence (1956–1957)

As predicted, the political and diplomatic conflict brought before the General Assembly, between the Arab States on one side and the British delegation and their allies on the other, led the Arab representatives to ask the member states of the United Nations to refer to the terms of the treaty of al-Sīb, which, in any case, had been imposed by Great Britain, signed by her agent, Wingate, then ratified by both the sultan and the *imām* in 1920. Was it not, in fact, by virtue of this treaty that Oman had been divided into two parts, 'the *imāma* of Oman' and 'the sultanate of Muscat'?[578]

The United States, which had not forgotten the attitude of Great Britain and her military activities at the time of the al-Buraimi crisis, saw in the treaty of al-Sīb a pretext for putting pressure on the British to recognise American interests in the region and making some strategic gains. The more so as the perpetuation of an implicit dispute between the two powers in that area allowed certain American correspondents in London to foresee 'a possible clash between British and American interests'.[579]

In fact, in spite of Great Britain's recognition of American interests inseparable from Western interests in the region, and despite British readiness to co-operate with the United States, the Foreign Office felt obliged to reassert clearly her position of principle:

> We should continue to make it clear that the special responsibilities which we exercise in the Gulf are ours alone; and that what we need is American understanding and even support but not American intervention (...) [The British have assured that] if their influence goes, it will give place to Arab nationalism.
>
> And the report concludes briefly that 'there *is* a British position but there *will* not be an American or Anglo-American one'.[580]

But what soured relations between the two powers still further is the fact that in August 1957, British forces confiscated American arms that had been sent to the imamites by the Saudis. Great Britain was annoyed by this practice, knowledge of which in any case, got no further than the Ministry of Defence and the Home Office. Indeed the British political line was to avoid making Oman a subject of confrontation with the United States.

In November 1957, the British prime minister started serious conversations with the American President Eisenhower so as to resolve the differences between the two countries. These discussions resulted in the 'Declaration of Common Purpose', which settled a new strategy and launched a period of cooperation between the two countires.

> [This] is a declaration of inter-dependence recognising that the old concept of national self-sufficiency is out of date and that the countries of the free world can maintain their security only by combining their resources and sharing their task. The United Kingdom and United States Governments have agreed to act henceforth in accordance with this principle.[581]

And this principle would in fact mark the history of the region down to the present day. The British and American spheres of influence were clearly outlined. The region was officially divided as follows: Oman, the region of '*Sāḥel Oman*', the Yemen, Bahrein, Qatar and Kuweit would come under the British sphere of influence; Saudi Arabia and Iran would remain dependent on American influence. But the share out of post-colonial influence did not settle the fate of Oman, which Great Britain still seemed determined to keep under her tutelage, even at the expense of engaging in a fierce juridico-political battle over the treaty of al-Sīb.

Discussion of identity and legitimacy

Although the principle of common co-operation between the two great powers remained one of the constant factors in international politics, the American attitude was not conducive to settling the dispute over al-Buraimi. In fact the United States attempted to play the *imāma* card through their Saudi allies, who had until then supported the cause of the imamites, as being in their own interest. Placed in this difficult situation, the behaviour of the imamites displayed both spontaneity and lack of experience. Their attitude was to be one of the factors in hastening their end. As for American policy, it focussed on two points; first of all they were concerned with preserving their strategic and oil interests and then it was important to maintain American influence in Saudi Arabia so as to prevent her aligning herself with the Egyptian position. Such a shift would inevitably reverberate on American interests throughout the region.

Meanwhile, in the terms of the claim seeking reference to the al-Sīb treaty of 1920, Mr Hassouna, the secretary general of the Arab League, asked the sultan to provide him with a copy of the treaty. But Great Britain rejected this approach, being well aware that reference to a 'treaty', which in international law meant an accord between two independent sovereign states, was going to weaken her position:

> We are doubtful how far the terms of the Treaty, which is loosely worded, might not be twisted so as to give a handle to our opponents. It was with this possibility in mind that we decided against letting the Americans have a copy when they asked for one recently.[582]

Henceforth, Great Britain was determined to use every means at her disposal to conceal the tenor of the treaty, even from her allies. What is more, her anxiety prompted her to seek out the address of the architect of the treaty, Sir Ronald Wingate, so as to know whether or not he was still alive.

She found him in Dublin and instructed him that, should journalists come to question him, his response should be that this treaty dealt only with the internal affairs[583] of the country concerned, in line with previous British statements. Sir Wingate, happy to be of use again thirty seven years on, tried to explain a posteriori the circumstances that affected the conclusion of the treaty: the situation at the time was so dangerous that they could not be sure to maintain the sultan, even on the coastal strip, unless they reached a general agreement with the tribes of the interior. It was on that basis that the treaty had been drawn up.

Wingate suggested that the British position could be founded on the fact that the *imām* had not signed the treaty, which thus was just an agreement with the tribes.[584] This was not in fact the case, since in the historical context of the time, the tribes could not sign the treaty without the agreement of the *imām*. We saw earlier that the *imām* had instructed his delegates to sign the treaty and that both he and the sultan had subsequently ratified it.

Finally, on 13 August 1957, the *New York Times* published three different 'copies' of the treaty of al-Sīb. The first originated in the office of the *imām* in Cairo, the second emanated from Sheikh Ṣāleḥ bin ʿIssa al-Ḥārthi, the son of ʿIssa bin Ṣāleḥ al-Ḥārthi, who had signed the treaty in the name of the *imām*, and the third belonged, apparently, to the Arab Information Centre in New York.[585] There was no great difference between these copies, except that the one in the *New York Times* had been touched up linguistically. When compared with the first copy belonging to the *imām* and with the English original (printed in the preceding chapter), they are found to be completely identical.

Great Britain tried in vain to disclaim responsibility for this treaty, by claiming that the sultan was entirely responsible and asserting that the treaty dealt only with internal affairs. She likewise attempted to minimise the value of the act by observing that it was just an 'agreement' and not a treaty.[586]

In the eyes of Great Britain it was important to prove that she had never recognised the *imāma*'s sovereignty in the interior. Following the same line of thought, she alleged that external relations had remained in the hands of the sultan. But in fact the sultanate's relations with the outside world were actually in the hands of the English.

As for the *imāma*, it is true that it did not maintain extensive relations with the outside world, but that was due in the first place to the state of siege imposed on it by Great Britain all through this period. On the question of passports, the sultan did issue some, it is true, but *imām* Muḥammad al-khalīlī also issued passports in his name and capacity. Moreover these passports stated unequivocally:

> The bearer of this passport is a subject of Imam Mohammed bin Abdullah al-Khalili. He is authorised to go to the above-mentioned countries. I ask all those concerned in the friendly kingdoms to allow the bearer freedom of passage and to grant him the necessary facilities.[587]

Commenting on the treaty in August 1957, in a conversation with the British ambassador in Washington, the American foreign affairs minister stated:

> ...There were several clauses in this arrangement which were unusual between sovereign and subject. What is more, there was the fact of British participation and the arrangement was called a treaty.[588]

In short, the controversy surrounding this treaty did not in reality concern its legal content, which effectively established the independence of the *imāma* by establishing its contracting status. It was more a question of acceptance or non-acceptance of the treaty, which of necessity resulted in recognising the *imāma* as an independent system and State. By repudiating the treaty of al-Sīb, Great Britain was seeking to raise again the real question, that of the unity of Oman, which, incidentally was not a British matter. But the true question – and it was implicit – was this: under what regime or system should the unity of Oman be reconstructed? Sultanate or *imāma*?

It was an irony of history that, in the end, the treaty of al-Sīb, imposed in 1920 by a Great Britain proud, at the time, of her achievement, became the first foundation of the legitimacy of the *imāma* in the eyes of international law and in that capacity, the chief subject of disclaim by that same Great Britain.

As for Oman, the party chiefly interested in the affair, ever since the second half of the eighteenth century, it had witnessed the co-existence of two realities which had become indefeasible. The first was the system of the *imāma*, which had preserved its traditional independence in the interior; the second, the sultanate, which had prevailed in Muscat and on the coastal fringe. If the former enjoyed doctrinal and historic legitimacy and the affection of the populations, the sultanate system, admittedly with external support, had none the less been in existence for almost a century and a half, long enough to establish historic and dynastic legitimacy and to be accepted as the second reality in Oman.

The Special Committee on Oman (1963–1964)

In spite of all the efforts made, it proved impossible to bring to a close the long political and legal debate about both the treaty of al-Sīb and Omani national identity nor the political and diplomatic dispute that had been taken to the United Nations. Neither the meetings of the special political committee nor the votes in the General Assembly produced positive results. And so the Omani cause came to be adjourned from one session to another until 1963.

Because of the pressures he was faced with, the representative of the United Kingdom finally, in the name of the sultan, invited a personal representative of the secretary general of the United Nations to visit Oman and present a report on the situation in the country, on condition that the Assembly would take no formal action at this stage. The chosen representative was the Swedish ambassador to Spain, Mr Herbert de Ribbing. The emissary paid a visit to Oman and met both the sultan and *imām* Ghāleb, then in exile in the kingdom of Saudi Arabia. On his return from the visit, which had lasted from 25 May to 9 June 1963, he presented his report to the secretary general. But the document aroused dissatisfaction among the Arab representatives, who claimed that it was far from objective.

Following a request made by the Arab group at the eighteenth session of the General Assembly, the 'Omani cause' was referred, despite British opposition, to the fourth committee, specialising in the elimination of colonialism. A heated debate took place on the simple question of whether the state of Muscat had attacked the state of Oman. Faced with this argument, the committee, not without considerable confusion, asked itself what could be meant by the very name of Oman! This vital point was still quite obscure.

A certain number of fundamental questions revolved around this problem of definition:

(1) The term 'Oman' was used sometimes in its broad sense to include the territories controlled by the *imāma* under the terms of the treaty of al-Sīb, as well as those of Muscat, and sometimes in a narrower sense.

(2) Did Muscat and Oman constitute two entities or one?
(3) Was it desirable to encourage the separation of Oman from Muscat, even in the name of self- determination principle, if, in fact, the two areas constituted a single entity.
(4) If the situation was not a case of colonialism, was it a case of neo-colonialism and was it within the province of the Special Committee charged with studying the implementation of the Declaration on the Granting of Independence to Colonial Countries and Peoples? One thing alone was clear: the problem was well and truly on an international scale; as such it must continue to hold the attention of UNO.[589]

In December 1963, Brazil presented a draft resolution in the name of thirteen states of Latin America asking the fourth committee to create a 'Special Committee on Oman', consisting of five members nominated by the president of the General Assembly. Its task would consist in making a thorough study of the Omani cause, carrying out on-the-spot inquiries and meeting all the interested parties face to face so as to present a detailed and accurate report to the secretary general.

In accordance with the resolution of the General Assembly of 1948, a 'Special Committee on Oman' was set up in December 1963; it was made up of five members: Costa Rica, Nepal, Nigeria, Senegal and Afghanistan. Mr Abdel Raḥmān Pazhwak, the representative of Afghanistan, was appointed chairman.

The committee had no easy task. One of the first difficulties it came up against had to do, as before, with the actual definition of the term 'Oman'. The committee noted that it had sometimes been used to designate a huge geographic area, at other times more restricted zones and at still others a political entity. Often the term had been used in a vague, generalised sense without understanding precisely whether it was a matter of a geographical or a political entity, and at times it even clearly designated both.[590]

The committee had worked out a methodical plan for studying the Omani question, starting with a study of Omani history using the principal works published on the subject. The committee likewise looked closely into the agreements between the sultan and Great Britain. It also contacted the parties concerned, the sultan, the *imām*, the states of the region and the Omanis in exile in the Gulf.

In line with this plan, the committee sent a letter to the sultan asking him to approve a visit by the committee to Muscat and Oman. But the sultan refused to allow the committee to enter the country, considering it to amount to interference in his internal affairs. However, he agreed to meet one of the committee members in the course of a visit he would shortly be making to London. Two meetings between the chairman of the committee, Mr Pazhwak, and the sultan actually took place on 21 August and 2 September 1964. At the same time, the members of the committee met British officials at the Foreign Office.

In order to determine in an objective and unbiased way, the nature of the relations between the sultan of Muscat and Great Britain, of the 23 agreements and treaties signed between the two countries, the committee studied the ones that were deemed to be the most important, dating from 1798, 1800, 1839, 1862, 1951 and 1958.

But the committee was not informed about the '1891 engagement concerning the cession of territories' which had been imposed on Fayṣal in 1891 and on the sheikhs of '*Sāḥel Oman*' in 1892. This 'engagement' was undoubtedly the most convincing and significant for the sultanate's dependence on Great Britain. In effect it amounted to an unofficial proclamation of a protectorate. This document alone would have sufficed to refute and demolish the British arguments about the 'independence of Muscat and Oman'. But the committee was unaware of it.

In the light of the documents at its disposal, the committee rehearsed the various points of view of the different parties concerned. And it noticed that the defenders of the Omani caused had considered these treaties imposed on Muscat to have been the first manifestations of British colonialism. For these agreements and treaties stipulated undertakings fraught with consequences, which in the end placed the sultanate under a protectorate. Any country whatsoever that found itself approving such obligations minimising its freedom and sovereignty could not be an independent country. And if Muscat was an independent country, why did it not send its own representative to the United Nations Organisation instead of leaving that task to Great Britain? Similarly, as the defenders had pointed out, the continual interference in the internal affairs of Muscat and Oman and the launching of military expeditions to strike the citizens of the interior and destroy their towns and villages were another aspect of colonialism.

On his side, the representative of the United Kingdom, who was also speaking in the name of the sultan, stated that the sultanate (Muscat and Oman) was indeed an independent state and should not be considered either as a British colony or as a semi-colony. He maintained that these treaties and agreements had been concluded between two independent countries and that the decision of the international court of justice at The Hague 1904 recognised the independence of Muscat and Oman.[591] Replying to the argument of interference, the representative indicated that, as it happened, this was only a matter of aid offered by Great Britain to a friendly country, in line with undertakings contracted between the sultan and herself.

Sheikh Ṣāleḥ responded by invoking Hyde, a British lawyer and an authority, according to whom the principles of international law did not allow one state to intervene in the internal affairs of another state with the object of suppressing a popular revolution, even under the terms of a treaty that permitted intervention of that nature. Still according to Hyde, such interference could not legally be authorised on the basis of a treaty, since to undertake such an action against the population of a foreign country constituted a legal violation and was denying the right of the peoples to rebel against their government. These were simple and well known principles that formed the basis of international law.[592]

While this debate was going on, the committee had met the *imām* at al-Dammām in Saudi Arabia and had asked him the following question: was he disposed, by way of compromise, to return to the situation before 1955? The *imām* replied that the most important thing was that the English leave Oman.

Once the English had gone, the population would be able to decide for itself what it wanted. If the population wanted to replace him, the *imām* would be the first to conform to that decision.[593]

Furthermore the committee met a group of Omani immigrants in Saudi Arabia, in Kuwait and in Cairo; they introduced themselves as political refugees. The committee questioned them face to face and their answers were significant. These personages, all of whom were opposed to sultan Sa'īd bin Taymūr's regime, insisted that what mattered was first and foremost to drive the English out of Oman.[594] In response to the questions put to them by the committee as to the future system of government, the majority of those questioned stated that it would be for the people to decide and that they themselves would abide by that decision. An influential member of the revolutionary council made it clear that the council was not fighting to give power to this or that *imām*, but for the freedom and independence of the country; afterwards, the population would choose the system of government that suited it.[595]

It is worth noting, incidentally, that when these inquiries were being made by the committee, a group of militant imamites close to the *imām* began to register divergences from him. Part of this group was composed of Omanis from the interior, 'orthodox' Ibāḍis who denied the legality of *imām* Ghāleb bin 'Ali because he had deserted his post at Nazwa in 1959, leaving his people to fight alone against the colonialists. The *imām* had abandoned Oman instead of fighting to the death as his mission of *imām* demanded; it was unpardonable in the eyes of the members of this group. A second group did not deny the *imām*'s legality and continued to fight within the framework of the *imāma* but, influenced by nationalist and Nasserite currents, it was beginning to see the *imām* as an outmoded, even obsolete system. According to the report of the Special Committee on Oman:

> Some members of the Revolutionary Council, the Committee reports, said that they favoured a Republic and one said that this was what the Revolutionary Council had in mind for the future. He stated that the Revolutionary Council believed that the Imāma was an old system that was outdated.[596]

These responses reflected a significant evolution in political consciousness. Born of the uprising and within the frame of the *imāma*, the thinking of the opposing elites was starting to open on to new horizons, foreign to the traditional imamite view.

Had the *imāma* failed to adapt to the new realities? It is difficult to offer objective replies to that proposition. Yet it is impossible to remain silent concerning the fact that new political and cultural circumstances were influencing the representations and opinions of the personalities in exile.

Thus the spread of Arab nationalist consciousness following the period of recovery embodied by Gamal 'Abdel Nasser, had left a deep mark on the opposing Omani elites. It was a time dominated by reflection and liberating values in the Arab world and the 'Third World' as a whole. At last the young Omanis in exile were finding moral, political and military support in their host countries (Egypt, Syria, Iraq).

The Special Committee on Oman had noticed the insistent predilection of all the Omanis for the principle of the elective system, either in the frame of the *imāma* or otherwise. The committee also noted the repeated use of the term 'will of the people'. And when the question was asked as to how that will of the people should be realised, some replied that they valued the traditional method, that is to say the election of the *imām*, because it expressed the aspirations of the people through their spiritual leaders and tribal chiefs. Others answered that they tended to favour a new method that would allow every individual a single and direct vote.[597]

From these various opinions, it is appropriate to single out at least one constant factor peculiar to the political culture of the Omanis: an attachment to the elective system, of which the *imāma* had been the repository and model throughout twelve centuries. If the *imāma* itself no longer enjoyed general support, election, one of its key principles, appeared to be a fundamental part of Omani culture and an element likely to accompany future developments.

For his part, the *imām* had declared himself willing to accept the popular will, to live in the modern age and to relinquish power if the people so wished. Furthermore the committee recorded that certain members of the revolutionary council, far from wanting to keep the old regime intact, were envisaging an electoral system along modern lines.[598]

The attitude of the *imām* and of members of his council could only be seen as a radical transformation in modern *Ibāḍi* thinking. Did this evolution mean the end of the *imāma* in its doctrinal, traditional and political aspect, as Oman had known it all through her history? Yet was it, on the contrary, a sign that *Ibāḍi* political thinking was capable of evolving in order to adapt to events and to the modern age? Oman might indeed benefit from its democratic heritage so as to invest in the building of a new Oman. And in fact the *imām* had expressed his readiness to negotiate with the sultan, in the hope of a return to the situation before 1955. But the sultan, anticipating the end of the *imāma*, refused to follow up these new tendencies.

The Special Committee on Oman finally completed its report towards the middle of 1964, with the prospect of presenting it to the nineteenth session of the General Assembly of the United Nations in September of that year. It concluded this long and important report by presenting certain recommendations: the question of Oman constituted a grave international problem to which the General Assembly should devote special attention. It estimated that the fundamental problem had been generated by imperialist policies and by foreign intervention in Muscat and Oman. The committee therefore considered that all the interested parties should enter into negotiations with a view to settling the question without prejudicing the positions adopted by any of them and should abstain from any action that might obstruct a peaceful settlement.[599]

This process of regularisation could get under way *a priori*. The military operations in the interior of Oman had been over since the end of 1961. But meanwhile, a dispute had broken out between the rulers of the *imāma*, who had started levelling mutual accusations; and a group of militants led by Ṣāleḥ bin ʿIssa al-Ḥārthi, speaking in the name of the 'National Council of the Omani Revolution', had set up the 'Omani Liberation Front'. But as 1965 dawned, both the Front and Ghāleb's *imāma* came to an end.

With this last *imāma*, the *imām* itself as a political, national and traditional concept disappeared.[600] But had Ghāleb's *imāma* been a genuine traditional and spiritual *imāma*? It was doubtful, to say the least, and it might be said that the last *imāma* was in fact that of Muḥammad bin ʿAbdullah al-khalīlī (1919–1954).

The committee finally completed its report on the possible nature of the desired regime:

> The Committee believes that, at least among Omanis who have left their country for one reason or another there is a strong attachment to the principles of representative democracy and that all, including the present Imam, are anxious to see a democratic system in their country.[601]

Oman: from the 'Middle Ages' to the future

'The future of Oman' is the title given at the end of the 1950s to an important collection of British documents. So at the very moment when Great Britain was 'defending' the independence of Muscat and the unity of Oman at the United Nations, she was claiming to work out plans for that country's future and outline its destiny in the twentieth century.

Following the Omani uprising, which was to last almost six years (1955–1961), and as a consequence of international pressures, Great Britain actually intensified her studies of Omani–British relations and she also studied the formulae appropriate to her post-uprising strategy. At the end of these investigations, she set out a certain number of scenarios. Given the importance of this documentation, we shall cite the main points as they appear in the report which concluded this work:

> If the present situation cannot endure, the following broad possibilities present themselves:
>
> (a) As we are so involved anyway, we should declare Muscat and Oman a protectorate and be done with it.
>
> (b) As Oman may be a bottomless pit and indefinite help required for the Sultan if he is to hold it, we should wash our hands of the whole business, perhaps telling the Sultan that we will help him in the coastal areas only.
>
> (c) We could maintain the present position with some improvements.
>
> The objections to paragraph (a) concerning the protectorate are:
>
> It would probably not be accepted by either the sultan or the tribes, and anyway, this policy is no longer in line with the spirit of the times. Moreover it may be costly on a material level and probably also in human lives.
>
> The objections to (b) are:
>
> It would seriously shake the confidence of the Sultan in us.

> It would similarly shake confidence throughout the rest of the Gulf after our prestige had become so involved in defending Oman against the Saudis.
>
> There may be oil in Oman. The discovery of a real field would have a most beneficial effect on our whole strategic position in the Gulf area... These objections rule out a) and b) and we are left with an attempt to improve the present position.[602]

As predicted in this memorandum, the objections, both to the protectorate and to a withdrawal from the affairs of Muscat pure and simple, were to carry the day. The final decision was taken with the aim of preserving the *status quo* by introducing certain improvements in the administrative and security arrangements. The policy therefore was determined on the basis of the continuity of relations between the two countries in their traditional, vague form, as described in the report written at the time.[603]

But in reality, Great Britain introduced improvement only in the military sphere. She preferred to maintain total immobility. The British political officials even hoped that the official relations between the two countries might remain ambiguous. That, then, was the 'future' envisaged for the country. And that is how Oman was to remain for the last decades of the reign of sultan Saʿīd bin Taymūr (1932–1970), in a lamentable state.

The decline of Oman and Muscat had certainly started with the reign of Thūwayni (1856–1866), after the separation from Zanzibar and the proclamation of the British protectorate in 1861. And when sultan Saʿīd bin Taymūr picked up the reins of power in succession to his father in 1932, Oman had already lived through almost seventy years of quasi continuous decline. But the new sultan did not attempt to reform the situation, quite the contrary, he was fiercely opposed to reform. According to an English observer, 'the sultan had wanted to prevent the twentieth century from contaminating the fifteenth century in which he had imprisoned his people'.[604] Naturally, this British national did not make any mention of his own country's share of responsibility for this medieval situation. In fact 'medieval' is a euphemism for, in many respects, Oman was much more to be envied in the Middle Ages than in the reign of Saʿīd bin Taymūr at the beginning of the twentieth century.

In fact, sultan Saʿīd established laws and measures that were disquieting. With the exception of a few Koranic schools, he banned public education in his country. During his reign there were only three primary schools in Oman, a country of one and a half million inhabitants. In 1970, he even had those schools closed, confiding to one of his British advisers: 'That is why you lost India, because you educated the people.'[605] 'Semi-public' education had started in Oman at the end of the seventeenth century, in the days of *imām* Bel'arab ibn Sulṭān (1688–1711), who founded the first official school.

Moreover, right up until the end of sultan Saʿīd bin Taymūr's reign, there was only one dispensary in the whole country. It was in Maṭraḥ and the only medication it had was aspirin. The British writer Fred Halliday quotes several people in this regard, who were able to visit Oman in 1950 and testify to this deprivation: 'In the villages of Oman, there is often not a single inhabitant in good health as far as the eye can see'; 'In twenty years experience of most of the countries of the Middle East, he had never seen a people so ground down by poverty and weakened by diseases that could be cured with treatment and care.'[606]

At this period, then, Oman was the country of prohibitions: it was prohibited to build houses of cob, to wear sunglasses, to smoke tobacco, to own books, for women to travel abroad, etc.; all these actions were deemed to be offences and were punishable by 'the laws'. The inhabitants had to pay particularly heavy taxes. For years, the gates and walls of the capital, erected during the Portuguese occupation (1508–1650) were closed every evening at sunset and a curfew began; the inhabitants could only move about by lantern light, torches being banned.

All these laws affected the person, dignity and spirit of the Omanis. Fearful of losing power, the sultan believed that power could be maintained by imprisoning his people, confiscating the country and stopping the clock. The Omanis were exiled from history.

Yet the Omani conscience did not allow all these measures to crush it; it found in the long history of Ibadhism a bastion of national identity and a good reason to hope for political change. So some Omanis gave expression to their rejection of an oppressive reality by getting involved in political movements of a modern kind. Hence the outbreak of the revolution of 1955–1964. However, although it embodied the hopes of the Omani elites and the generation of the sixties, the revolution was just a footnote in Omani history. Its merit is that it accelerated the movement of history. It permitted the advent of a sultan in 1970 who gave the sultanate system its most modern aspect, with a remarkably advanced programme of development.

Conclusion of Part II

The strategy put in place by the British at the beginning of the nineteenth century had progressed systematically. The great prosperity enjoyed by Oman under the reign of sultan Saʿīd ibn Sulṭān (1806–1856), one of the most important periods of the sultanate, had been ended by England. A strong Oman was of necessity an adversary of British power in the region.

Great Britain therefore spared no effort in establishing definitive domination, including restrictive treaties and control of the shipping lanes or the introduction of steamboats and modern means of communication. All this led to the progressive weakening of Oman, first as a commercial force, leading subsequently to its isolation as a regional power and its marginalisation. Following the death of sultan Saʿīd and after the separation from Zanzibar, Oman was a feeble country, completely cut off from the political chequerboard in the region. In order to achieve her ends, Great Britain had no hesitation in using all the tricks in the book. She destroyed Omani merchant ships, confiscating and burning them, and all on the pretext of fighting the slave trade, 'piracy' or, later, the arms trade.

Yet it is clear that the increase in British influence and the deterioration of the economic situation prompted Omanis who were looking for a way out for their country, to rally round the Ibadhite movement. Recourse to revolution then became ineluctable.

The revolution of ʿAzzān ibn Qays (1869–1871) was the outcome of this whole period. It could have constituted a decisive turning point for the political history of Oman. However, Great Britain, assisted by a number of other circumstances, thwarted that development.

Thereafter, the natural adversary of Great Britain in the region was the Ibadhite movement, once more promoted to being a historic national movement. Although England had restored the sultanate system in the person of Turki, she did not allow the new sultan to enjoy full independence. She imposed such political and financial pressures that his activity was entirely frustrated. She did the same with his successor, Fayṣal, who tried in vain to escape from the British grasp.

However, the Ibadhite movement still had a date with history. The revolution of *imām* al-Khārūsi (1913–1920), spread over seven years, was the longest the Arab world had known at the time. An attachment to national independence was undoubtedly a constant factor in the political thinking and culture of the Omanis.

But the uneven balance of forces in the end allowed Great Britain in 1920 to impose the treaty of al-Sīb, which tended to isolate the imamites of the interior.

For twelve years, Muscat had no sultan. Great Britain governed the country through the expedient of a 'regency council' until Saʿīd bin Taymūr came to power in 1932. His long reign (1932–1970) was to be known as 'the Omani Middle Ages'. Great Britain, having, for a century and a half, applied herself to obliterating Omani history, would proceed in the days of Saʿīd bin Taymūr quite simply to remove Oman from history altogether. During that period the Omani people were doomed to a dual exile, both outside and inside the country.

But when the region entered the oil age, the persistent presence of the imamites became a handicap to British strategy and an obstacle to her aims. Early in the 1950s, therefore, England resorted to military action and her forces occupied the chief towns of the *imāma*, Abri, al-Rustāq and the capital, Nazwa. Faced with this aggression, the imamites launched an uprising (1955–1964), which enabled them to begin to break their political isolation and counter the general stagnation in the country. However, although the Omanis rallied round the uprising and it was supported in the Arab countries and in the world, Great Britain managed to quash it.

General conclusion

The course of Omani politics, culture and history is very eccentric. The key to this eccentricity lies indisputably in the way Ibadhism thinks and operates. As an ideal in the early days and in times of adversity, with experience of power in the age of maturity and as a heritage in the present time, Ibadhism is identified with Omani history and is an intrinsic part of it.

Three main conclusions emerge from a study of the political evolution of the country: one has to do with the original model of an Islamic state proposed by the *Ibāḍi* doctrine from the earliest times; another stresses the durability of the myth and the robustness of the *Ibāḍi* experience all through the country's political history and the last is connected with the strength of the democratic heritage bequeathed by Ibadhism to current Omani culture.

The principles of *al-shūrā wal-bay'a* (consultation and allegiance) or of *al-ijmā' wal-ta'āqd* (consensus and contract) and, in addition, the values and principles of social equality and equality before the law, represent the main foundations of Omani Islamic democracy and of the philosophy peculiar to the social and political culture of the imamite state. It has been the constant concern of the Ibadhite movement, characterised by exceptional perseverance, to construct a state and an ideal Islamic society, both inspired by the example of the caliphate state.

One of the first characteristics of the *Ibāḍi* imamite system is that it cannot be assimilated to a theocratic system or to power by divine right. The *imām* is merely an elected ruler and a representative of *al-umma*. And by maintaining the essential principle of the free election of the *imām*, together with the commitment characterised by *al-bay'a*, *Ibāḍi* practice has conferred on the state a democratic foundation and democratic values, an ideal very close to what is called democracy today.

Democracy, the democracy of *al-shūrā*, had entered Oman with the *Ibāḍi* doctrine, with the religion. It was thus identified with the spirit of Omani culture. But it must be remembered that Omani democracy does not represent just a political model, it is also, and above all a social and cultural behaviour, an attitude and principles of value. This democracy, which is embodied in the free and continued election of the *imām*s and in the active role of the *'ulamā'*, was the chief characteristic of Omani political culture. It was its spiritual characteristic. And thanks to long practice, it became a defining tradition for Omani society. It became a law of collective life, a state.

Throughout the centuries it was by practising this democracy that the Omanis were able to realise principles such as justice, equality before the law, social peace and national unity and independence. Furthermore, it allowed them to achieve a form of harmony between the *umma*, the nation and its rulers. Thus attachment to the practice of Omani spiritual democracy appears as a guarantee of the continuity of the imamite system for more than a thousand years and in return, the system has guaranteed the continuity of democracy.

Although the position of *imām* has a fundamentally spiritual connotation, the functions of the *imām* are by no means restricted to practices of religion and worship; they encompass all the affairs of state, political, military and financial. Moreover, the position of *imām* is not reserved exclusively to the *'ulamā'*; for much of the history of the *imāma*, it has been occupied by national figures who do not belong to that group.

If the sovereignty of the people and freedom have been the basis of Omani political culture, the political power of the *imāma* also rested on the principle of the participation of the people as a whole in political life, indeed at all levels, regional as well as state, through representatives such as the *'ulamā'* and tribal personalities.

Moreover, the imamite state is founded on the principle of the separation of legislative and executive powers, although there is no explicit distinction between the two. It is worth emphasising that the *'ulamā'* have constituted a 'permanent legislative assembly' all through the imamite history of Oman. From another angle, the delegation of power in the various regions supervised by *wālis* (governors) with the support of *majlis* (councils) and independent *qāḍīs* (judges), gave the regions wide administrative autonomy within the *imāma*. This decentralised structure of the *imāma* was merely the implementation in space of the principle of active participation by the citizens in political life.

The fact that stands out clearly from Omani history is that the *'ulamā', ahl al-ḥall wal-'aqd* (those who make and break), the political conscience and representatives of society, played a pre-eminent role in perpetuating the system of the *imāma* and of the Ibadhite movement. Beside their role as spiritual guides of society, as judges, as guardians of the application of the principles of *shūrā* and social equality etc., they were also responsible for legislating within the framework of the *al-ijtihad* principle, notably in matters of commerce, taxation and external relations. As privileged custodians of the political culture of their country, they set great store by acting, through their theoretical, legal and historical works, as the memory of that political culture. Without that memory, any civilisation is liable to lose its cultural landmarks and its identity.

Heir to the tradition of the state of the Rashidite caliphate and with its own vision and experience of what the ideal Islamic state must be, the Ibadhite movement a fundamentally important point of view concerning the caliphate period. No one can claim to have a thorough knowledge of Islamic history without taking that into consideration.

The fact remains that constant practice of the principles of *al-ijmāʿ wal-taʿāqd* throughout twelve centuries (when that practice had been suspended since the second AH/eighth AD century in the other Arab societies) rendered the stability of society and the security of the *imāma* system possible, while ensuring its continuity. In fact, this political culture was also marked by pacific values. Apart from disputes of a tribal nature, we can find no instance of revolt against a legitimate *imām;* peace guaranteed the sovereignty of the *imāma.*

The principles of social equality and equality before the law were among the pillars of Omani political culture, a culture that asserted unequivocally the place of man as a human being by constantly affirming the general interest of society and of the nation. For this culture, human dignity could be achieved only through the collective dignity of *al-umma*. Active participation in social and political life, either directly or indirectly, fortified and reinforced the citizenship of the Omani man. Thus, Omani political culture is, centrally, an autonomous democracy that leaves its marks on society and on the very personality of the Omani citizen.

Finally, in spite of its tribal component, often associated with the idea of centrifugal forces, Omani society has shown itself to be organised and structured. Nor should it be forgotten that the tribes, with their characteristically acute sense of freedom, had helped to consolidate the non-centralised nature of the imamite system and therefore to assert the identity of Omani democracy.

If to these components we add the structures of an open economy, resting notably on important shipping activity, we are bound to acknowledge that the long experience of the *Ibāḍi imāma* had in no way harmed the development of the country. Ibadhite Oman was quite the opposite of an 'archaic state, turned in on itself and underdeveloped'. Its political culture, based on the responsibility of the citizens and their rulers, made it a nation at once sovereign and respected, but also stable and peace loving.

However, Oman's strategic and privileged position inevitably aroused envy and attacks from outside. And the fact that the Omanis had to face quasi continuous challenges and defend their country had further affirmed the national identity and ensured that the principle of national independence became deeply rooted in their political culture. It is interesting to note in this connection that the Omani preferred to be seen as an Omani rather than an Ibadhite or an imamite.

Nevertheless, in the course of the nineteenth century, Great Britain was to succeed in breaking down Omani unity and putting an end to the unified Islamic state. For a century and a half she would apply herself to destroying its political culture so as to re-fashion the country and its history to meet the demands of colonialism. She succeeded in separating the coastal region from its roots and confining the imamite system to the interior. However, it was impossible completely to uproot Omani culture with its spiritual foundation.

In the contemporary period, the *imāma* came to an end as a political system and institution, after the *imāma* of al-Khalīlī (1919–1954). Its now outdated institutions had ceased to make it the historical alternative it once was and its political role no longer met the demands of contemporary Omani society. Yet the *Ibāḍi* experience will always remain as an invaluable inheritance and national patrimony, not just for the Ibāḍis but also certainly for the Omanis as a whole, Ibāḍis and non-Ibāis; in short, it remains an Arab-Islamic experience.

In the long run, although the Ibadhite movement is not present on the political stage today, it remains very much present and active in religious and social life. It has a place in the Omani consciousness. And as a doctrine, it still represents the ultimate point of reference for Oman and the Omanis.

In the final analysis, Omani historical logic, cultural specificity and socio-political reality bring us back to the conviction that the western democratic system does not constitute an ideal model, applicable and desirable everywhere and in every epoch. The more so as Omani society had conceived and elaborated its own appropriate democratic paradigm, taking account of the cultural and religious environment and the prevailing values. While preserving its autonomy, this paradigm could be developed, adapted, even modernised progressively in the context of the political culture of Oman. Besides, it is permissible to think that if the government of the country rested on the rich political heritage of Oman, it might offer the present period a model appropriate to Omani democracy.

The marriage of the heritage and values of Oman with the demands of the present is a historic necessity if both the wealth of the past and the dreams of the future are to be safeguarded. Oman cannot win the future without adopting its own past. To shut the door on the past would be to shut the door on truth itself, on the sources of Oman's identity, on its civilisation.

Politically, it is imperative for the security and stability of the country that it draw resources from its heritage. Today it is up to Oman to find, between the experience of the past and the demands of the present, the balance necessary for consolidating the Omani state in its exemplary role as a modern Arab–Islamic state and as a force essential to the balance and peace of the Gulf region.

For some twenty years now, a genuine Omani renaissance has been making an appearance. A modern state has been built, uniting the country again and endowed with advanced institutions. In a spirit of national reconciliation and clearsightedness, the Omani government has brought in patriotic political figures, formerly in opposition, to share in constructing the country and reinforcing its image as a modern state. It has done the same with the imamites, who have given it their blessing, although they have reservations and remain cautious with regard to the penetration of western influence, particularly cultural, in the country.

During the last quarter of a century, Oman has emerged from a state almost of medievalism to take root firmly in the twentieth century. On the economic front and that of development in general, the government has, in spite of limited economic resources, put in place projects unmatched in the developing countries, including the oil countries of the Gulf. This has enabled it to construct the economic infrastructure of the country and launch developments in education at all levels following a genuine socio-economic and political plan for the way ahead. In a serious but prudent attempt to exploit the national heritage so as to introduce political reforms, the government of Oman took an important decision in 1991: for the first time in the history of the sultanate, a *majlis* of *shūrā* of 59 members has been set up. In its second session in 1994, the membership of the *majlis* was raised to 80. And for the first time, two women have been elected, a particularly significant move. In November 1996, sultan Qābūs, took the initiative of issuing a white paper, a 'fundamental law of the state' which, among other things, will settle the question of the succession to the throne as well as that of political power in the country. This measure will contribute further to the political stability of the country.

So the processes of 'Omani democracy' have begun to set their mark on the political and cultural life of this new Oman. It is true that the restrictive system of election and especially the margin of legislative power in the hands of the *majlis* can be criticised. And there will no doubt always be demands for the improvement of that institution, but Oman, which has chosen the path of reason and a policy of prudence, will henceforth know how fast to proceed on the road of political reform and the development of a modern Omani democracy. The leadership that succeeded in bringing Oman out of its 'medieval condition' knew too how to enrol it definitively in the twentieth century and beyond.

Annexes

Annex I

Table of imams *and* 'seyyids' *of Oman:* name of their tribes, of their residence and dates of their reigns

Imâms	*Tribus*	*Residences*	*Anee de debut de regne*	
			Hégire	*Ère chrétienne*
Jalanda ibn Mas'ûd	Azd	—	135	751
Muhammad ibn'Affân	*Id*	Nazwa	—	—
al-Wârith ibn Ka'ab	Yahmad (branche de la tribu de Azd)	*Id*	185	801
Ghassân ibn'Abd Allâh	*Id*	*Id*	192	807
'Abadal Malik ibn Hamid	Azd	—	208	824
al-Muhannâ ibn Ja'far	Yahmad	Nazwa	226	840
al-Salt ibn Mâlek	Azd	—	237	851
Râshed ibn an-Nadhir	—	—	273	886
'Azzân ibn Tamîm	—	Nazwa	277	890
Muhammad ibn al-Hassan	Azd	—	284	897
'Azzân ibn al-Hir	Yahmad	—	285	898
'Abd Allâh ibn Muhammad	—	—	286	899
al-Salt ibn al-Qâsim	—	—	287	900
Hassn ibn Sa'id	—	—	287	900
al-Hawârî ibn Matraf	—	—	292	904

(continued)

Continued

Imâms	*Tribus*	*Residences*	*Anee de debut de regne*	
			Hégire	*Ère chrétienne*
'Umar ibn Muhammad	—	—	300	912
Muhammad ibn Yazid	Kind	—	—	—
Mollah al-Bahâri	Sa'âl	Nazwa	—	—
Sa'id ibn 'Abd Allâh	—	—	328*	939
Râshed ibn al-Walid	—	Nazwa	—	—
al-Khalil ibn Shâthân	—	—	400	1009
Râshed ibn Sa'id	—	—	445*	1053
Hafs ibn Râshed	—	—	445	1053
Râshed ibn 'Alî	—	—	446	1054
Ibn Jâbir Mûssâ	—	Nazwa	549*	1154
Mâlek ibn 'Ali	—	—	809	1406
al-Fallâh ibn al-Mohsin	Nabhân	Makniyât	549	1154
'Arâr ibn Fallâh	*Id*	*Id*	—	—
Modhafar ibn Solaymân	*Id*	—	809	1406
Makhzûm ibn al-Fallâh	*Id*	Bahlâ	—	—
Abû al-Hassan ibn Khamys	Azd	—	839	1435
'Umar ibn al-Khattâb	Yahmad	—	855	1451
'Umar al-Sharif	—	—	896	1490
Ahmed ibn Muhammad	Yahmad	Bahlâ	—	—
Abû al-Hassan	—	—	—	—
Muhammad ibn Ismâ'il	—	Azka	906	1500
Barâkat ibn Muhâmmad	—	Nazwa	936	1529
'Abd Allâh ibn Muhammad	Hinâ' î	Bahlâ	967	1560
Nâser ibn Murshed	Ya'rubi	al-Rustâq	1034	1624
Sultân ibn Sayf I	*Id*	*Id*	1059	1649
Bel'arab ibn Sultân	*Id*	Yabrîn	1078	1688
Sayf ibn Sultân I	*Id*	al-Rustâq	1123*	1711
Sultân ibn Sayf II	*Id*	al-Nazrn	1123	1711
Sayf ibn Sultân II	*Id*	—	1131	1718

Continued

Imâms	*Tribus*	*Residences*	*Anee de debut de regne*	
			Hégire	*Ère chrétienne*
Muhanna ibn Sultân	*Id*	al-Rustâq	1131	1719
Ya'rûb ibn Bel'arab	*Id*	Nazawa	1134	1721
Sayf ibn Sultân II	*Id*	al-Rustâq	1135	1722
Muhammad ibn Nâser	Ghâfer	Yabrîn	1137	1724
Sayf ibn Sultân II	Ya'rûbi	al-Rustâq	1140	1728
Sultân ibn Murshed	*Id*	*Id*	1151	1738
Ahmed ibn Sa'id	al-Bû Sa'idi	*Id*	1154	1741
Sa'id ibn Ahmed	*Id*	*Id*	—	1783
Seyyids-sultans				
Hamad ibn Sa'id	*Id*	Mascate	1193	1792
Sultân ibn Ahmed	*Id*	*Id*	1206	1792–1804
Sa'id ibn Sultân	*Id*	Mascate et Zanzibar	1249	1806
Thûwayni ibn Sa'id	*Id*	Mascate	1273	1856
Sâlem ibn Thûwayni	al-Bû Sa'idi	Mascate	1283	1866
'Azzan ibn Qays (*imâm*)	*Id*	*Id*	1285	1869
Turki ibn Sa'id	*Id*	*Id*	1291	1871
Faysal ibn Turki	*Id*	*Id*	1305	1888

OMAN APRÈS 1913

Sultanat de Mascate		imama *d'Oman*	
Sultans		Imâms	
Taymûr bin Faysal	1913-abdication 1931	Sâlem bin Râshed al-Kharûsi	1913–1919
Sa'id bin Taymûr	1932-détrôné 1970	Muhammad bin 'Abd Allâh al-Khaîlî	1919–1954
Qâbûs bin Sa'id	1971–	Ghâleb bin 'Ali al-Hinâ'i	1954–1965

Source: See Ibn Ruzayq (Humayd), al-Fath al-mubīn fi sīrat al-bu Sa'īdiyīn (m. 1873). Translated and published under the title of: History of the Imāms and Seyyids of Oman, by GP Bager, London, Draf Publishers, Ltd, 1986. We have corrected some dates and names and updated this list from 1920 till 1970.

Notes
* indicates approximate dates; — indicates the uncertainty of dates or data.

Annex II

The dynasty of al-Bū Sa'idī

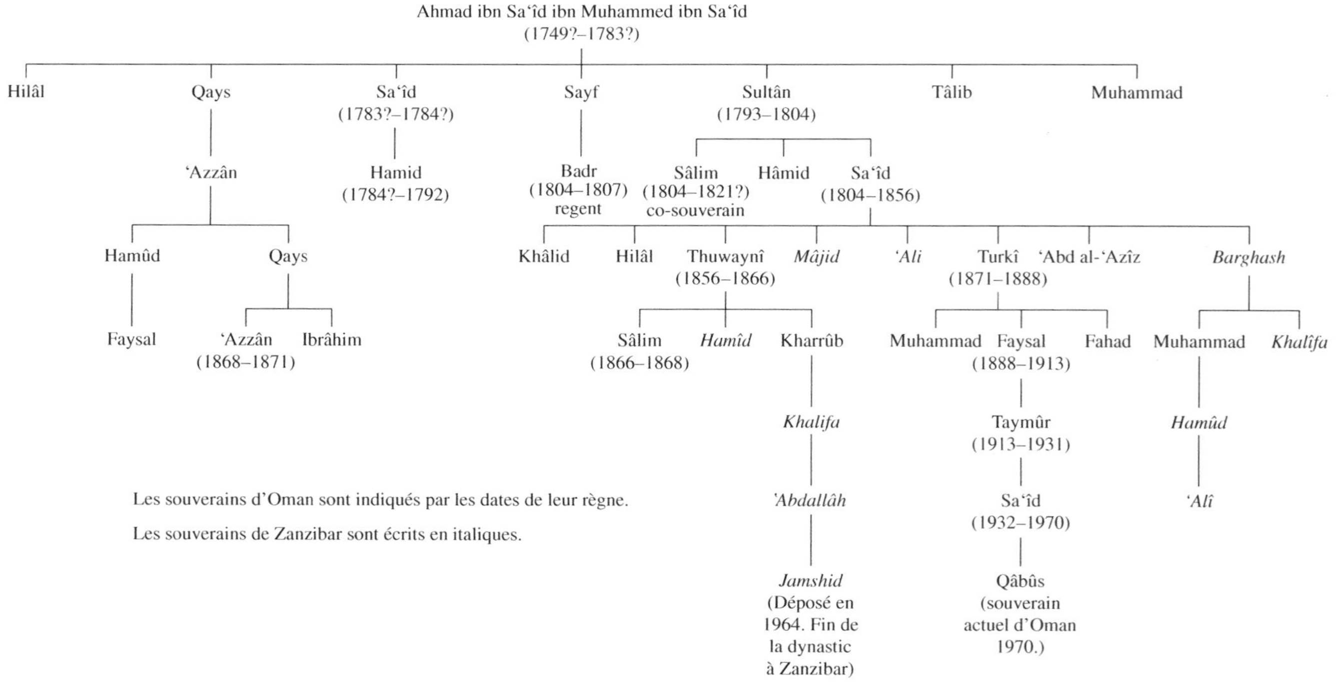

LA DYNASTIE DES ÂL BÛ SA'ÎD
Tableau généalogique simplifié, On trouvera dans LORIMER, *Gazetteer of the Persian Gulf*, Vol. VI, la généalogie complète de la famille de 1744 à 1902: Table of the principal descendants of Ahmad-Bin-Sa'id, al Bu Sa'idi Founder of the present rulling families of Oman & Zanzibar.

Source: 'La Péninsule arabique d'aujourd'hui', under the direction of Paul Bonnenfant, Paris, end. CNRS, 1982, vol. II.

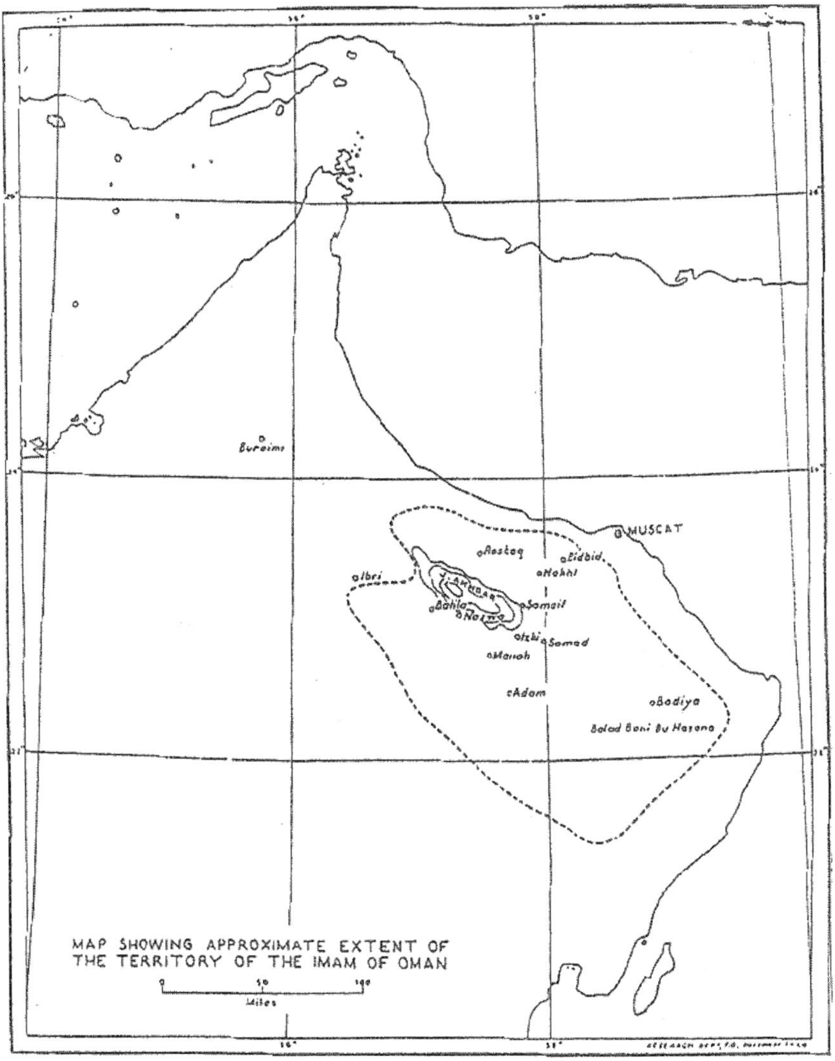

Map 1 The territory of the *imāma* of Oman.

Source: FO 371/1/114578.

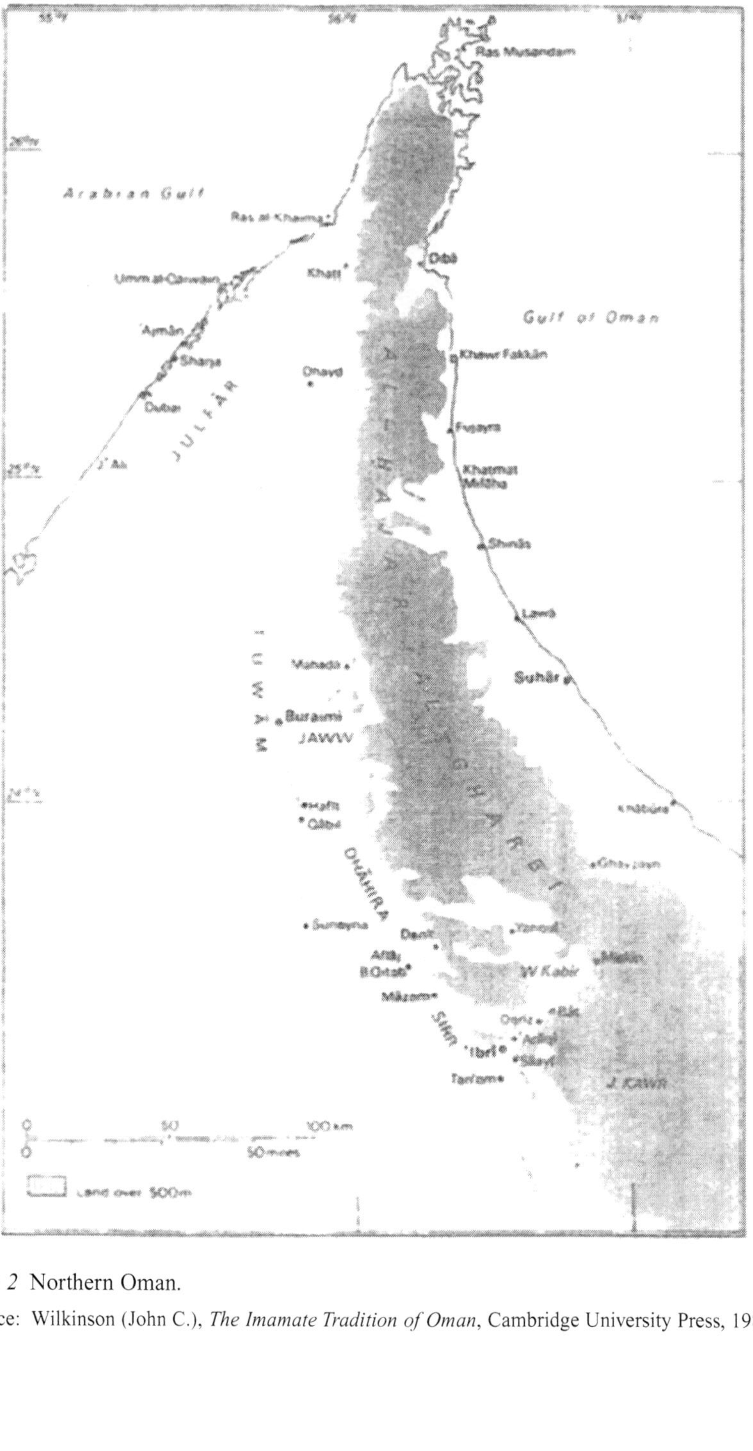

Map 2 Northern Oman.

Source: Wilkinson (John C.), *The Imamate Tradition of Oman*, Cambridge University Press, 1987.

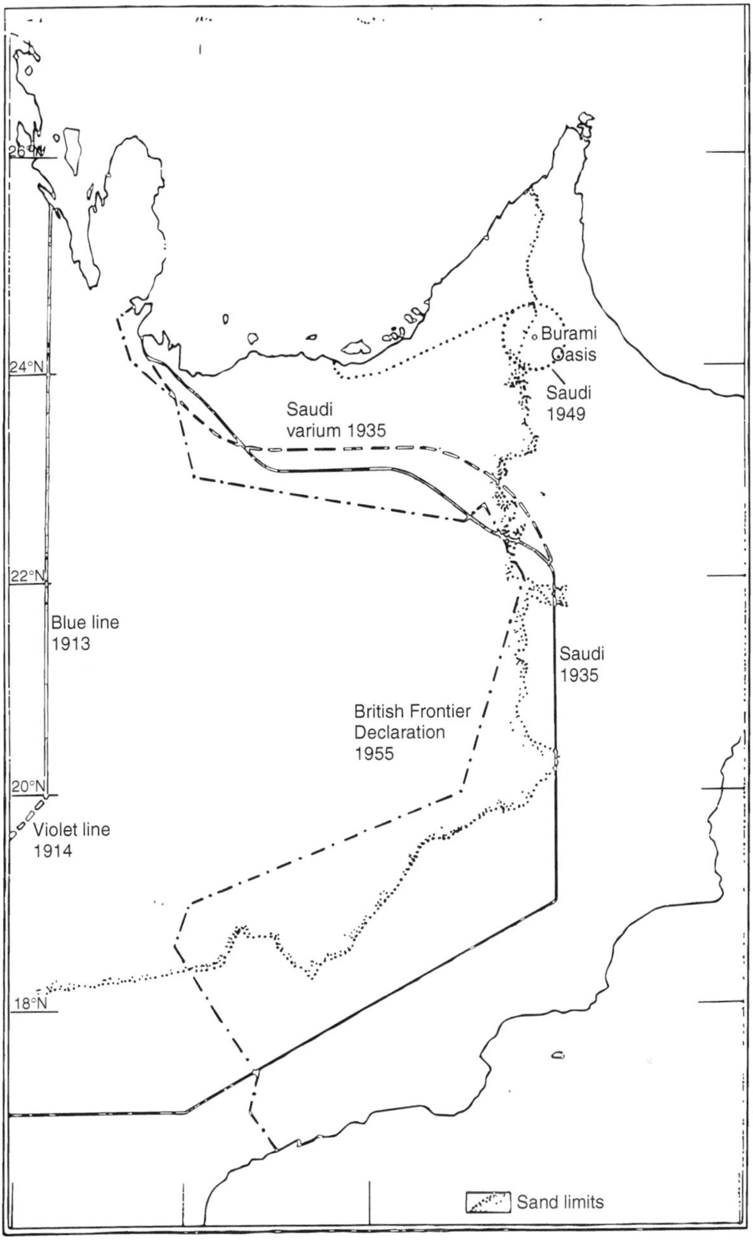

Map 3 Frontier claims in south-east Arabia.

Source: Wilkinson (John C.), *The Imamate Tradition of Oman*, Cambridge University Press, 1987.

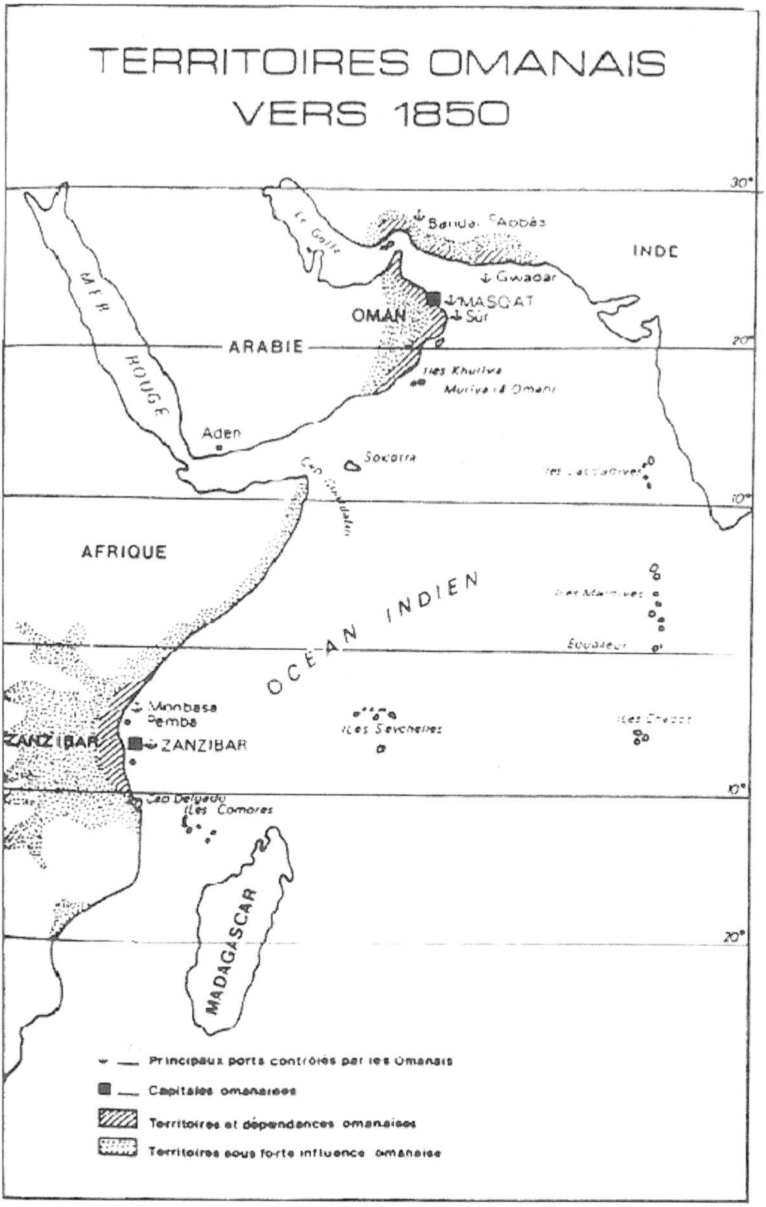

Map 4 Omani territories, *c.*1850.

Source: *Carte* Paul Bonnenfant Michel RIVAL.

Glossary

'adl	justice
ahl al-bilād	people of the country (citizens)
ahl al-hall wa l-'aqd	those who can make and break
ahl al-da'wa	people with a vocation
ahl al-Nahr	'people of the river'
ahl al-sunna	people of Tradition
'ālim **(pl.** ***'ulamā'*****)**	religious scholar
aṇs'ār	supporters
'aqd	contract, engagement
awqāf **(sing.** ***waqf*****)**	property in mortemain
bay'a	allegiance
bayt al-māl	public assets
calife (khalīfa)	Chief of the Muslim community. Khalīfa, a post of the head of the community created after the death of the Prophet. It should be elected by the *umma*.
ḍa'īf	weak
dawla	state
difā'	defence
dīn wa dawla	religion and state
dhuhūr	demonstration (manifestation)
dustūr	constitution
faqīh **(pl.** ***fuqahā'*****)**	legal, religious expert
firqa **(pl.** ***firaq*****)**	'sect', school, spiritual family
fitnah	discord, a religious conflict
ghanīma **(pl.** ***ghanāyem*****)**	booty, spoils of war
ḥadīth	'transmitted saying' (by the Prophet himself or by one of his companions with reference to him)

ḥākim	governor
ḥukūma	government
ḥurriyah	liberty, freedom
ibn **(*bin*** **or** ***ben*)**	son of…
ijmā'	consensus
ijtihād	personal effort on religious interpretations
'ilm	knowledge, learning
imām	guide, leader: a supreme ruler of the Muslim community b guide of the prayer
imāma	Ibadhite political system of Oman
istidlāl	induction
jamā'a	community
jaysh	army
jihād	effort, combat, struggle against
jizyah	a duty tax on non-Muslims
khārijites	leavers, secessionists
khuṭba	a religious preach
khūrūj	exit from Islamic legitimacy
kitmān	dissimulation
kufr	non-faith
al-majālis **(sing.** ***majlis*)**	council
al-majlis al-'ām	general council
majlis al-shuyūkh	(senate), the upper council
majlis al-shūrā	consultative council
majlis ḥamalat al-'ilm	the council of bearers of knowledge
manātiq	provinces
masālek al-dīn	the paths of faith
muftī	a religious authority
muhājirūn	emigrants
al-muḥakkimah	the party of the arbitrated
mushrikūn **(sing.** ***shirk*)**	idolaters, polytheists (those who associate)
muwāṭin	citizen
nahḍa	renaissance
qawī	strong
qāḍī	judge
al-qa'ūd	quietism
qiyās	reasoning by analogy

raḥmān	merciful
rāshidūn	the well advised caliphs
al-sādah (sayyid)	title of nobleness attributed to the descendants of the Prophet (used as a political title of the ruling family in Oman)
al-ṣalāḥ	virtue, right path
shar'	revealed law
sharī'a	legal code based on the shar',
shirā'	sacrifice
shūrā	consultation
sunna	Tradition
umma	community, nation
'urf	common law
Wāli (**pl.** ***wūlāh***)	governor
Waṭan	homeland
Al-waṭan al-rūḥi	spiritual home
zakāt	legal alms

Notes

Introduction

1 '*A prendre le terme dans la rigueur de l'acception, il n'a jamais existé de véritable démocratie, et il n'en existera jamais. Il est contre l'ordre naturel que le grand nombre gouverne et que le petit soit gouverné*'. Rousseau, Jean-Jacques, *Du Contrat Social*, Paris, Flammarion, 1966, p. 107.

2 '*Suivant la vraie signification des mots* [la démocratie consiste en]*: un gouvernement auquel le peuple prend une part plus ou moins grande'*... '*Son sens est intimement lié à l'idée de liberté politique'*... '*la liberté n'est pas l'état principal et continu du désir du peuple dont l'état social est démocratique. Ce qu'ils aiment d'un amour éternel, c'est l'égalité*'. Prélot, M., Lescuyer, G., *Histoire des idées politiques*, Paris, Dalloz, 1990, p. 561.

3 '*La loi, en général, est la raison humaine, en tant qu'elle gouverne tous les peuples de la terre; et les lois politiques et civiles de chaque nation ne doivent être que les cas particuliers où s'applique cette raison humaine. Elles doivent être tellement propres au peuple pour lequel elles sont faites, que c'est un très grand hasard si celles d'une nation peuvent convenir à une autre*'. Montesquieu, C. de S. de, *De l'esprit des lois*, Paris, Flammarion, 1979 tome 1, p. 128.

4 See Farghot, A., 'al Dīn wal 'Ilmaniyya fi Uroba al-Gharbiyya...' (Religion and the secular in western Europe...), in *al-'alāqāt bayn al-Hadạrāt al-'Arabiyya wal Urobiyya*, Conference of Hamburg, April 1983), al-Dar al-Tunisiyah, 1985.

5 Sura 4 Women (*An-Nisā'*), verse 59.

6 Sura 3 The Family of Imran (*Āl 'Imrān*) verse 159.

7 Gardet, L., *La Cité musulmane, vie sociale et politique*, Paris, Librairie philosophique J. Vrin, 1981, p. 34.

8 Laoust, H., *Le Califat dans la doctrine de Rashid Rida*, annotated translation of *al-Khilafa au al-Imāma al-'uzma* (The supreme Caliphate or *Imāma*), Paris, Librairie d'Amérique et d'Orient, 1986, p. 156.

9 'Abduh, M., *al-Islām wan Nasrāniyyah bayna al-'ilm wal madaniyyah* (Islam and Christianity Between Science and Civilisation), Algiers, Entreprise nationale du Livre, 1988, p. 53.

10 Sura 3 The Originator of Creation (*Fatiṛ*) verse 24.

11 Laoust, H., op. cit., p. 23.

12 Gardet, L. in his book *L'Islam* notes that Muslim values have a specificity, of which European languages almost always give only an approximation. The West, he says, even de-Christianised, spontaneously refers any religious notions of which it makes to Christian values. (Gardet, L., *L'Islam, religion et communauté*, Paris, Desclée de Brouwer, 1967, p. 29.)

13 Gardet, L., 1981, op. cit., p. 51.

14 Sura 4 Women (*An-Nisā'*) verse 58.

15 Sura 42 The Counsel (*As Shūrā*) verse 36.
16 *Al-Manār*, section 10, no. 23, 1922, p. 750.
17 Ibid.
18 Ibid., p. 750.
19 Ibid., p. 751.
20 Ibid., p. 750.
21 Ibid., p. 750.
22 The Muslim philosopher, Muḥammad Iqbal, testified in 1930 that humanity today needs three things: a spiritual interpretation of the universe, spiritual emancipation of the individual, and far-reaching fundamental principles guiding the evolution of human society along spiritual lines. In his view, Europe's idealism has never become a vibrant factor in its life; the result is a perverted ego, trying to find itself through intolerant democracies whose sole function is to exploit the poor in the interests of the rich. Europe today, he concludes, is the greatest obstacle on the road to the ethical progress of mankind (Iqbal, M.), *Reconstruire la Pensée Religieuse de l'Islam*, Paris, Librairie d'Amérique et d'Orient Adrien Maisonneuve, 1955, p. 193.
23 *Al-sharīʿa* is not simply the juridical code, based on the *sharʿ*, it also represents the ethical framework of Islam.

Preliminary chapter

24 Stevens, A., *Oman, citadelle entre sable et mer*, [s.l., Belgium] ed. Terra Incognita, 1990, p. 7.
25 Kelly, J.B., *Britain and the Persian Gulf, 1795–1870*, Oxford, 1979.
26 Stevens, A., op. cit., p. 10.
27 Ibn ʿAmer (bin ʿAli bin ʿUmayr), *Hadāṛat Umān al-Qadimah*, 'The ancient civilisation of Oman', Sultanate of Oman, Ministry of National and Cultural Heritage, [undated] p. 14.
28 Ibid., p. 19.
29 Miles, S.B., *The countries and tribes of the Persian Gulf*, London, Frank Cass, 1900 (2nd edition, 1966).
30 Miles, S.B., op. cit.
31 Al-Sabah (Sālem al-Jabir), *Les Emirats du Golfe. Histoire d'un peuple*, Paris, Fayard, 1980, p. 18.
32 Kāshef (Sayyeda Isma'īl), *'Umān fi fajr al-islām*, 'Oman at the dawn of *Islām*', Sultanate of Oman, Ministry of National and Cultural Heritage, 1989, p. 14.
33 Wilson, A.T., *The Persian Gulf: a historical sketch from the earliest times to the beginning of the 20th century*, Oxford, Clarendon Press, 1928.
34 Miles, S.B., op. cit., p. 16.
35 Kelly, J.B., 1968, op. cit., p. 4.
36 Wilson, A.T., op. cit., p. 8.
37 Miles, S.B., op. cit., p. 19.
38 Al-Azkawi (Sarhan bin Saʿīd), *Tārīkh 'Umān: kāshf al-Ghamma al-Jama' li Akhbār al-Umma*, reviewed by ʿAbdal-Majid Hassib al-Qaysi, Abu Dhabi, Dar al-Dirasat al-Khalījya, [1976], p. 31.
39 Ibid., p. 32.
40 Kāshef, S.I., op. cit., p. 23.
41 The word 'Tradition' will always be written with a capital letter when it is a translation of *sunnat* Islamic law; the *ḥadīth* means literally 'transmitted saying' (by the Prophet himself or by one of his companions with reference to him).
42 Al-Sālmī (ʿAbd Allah bin Ḥumayd), *Tuḥfat al-A ʿyān bi Sīrat ahl ʿUmān*, 'Chef d'oeuvre of the people of note: biography of the people of Oman', Cairo, Matbaʿat al-Imām, vol.1, 1961, p. 8.
43 Ibid., p. 9.

44 Al-Shahrestani (Muḥammad bin 'Abd al-Karim), *al-Milal wal Neḥal*, 'The doctrines and schools of thought', ed. 'Abd al-Aziz Muḥammad al-Wakil, Beirut, Dar al Fikr, [undated] p. 120.
45 Al-Sālmī (A.H.) op. cit., p. 12.
46 Al-Qalhāti (Muḥammad bin Sa'īd al-'Azdi), *al-Kashf wal-Bayān*, 'The discovery and the manifesto', reviewed by Sayyeda Isma'īl Kāshef, Sultanate of Oman, Ministry of National and Cultural heritage, Cairo, 1980, vol. II, pp. 240–241.
47 Ibid., p. 252.
48 Al-Sama'īlī (Sālem bin Ḥamad bin Shamis al-Sayyābi), *Izalet al-Wa'thā' 'An Atbā'Abi al-Sha'thā'*, 'Highlighting the disciples of Abu Sha'tha', reviewed by Sayeda Ismaīl Kāshef, Sultanate of Oman, Ministry of National and Cultural Heritage, Cairo, 1979, p. 11.
49 al-Braki (Nāṣer al-Murshed), *al-Ibāḍiyyah fi al-Fikr al-Siyāsi al-Islāmi wa Atharuha fi Qiyām al-Duwal*, 'Ibadhism in Islamic political thought and its influence on the establishment of States', in *Al-Ijtihad*, no. 13, Beirut, 1991, p. 117. See also the *Encyclopédie Islamique*, new edition, Paris, 1975, tome III, p. 672.
50 Kāshef, S.I., op. cit., p. 279.
51 Al-Shammākhi (Aḥmed bin Sa'īd bin 'Abdel Wāḥed), *Kitāb al-Siyar*, 'The book of biography and responses', reviewed by Aḥmed bin Sa'ūd al-Sayyābi, Sultanate of Oman, Ministry of National and Cultural Heritage, 1987, tome 1, p. 91. This *'ālim* is one of the principal references for the *Encyclopédie Islamique*.
52 Kelly, J.B., 1968, op. cit., vol. 1, p. 15.
53 Ibid., p. 7. It is worth pointing out that the term 'secular' here is not to be taken literally but rather in the sense of 'tolerant'.
54 *Encyclopédie Islamique*, new edition, Paris, 1975, vol. III, p. 673.
55 *Kitāb al-Siyar wal-Jawābāt*, op. cit., tome I, pp. 121 and 124. See also al-Kindi (Aḥmed bin 'Abd Allah), *Kitab al-Ihtidā'*, 'The book of the guide', Sultanate of Oman, Ministry of National and Cultural Heritage, 1985.
56 See Wilkinson, J.C., 'Bio-bibliographical background to the crisis period in the Ibadhite *Imāma* of Oman (end of 9th to end of 14th century)', *Arabian studies*, vol. III, London, 1976, p. 139.
57 Ibid.
58 The book of *al-'ālim* Abi Sa'īd Muḥammad ibn Sa'īd al-Kidmi, surnamed the *imām* of the *Ibāḍi* doctrine (AH third century/ninth century AD) and a member of the *al-Istiqamah* school at Nazwa, was intended as a response to the writings of the Rustaq school, calling for reform, unity and the setting aside of precedents. In similar vein, the book by *al-'ālim* Abu Baker ibn Ahmed ibn 'Abd Allah ibn Mūssa al-Kindi al-Nazwi (AH fifth or sixth century/AD eleventh or twelfth century), *Kitāb al-Iḥtidā'*, went more deeply into the constitutional debate of the day. Nor should *Kitāb al-Siyar wal-Jawābāt*, already mentioned, be forgotten.

1 The *Ibāḍi* doctrine: origin, thought and tradition

59 Al-Qalhāti, M.S., op. cit., tome II, p. 421.
60 Ennami ('Amr Khalīfah), *Studies in Ibadhism*, thesis, University of Cambridge, 1971, p. 13.
61 Ibid.
62 *Al-Ansār*, a name given by the Prophet to the believers in Medina in order to honour them and distinguish them from the *Muhājirūn*, the immigrants from Mecca. See the Encyclopaedic Dictionary of Islam by Cyril Glassé.
63 Al-Qalhāti, M.S., op. cit., tome II, p. 239.
64 Al-Shahrestan, M.A., op. cit., p. 114.
65 Sura 4 Women (*An-Nisā'*), verse 74.
66 Sura 9 Repentance (*At-Tawba or Bara' a*), verse 111.
67 Gardet, L., *Les Hommes de l'islam*, Paris, Hachette, 1977, pp. 209–210.

68 Ibid., p. 199.
69 Muʿmmar (ʿAli Yahya), *al-Ibaḍiyyah Bayn al-Firaq al-Islamyah*, 'Ibadhism among the Islamic sects', Sultanate of Oman, Ministry of National and Cultural Heritage, 1986, tome II, p. 166. See alsoal-Qalhati, M.S., op. cit. tome II, p. 240.
70 Al-Qalhati, M.S., op. cit., tome II, p. 240.
71 Ibid., p. 241.
72 Al-Shammakhi, A.S., op. cit., tome I, p. 51.
73 Ibn Katheer (Isma'īl bin 'Umar), *al-Bidāya wal-Nihāya*, 'The Beginning and the End', Cairo, Dar Abi-Hayan, 1966, tome IV, p. 345.
74 Al-Qalhati, M.S., op. cit., tome I, p. 252. See also al-Shammakhi, A.S., op. cit., p. 52.
75 Al-Qalhati, M.S., op. cit., tome II, p. 252.
76 Cf. *imām* ʿAli (ibn Abi Talib), *Nahjal-Balagha*, 'The Way of Eloquence', 2nd edition, Cairo, Dar al-Kitab al-Maṣri, 1990, p. 399.
77 Ibn Katheer (Ismaʿīl bin ʿUmar), op. cit., p. 347.
78 Al-Maamiry (Aḥmed Hamoud), *Oman and Ibadhism*, New Delhi, Lancers Booms, 1989, p. 33. He was born *probably* in AH 18/AD 639 and the date of his death is given as AH 93–94, or even 103, cf. *Encyclopédie islamique*, op. cit. tome III p. 670.
79 Khleifat (ʿAwad Muḥammad), *al-Ūsūl al-Tarīkhiyah lil Firaq al-Ibāḍiyyah*, 'The historical origins of the Ibāḍite sects', 2nd ed., Sultanate of Oman, Ministry of National and Cultural Heritage, 1988, p. 7. See also al-Sama'ili, S.H., op. cit., pp. 13–39.
80 Ennami, A.K., op. cit., p. 95.
81 Ibid., p. 2.
82 *Encyclopédie islamique*, op. cit., tome III, p. 670.
83 Ibid., p. 669.
84 Ennami, A.K., op. cit., pp. 104–109.
85 Ibid. op. cit., p. 85.
86 Khleifat, A.M., '*The historical origin of the Ibadites sect*', Sultanate of Oman, Ministry of National and Cultural Heritage, 1988.
87 *Kitāb al-Siyar wal-Jawābāt*, op. cit., 1986, tome II, pp. 325–345.
88 The disciples of Ibn al-Azraq.
89 *Kitab al-Siyar wal-Jawābāt*, op. cit., tome II, p. 333. See also *al-Qalhāti*, M.S., op. cit., p. 207.
90 *Kitab al-Siyar wal-Jawābāt*, op. cit., tome II, p. 329.
91 Ibid., p. 341.
92 Ibid., p. 342.
93 Ibid.
94 Ibid.
95 Mrûa (Hussein), *al-Nazaʿāt al-Mādiyya fi al-Falsafa al-ʿArabiyya al-Islamiyya*, 'Materialist tendencies in Arab–Islamic philosophy', Beirut, al-Fārābi, 4th ed., 1981, tome I, p. 496.
96 Ibid., p. 497.
97 Gardet, L., 1977, op. cit., p. 246.
98 Ibid., p. 209.
99 Ibid., p. 211.
100 Muʿamar, A.Y., *al-Ibadiyaah bayn al-Firaq al-Istamyah* (Ibadhism among the Islamic Sects), 1986, 2 volumes, tome II, p. 197.
101 Al-Kindi (Aḥmed bin ʿAbd Allah), *al-Muṣannaf*, 'The Classifier', Sulanate of Oman, Minstry of National and Cultural Heritage, 1983, tome X, p. 27. This tome is devoted to the Ibadhite constitution. In view of its specialised language, we have been anxious to keep the exact sense of the text, as far as possible.
102 Ibid., p. 27.
103 Gardet, L., 1977, op. cit., p. 216.
104 Ibid., p. 215.
105 Sura 32 Prostration (*As Sadjdat*), verse 23.

106 Al-Kindi, A.A., 1983, op. cit., tome X, pp. 39, 63 and 65.
107 Ibid., p. 80.
108 Ibid., p. 81.
109 Ibid., p. 81.
110 They were: Sa'īd ibn Abī Waqqās, Ali ibn Abī Tāleb, 'Uthmān ibn 'Affān, 'Abdul Rahmān Abī 'Aouf, al-Zubayr ibn 'Awām and Talhat ibn 'Ubeyd Allah.
111 Mrûa, H., op. cit., tome I, p. 397.
112 In this respect, a significant tradition tells that, when the *'ulamā'* chaired by 'Abd Allah al-Sālmī, decided to grant the *imāma* to Sālem ibn Rashed al-kharūsi (1913–1919), al-Sālmī, when informing him, asked the *'ulamā'* in the candidate's presence, but without his knowing: 'Who is your *imām*?' The *'ulamā'* replied with one voice: 'Sālem ibn Rashed al-kharūsi'. The candidate, who was standing, fainted, not from joy but from fear. He tried to excuse himself. But the learned 'Abd Allah ibn Humaid al-Sālimi asked one of his pupils to strike the candidate on the neck. When the candidate asked why, al-Riyāhi replied: 'Your refusal is going to divide the ranks of the Muslims'. Al-kharūsi then accepted the post and ruled the imāma until he was assassinated in 1919.
113 *Report of the Special Committee on Oman*, United Nations General Assembly, New York, 1964–1965, document A/5846, p. 38.
114 *Report of the Special Committee on Oman*, op. cit., pp. 38–39.
115 Al-Kindi, A.A., 1983, op. cit., tome X, p. 58.
116 Ibid., p. 68. See also pp. 23 and 57.
117 Al-Azkāui, 1976, op. cit., p. 111.
118 Al-Kindi, 1983, op. cit., tome X, p. 58.
119 Ibid., p. 229.
120 Ibid., p: 220.
121 Ibid., pp. 223 and 234.
122 Ibid., p. 215.
123 *Report of the Special Committee on Oman*, op. cit., p. 39. According to the Arab text of the report, decisions are taken by majority vote.
124 Ibid., p. 39.
125 Ibid.
126 Here is the model of a *bay'a* used by *imām* Nāṣer ibn Murshed (1624–1649):

> To sheikh (*al-wāli* Abi al-Hasan): We declare you to be governor of the village of Liwā' in the region of al-Bāṭina; we entrust you with the village and its region, whether inhabited or desert, and we order you to govern the whole population with justice, whether they be slaves or free, poor or rich, important or insignificant, and to preserve them from evil. You must be firm and also kind; you must be upright with the Muslims, your followers: you must accord to each the enjoyment of his rights; never allow faults to pass unpunished and do your best to guide your subjects towards what is good and to keep the canals and their fields in good order; you must enable their mosques to prosper and pardon the guilty; watch over the poor and weak that they may have their share in God's gift. You must make known to them those of your friends who can solace them by attending to their needs from time to time, for most poor people will not generally come to you from shame or weakness and although they are Muslims, and they will not come to ask you what you hold to be just; you must imprison those who justly deserve prison… and you must feed the weak among the Muslims, especially those who are deserving. Entrust to no man the charge I have given you except to one who can truly defend the religion of the Muslims. I entrust to you the protection of the country and its defence; I entrust to you the women and the citizens; I have ordered all the villages to obey you and I formally forbid anyone to disobey you as long as you carry out these precepts. But if you defy my orders, I shall not

> answer for the money you have collected from your subjects and you will take the consequences yourself... my only wish is to exalt the Muslim religion, to follow the precepts of the prophet Mohammed, to stimulate the faith and combat iniquities.
>
> (Al-Wasmi (Khalid), *Oman entre l'indépendance et l'occupation coloniale*, Geneva, Labor et Fides; Paris, Publications orientalistes de France, 1986, p. 78)

For further details on the *wālis* and their *bay'a*, see al-Kindi, A.A., op. cit., tome X, p. 175 and also *Kitāb al-Siyar wal-Jawābāt*, op. cit., tome II, p. 184.

127 *Qāḍī* in the singular and *quḍāh* in the plural.
128 *Report of the Special Committee on Oman*, op. cit., p. 39.
129 Gardet, L., 1977, op. cit., p. 48.
130 Al-Kindi, A.A., 1983, op. cit., tome X, p. 127.
131 Ibid., p. 126. See also *Kitāb al-Siyar wal-Jawābāt*, op. cit., tome II, p. 178.
132 Al-Kindi, A.A., 1983, op. cit., tome X, p. 219.

2 The Portuguese period: 1500–1650

133 Lorimer, J.G., Gazetteer of the Persian Gulf, Oman and Central Arabia, ed. and completed by R.J. Birdwood, Calcutta, Superintendant Govt. Printing, 1908–1915.
134 Miles, S.B., op. cit., p. 137.
135 Wilson, A.T., op. cit., p. 83.
136 Al-'Aqād (Salāḥ), *al-Tayārāt al-Siyāsiah fi al-Khaīij al-'Arabi*, 'Political currents in the Arabian Gulf', Anglo-Egyptian Library, 1974, p. 10.
137 Wilson, A.T., op. cit., pp. 106–108.
138 Miles, S.B., op. cit., pp. 133–134.
139 Al-Sālmī, A.H., op. cit., tome I, p. 246.
140 See ibn Rustaq (Ḥumayd) (d. 1873), *al-Fatḥ al-mubīn fi Sīrat al-Bū Saīdiyyīn*, 'History of the Imams and Seyyids of Oman', translated and edited by G.P. Badger, London, Drak Publishers Ltd., 1986, p. XXV (the author's name in the English edition appears as Salil ibn Razik).
141 Wolpert, S., *A new History of India*, 2nd edition, Oxford University Press, New York, 1982, p. 136.
142 Al-Sabah, S.A., op. cit., p. 21.
143 It must be emphasised that some historians are reluctant to accept that Aḥmed ibn Mājed agreed to help Vasco de Gama in his mission. Some think he died before that date.
144 Wolpert, S., op. cit., p. 136.
145 Barros, João de, *Da Asia*, Lisbon, Regia Officina Typographica, 1781 (reprinted, Paris, 1981, pp. 1–2).
146 Wilson, A.T., op. cit., p. 112.
147 Barros, J. de, op. cit., pp. 3–5.
148 Mies, S.B., op. cit., p. 151.
149 Wilson, A.T., op. cit., p. 124.
150 Bondarevsky, G., *Hegemonists and Imperialists in the Persian Gulf*, Moscow, Novosti Press Agency Publishing House, 1981, p. 37.
151 Wilson, A.T., op. cit., pp. 118–119.
152 Ibid., p. 82.
153 Al-Sabah, S.A., op. cit., p. 22.
154 Barros, J. de, op. cit., p. 2.
155 Al-'Aqād, S., op. cit., p. 12.
156 Miles, S.B., op. cit., p. 164.
157 Al-'Aqād, S., op. cit., p. 12.

158 Miles, S.B., op. cit., pp. 156–158.
159 Ibid., p. 163.
160 Ibid., pp. 182–183.
161 Bondarevsky, G., op. cit., p. 39.
162 Lorimer, J.G., op. cit., vol. 1, p. 9. See also Wilson, A.T., op. cit., p. 159.
163 Wilson, A.T., op. cit., p. 139.
164 Bondarevsky, G., op. cit., p. 41.
165 Ibid., p. 41.
166 Miles, S.B., op. cit. p. 184.
167 Lorimer, J.G., op. cit. p. vol. 1, p. 24.
168 Ibid., p. 26.
169 al-Sabah, S.A., op. cit., p. 23.
170 Cf. Wilson, A.T., op. cit., p. 165.
171 See al-Sabah, S.A., op. cit., p. 24.
172 Lorimer, J.G., op. cit., vol. 1, p. 46.
173 Ibid., p. 46.
174 Wilson, A.T., op. cit., p. 168.
175 Lorimer, J.G., op. cit., vol. 1, p. 48.
176 al-Sabah, S.A., op. cit., pp. 24–25.

3 The example of the Ibadhi Islamic State in modern history

177 Ibn Ruzayq, H., op. cit., p. 54.
178 Ibid., p. 53.
179 Ibid., p. 54.
180 Cf., above, Chapter 1 for more details on the 'states' of the *imāma*.
181 Miles, S.B., op. cit., p. 202.
182 Al-*Sayār* ('A 'Īsha), *Dawlat al-Ya'āribah, 'Umān wa sharq Afriqiyā*, 1624–1741, 'The Ya'rūbite State, Oman and East Africa', Beirut, Dar al-Quds, 1975, p. 50.
183 Miles, S.B., op. cit., p. 192.
184 Al-Sālmī, A.H., op. cit., tome II, p. 16. See also al-Azkawi, S., op. cit., pp. 104–105.
185 The Banī Yās tribes are the ancestors of al-Nahyān, the current rulers of Abu Dhabi.
186 Al-Sālmī, A.H., op. cit., tome II, p. 13.
187 Le Cour Grandmaison, C., 'Présentation du sultanat d'Oman', in *La Péninsule arabique aujourd'hui*, under the direction of Paul Bonnenfant, Paris, éd. Du C.N.R.S., 1982, tome II, p. 276.
188 Miles, S.B., op. cit., p. 198.
189 See al-Sālmi, A.H., op. cit., tome II, p. 17.
190 Le Cour Grandmaison, C., op. cit., p. 276.
191 Ibid., p. 270.
192 Ibid., p. 276.
193 Chapter 6 will deal more particularly with the development of the Omano-African axis.
194 *Oman*, Damascus, ed. of the Bureau de 'série de recherches arabes', 1964, p. 67.
195 The Diu and Goa regions remained under Portuguese control until 1961.
196 *Oman*, op. cit., p. 52.
197 The reigns of Bel'arab ibn Sulṭan and his brother Sayf ibn Sulṭān overlapped, due, perhaps, to the fact that Sayf had been approved by some of the tribes in 1692, four years after the beginning of his brother Bel'arab's reign (1688–1711). In other words, until 1711 there were two *imāms* in Oman. Certain external acquisitions from 1696 are Sayf ibn Sulṭān's by right. However, uncertainties about this period remain and it is difficult to be precise. It is noteworthy that Bel'arab died in 1711, the year that also marks the end of Sayf's reign: both brothers passed away on the same date.

198 *Oman*, op. cit., p. 67.
199 Landen, R.G., op. cit., p. 55.
200 Ibn Ruzayq, H., op. cit., p. 93.
201 *Al-awqāf* are the properties and possessions of orphans and old people, properties of the mosques taken over by the State. Al-sharī'a, Muslim law, prohibits their disposal under any circumstances.
202 Ibn Ruzayq, H., op. cit., p. 94.
203 See al-Sayār, A., op. cit., p. 112.
204 Cf., above, Chapter 1 (Exclusions from the *imāma*), and al-Azkawi, S.S., op. cit., p. 111.
205 Al-Kindi, A.A., op. cit., tome X, p. 58. Cf. above, Chapter 1.
206 See Bathurst, R.D., 'Maritime trade and imamate government: two principal themes in the history of Oman to 1728', in Hopwood, D. *et al.*, *The Arabian Peninsula: society and politics*, London, George Allen and Unwin, 1972, p. 104.
207 Al-Azkawi, S.S., op. cit., p. 113.
208 Ibid.
209 Ibn Ruzayq, H., op. cit., p. 102.
210 Al-Azkani, S.S., op. cit., p. 114.
211 Ibid., p. 116.
212 Ibid., p. 115.
213 Le Cour Grandmaison, C., 'Présentation du sultanat d'Oman', op. cit., p. 276.
214 *L'Oman et la France, quelques éléments d'histoire. Archives et documantation*, Paris, Ministère des Affaires étrangères, 1989, p. 3.
215 Kelly, J.B., 'A prevalence of furies: tribes, politics and religion in Oman and Trucial Oman', in Hopwood, D. *et al., The Arabian Peninsula: society and politics*, London, George Allen and Unwin, 1972, p. 108 (*Studies in Modern Asia and Africa*, no. 8).
216 Al-Azkawi, S.S., op. cit., p. 127.
217 Bathurst, R.D., op. cit., p. 105.
218 Al-Sālmi, A.H., op. cit., tome II, p. 118, and Al-Azkawi, S.S., op. cit., p. 113.
219 Al-'Aqād, S., op. cit., p. 48.
220 Ibid., p. 49.
221 Quoted by al-Sayār, A., op. cit., p. 199.
222 Ibid., p. 200.
223 Al-Sayār, A., op. cit., p. 202.
224 Ibid., p. 202.
225 Ibn Ruzayq, H., op. cit., p. 151.
226 Kajare (Firouz), *Le Sultanat d'Oman, étude d'histoire diplomatique et de droit international*, Paris, A. Pedone, 1914, p. 66.
227 Ibid. See also Ibn Ruzayq, H., op. cit., p. 155, and al-Sālmī, A.H., op. cit., tome II, p. 128.

4 Al-Bū Sa'īdi's state: the origin of the sultanate system

228 The history of Aḥmed's accession to power is not well established. Some hold that he obtained his *bay'a* after driving the Persians out in 1741. Others claim he got it in 1744, that is to say after restoring order in internal affairs and liquidating the opposition; we find this the more plausible hypothesis. In fact it is even difficult to determine how long he remained in power. It is astonishing to see A.H. Sālmī saying he exercised power for 29 years (op. cit., tome II, p. 139). If we accept the date given above, we find he was in power for 39 years.
229 'Abd Allah (Muḥammad Mursi), *Emarat Sāḥel Umān wa al-Dawla al-Sa'ūdiya al-'Ūlla*, 'The emirates of the coast of Oman and the first Saudi State', Cairo, vol. I Librairie égytienne, (1793–1918), 1978, pp. 91–93.
230 Al-Sālmī, A.H., op. cit., vol. II, p. 137.

231 Lorimer, J.G., op. cit., vol. 1, p. 135.
232 Al-'Aqād, S., op. cit., p. 50.
233 Al-Sālmī, A.H., op. cit., tome II, p. 137.
234 Nāṣer ibn Muḥammad is the son of Muḥammad ibn Nāṣer al-Ghāfiri, who contributed to the great division of Oman between the Ghafirite and Hanawite factions.
235 Kajare, F., op. cit., p. 69.
236 This question will be dealt with later, in the chapter on the sultanate of Muscat and Zanzibar.
237 Wilson, A.T., op. cit., p. 189.
238 Al-Sayyābi (Sālem bin Hamūd bin Shamis), *'Umān 'abr al-Tārikh*, 'Oman through history', Sultanate of Oman, Ministry of National and Cultural Heritage, 1986, tome IV, p. 154.
239 Kajare, F., op. cit., p. 68.
240 Miles, S.B., op. cit., vol.1, part 1, p. 274.
241 See Lorimer, J.G., op. cit. pp. 145–147.
242 This matter will be dealt with in detail in Chapter 5 on the *'Saḥel Oman'*.
243 Al-Sayyābi, S.H., op. cit., tome IV, p. 182.
244 Ibid., p. 184.
245 Al-Sālmī, A.H., op. cit., tome II, p. 140.
246 Bondarevsky, G., op. cit., p. 59.
247 Ibid., p. 60.
248 Lorimer, J.G., op. cit., vol. 1, p. 151.
249 Kajare, F., op. cit., p. 74.
250 Ibid., p. 75.
251 Ibid.
252 Bondarevsky, G., op. cit., pp. 60–61.
253 Lorimer, J.G., op. cit., vol. 1, pp. 151–155. See also Bondarevsky, G., op. cit., p. 57.
254 Al-'Aqād, S., op. cit., p. 63.
255 In Ventôse year IV (4 February 1796): That is the date indicated in the diplomatic document of the Ministère des Affaires Etrangères. In fact, the Committee of Public Safety and the Convention, of which it was an offshoot, were separated in October 1795. So an error that is either chronological or institutional casts doubt on the reliability of the document in question.
256 Aff. étr. N.S. Mascate, vol. 37, p. 168.
257 Aff. étr. N.S. Mascate, vol. 37, p. 171.
258 Ibid., p. 172.
259 For details of the instructions to citizen Beauchamp, see the memo in Aff. étr. N.S. Mascate, vol. 37, pp. 168–176.
260 Auzoux, A., 'La France et Mascate aux XVIII et XIX siècles', *Revue d'histoire diplomatique*, 1910, p. 235.
261 Al-'Aqād, S., op. cit., p. 63.
262 Graz, Liesl, *Les Omanais, nouveaux gardiens du Golfe*, Paris, Albin Michel 1981, p. 22.
263 Al-'Aqād, S., op. cit., p. 66.
264 See the text in Aitchinson, C.U., *Collection of treaties, engagements and sanadss relating to India and neighbouring countries*, Delhi, Manager of Publications, 1933, vol. XI, pp. 287–288.
265 Al-'Aqād, S., op. cit., pp. 68–69.
266 Al-Naqib (Khaldun Hassan), *al-Mujtama' wal-Dawla fi al-Khalīj wal-Jazirah al-'Arabiyyah*, 'Society and State in the Gulf and the Arabian Peninsula', Beirut, Markaz Dirasat al-Waḥda al-Arabiyya', 1987, p. 83.
267 Al-'Aqād, S., op. cit., p. 69.
268 Wilson A.T., op. cit., p. 189.
269 Al-'Aqād, S., op. cit., p. 77.

270 Aitchinson, C.U., op. cit., p. 288.
271 Auzoux, A., op. cit., p. 239.
272 Ibid., p. 239.
273 Al-'Aqād, S., op. cit., p. 77.
274 The Wahhābis form a sect that arose in the second half of the eighteenth century and later provided the official doctrine of Saudi Arabia. We shall return to that later.
275 Auzoux, A., op. cit., p. 240.
276 Ibid.
277 Ibid., p. 241.
278 Al-'Aqād, S., op. cit., p. 78.
279 Auzoux, A., op. cit., pp. 242–243.
280 Aff. étr. N.S. Mascate, vol. 37, p. 162.
281 Kajare, F., op. cit., p. 80.
282 Auzoux, A., op. cit., p. 252.
283 See al-'Aqād, S., op. cit., p. 58.
284 The Buraymi oasis groups together nine villages, six, including al-'Ain, dependant on Abu Dhabi, the other three, Sa'ra, Hamāssa and the village of al-Buraimi are dependant on the sultanate of Muscat. We shall return to the al-Buraimi question later.
285 Kelly, J.B., *The eastern frontiers of the Arab Peninsula*, trans. By Kheyri Hammad, Beyrouth, ed. Al-Hayar, 1971, p. 85.
286 Al-Sālmī, A.H., op. cit., tome II, p. 157.
287 Maurizi, V., *History of Sayid Sa'id*, Cambridge, Oleander Press, 1954, pp. 5–6.
288 Sa'id, the sayyid or sultan, who was occasionally, addressed using the title of *imām*. This usage is to be found particularly in the documents of the French Foreign Ministry.
289 Kajare, F., op. cit., p. 85.
290 Ibid., p. 85.
291 Auzoux, A., op. cit., p. 258.
292 Kajare, F., op. cit., p. 86.
293 See the text in al-Wasmi, op. cit., p. 139.
294 Kajare, F., op. cit., p. 87.

5 *'Sāḥel Oman'*: the common history (1750–1850)

295 We shall put 'Sāḥel Oman' in inverted commas to distinguish it from the coast of Oman, the coastal region (the same word in Arabic).
296 Heard-Bey, Frauke, 'Le développement d'un Etat-cité maritime dans le Golfe: l'exemple de Dubayy', in *La Péninsule arabique d'aujourd'hui*, directed by Paul Bonnenfant, Paris, éd. C.N.R.S., 1982, tome II, p. 523.
297 Al-Sabah, S.A., op. cit., p. 61.
298 The well-known story going the rounds concerning the naming of Ra's al-Khaymah tells that sheikh Qasim had pitched a tent at the entrance to the little gulf on which the town of Julfar is situated; on it he placed a lantern to guide the fishermen and merchant ships entering the port. Because of this the region was known by the name of Ra's al-Khaymah and, in time, the name Julfar disappeared altogether.
299 Kelly, J.B., op. cit., p. 18.
300 Nawfal (Sayyed), *al-Khalīj al-'Arabi aw al-Hadūd al-Sharqiyya lel Jazirah al-'Arabia*, 'The Arabian Gulf or the eastern frontiers of the Arab homeland', Beirut, Dar Attali'a, 1969, p. 253.
301 Al-Shaḥūḥ are the tribes living in the region of Ru'ūs al-Jibāl, 'the mountain tops', lying between Oman and '*Sāḥel Oman*'. Al-Shaḥūḥ are distinguished by their specific dialect, which is hard to understand. When they arrived, the Omanis were amazed that some people thought they were not Arabs.
302 See ibn Ruzayq, H., op. cit., p. 111.

303 'Abd Allah, M.M., op. cit., p. 93.
304 Miles, S.B., op. cit., p. 269.
305 Quoted by Ibrahim ('Abdel Aziz 'Abdel Ghani), *Ṣirā' al'Omarā'*, 'A combat of the princes', London, Dar al-Saqi, 1990, p. 36.
306 Al-'Abed, F.S., *Syāsat Briṭṭānia fi al-Khalīj al-'Arabi*, 'British policy in the Arabian Gulf', Kuwait, Dar That al-Salasel [d.], p. 43.
307 Al-Sabah, S.A., op. cit., p. 65.
308 Al-'Abed, F.S., op. cit., pp. 42–43.
309 Bondarevsky, G., op. cit., p. 75.
310 Al-'Abed, F.S., op. cit., p. 50.
311 Bondarevsky, G., op. cit., p. 75.
312 Ibid., pp. 73–74.
313 Maurizi, V., *History of Sayid Sa'īd*, Cambridge, Oleander Press, 1954, p. 52.
314 Bondarevsky, G., op. cit., p. 76.
315 Ibrahim, A.A., Sirā' al-'Omarā', (combat of the Princes), London Saqi Books, 1990, p. 65.
316 See Lorimer, J.G., op. cit. vol. 2, p. 643.
317 Al-'Abed, F.S., op. cit. p. 73.
318 Bondarevsky, G., op. cit., p. 77.
319 Ibid.
320 It is worth noting here that 'Ajmān and Umm-al-Qaywaīn, being under the authority of al-Qawāsim, did not sign this undertaking. This situation would change, however, in order to fit in with British strategy in the region.
321 Aitchinson, C.U., op. cit., p. 241.
322 Ibid.
323 See the text ibid., p. 245.
324 Al-'Aqād, S., op. cit., p. 107.
325 Bondarevsky, G., op. cit., p. 78.
326 'Abd Allah, M.M., op. cit., p. 260.
327 Kelly, J.B., op. cit., vol. 1, p. 173.
328 Ibid., p. 176.
329 Ibid., pp. 177–180.
330 Al-'Abed, F.S., op. cit., p. 96.
331 Al-'Aqād, S., op. cit., p. 112.
332 Al-'Aqād, S., op. cit., p. 114.
333 Cf. text in Aitchinson, C.U., op. cit., p. 256.

6 The Omani–African state (1650–1860): the sultanates

334 See al-Qāsīmī (Sultan ibn Muḥammad), *Taqsim al-Imbarātoriyyah al-'Umāniyyah 1856–1862*, 'The partition of the Omani empire', Dubai (UAE), al-Bayan, 1989, p. 14 (Sheikh Dr Sultan ibn Muḥammad al-Qāsīmī is the present governor of Sharjah).
335 Al-Sayat, A., op. cit., p. 82.
336 Al-Qāsīmī, S.M., op. cit., p. 15.
337 Le Cour Grandmaison, op. cit., tome I, p. 278.
338 Phillips, Wendell, *Oman, a history*, Beirut, Librairie du Liban, 1971, p. 101.
339 Al-Maghairi, Sa'īd ibn 'Ali, *Jahinat al-akhbār fi tarīkh Zanzibar*, Sultanate of Oman, Ministry of National and Cultural Heritage, 2nd edition, 1986, p. 80.
340 The French *Journal des débats* describes the wealth of Zanzibar at that time in these terms: 'The Sultan himself worked to combine sugar, cotton, indigo, spices and coffee with the clove industry. This diversity of products is characteristic. Some are purely African, others have analogues in Arabia and India, still others seem to have been taken from the European colonies in South America and even the islands of the

Pacific, a faithful reflection of a country in which the characters of several others are combined and which at the same time belongs to Africa in respect of situation and climate, to the Muslim Orient by its neighbours and rulers, to India and the South Sea Islands by some items of its flora, to Spanish America by its burgeoning plantations.' (*Journal des débats*, in Aff. étr. M.D. Afrique, vol. 149).

341 *Journal des débats*, in Aff. étr. M.D. Afrique, vol. 149.
342 Miège, J.L., 'Oman et l'Afrique centrale au XIXe siècle' in *La Péninsule arabique d'aujourd'hui*, under the direction of Paul Bonnenfant, Paris, éd. du C.N.R.S., 1982, tome II, p. 294.
343 Ibid., p. 301. See also Landen, R.G., *Umān menthu 1856*, 'Oman depuis 1856', trans. Muḥammad Amin Abdallah, Beirut, 1970, p. 219.
344 Kajare, F., op. cit. p. 95.
345 Aff. étr. N.S. Mascate, vol. 37, pp. 162–167.
346 See Kelly, J.B., op. cit. p. 550.
347 Kajare, F., op. cit. p. 93.
348 Ibid., p. 97.
349 Stevinson, Richard, 'Aperçu sur le début de la relation commerciale et consulaire américaine avec le sultanat d'Oman (1833–1856)', in *Journal of the Gulf and Arabian Peninsula Studies*, University of Kuweit, N ° 11, 2nd year, July 1977, pp. 125–126. In an attempt to develop Omano-American relations, the sultan sent an emissary, Aḥmad bin Naʿmān, to the United States in 1840, on board his ship *Ṣulṭānah*: it was the first official voyage of an Arab emissary to America and the first Arab ship to moor in the port of New York. It's arrival caused a sensation in the American press, to the extent that the American elections were relegated to second place (the arrival of this ship coincided with the end of Martin Van Born's presidency). See Ibets, H.F., *Sultanah à New York*, Sultanate of Oman, Ministry of National Heritage and Culture; Cairo, Archives des Arabes, 1980.
350 See al-Qāsīmī, S.M., op. cit., pp. 49–50.
351 Aff. étr. M.D. Afrique, vol. 149, folio 6.
352 Aff. étr. M.D. Afrique, vol. 149, folio 6–7.
353 Aff. étr. N.S. Mascate, vol. 37, folio 167. See the text of the agreement in al-Wasmi, K., op. cit. p. 230.
354 *Le Journal des débats*, in Aff. étr. M.D. Afrique, vol. 149.
355 Miles S.B., op. cit., p. 246. The Kuria Muria Islands, in the 'Arabian Sea', a few kilometres from the Omani-Yemeni maritime frontier, have quite an interesting history. With the exacerbation of the Franco-British conflict in the reign of sultan Saʿīd ibn Sultan (1806–1856), France announced her intention to rent them. But by a rather British arrangement they were offered as a present to Queen Victoria. During the reign of sultan Saʿīd ibn Taymūr (1932–1970), Great Britain, deeming the islands to be of no further strategic use, returned them to Oman without the sultan having claimed them. But she asked in return that the sultan consent to rent the island of Gwader, then under Omani jurisdiction, to Pakistan. British reports in the Public Record Office show that the restoration of the Kuria Muria Islands was to cover the sultan's decision about Gwader and give an image of the sultan as a nationalist.
356 Kelly, J.B., op. cit., p. 557.
357 Cf. above, Chapter 5.
358 See Kelly, J.B., op. cit., p. 579.
359 Kajare, F., op. cit., pp. 108–109.
360 Kelly, J.B., op. cit., p. 583.
361 Kajare, F., op. cit., p. 109.
362 The eldest, Khāled, died before his father in 1854 and Hilāl had been ruled out by his father.

363 Kajare, F., op. cit., p. 112.
364 See also al-Qāsīmī, S.M., op. cit., p. 81; Lorimer, J.G., op. cit. vol. 2, pp. 469–472, and Aff. étr. N.S. Mascate, vol. 1, folio 53.
365 Aff. étr. N.S.Mascate, vol. 1, folio 53.
366 Al-Wasmi, K., *Oman entre l'indépendance et l'occupation coloniale*, Genève, Labor et Fides; Paris, Publications orientalistes de France, 1986, p. 238.
367 Ibidem.
368 See the section on the separation in Chapter 4.
369 Qasim, J.Z., *Dirāssa li tārīkh al-Emārāt al-Arabyyiah (1840–1914)*, 'Study of the history of the Arab Emirates', Kuweit, Centre of Scientific Studies, 1974, p. 86.
370 Aff. étr. N.S. Mascate, vol. 1, folio 53 and 54.
371 Kajare, F., op. cit., p. 115.
372 See al-Qāsīmī, S.M., 1989, op. cit., p. 8.
373 Landen, R.G., op. cit., p. 114.
374 Cf. above, Chapter 4.
375 Kajare, F., op. cit., p. 116.
376 Report of the Special Committee on Oman, op. cit., p. 27.
377 Landen, R.G., op. cit., p. 26.
378 Kelly, J.B., op. cit., vol. 1, p. 247.

7 The revolution of *imām* 'Azzān ibn Qays al-Bū Sa'īdi (1869–1871)

379 Landen, R.G., op. cit, p. 178.
380 Ibid., p. 181.
381 Lorimer, J.G., op. cit., vol. 1, p. 472.
382 Al-Sālmī, A.H., op. cit., tome II, p. 186.
383 Ibid., p. 188.
384 See Lorimer, J.G., op. cit., vol. 2, pp. 474–475.
385 Ibid., p. 475.
386 Ibid., p. 476. See Qasim, J.Z., op. cit., p. 97.
387 Al-Sālmī, A.H., op. cit., tome II, p. 190.
388 Lorimer, J.G., op. cit., vol. 2, p. 478.
389 Ibid., p. 481.
390 Wilkinson, J.C., *The Imamate Tradition of Oman*, Cambridge University Press, 1987, p. 230.
391 Landen, R.G., op. cit., p. 292 and al-Sālmī, A.H., op. cit., tome II, pp. 196–197.
392 See Lorimer, J.G., op. cit., tome II, p. 482. See al-Sālmī, A.H., op. cit., p. 198.
393 Landen, R.G., op. cit., p. 293.
394 Wilkinson, J.C., op. cit., p. 235.
395 Landen, R.G., op. cit. p. 295.
396 Al-Sālmī, A.H., op. cit., tome II, p. 196.
397 Wilkinson, J.C., op. cit., p. 231.
398 Cf. the integral text of the *bay'a* in Chapter 1.
399 For more details on the content and specific language of this letter, see al-Sālmī, A.H., op. cit., tome II, p. 200.
400 Ibid., p. 206.
401 Lorimer, J.G., op. cit., vol. 1, p. 483.
402 Landen, R.G., op. cit., p. 300.
403 Quoted by Kelly, J.B. *Britain and the Persian Gulf 1795–1870*, op. cit., p. 710.
404 Al-Sālmī, A.H., op. cit., tome II, pp. 211–212.
405 Cf. above, Chapter 6 and below, Chapter 10.
406 Al-Sālmī, A.H., op. cit., tome II, p. 208.
407 Kelly, J.B., *Britain and the Persian Gulf 1795–1870*, op. cit., p. 702.

408 Landen, R.G., op. cit., p. 306.
409 IOR: R/15/6/36, *The Clyde Affair*, p. 11.
410 Lorimer, J.G., op. cit., vol. 1, p. 487.
411 Landen R.G., op. cit., p. 314.
412 Lorimer R.G., op. cit., vol. 1, p. 488.
413 IOR: R/15/6/36, *The Clyde Affair*, p. 7.
414 Lorimer, J.G., op. cit., vol. 1, p. 489.
415 IOR: L/PS/9/50, *Letter from imām 'Azzan to Colonel Pelly*, p. 1159.
416 IOR: L/PS/9/50, *Letter from Colonel Pelly to Desbrew*, p. 1159.
417 IOR: R/15/6/36/, *The Clyde Affair*, pp. 11 and 21.
418 Ibid., p. 10.
419 Ibid., p. 15.
420 Ibid., pp. 22–23.
421 Ibid., p. 11.
422 Ibid., *The Clyde Affair*, pp. 28 and 32.
423 Ibid., pp. 32–33.
424 Al-Sālmī, A., op. cit., tome II, p. 226.
425 IOR: R/15/6/36, *The Clyde Affair*, p. 34.
426 IOR: R.15/6/52, *Confidential letter from Political Agent, Muscat, to Political Resident, Bushehr, June 27, 1929*, p. 219. See also Wilkinson, J.C., *The Imāma Tradition of Oman*, op. cit., p. 237.
427 Wilkinson, J.C., op. cit., p. 237. See also Kelly, J.B., *Britain and the Persian Gulf 1795–1870*, op. cit., p. 708.
428 Quoted by Wilkinson, J.C., op. cit., p. 237.
429 Ibid., p. 236.
430 Badger, G.P., 'Introduction and analysis', in *History of the Imams and Seyyids of Oman*, op. cit., p. CXIX.
431 IOR: R15/6/36, *The Clyde Affair*, p. 29.
432 Cf. Kelly, J.B., *Britain and the Persian Gulf 1795–1870*, op. cit., p. 709.
433 Lorimer J.G., op. cit., vol. 1, p. 492.
434 IOR: L/PS/9/17, *Muscat*, 1869, pp. 223–231.
435 Wilkinson, J.C., *The Imamate Tradition of Oman*, op. cit., p. 238.
436 IOR: R/15/6/36, *The Clyde Affair*, p. 36.
437 Cf. above, Chapter 4. We shall return to this point in the following chapter.
438 Lorimer, J.G., op. cit., vol. 1, p. 499.
439 IOR: R/15/6/36, *The Clyde Affair*, p. 44.
440 Lorimer, J.G., op. cit., vol. 1, p. 520.

8 Oman between independence and dependence

441 Landen, R.G., op. cit., p. 365, vol. 1, pp. 536–537.
442 Aff. étr. N.S.Mascate, vol. I, p. 65.
443 Lorimer, J.G., op. cit., vol. 1, pp. 536–537.
444 Lorimer, J.G., op. cit., vol. 1, p. 551.
445 See the proclamation the sultan issued to the Omanis in Aff. étr. N.S. Mascate, vol. II, p. 172.
446 Aff. étr. N.S. Mascate, vol. II, p. 48.
447 Aff. étr. N.S. Mascate, vol. I, p. 135.
448 Lorimer, J.G., op. cit., vol. 1, pp. 499–500.
449 Af. Étr. N.S. Mascate, vol. I, p. 56.
450 Aff. Étr. N.S. Mascate, vol. I, p. 44.
451 Lorimer, J.G., op. cit., vol. 1, p. 535.
452 Aff. étr. N.S. Mascate, vol. I, p. 84.

453 Aff. étr. N.S. Mascate vol. I, p. 61.
454 Aff. étr. N.S. Mascate, vol. I, p. 62.
455 Journal des débats, 25 February, 1899. See also Aff. étr. N.S. Mascate, vol. 33, p. 3.
456 Journal des débats, 20 November, 1898.
457 Le Cour Grandmaison, C., 'Présentation du sultanat d'Oman', op. cit., p. 279.
458 *Letter from Lord Curzon to Lord Hamilton*, 12 January 1899. IOR MSS. Eur. D 510/1.
459 Aff. étr. N.S.Mascate, vol. I, folio 56.
460 *Letter from Lord Hamilton to Lord Curzon*, 14 April, 1899. IOR MSS. Eur. C 126/1.
461 See the text in: al-Wasmi, K., op. cit., p. 230.
462 *Letter from Lord Curzon to Lord Hamilton*, 19 January 1899. IOR MSS. D 150/1.
463 Ibid.
464 *Letter from Lord Curzon to Lord Hamilton*, 9 February, 1899. IOR MSS. D 150/1.
465 *Letter from Lord Hamilton to Lord Curzon*, 3 March, 1899. IOR MSS. C 126/1.
466 *Letter from Lord Curzon to Lord Hamilton*, 23 March, 1899. IOR MSS. D 150/1.
467 Cf. above, Chapter 6.
468 *Letter from Lord Hamilton to Lord Curzon*, 10 March, 1899. IOR MSS. Eur. C 120/1.
469 See Lorimer, J.G., op, cit., vol. 1, p. 558.
470 Ibid., p. 558.
471 Ibid., p. 559.
472 Ibid., p. 559.
473 Dawud, M.A., *al-Khalīj al-'arabi wal-'alāqāt al-dawaliyyah*, 'The Arabian Gulf and international relations 1890–1914', Cairo [undated] tome I p. 99.
474 *Letter from Lord Curzon to Lord Hamilton*, 23 February, 1899. IOR MSS. Eur. D 150/1.
475 *Letter fromLord Curzon to Lord Hamilton*, 23 March 1899. IOR MSS. Eur. D 150/1.
476 *Letter from Lord Hamilton to Lord Curzon*, 3 March 1899. IOR MSS. Eur. C 126/1.
477 The boutres are Arab sailing ships.
478 Miège, J.L., 'L'Oman et l'Afrique orientale au XIX siècle', in *La Péninsule arabique d'aujourd'hui*. Under the direction of Paul Bonnenfant, Paris, éd. du C.N.R.S., 1982, tome II, pp. 300–301.
479 Kajare, F., op. cit., p. 142.
480 Ibid., pp. 147–148.
481 Ibid., p. 142.
482 Aff. étr. N.S. Mascate, vol. 27, p. 211.
483 Aff. étr. N.S. Mascate, vol. 27, p. 212.
484 *Journal officiel*, in Aff. étr. N.S. Mascate, vol. 33, folio 33.
485 These were Jonkheer de Savornin Lohman, a former minister of the interior in the Netherlands, a member of the permanent arbitration court, Mr Melvin W. Fuller, chief justice of the supreme court of the United States of America, a member of the permanent arbitration court, and M. Henri Lammasch, a member of the house of Lords of the Austrian parliament, a member of the permanent arbitration court (Aff. etr. N.S. Mascate, vol. 33, folio 202); Mr Lohman represented France, Mr Fuller Great Britain and Mr Lammasch was the supreme arbiter.
486 Aff. étr. N.S.Mascate, vol. 33, folio 52.
487 *Report of the Special Committee on Oman*, op. cit., p. 26.
488 Aff. étr. N.S.Mascate, vol. 33, pp. 117–118.
489 Aff. étr. N.S.Mascate, vol. 33, p. 119.
490 Aff. étr. N.S.Mascate, vol. 33, p. 126.
491 Al-'Aqād, S., op. cit., p. 209.
492 Lorimer, J.G., op. cit., vol. 1, pp. 393–394.
493 IOR: R/15/6/51, pp. 4–5.
494 IOR: R/15/6/51, pp. 5–6.
495 Le Cour Grandmaison, C., 'Présentation du sulanat d'Oman', op. cit., p. 280.

9 The sultanate of Muscat and the *imāma* of Oman

496 Nawfal, Sayeed, *al-Awdā' al-Siyāsiyyah li Emarat al-Khalīj al-'Arabi wa Janūb al-Jazīrah*, 'The political situations in the Emirates of the Arabian Gulf and the southern Peninsula', Cairo, Institut de recherches et d'études arabes, UNICEF. Book 2, 1972, p. 79. See also Zorgbibe, Charles, *Géopolitique et histoire du Golfe*, Paris, PUF, 1991, p. 36.
497 Landen, R.G., op. cit., p. 267.
498 Ibid.
499 Bondarevsky, G., op. cit., p. 102.
500 Kelly, J.B., op. cit., p. 833.
501 Wingate, R. *Not in the limelight*, London, Hutchinson & Co. Ltd., 1959, p. 82.
502 Landen, R.G., op. cit., p. 401.
503 Al-Sālmī, Muḥammad bin 'Abd Allah, *Nahḍat al-a'yān bi ḥuriyyat 'Uman*, 'The renaissance of the men of note in the freedom of Oman', Cairo, [undated] p. 130.
504 Wilkinson, J.C., *The Imamate Tradition of Oman*, op. cit., p. 243.
505 Al-Sālmī (Muḥammad bin 'Abd Allah), op. cit., p. 138.
506 Cf. above, Chapter 1.
507 Al-Sālmī (Muḥammad bin 'Abd Allah) op. cit., p. 151.
508 Cf. above, Chapter 1.
509 IOR: R/15/6/337, *Administration report of the Muscat agency for the year 1913*, p. 51.
510 Al-Sālmī, Muḥammad bin 'Abd Allah, op. cit., p. 181.
511 IOR: R/15/6/337, *Administration report of the Muscat agency for the year 1913*, p. 52.
512 Al-Sālmī, Muḥammad bin 'Abd Allah, op. cit., pp. 197–198.
513 IOR: R/15/6/337, *Administration report of the Muscat agency for the year 1913*, p. 49.
514 Al-Sālmī, Muḥammad bin 'Abd Allah, op. cit., p. 200.
515 IOR: R/15/6/337, *Administration report of the Muscat political agency for the year 1913*, pp. 122–123.
516 Ibid., p. 123.
517 Al-Sālmī, Muḥammad bin 'Abd Allah, op. cit., p. 218 (we have adapted the language of the text without in any way modifying the content).
518 IOR: R/15/6/337, *Confidential: Report from political agent, Muscat, to S.G.Knox, Bushehr, 8 Feb. 1916*, p. 75.
519 *Report of the Special Committee on Oman*, op. cit., p. 29.
520 Peterson, J.E., The revival of the Ibāḍi Imamate in Oman and the threat to Muscat, 1913–1920', *Arabian Studies*, vol. III, Middle East Centre, University of Cambridge, 1976, p. 175.
521 IOR: R/15/6/337, *Administration report of the Muscat political agency and consulate 1920*, p. 196.
522 Landen, R.G., op. cit., p. 399.
523 IOR: R/15/6/337, *Administration report of the Muscat politcal agency 1916*, p. 130.
524 IOR: R/15/6/337, *Confidential: Administration report of the Muscat political agency 1919*, p. 175.
525 Aff. étr. Asie 1918–1929, Golfe Persique-Mer Rouge, vol. II, p. 20.
526 *Report of the Special Committee on Oman*, op. cit., p. 29.
527 Ibid.
528 Ibid., p. 30.
529 Aff. étr. Asie 1918–1929, Golfe Persique–Mer Rouge, vol. II, pp. 22–23.
530 IOR: R/15/6/337, *Confidential: Administration report of the Muscat political agency and consulate 1920*, p. 220.
531 Ibid., p. 196.

532 Wingate, R., op. cit., p. 86.
533 Ibid.
534 Ibid., p. 89.
535 Ibid., p. 90. See also the *Report of the Special Committee on Oman*, op. cit., p. 31.
536 *Report of the Special Committee on Oman*, op. cit., pp. 92–93. See also *The Treaty of Sib 1920*, in FO 371/126, p. 884.
537 *Report of the Special committee on Oman*, op. cit., p. 92.
538 IOR: R/15/6/337, *confidential: Administration report of the Muscat political agency and consulate 1920*, p. 200.
539 Quoted by Wilkinson, J.C., *The Imamate Tradition of Oman*, op. cit., p. 251.
540 IOR: R/15/6/52, *Secret: Report from the political agent, Muscat, to the civil commissioner, Baghdad, 28 April 1920*, p. 35.
541 Ibid., p. 37.
542 Aff. étr. Asie 1918–1929, Golfe Persique, vol. 2, p. 53.
543 Ibid., p. 108.
544 Ibid., p. 109.
545 Ibid., p. 111.
546 IOR: R/15/6/52, *From political agent, Muscat, to the deputy political resident, Bushehr, 26 June 1920*, p. 54.
547 IOR: R/15/6/52, *Telegram. From political agent, Muscat, to political resident, Bushehr, 17/7/1920*, p. 60.
548 IOR: R/15/6/52, *Confidential: Deputy secretary, Foreign. 18 August, 1920*, p. 69.
549 IOR: R/15/6/52, *Air Force mess, Ambala, 8/9/1920*, p. 78.
550 IOR: R/15/6/52, *From the secretary to the government of India in the Foreign and political department, to the political resident, Bushehr, 1 Dec. 1920*, p. 114.
551 IOR: R/15/6/54, *From political resident, Bushehr, to the Foreign secretary, to the government of India, Nov. 1931*, p. 369.
552 Cf. Wilkinson, J.C., op. cit., p. 274; Aitchinson, C.U., op. cit., p. 319. Note that the same type of agreement was signed by the rulers of other Gulf countries.
553 IOR: R/15/6/52, *From British resident and consulate general, Bushehr, to Sir Denis Bray, Foreign secretary of the government of India, 6 August, 1920*, p. 230.
554 Ibid., p. 231.
555 IOR: R/15/6/54, *Translation: Letter of abdication of Sultan Taymur to the political resident in the Gulf, 17 Nov. 1931*, p. 376. See the original of the letter of abdication in IOR: R/15/6/52, 22 July 1929, p. 224.
556 IOR: R/15/6/54, *Letter from Said bin Taimur to the political resident in the Persian Gulf, 10/2/1932*, p. 419.

10 The revolution of 1955–1964: towards the end of colonial partition and chaos

557 See Heard-Bey, F., *From Trucial States to United Arab Emirates*, London, Longman, 1982, p. 303.
558 FO 371–126 881, *The Sultans of Muscat and Oman*, 28/07/1957.
559 *Le Monde*, of 24 January, 1956.
560 FO 371–114 578, *Letter from residency in Bahrein to the Foreign Office*, April 5, 1955.
561 FO 371–114 583, *Letter from Shuckburgh to Sir H. Trevelyan, Cairo, Nov. 18, 1955.*
562 FO 371–144 583, Confidential: *Foreign Office to 10 Downing Street, Nov. 16 1955.* See also FO 371–144 583, *Advance warning of the Nazwa operation, Nov. 30, 1955.*
563 See the text of the declaration in FO 371–126 908.
564 FO 371–114 585, *Secret telegram from Bagdad to Foreign Office, December 16, 1955*. The subject is Rashid 'Ali al-Kilani, former prime minister of Iraq and a fierce

opponent of English colonialism. As for the mufti al-Qadsi, he is sheikh Amin al-Husseini, leader of the Palestinian nationalist movement.

565 FO 371–126 869, *Annual report on territories in Persian Gulf*, Muscat 1956.

566 FO 371–126 879, *Internal political situation in Muscat and Oman.*

567 FO 371–126 880, letter dated 23 July 1957, in *Internal political situation in Muscat and Oman.*

568 FO 371–120 576, *Confidential: Letter from the British consulate in Muscat to the British residency in Bahrain, August 16, 1956.*

569 *Oman*, op. cit., p. 120.

570 *Report of the Special Committee on Oman*, op. cit., p. 54.

571 *Oman*, op. cit., pp. 102–103.

572 *Report of the Special Committee on Oman*, op. cit., p. 12. See also FO 371–126 883, *Confidential: from Foreign Office to Baghdad, August 16, 1957.*

573 *Report of the Special Committee on Oman*, op. cit., p. 12.

574 *Oman*, op. cit., p. 132.

575 *Report of the Special Committee on Oman*, op. cit., p. 13.

576 Muḥammad Amin 'Abd Allah, a militant nationalist, was a member of the 'Liberation Front', which was to be established at the same time. He translated a number of books on Oman. He died in his homeland, Muscat, in 1982.

577 *Report of the Special Committee on Oman*, p. 13.

578 Cf. Chapter 9.

579 FO 371–128 76, *From Washington to Foreign Office, July 23, 1957.*

580 FO 371–120 575, *Foreign Office letter dated March 2, 1956.*

581 CAB. 129/90, *Secret, Cabinet. Anglo-American co-operation. Note by the Prime Minister, 15 Nov. 1957.*

582 FO 371–114 581, *Letter from Eastern Dept. to Chancery, Cairo, 23/8/55.*

583 FO 371–126 884, *The agreement of Sib. August 16, 1957.* See also FO 371–884, *Confidential Foreign Office correspondences. August 21, 1957.*

584 FO 371–126 887, *Confidential: Sir Ronald Wingate and the agreement of Sib, Sept. 1957.*

585 It should be noted that the copy presented was not the original for two reasons: the first is that the English were in possession of one of the copies and refused to show it. As for the *Imām*'s copy, it had been kept in the home of a certain 'suffin' (Shabān) bin Ḥamed in Oman but he had been attacked in his house and all his documents, including the treaty, had been stolen. *Report of the Special Committee on Oman* op. cit., p. 32.

586 It is interesting to note that when the *imām* had sent sheikh Ṣāleh to Bahrein in 1953 to discuss certain modifications to be made to the treaty, the resident had declared that the United Kingdom insisted that the integral version of the treaty be maintained. See *Report of the Special Committee on Oman*, op. cit., p. 33.

587 *Report of the Special Committee on Oman*, op. cit., p. 39.

588 FO 371–126 883, *Secret: Telegram from Washington to Foreign Office, August 20, 1957.*

589 *Report of the Special Committee on Oman*, op, cit., p. 17.

590 Ibid., p. 18.

591 In fact the discussion about the Franco-British differences over the flying of the French flag by Omani ships went on in the absence of Oman, the country most concerned but represented by Great Britain. Cf. Chapter VIII.

592 *Report of the Special Committee on Oman*, op. cit., p. 53.

593 Ibid., p. 65.

594 There were some 10 000 Omani refugees in Saudi Arabia, 5000 in Kuweit, 200 in the United Arab Republic (Egypt) and 300 in Iraq. Ibid., p. 63.

595 *Report of the Special Committee on Oman*, op. cit., p. 65.

596 *Report of the Special Committee on Oman*, op. cit., p. 65.
597 Ibid., pp. 78–79.
598 Ibid., p. 78.
599 Ibid., p. 79.
600 *Imām* Ghāleb is still living in Saudi Arabia, although some members of his family and friends are living and working in present-day Oman.
601 *Report of the Special Committee on Oman*, op. cit., p. 79.
602 FO 371–126919, *Secret: Memorandum, Muscat and Oman, August 7th, 1957.*
603 FO 371–126 904, *Confidential: Foreign Office to Sir B. Burrows, Bahrein, August 30th, 1957.*
604 Quoted by Eric Rouleau, 'Oman ou la révolution refoulée', ['Oman, or the repressed revolution'], *Le Monde*, 28 May 1971.
605 Halliday, Fred, *Arabia without sultans*, New York, Random House, 1975, p. 276.
606 Ibid., p. 275.

Sources and bibliography

This bibliography is divided into several parts. It mainly consists of, first, the 'ibādites manuscripts', dated from many centuries, and recently published by the Ministry of National and Cultural Heritage. However, they do not represent the official opinion of the Omani government. Second, the official documents from the French and English public archives (French Ministry of Foreign Affairs, Indian Office Record, IOR), as well as the records of the Foreign Office (FO).

In fact, the French represent nearly all the documents registered in the French Ministry of Foreign Affairs that are related to the present subject.

In respect to the alphabetical order, the article 'al' (the) along with the words 'ben', 'bin' and 'ibn' (son of) have been ignored.

Bibliography

Monographs

Ibadites sources

PUBLICATIONS OF THE SULTANATE OF OMAN, MINISTRY OF CULTURAL AND NATIONAL HERITAGE

'Amer, ibn 'Ali bin 'Umayr, *Ḥadhārat 'Umān al-Qadīmah* (The Ancient Civilisation of Oman), undated.

al-Azkāwi, Sarhān bin Sa'īd, Tārikh 'Umān: *Kashf al-Ghamma al-Jāma' li Akhbār al-Umma*, (Oman History), revue par 'Abd al-Majed Ḥassib al-Qaysi, Abu-Dhabi, Dār al-Dirāsāt al-Khalījiya, 1976.

al-Kidmi, Muḥammad bin Sa'īd, *al-Istiqāmah* (Rectitude), 1985, 3 volumes.

al-Kindi, Ahmed bin 'Abd Allāh bin Mūssa al-Nazwi, *al-Muṣannaf* (The Classifier), 1983, 42 volumes.

——, *Kitāb al-Ihtidā'* (The Guide Book), reviewed by Sayeda Ismā'īl Kāshef, 1985, 3 volumes.

al-Kindi, Muḥammad bin Ibrāhim, *Bayān al-Shara'* (Manifesto of the Religious Law), 73 volumes.

Kitāb al-Siyar wal-jawābāt (The Book of Biography and Responses), reviewed by Sayeda Ismā'īl Kāshef, 1986, 2 volumes.

al-Maghairi, Sa'īd ibn 'Ali, *Jahinat al-akhbār fi tārikh Zanzibar* (History of Zanzibar) revue par Muhammad 'Ali al-Sulaybi, 2nd edition, 1986.

Mu'ammar, 'Ali Yaḥya), *al-Ibādiyyah bayn al-Firaq al-lslāmyah* (Ibadhism among the Islamic Sects), 1986, 2 volumes.

al-Qalḥāti, Muḥammad bin Sa'īd al-Azdi, *al-Kashf wal-Bayān* (Discovery and the Manifesto), reviewed par Sayeda Ismā'īl Kāshef, Cairo, 1980, 2 volumes.

al-Sa'di, Jamīl bin Khamīs, *Qāmūs al-Sharī'a* (Encyclopaedia of al-Sharī'a), 1982, 93 volumes.

al-Sālmī, 'Abd Allāh bin Ḥumayd Nūr al-Dīn, *Tuḥfat al-A'yān bi Sīrat ahl 'Umān* (Masterpiece of the Notables: Biography of the People of Oman), Cairo, Matba'at al-Imām, 1961, 2 volumes.

al-Sālmī, Muḥammad bin 'Abd Allāh, *Nahḍat al-a'yān bi ḥuriyat 'Umān* (The Rebirth of Notables in the Freedom of Oman), Cairo, undated.

al-Samāīlī, Sālem bin Ḥamād bin Shāmis al-Sayyābi, *'Izālet al- Wa'thā' 'An Atbā' Abi al-Sha'thā'* (Highlighting the Disciples of Abu Sha'tha), reviewed by Sayeda Ismā'īl Kāshef, Cairo, 1979.

al-Sayyābī, Sālem bin Ḥamūd bin Shāmis, *'Umān 'abr al-Tārikh* (Oman through History), 1986, 4 volumes.

al-Shammākhi, Aḥmed bin Sa'īd bin 'Abdel Wāḥed, *Kitāb al-Siyyar* (The Book of Biography), reviewed by Aḥmed bin Sa'ūd al-Sayyābi, 1987.

Arabic sources

'Abd Allāh, Muḥammad Mūrsi, *Emārāt al-Sāḥel wa 'Umān wa al-Dawlah al-Sa'ūdiyyah al-'Ulla* (The Emirates of the Oman Coast and the First Saudi State (1793–1918)), volume I, Cairo, Egyptian Library, 1978.

'Abduh, Muḥammad, *al-lslām wal-Naṣrāniyyah bayna al-'ilm wal-ḥaḍāra* (Islam and Christianity between Science and Civilization), Algiers, National book Enterprise, 1988.

al-'Abed, F.S., *Siyāsāt Briṭānia fi al-Khalīj al-'Arabi* (British Policy in the Arabian Gulf), Kuwait, Dār That al-Salāsel, [undated].

Ali ibn Abi Tālib, *Nahj al-Balāgha* (The Way of Eloquence), 2nd edition, Cairo, Dār al-Kitāb al-Maṣri, 1990.

al-'Aqād, 'Abāss Maḥmūd, *al-Dimoqrāṭiyyah fi al-lslām* (Democracy in Islam), Cairo, Dār al-Ma 'āref, 1981.

al-'Aqād, Ṣalāḥ, *al-Tayārāt al-Siyyāsiah fi al-Khalīj al-'Arabi* (Political Currents in the Arabian Gulf), Cairo, Anglo-Egyptian Library, 1974.

al-Bāker, 'Abd al-Raḥmān, *Min al-Baḥrain ilā al-Manfā* (Bahrein in Exile), Beirut, al-Ḥayāt Library, 1965.

Dāwūd, M.A., *al-Khalīj al-'Arabi wal-'alāqāt al-duwalyyah* (The Gulf and International Relations 1890–1914), Cairo, volume I, [undated].

Ibets, H.F., *Sulṭānah in New York*, Sultanate of Oman, Ministry of National and Cultural Heritage, Arab Archives, Cairo, 1980.

Ibrāhīm, 'Abdel 'Azīz 'Abdel Ghani, Ṣirā' al-'Omarā' (Combat of the Princes), London, Saqi Books, 1990.

Kāshef, Sayeda Ismā'īl, *'Umān fi fajr al-Islām* (Oman at the Dawn of Islam), Sultanate of Oman, Ministry of National and Cultural Heritage, 1989.

ibn Katheer (Ismā'īl bin 'Umar), *al-bidāya wal-nihāya* (The Beginning and the End), volume 4, Cairo, Dār Abi-Hayan, 1996.

Kelly (J.B.), *al-Ḥudūd al-sharqiyyah li shibh al-Jazīrah al-'Arabiyya* (Eastern Arabian Frontiers), translated by Kheyri Ḥammād, Beyrouth, ed. al-Ḥayāt, 1971. Original title in English: *Eastern Arabian Frontiers*, London, 1964.

——, *Briṭānia wal-Khalīj*, 1795–1870 (Britain and the Persian Gulf 1795–1870), translated by Muḥammad Amīn 'Abd Allāh, Sultanate of Oman, Ministry of National and Cultural Heritage, 1979, 2 volumes.

Khleifat, 'Awaḍ Muḥammad, *Nash'at al-Ḥarakah al-Ibādiyyah* (The Emergence of the Ibadhite Movement), Amman, Dār al-Sha'b, 1978.

——, *al-'Uṣūl al-tārikhiyah lil firaqah al-Ibādiyyah* (The Historical Origins of the Ibadhite Sects), Sultanate of Oman, Ministry of National and Cultural Heritage, 2nd edition, 1988.

Landen, Robert Geran, Oman since 1856: Disruptive Modernization in a Traditional Arab Society, Princeton, NJ, Princeton University Press, 1967. Translated into Arabic by Muḥammad Amīn 'Abd Allāh, Beirut, 1970.

Lorimer, John Gordon, Dalīl al-Khalīj (Gazetteer of the Persian Gulf, Oman and Central Arabia), completed and edited by R.L. Birdwood, Calcutta, Superintendent Govt. Printing, 1908–1915. Translated into Arabic by the Government of Qatar, 2nd edition, [1975–?], 14 volumes.

Miles, Samuel Barrett, *al-Khalīj, bildāneh wa Qabā'īleh* (The Countries and tribes of the Persian Gulf), London, Frank Cass, 1900 (2nd edition, 1966). Translated into Arabic by Muḥammad Amīn 'Abd Allāh, Sultanate of Oman, Ministry of National and Cultural Heritage, 1982.

Mrûa, Ḥussein, *al-Nazā'āt al-Mādiyya fi al-falsafah al-'Arabiyya al-Islāmiyya* (Material Tendencies in Arab Islamic Philosophy), Beirut, al-Fārābi, 4th edition, 1981, 2 volumes.

al-Naqib, Khaldūn Ḥassan, *al-mujtama 'wal-dawla fi al-Khalīj wal-Jazīrah al-'Arabiyya* (Society and the State in the Gulf and the Arabian Peninsula), Beirut, Markaz Dirāsāt al-Waḥda al-'Arabiyya, 1987.

Nawfal, Sayyed, *al-Khalīj al-'Arabi aw al-Hudūd al-Sharqiyya lel Jazīrah al-'Arabiyya* (The Arabian Gulf or the Oriental Frontiers of the Arab Homeland), Beirut, Dār al-Talī'a, 1969.

——, *al-awḍā' al-Siyāsiyya fi Emārāt al-Khalīj al-'Arabi wa janūb al-Jazīrah* (The Political Situations in the Emirates of the Arabian Gulf and the Saudi Peninsula), Cairo, Institute of Arab Research and Studies: UNICEF, Book 2, 1972, volume 2.

al-Qāsīmī (Sulṭān ibn Muḥammad), *Taqsīm al-imbarāṭoriyya al-'Umāniyya 1856–1862* (The Division of the Omani Empire), Dubai (U.A.E.), al-Bayān, 1989.

——, *al-'Alāqāt al-'Umāniyya al-Farensyya* 1715–1905 (Omani-French Relations 1715–1905), The Emirates, Al Ghurair Printing & Publishing House, 1993.

Qāsim (Jamal Zakariya), *Dirāssa li tārīkh al-Emārāt al-Arabiyya (1840–1914)* (Study of the History of the Arab Emirates), Kuwait, Establishment for Scientific Studies, 1974.

al-Sayār, 'A'īsha, *Dawlat al-Ya'āribah, 'Umān wa sharq Afriqyā, 1624–1741* (The Ya'rūbite State, Oman and North Africa), Dār Beirut, al-Quds, 1975.

al-Shahrestani, Muḥammad bin 'Abd al-Karim, *al-Milal wal-Nehal* (Les doctrines et les écoles de pensée), ed. 'Abd al-Azīz Muḥammad al- Wakil, Beirut, Dār al-Fikr, [undated].

al-Shiṭi 'Abd Allāh, *Fi Ma'rakat al-Ḥurriyah* (Oman in the Battle for Freedom), Damascus, 1962.

al-'Ubeidli, Aḥmed, *al-'Imām 'Azzān ibn Qays, 1868–1871*, Beirut, Dār al-Ḥadātha, 1984.

Wilson, Arnold Talbot, *Tārikh al-Khalīj* (The Persian Gulf: a historical sketch from the earliest times to the beginning of the 20th century), Oxford, Clarendon Press, 1928.

Translated into Arabic by Muḥammad Amīn 'Abd Allāh, Sultanate of Oman, Ministry of National and Cultural Heritage, 1985.
al-Zarqā (Muḥammad 'Ali), *'Umān Qadimanwa Hadithan* (Oman ancient and modern), Damascus, 1959.

Anonymous Arabic sources

Kifāḥ 'Umān bayn al-Ams wal-yawm (Oman's Struggle Between Yesterday and Today), Damascus, Bureau of the *imāma* of Oman, [1960-?].
Oman, Bureau (Arabic Research Series), Damascus, 1964.
Qaḍyat 'Umān fi al-jam'ya al-'āmah lil Umam al-Muttaḥida (The Omani Cause at the General Assembly of the United Nations), Cairo, Bureau of the *imāma* of Oman, 1961.
'Umān fi al-Maḥāfel al-Dwaliyeh (Oman in the International Stage), Damascus, 1966.

French sources

Barros, João de, Da Afia, Lisboa, Regia Officina Typografica, 1781, réimpr. Paris, 1981 (Translated by the Omani embassy in Paris).
Benoist-Méchin, Jacques, *Ibn-Séoud ou la Naissance d'un royaume*, Paris, Albin Michel, 1955.
Berreby, Jean-Jacques, *La Péninsule arabique, terre sainte de l'islam, patrie de l'arabisme et empire du pétrole*, Paris, Payot, 1958.
Braudel, Fernand, *Écrits sur l'Histoire*, Paris, Flammarion, 1969.
Burdeau, Georges, *La Démocratie*, Paris, Seuil, 1966.
Chelbod, Joseph, *Le Droit dans la société bédouine*, Paris, Librairie Marcel Rivière et Cie, 1971.
Djalili, Mohammad-Reza, *Le Golfe Persique, problèmes et perspectives*, Paris, Dalloz, 1978.
Gardet, Louis, *L'Islam, religion et communauté*, Paris, Desclée de Brouwer, 1967.
——, *Les Hommes de l'Islam*, Paris, Hachette, 1977.
——, *La Cité musulmane, vie sociale et politique*, Paris, Librairie philosophique J. Vrin, 1981.
Graz, Liesl, *Les Omanais, nouveaux gardiens du Golfe*, Paris, Albin Michel, 1981.
Hegel, G.W.F., *La Raison dans l'Histoire*, Paris, Christian Bourgois, 1990.
Humaidan, Ali, *Les Princes de l'or noir*, Paris, Hachette, 1968.
Iqbal, Mohammed, *Reconstruire la pensée religieuse de l'Islam*, Paris, Librairie d'Amérique et d'Orient Adrien Maisonneuve, 1955.
Kajare, Firouz, *Le Sultanat d'Oman, étude d'histoire diplomatique et de droit international*, Paris, A. Pedone, 1914.
Laoust, Henri, *Le Califat dans la doctrine de Rashīd Ridā*, annoted translation of al-Khilāfa aw al-lmāma al-'uzmā (The Califate of the supreme *imāma*), Paris, Librairie d'Amérique et d'Orient, 1986.
Montesquieu, Charles de Secondat, baron de, *De l'esprit des lois*, Paris, Flammarion, 1979.
L'Oman et la France, quelques éléments d'histoire. Archives et documentation, Paris, Ministère des Affaires étrangères, 1989.
Prélot, Marcel and Lescuyer (Georges), *Histoire des idées politiques*, Paris, Dalloz, 1990.
Robin, Maurice, *Histoire comparative des idées politiques*, Paris, Economica, volume I, 1988.
Rousseau, Jean-Jacques, *Du contrat social*, Paris, Flammarion, 1966.

Ruethe, Emily, *Mémoires d'une princesse arabe*, Paris, Karthala, 1991.
al-Sabah, Salem al-Jabir, *Les Émirats du Golfe, histoire d'un peuple*, Paris, Fayard, 1980.
Stevens, A., *Oman citadelle entre sable et mer* [s. I., Belgique,] éd. Terra Incognita, 1990.
Tur, Jean- Jacques, *Les Émirats du Golfe Arabe*, Paris, P. U. F., 1976.
al-Wasmī, Khālid, *Oman entre l'indépendance et l'occupation coloniale*, Genève, Labor et Fides; Paris, Publications orientalistes de France, 1986.
Zakariya, Fouad, *Islamisme ou laïcité, les Arabes à l'heure du choix*, Cairo, al-Fikr; Paris, La Découverte, 1991.
Zorgbibe, Charles, *Géopolitique et histoire du Golfe*, Paris, P. U. F., 1991.

English sources

Barbu, Z., *Democracy and dictatorship*, New York, Grove Press, 1956.
Bondarevsky, G., *Hegemonists and imperialists in the Persian Gulf*, Moscow, Novosti Press Agency Publishing House, 1981.
Halliday, Fred, *Arabia without sultans*, New York, Random House, 1975.
Heard-Bey, Frauke, *From Trucial States to United Arab Emirates*, London, Longman, 1982.
al-Maamiry, Ahmed Hamoud, *Oman and Ibadhism*, New Delhi, India, Lancers Booms, 1989.
Mansfield, Peter, *History of the Middle East*, London, Viking, 1991.
Maurizi, Vicenzo, *History of Sayid Sa'īd*, Cambridge, Oleander Press, 1954.
Peterson, J.E., *Oman in the twentieth century*, London, Croom Helm, 1978.
Phillips, Wendell, *Oman a history*, Beirut, Librairie du Liban, 1971.
al-Qasimi, Sultān ibn Muhammad, *The Myth of Arab piracy in the Gulf*, London, Croom Helm, 1986.
ibn Ruzyaq, Humayd, *al-Fatḥ al-mubīn fi sīrat al-bū Sa'īdiyīn, History of the lmāms and Seyyids of Oman*, translated and edited by G.P. Badger, London, Draf Publishers Ltd., 1986.
Said Zahlan, R., *The Origins of the United Arab Emirates*, London, Macmillan Press Ltd., 1978.
Weber, Max, *Economy and society*, New York, Bedminster Press, 1968.
Wilkinson, John C., *Water and tribal settlement in South-East Arabia. A study of the Aflāj of Oman*, Oxford, Clarendon Press, 1977.
——, *The Imamate tradition of Oman*, Cambridge University Press, 1987.
Wingate, Ronald, *Not in the limelight*, London, Hutchinson and Co Ltd., 1959.
Wolpert, Stanley, *A new history of India*, Oxford University Press; New York, 1982 (2nd edition).

Articles of periodicals and journals, contributions to Arabic collective sources

Arabic books

al-Braki, Nāṣer al-Murshed, *al-Ibādiyyah fi al-Fikr al-Siyāsi al-lslāmi wa Athāruha fi Qiyâm al-Duwal* (Ibadhism in Islamic Political Thought and its Influences on the Establishment of States), in *al-Ijtihād*, Beirut, no: 13, 1991.
Farghot, Antoine, *al-Dīn wal 'Ilmāniya fi Uroba al-Gharbiya* (Religion and Laity in Western Europe), in *al-'Alāqāt bayn al-Ḥaḍārāt al-'Arabiyya wal Urobiya* (conférence de Hambourg, avril 1983), al-Dār al-Tunisiyyah, 1985.

Stevinson, Richard, Aperçu sur le début de la relation commerciale et consulaire américaine avec le sultanat d'Oman (1833–1856) (Brief Account in the Beginning of the American Commercial and Consular Relationship with the Sultanate of Oman (1833–1856)), in *Journal of the Gulf and Arabian Peninsula Studies*, Kuwait, no: 11, second year, July 1977.

Arabic journals and periodicals

Journal *al-Khalij*, Sharjah (UAE), 17 August 1991.
Al-Manār, section 5, no: 23, 1922, pp. 361–372.
Al-Manār, section 10, no: 23, 1922, pp. 729–752.
Al-Manār, section 2, no: 26, 1925, pp. 100–104.
Al-Manār, section 3, no: 26, 1925, pp. 212–217.
Al-Manār, section 5, no: 26, 1925, pp. 362–393.

French books

Auzoux, A., 'La France et Mascate aux XVIIIe et XIXe siècles', *Revue d'histoire diplomatique*, 1910.
Heard-Bey, Frauke, 'Le développement d'un État-cité maritime dans le Golfe: l'exemple de Dubayy', in *La Péninsule arabique d'aujourd'hui*, directed by Paul Bonnenfant, Paris, éd. du CNRS, 1982, volume II.
Le Cour Grandmaison, C., 'Présentation du Sultanat d'Oman', in *La Péninsule arabique d'aujourd'hui*, directed by Paul Bonnenfant, Paris, éd. du CNRS, 1982, volume II.
Miège, J.-L., 'Oman et l'Afrique centrale au XIXe siècle', in La Péninsule arabique d'aujourd'hui, directed by Paul Bonnenfant, Paris, éd. du CNRS, 1982, volume II.
Rouleau, Éric, 'Oman ou la révolution refoulée', *Le Monde*, 28 May 1971.
Wilkinson, John C., 'Changement et continuité en Oman', in *La Péninsule arabique d'aujourd'hui*, directed by Paul Bonnenfant, Paris, éd. du CNRS, 1982, volume II.

French journals and periodicals

Le Figaro, 7 February 1992.
Journal des débats, in Aff. Etr., M. D. Afrique, vol. 149.
Journal des débats, 20 November 1898.
Journal des débats, 25 February 1899.
Journal officiel, in Aff. Etr., N. S. Mascate, vol. 33, f. 33.
Le Monde, 24 January 1956.
Le Monde diplomatique, March 1970.
Le Monde, 28 May 1971.

English books

Bathurst, R.D., 'Maritime trade and Imamate government: two principal themes in the history of Oman to 1728', in Hopwood, Derek *et al.*, ed., *The Arabian Peninsula: society and politics*, London, George Allen and Unwin, 1972.
Eickelman, Dale F., 'Religious tradition, economic domination and political legitimacy', *Revue de l'Occident musulman et de la Méditerranée*, Aix-en-Provence, no: 29, 1980.
——, 'Religious knowledge in inner Oman', *Journal of Oman studies*, 1983.

——, 'From theocracy to monarchy: authority and legitimacy in inner Oman, 1935–1957', *International Journal of Middle East Studies*, 1985.

Kelly, J.B., 'A prevalence of furies: tribes, politics and religion in Oman and Trucial Oman', in Hopwood, Derek *et al.*, ed., *The Arabian Peninsula: society and politics*, London, George Allen and Unwin, 1972.

Peterson, J.E., 'The revival of the Ibādi imamate in Oman and the threat to Muscat, 1913–1920', in *Arabian studies*, vol. III, Middle East Centre, University of Cambridge, 1976.

Wilkinson, John C., The origins of the Oman State, in Hopwood (Derek) *et al.*, ed., *The Arabian Peninsula: society and politics*, London, George Allen and Unwin, 1972.

——, 'The Julanda of Oman', *Journal of Oman studies*, 1975.

——, The Ibādi imāma, *Bulletin of the School of Oriental and African studies*, XXXIX, London, 1976.

——, 'Bio-bibliographical background to the crisis period in the Ibādī imamate of Oman (end of 9th to end of 14th century)', in *Arabian studies*, vol. III, Middle East Centre, University of Cambridge, 1976.

English Journals

The Times, 16 January 1956.

International Herald Tribune, 6 February 1992.

Thesis

Ennami, 'Amr Khalifah, *Studies in lbādism*, thesis, University of Cambridge, 1971.

Hamaidan, Ahmed, *Le Mouvement National Moderniste au Bahrein (1954–1980)*, thèse de doctorat, Université de Paris X, 1983.

Other sources

Aitchinon, C.U., *Collection of Treaties, Engagements and Sanads Relating to lndia and Neighbouring Countries*, Delhi, Manager of publications, vol. XI, 1933.

Le *Coran*, trans. Régis Blachère, Paris, G. P. Maisonneuve & Larose, 1980.

Encyclopédie islamique, new edition, Paris, 1975, volume III.

Glassé Cyril, 'New Encyclopedia of Islam', a revised edn of the 'Concise Encyclopedia of Islam', California, AltaMira, 2001; 'The Concise Encyclopedia of Islam', revised edition, London, Stacey International Publishers, 2003; translated and adapted Yves Thoraval as 'Dictionnaire Encyclopédique de l'Islam', Paris, Bordas, 1991.

Archives

French documents

ARCHIVES, MINISTRY OF FOREIGN AFFAIRS

NS Mascate, vol. 1 (Le Golfe Persique et les Puissances, volume I, 1891–1895)

NS Mascate, vol. 2 (Le Golfe Persique et les Puissances. Dossier général, volume II, 1895)

NS Mascate, vol. 4 (Le Golfe Persique et les Puissances. Dossier général, volume IV, 1899)
NS Mascate, vol. 5 (Le Golfe Persique et les Puissances. Dossier général, volume V, 1900)
NS Mascate, vol. 6 (Le Golfe Persique et les Puissances. Dossier général, volume VI, 1901)
NS Mascate, vol. 7 (Le Golfe Persique et les Puissances. Dossier général, volume VII, 1901–1902)
NS Mascate, vol. 8 (Le Golfe Persique et les Puissances. Dossier général, volume VIII, 1902)
NS Mascate, vol. 9 (Le Golfe Persique et les Puissances. Dossier général, volume IX, 1903)
NS Mascate, vol. 10 (Le Golfe Persique et les Puissances. Dossier général, volume X, 1903–1904)
NS Mascate, vol. 11 (Le Golfe Persique et les Puissances. Dossier général, volume XI, 1904–1905)
NS Mascate, vol. 14 (Le Golfe Persique et les Puissances. Dossier général, volume XIV, 1908–1910)
NS Mascate, vol. 17 (Le Golfe Persique et les Puissances. Démonstration navale franco-russe, 1902–1903)
NS Mascate, vol. 18 (Consulat de France 1893–1905)
NS Mascate, vol. 20 (Trafic d'armes. Dossier général, volume II, 1908–1910)
NS Mascate, vol. 22 (Trafic d'armes. Dossier général, volume IV, 1912)
NS Mascate, vol. 23 (Trafic d'armes. Dossier général, volume V, 1913–1914)
NS Mascate, vol. 24 (Arbitrage franco-anglais, volume I, 1912)
NS Mascate, vol. 27 (Boutres français, volume II, 1898–1900)
NS Mascate, vol. 30 (Contentieux franco-anglais, volume V, 1903)
NS Mascate, vol. 31 (Boutres français. Contentieux franco-anglais, volume VI, 1903–1904)
NS Mascate, vol. 33 (Boutres français, volume VIII, 1905)
NS Mascate, vol. 34 (Boutres français, volume IX, 1905–1906)
NS Mascate, vol. 35 (Boutres français, volume X, 1906–1916)
NS Mascate, vol. 36 (Affaires politiques générales, volume I, 1895–1898)
NS Mascate, vol. 37 (Affaires politiques générales, volume II, 1901–1907)
NS Mascate, vol. 39 (Affaires politiques générales, volume IV, 1913–1918)
NS Mascate, vol. 41 (Dépôt français de charbon, volume II, 1899–1900)
NS Mascate, vol. 42 (Dépôt français de charbon, Volume III, 1899–1900)
NS Mascate, vol. 43 (Dépôt français de charbon, volume IV, 1901–1918)
NS Mascate, vol. 45 (Boutres français. Traite des Noirs, volume II, 1897–1899)
NS Mascate, vol. 46 (Boutres français. Traite des Noirs, volume III, 1899–1902)
NS Mascate, vol. 47 (Boutres français. Traite des Noirs, volume IV, 1902–1914)

FOREIGN AFFAIRS

CCC Zanzibar, vol. 1
CCC Zanzibar, vol. 3 (Correspondance commerciale, volume III, 1866–1874)
CCC Zanzibar, vol. 4 (Correspondance commerciale, volume N, 1875–1880)
CCC Zanzibar, vol. 6 (Correspondance commerciale, volume VI, 1883)
CCC Zanzibar, vol. 9 (Correspondance commerciale, volume IX, 1890)

FOREIGN AFFAIRS

MD Afrique, vol. 149 (Mémoires et documents, volume III, 1842–1847)

FOREIGN AFFAIRS

Asie 1918–1929, Golfe Persique, vol. 1.
Asie 1918–1929, Golfe Persique, vol. 2.
Asie 1918–1929, Golfe Persique, vol. 3.

English documents

DOCUMENTS OF INDIAN OFFICE RECORDS (IOR)

R/15/1/436 *Muscat rising* 1913. 25 April 1917–26 Oct. 1920.
R/15/1/437 *Muscat Omani relations: renewal of 1920 treaty*. 4 April 1932–18 Oct. 1946.
R/15/2/626 *Function and powers of Council of State Muscat*. 19 Feb. 1947–4 March 1947.
R/15/2/743 *Middle East services Cairo*. Anglo-American policy in the Middle East. 2 May 1944–22 June 1944.
R/15/6/36 *Muscat précis. Printed narrative of Muscat affairs*. Oct. 1869–Dec. 1892.
R/15/6/46 *Peace negotiations between Imam and Sultan*. 14 June 1915–8 Nov. 1915.
R/15/6/50 *Succession and recognition of Sayyid Faysal*. 18 June 1888–23 April 1890.
R/15/6/51 *H.H. Sayyid Faysaf's proposal to abdicate in favour of Sayyid Taimur*. 26 Oct. 1903.
R/15/6/52 *Sultan's abdication plan*. 28 Dec. 1929–6 June 1932.
R/15/6/54 *Abdication of Sayyid Taimur & succession of Sayyid Said*. 11 Nov. 1931–2 Feb. 1932.
R/15/6/216 *Muscat State affairs. Sir Sayyid Saʿīd ibn Taimur: position and personality. Question of title and letters after Sultan's names*. 16 Aug. 1937–18 May 1946.
R/15/6/251 *Sultan's relations with tribes: future development Trucial States and central Oman*. 12 Jan. 1951–10 Dec. 1951.
R/15/6/337 *Muscat administrative reports and related correspondence*.
R/15/6/161 *Soviet broadcasting in Near and Middle East*. 16 March 1933–10 June 1933.
R/15/6/162 *Anti-communist publicity policy*. 21 May 1948–24 July 1948.
R/15/6/243 *Shaikh Sulaiman Ibn Himyar of Jabal Akhdhar*. 5 June 1949.
L/PS/9/50 Muscat 1869.
L/PS/9/17 Muscat 1869.

IOR: MSS. EUR.

D 510/1 Private correspondence India, Part II, Curzon to Hamilton, vol. XIII. 4 Aug. 1898–5 Jan. 1899.
D 510/13 Private correspondence India, Part I, Curzon to Hamilton, vol.XXIV. 1 Jan.–30 April 1903.
D 510/14 Private correspondence India, Part II, Curzon to Hamilton, vol. XXVI. 7 May–15 Oct. 1903.
C.126/5 Private correspondence India, Hamilton to Curzon, vol. IV, 1903.

DOCUMENTS FROM THE FOREIGN OFFICE (FO)

FO 371 1955 General Correspondence: Political Department. Index

114 561 *Visit to Middle East by UK representative.*

114 564 *Proposal to return Kuria Maria islands, ceded to Queen Victoria in 1854, to Sultan of Muscat.*

114 575 *Oil concessions in Dhofar.*

114 576 *Annual reviews for the P. Gulf and Trucial States for 1954.*

114 577 *Monthly summaries of events in P. Gulf Dec. 1954–Nov. 1955.*

114 578–114 585 *Situation among tribes & shaikhs of Muscat & Oman, involvement of Arab League in affairs of Oman: Saudi Arabian threat, and gun running operations against Imam of Oman headquarters at Nazwa.*

114 586–114 587 *Bahrain internal political situation. Demands for constitutional and administrative reforms following disturbances between Shia and Sunni communities.*

114 588 *Kuwait internal political situation.*

114 590 Views of Foreign minister of Iraq on possible confederation of Persian Gulf States and membership of Arab League.

114 591 Communism in the Persian Gulf.

114 592 Report from political agent Dubai for 6th and 7th meetings of Trucial council.

114 594 *Question of admittance of Persian Gulf States to Arab League.*

114 596 *Political relations between Egypt and the Trucial States: unauthorized visits. Egyptian diplomats to Persian Gulf Islamic conference at Mecca. Gulf rulers discouraged from attending.*

114 608–114 633 *Buraimi arbitration tribunal to establish frontier between Saudi Arabia and Abu Dhabi and sovereignty over Buraimi area.*

114 634–114 638 *Saudi Arabia infractions of Buraimi: arbitration agreement.*

114 639 Conflicting claims to the Sea-bed claims by Persia to Bahrain.

114 640–114 641 *Claims by Persia to Abu Musa & Tunbs and Bahrain, dispute between Kuwait and Saudi Arabia over lands in the neutral zone.*

114 642–114 643 *Negotiations between Sultan of Muscat and Pakistan for lease or sale of Gwader.*

114 646 *Frontier between Saudi Arabia and Kuwait, neutral zone.*

114 647 *Claims by rulers of Qatar & Abu Dhabi to ownership of island of Halul.*

114 648 *Land & sea boundaries of Trucial sheikhdoms.*

114 649 *Sharja & Sultan dispute to three villages boundary.*

114 707 *Relation between Qatar Petroleum Company & Government of Qatar; new agreement.*

114 708–114 712 *Kuwait oil company. Agreement between ruler of Kuwait and Kuwait oil Co.*

114 713 *Oil concessions in Persian Gulf States.*

114 714 *Operations of the Bahrain petroleum company.*

114 715 *Political agreement between UK and Petroleum Development Ltd concerning the exploration agreement between the company and the ruler of Fujairah.*

114 719 *Brief on use of oil reserves for development in Persian Gulf.*

114 746 *Anti-British propaganda in Persian Gulf.*

114 747 *Anti-British propaganda in P. Gulf from Egypt.*

FO 371 1956 General Correspondence: Political Department. Index

120 540 *Persian Gulf: annual report for 1955.*
120 541 *Periodic political reports on Persian Gulf.*
120 542–120 543 *Internal political situation in Muscat & Oman.*
120 552 *Internal political situation in Persian Gulf Interstate relations, confederation of sheikhdoms.*
120 553 *Internal political situation in Trucial States.*
120 555 *Call by Egypt for strikes and response from Persian Gulf States.*
120 557–120 559 *Security situation in Persian Gulf States.*
120 560 *Political relations between Persian Gulf States & other Arab countries.*
120 561 *Attitude of Egypt to Persian Gulf States.*
120 565 *Political relation between Iraq & Persian Gulf States.*
120 567 *Reaction of Persian Gulf States to UK policy towards Egypt & Israel.*
120 571 *Reappraisal of British policy in Persian Gulf States.*
120 574 *Attitude of Pakistan towards Persian Gulf States, diplomatic representation.*
120 575 *Brief for talks in Washington between UK & US on relation between countries in Arabian peninsula.*
120 576 *Oman & Arab League.*
120 577–120 589 *Negotiations between Saudi Arabia & UK over Buraimi.*
120 596–120 597 *Negotiations between Pakistan & Sultan of Muscat over Gwader oil rights.*
120 617–120 619 *British forces in Persian Gulf.*
120 620–120 622 *Persian Gulf defence, internal security schemes.*
120 640 *Radio and Tele in Persian Gulf.*
120 647 *Oil concessions in Muscat and Oman.*
120 650 *Oil interests of UK in Persian Gulf.*
120 651 *Oil interests of Arab League in Persian Gulf.*
120 654 *Oil surveys in the Gulf, particularly Muscat.*

FO 371 1957 General Correspondence. Political Department. Index

126 869 *Annual reports on territories in Persian Gulf.*
126 871–126 873 *Internal political situation in Persian Gulf.*

Oman 1957

126 874–126 892 *Internal political situation in Muscat & Oman.*
126 898 *Broadcasts in Arabic from Radio Cairo.*
126 900 *Internal political situation in Trucial States.*
126 903 *Press comment in foreign press on political situation in Oman.*
126 904 *UK policy on future of Muscat & Oman.*
126 908 *Political relation between Muscat and Oman and Saudi Arabia.*
126 910 *Political relation between States in Persian Gulf & US.*
126 919–126 920 *Political relation between Muscat & Oman & UK.*
126 923 *Importance of states in Persian Gulf to future of Middle East.*
126 924 *Talks between UK & US on situation in Persian Gulf.*
126 925–126 926 *Dispute between SA & UK over Buraimi.*
126 928–126 929 *Negotiations between Sultan of Muscat & Pakistan concerning Gwader oil rights.*

126 940 *Guerilla warfare & sabotage in Persian Gulf.*
126 941–126 943 *Development plan for Trucial States.*
126 951 *Armed forces of UK in Persian Gulf.*
126 956 *Development of agriculture in Trucial States.*
126 962 *Anti-British propaganda in Persian Gulf States.*
126 965 *Oil concessions in Muscat & Oman.*
126 975 *Mineral deposits in Muscat & Oman.*
126 989 *Sabotage in Persian Gulf.*
126 994 *Security in Persian.*

FO 371 1958
132 523 *Periodic reports of events in Persian Gulf.*
132 524–132 530 *Internal political situation in Muscat & Oman.*
132 554 *Press interview with ruler of Sharjah.*
132 563 *Method of addressing mail to Persian Gulf or Gulf of Arabia.*
132 566 *Development in Muscat.*
132 597 *Oil concessions & boundaries in Muscat & Oman.*
132 601 *Surrender of oil concessions in Persian Gulf.*
132 605 *Amendments to 1956 orders in council for Trucial States.*

Cabinet
128 *Minutes.*
129/60 *Saudi Arabian frontier dispute.*
129/65 *Persian oil.*
129/83 *Bagdad Pact Organisation: privileges and immunities.*
129/87 *Persian Gulf*

UN documents

Rapport du comité spécial de l'Oman, Assemblée générale, Narions unies, New York, 1964–1965.
Oman, Ref. A/6700/ Rev 1, NY 1967 (ch. XIII).
Oman, Ref. S/7200/ Rev 1, NY 1968 (ch. XVII).
Oman, Ref. A/7623/ Rev 1, NY 1969 (ch. XIV).

Index